VOLUME 4
A GHOST IN THE TOMB

GRAYSON

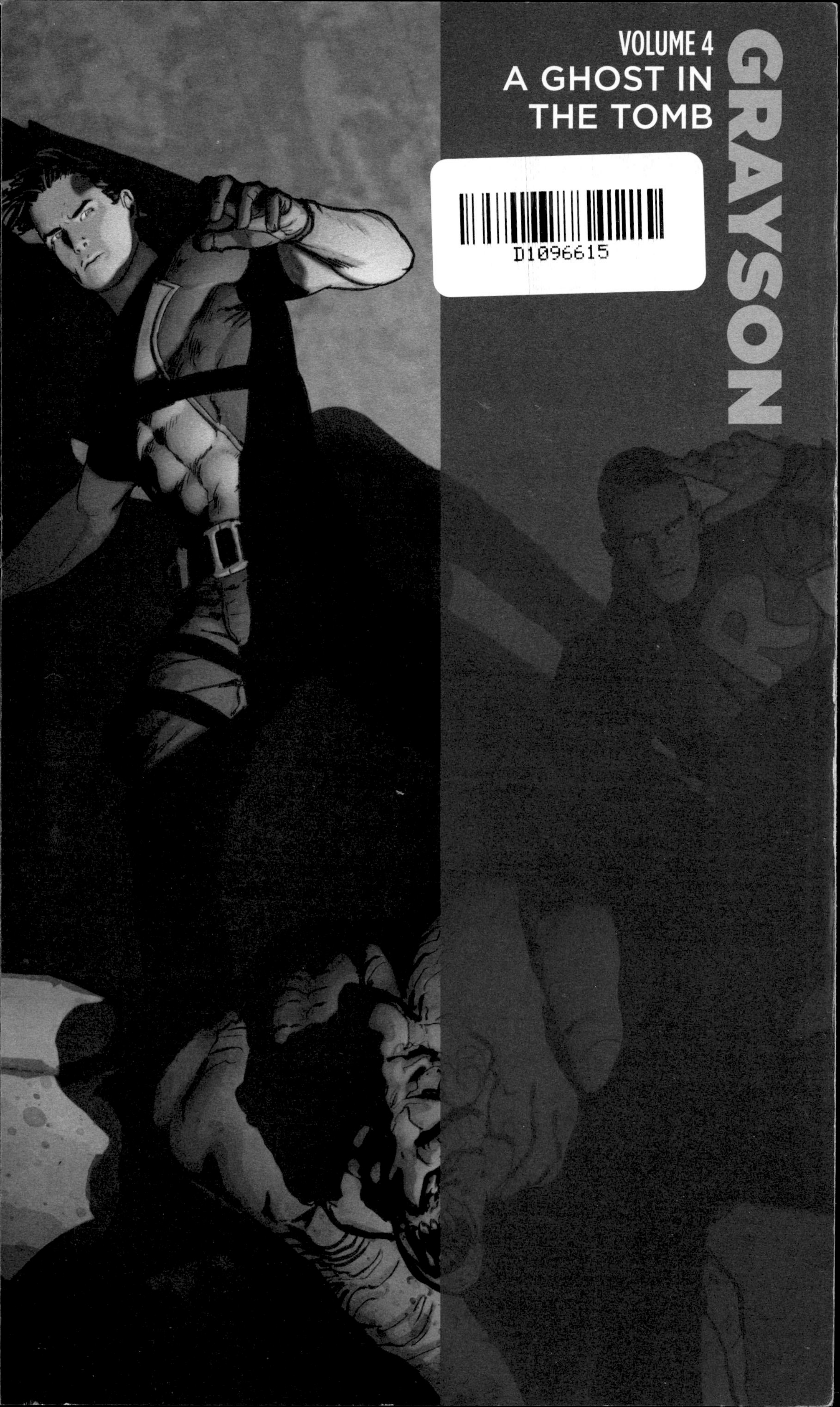

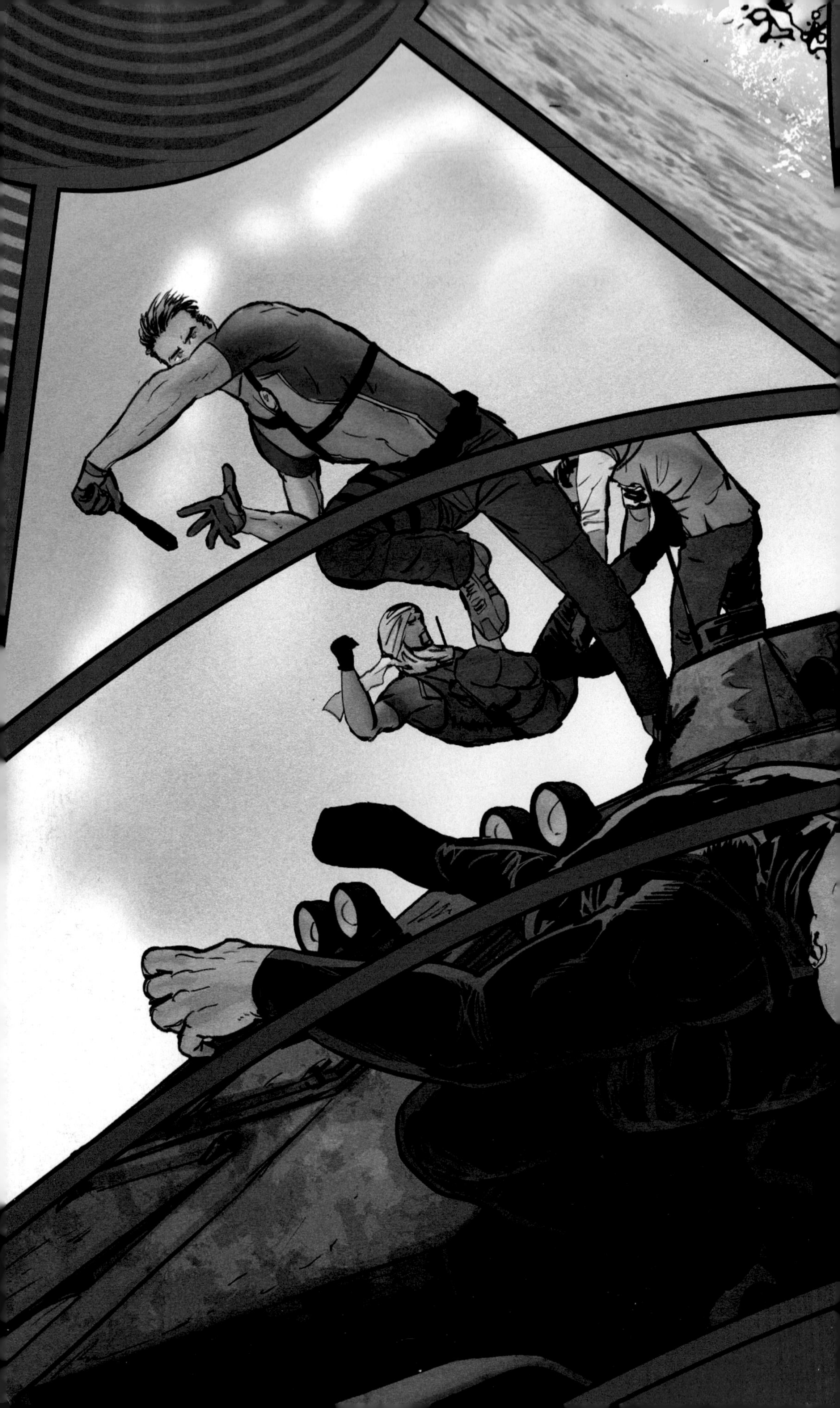

GRAYSON

VOLUME 4
A GHOST IN
THE TOMB

WRITTEN BY
TIM SEELEY
TOM KING

ART BY
MIKEL JANÍN
HUGO PETRUS STEPHEN MOONEY
JORGE CORONA
CARMINE DI GIANDOMENICO
RAUL FERNANDEZ ANDRES GUINALDO
ROB HAYNES ALVARO MARTINEZ
ALAIN MAURICET SCOTT MCDANIEL
ANDY OWENS STEVE PUGH
KHARY RANDOLPH WALDEN WONG

COLOR BY
JEROMY COX
EMILIO LOPEZ CHRIS SOTOMAYOR
GABE ELTAEB SANDRA MOLINA
MATT LOPES

LETTERS BY
CARLOS M. MANGUAL
TOM NAPOLITANO

COLLECTION COVER ARTIST
MIKEL JANÍN

BATMAN CREATED BY
BOB KANE WITH
BILL FINGER

GRAYSON VOLUME 4: A GHOST IN THE TOMB

Published by DC Comics. Compilation and all new material Copyright © 2016 DC Comics. All Rights Reserved. Originally published in sing
magazine form in GRAYSON 13-16, ROBIN WAR 1-2. Copyright © 2015, 2016 DC Comics. All Rights Reserved. All characters, their distinct
likenesses and related elements featured in this publication are trademarks of DC Comics. The stories, characters and incidents featured
this publication are entirely fictional. DC Comics does not read or accept unsolicited submissions of ideas, stories or artwork.

DC Comics, 2900 West Alameda Ave., Burbank, CA 91505
Printed by RR Donnelley, Salem, VA, USA. 9/2/16. First Printing.
ISBN: 978-1-4012-6762-9

Library of Congress Cataloging-in-Publication Data is Available.

PEFC Certified

Printed on paper from
sustainably managed
forests and controlled
sources

PEFC/29-31-75   www.pefc.org

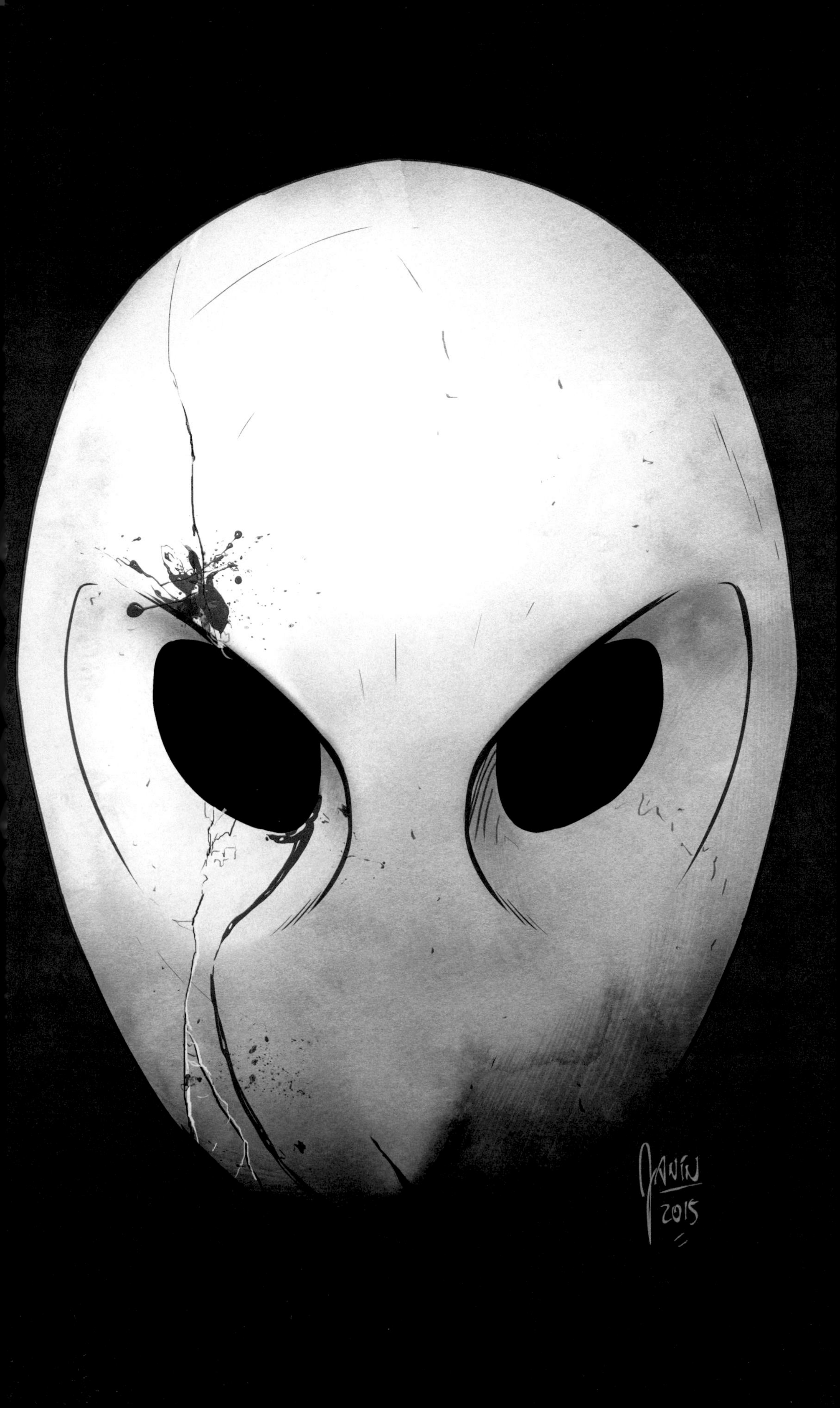
JANÍN
2015

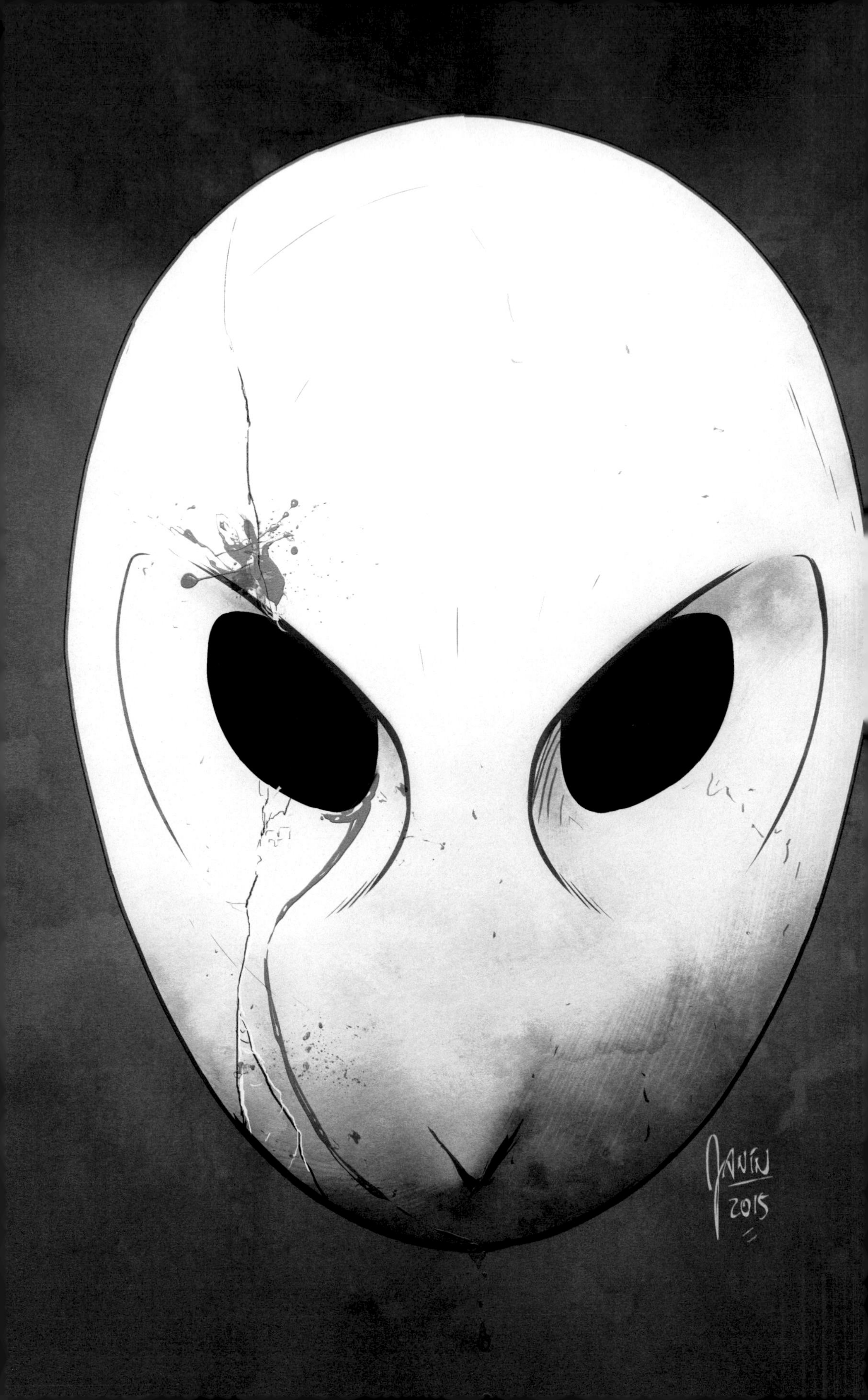
JANÍN
2015

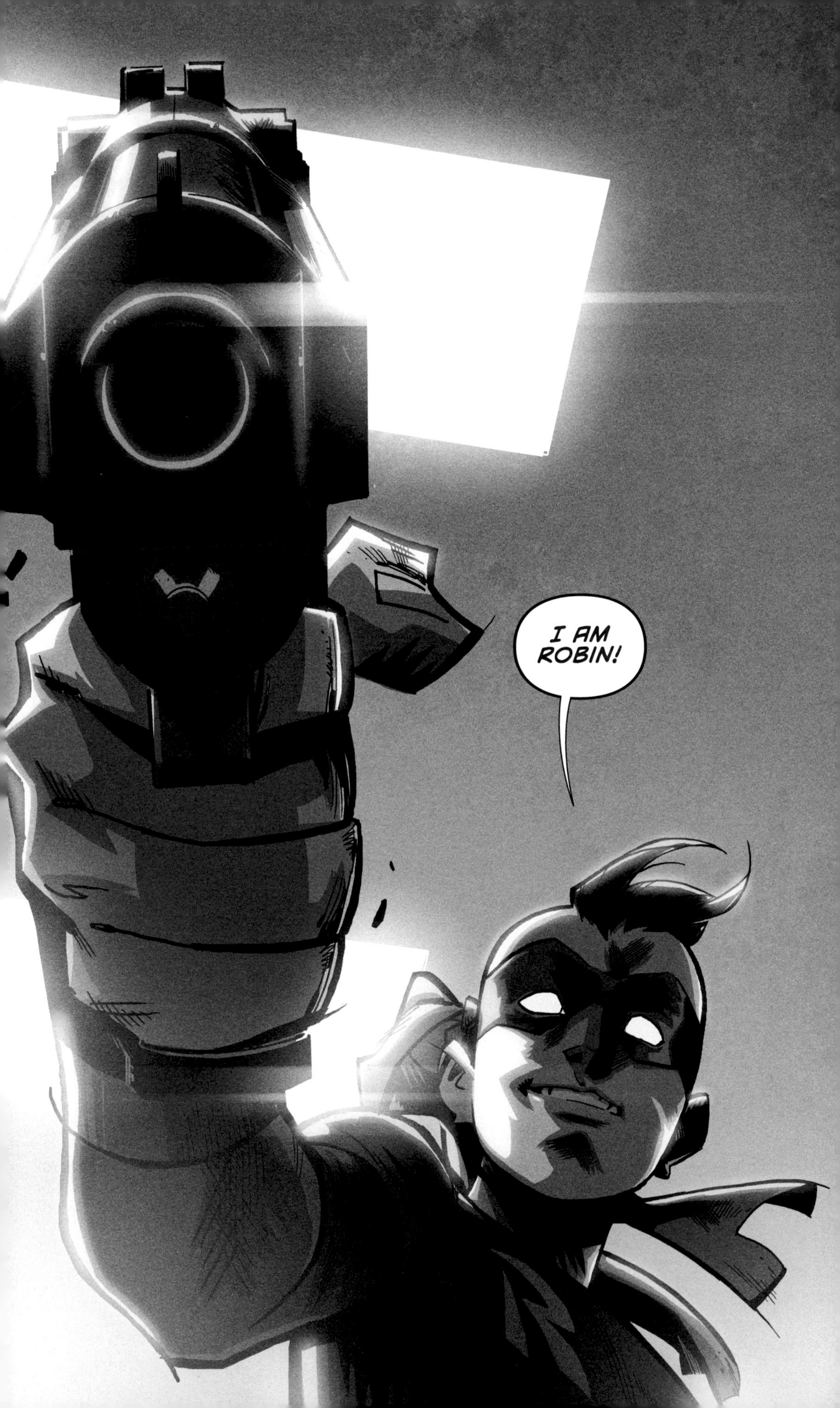
I AM ROBIN!

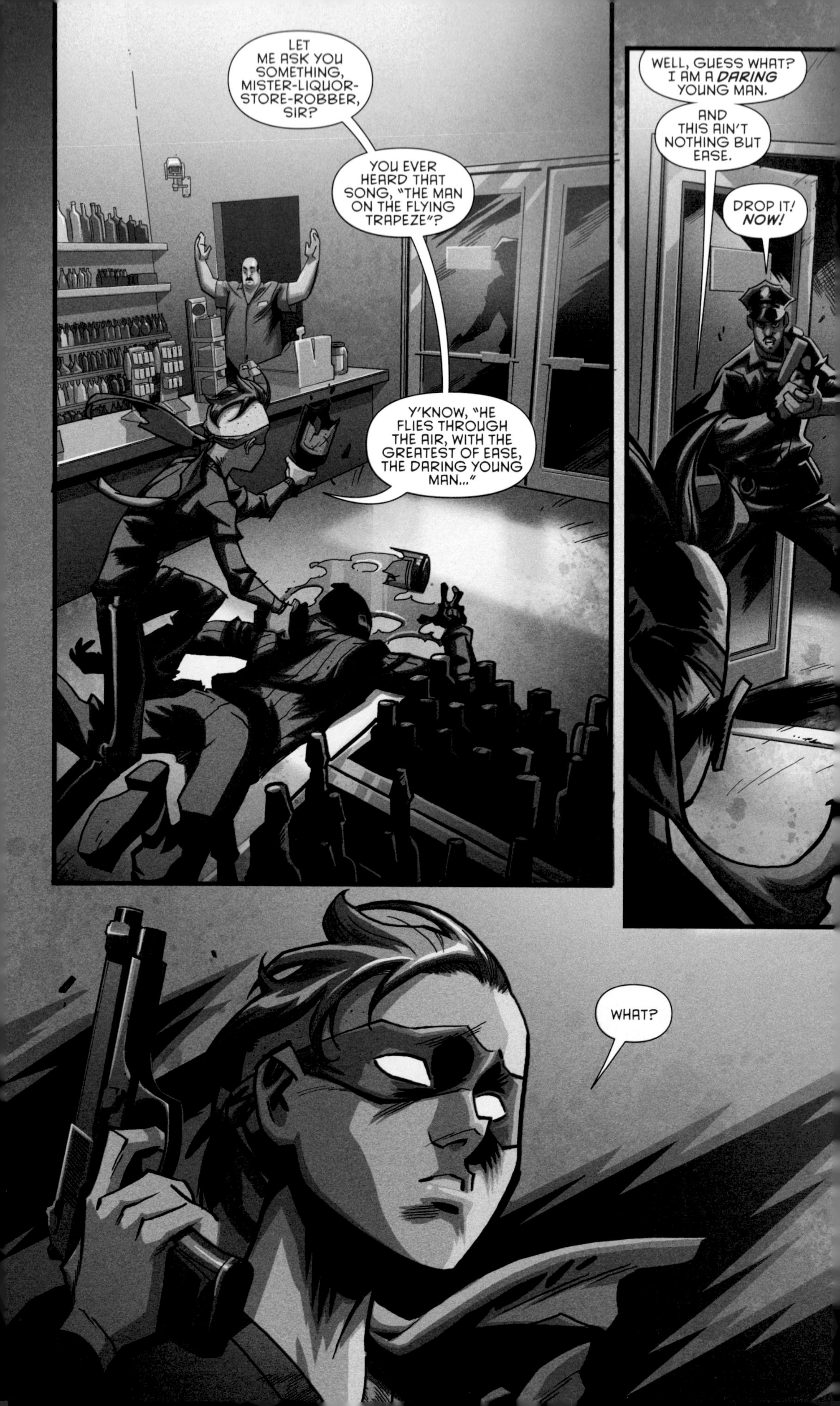
LET ME ASK YOU SOMETHING, MISTER-LIQUOR-STORE-ROBBER, SIR?
YOU EVER HEARD THAT SONG, "THE MAN ON THE FLYING TRAPEZE"?
Y'KNOW, "HE FLIES THROUGH THE AIR, WITH THE GREATEST OF EASE, THE DARING YOUNG MAN..."
WELL, GUESS WHAT? I AM A *DARING* YOUNG MAN.
AND THIS AIN'T NOTHING BUT EASE.
DROP IT! ***NOW!***
WHAT?

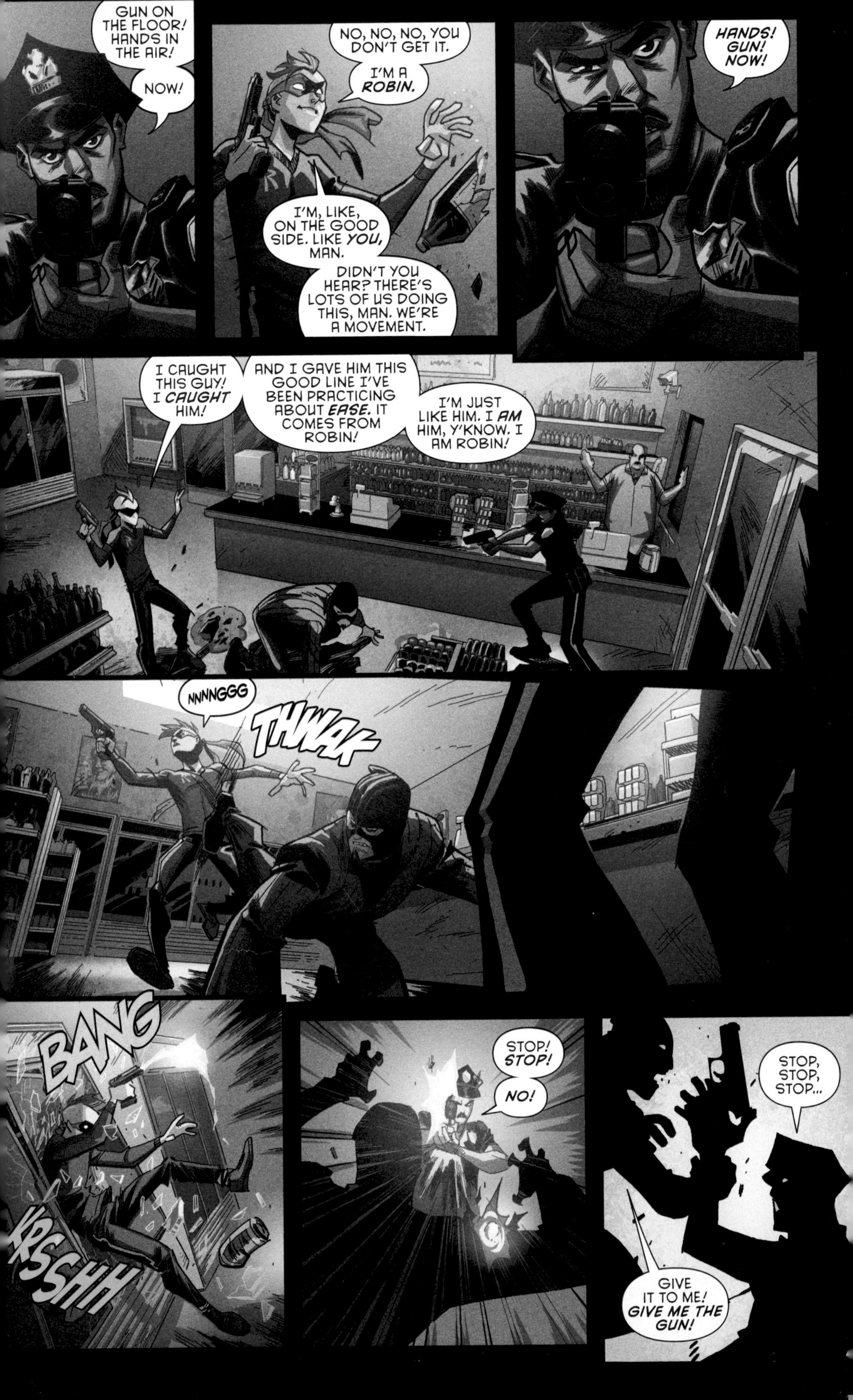

GUN ON THE FLOOR! HANDS IN THE AIR!
NOW!
NO, NO, NO, YOU DON'T GET IT.
I'M A *ROBIN.*
I'M, LIKE, ON THE GOOD SIDE. LIKE *YOU,* MAN.
DIDN'T YOU HEAR? THERE'S LOTS OF US DOING THIS, MAN. WE'RE A MOVEMENT.
HANDS! GUN! NOW!
I CAUGHT THIS GUY! I *CAUGHT* HIM!
AND I GAVE HIM THIS GOOD LINE I'VE BEEN PRACTICING ABOUT *EASE.* IT COMES FROM ROBIN!
I'M JUST LIKE HIM. I *AM* HIM, Y'KNOW. I AM ROBIN!
NNNNGGG
THWAK
BANG
KRSSHH
STOP! *STOP!*
NO!
STOP, STOP, STOP...
GIVE IT TO ME! *GIVE ME THE GUN!*

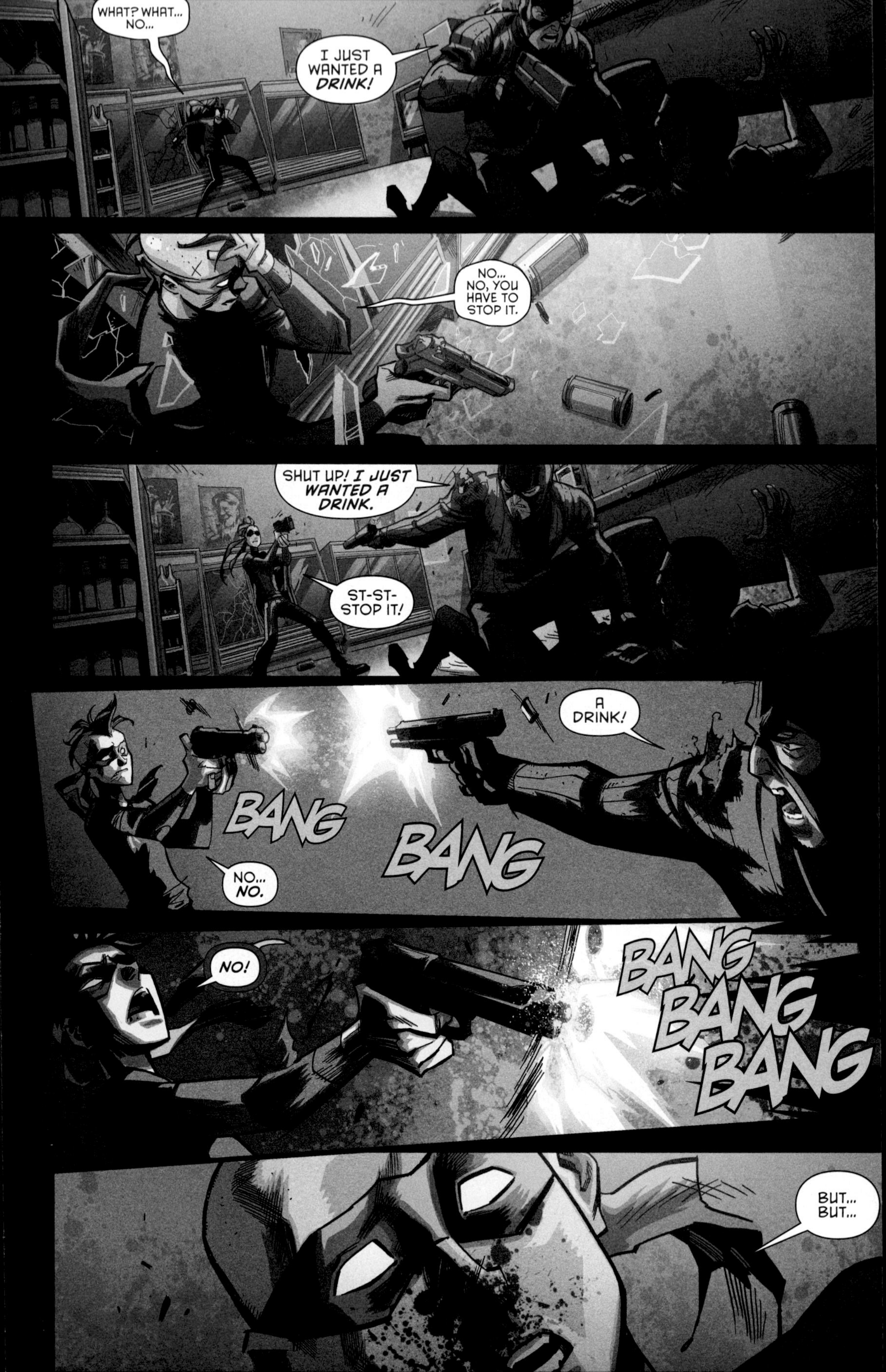
WHAT? WHAT... NO...
I JUST WANTED A DRINK!
NO... NO, YOU HAVE TO STOP IT.
SHUT UP! I JUST WANTED A DRINK.
ST-ST-STOP IT!
A DRINK!
BANG
BANG
NO... NO.
NO!
BANG
BANG
BANG
BUT... BUT...

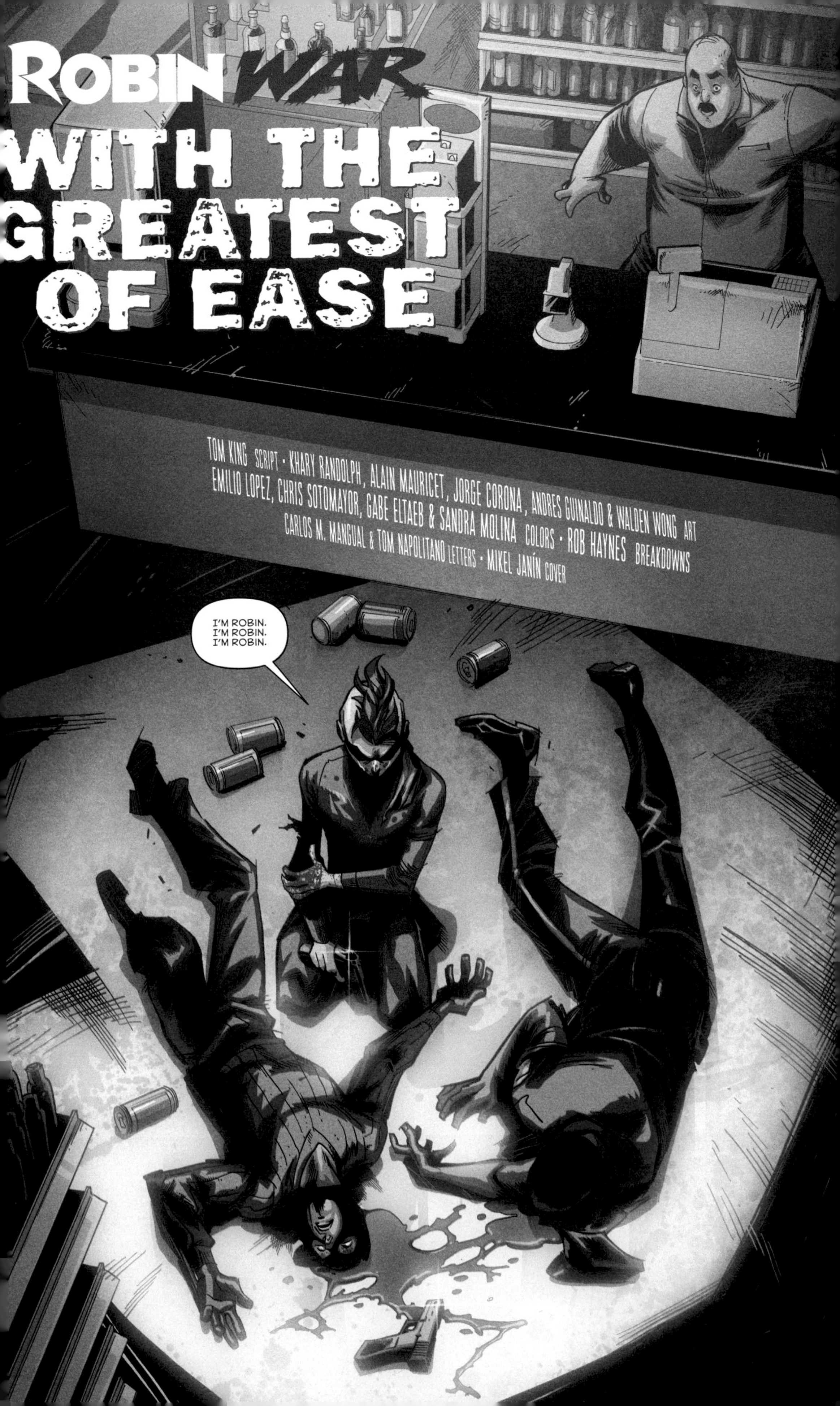

ROBIN WAR
WITH THE GREATEST OF EASE
TOM KING SCRIPT • KHARY RANDOLPH, ALAIN MAURICET, JORGE CORONA, ANDRES GUINALDO & WALDEN WONG ART
EMILIO LOPEZ, CHRIS SOTOMAYOR, GABE ELTAEB & SANDRA MOLINA COLORS • ROB HAYNES BREAKDOWNS
CARLOS M. MANGUAL & TOM NAPOLITANO LETTERS • MIKEL JANÍN COVER
I'M ROBIN. I'M ROBIN. I'M ROBIN.

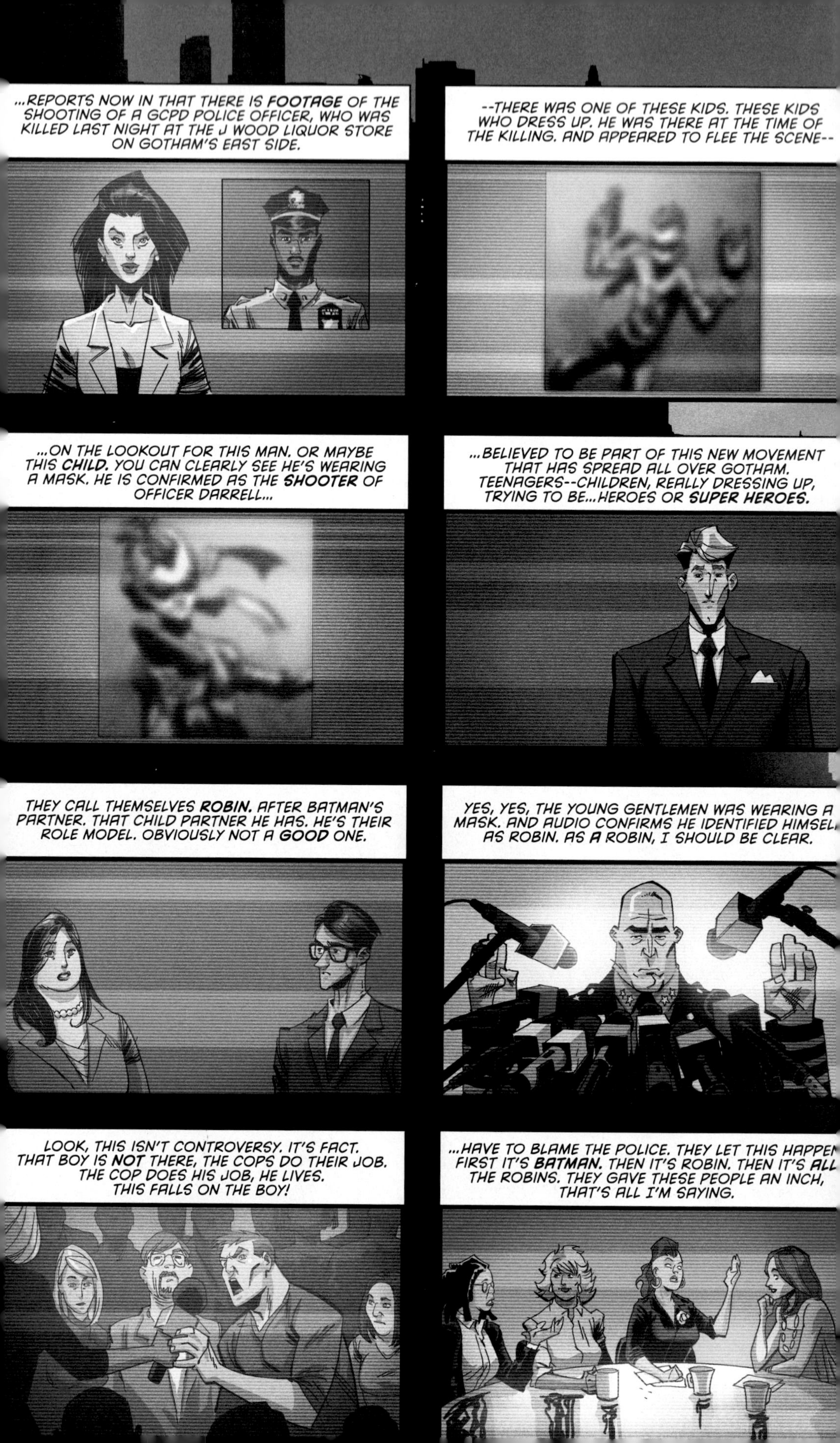
...REPORTS NOW IN THAT THERE IS FOOTAGE OF THE SHOOTING OF A GCPD POLICE OFFICER, WHO WAS KILLED LAST NIGHT AT THE J WOOD LIQUOR STORE ON GOTHAM'S EAST SIDE.
--THERE WAS ONE OF THESE KIDS. THESE KIDS WHO DRESS UP. HE WAS THERE AT THE TIME OF THE KILLING. AND APPEARED TO FLEE THE SCENE--
...ON THE LOOKOUT FOR THIS MAN. OR MAYBE THIS CHILD. YOU CAN CLEARLY SEE HE'S WEARING A MASK. HE IS CONFIRMED AS THE SHOOTER OF OFFICER DARRELL...
...BELIEVED TO BE PART OF THIS NEW MOVEMENT THAT HAS SPREAD ALL OVER GOTHAM. TEENAGERS--CHILDREN, REALLY DRESSING UP, TRYING TO BE...HEROES OR SUPER HEROES.
THEY CALL THEMSELVES ROBIN. AFTER BATMAN'S PARTNER. THAT CHILD PARTNER HE HAS. HE'S THEIR ROLE MODEL. OBVIOUSLY NOT A GOOD ONE.
YES, YES, THE YOUNG GENTLEMEN WAS WEARING A MASK. AND AUDIO CONFIRMS HE IDENTIFIED HIMSEL AS ROBIN. AS A ROBIN, I SHOULD BE CLEAR.
LOOK, THIS ISN'T CONTROVERSY. IT'S FACT. THAT BOY IS NOT THERE, THE COPS DO THEIR JOB. THE COP DOES HIS JOB, HE LIVES. THIS FALLS ON THE BOY!
...HAVE TO BLAME THE POLICE. THEY LET THIS HAPPEN FIRST IT'S BATMAN. THEN IT'S ROBIN. THEN IT'S ALL THE ROBINS. THEY GAVE THESE PEOPLE AN INCH, THAT'S ALL I'M SAYING.

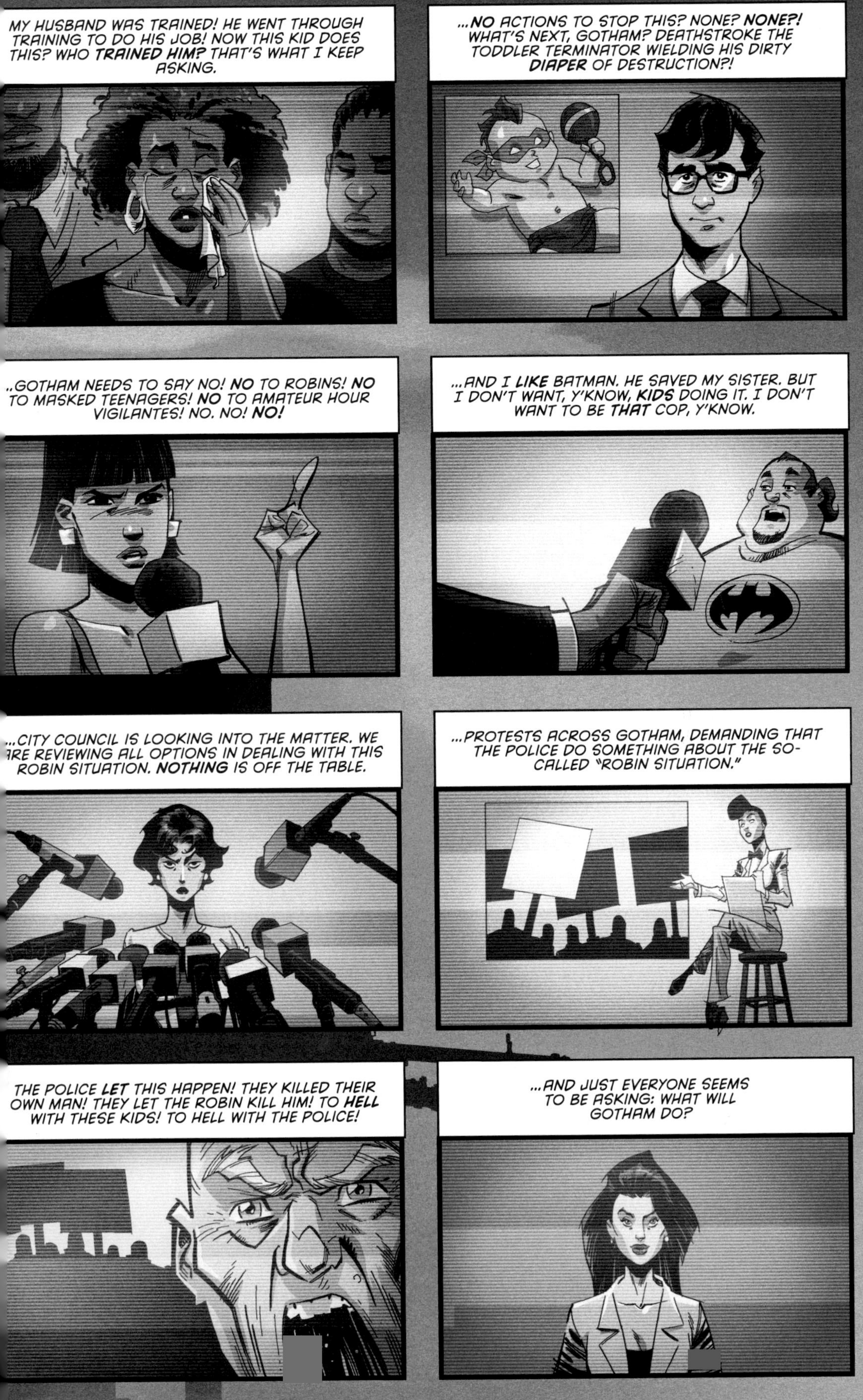
MY HUSBAND WAS TRAINED! HE WENT THROUGH TRAINING TO DO HIS JOB! NOW THIS KID DOES THIS? WHO TRAINED HIM? THAT'S WHAT I KEEP ASKING.
...NO ACTIONS TO STOP THIS? NONE? NONE?! WHAT'S NEXT, GOTHAM? DEATHSTROKE THE TODDLER TERMINATOR WIELDING HIS DIRTY DIAPER OF DESTRUCTION?!
..GOTHAM NEEDS TO SAY NO! NO TO ROBINS! NO TO MASKED TEENAGERS! NO TO AMATEUR HOUR VIGILANTES! NO. NO! NO!
...AND I LIKE BATMAN. HE SAVED MY SISTER. BUT I DON'T WANT, Y'KNOW, KIDS DOING IT. I DON'T WANT TO BE THAT COP, Y'KNOW.
...CITY COUNCIL IS LOOKING INTO THE MATTER. WE ARE REVIEWING ALL OPTIONS IN DEALING WITH THIS ROBIN SITUATION. NOTHING IS OFF THE TABLE.
...PROTESTS ACROSS GOTHAM, DEMANDING THAT THE POLICE DO SOMETHING ABOUT THE SO-CALLED "ROBIN SITUATION."
THE POLICE LET THIS HAPPEN! THEY KILLED THEIR OWN MAN! THEY LET THE ROBIN KILL HIM! TO HELL WITH THESE KIDS! TO HELL WITH THE POLICE!
...AND JUST EVERYONE SEEMS TO BE ASKING: WHAT WILL GOTHAM DO?

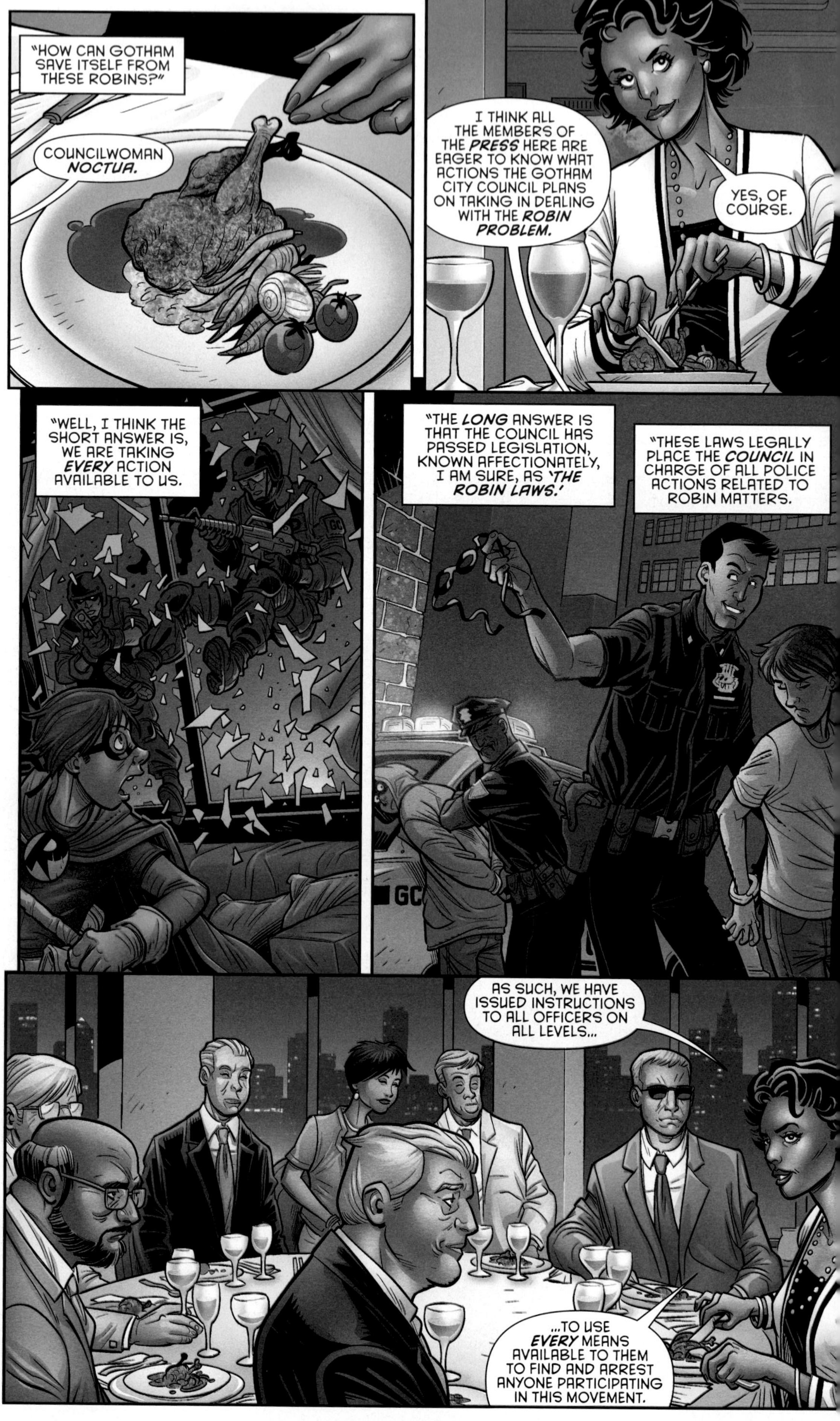
"HOW CAN GOTHAM SAVE ITSELF FROM THESE ROBINS?"
COUNCILWOMAN NOCTUA.
I THINK ALL THE MEMBERS OF THE PRESS HERE ARE EAGER TO KNOW WHAT ACTIONS THE GOTHAM CITY COUNCIL PLANS ON TAKING IN DEALING WITH THE ROBIN PROBLEM.
YES, OF COURSE.
"WELL, I THINK THE SHORT ANSWER IS, WE ARE TAKING EVERY ACTION AVAILABLE TO US.
"THE LONG ANSWER IS THAT THE COUNCIL HAS PASSED LEGISLATION, KNOWN AFFECTIONATELY, I AM SURE, AS 'THE ROBIN LAWS.'
"THESE LAWS LEGALLY PLACE THE COUNCIL IN CHARGE OF ALL POLICE ACTIONS RELATED TO ROBIN MATTERS.
AS SUCH, WE HAVE ISSUED INSTRUCTIONS TO ALL OFFICERS ON ALL LEVELS...
...TO USE EVERY MEANS AVAILABLE TO THEM TO FIND AND ARREST ANYONE PARTICIPATING IN THIS MOVEMENT.

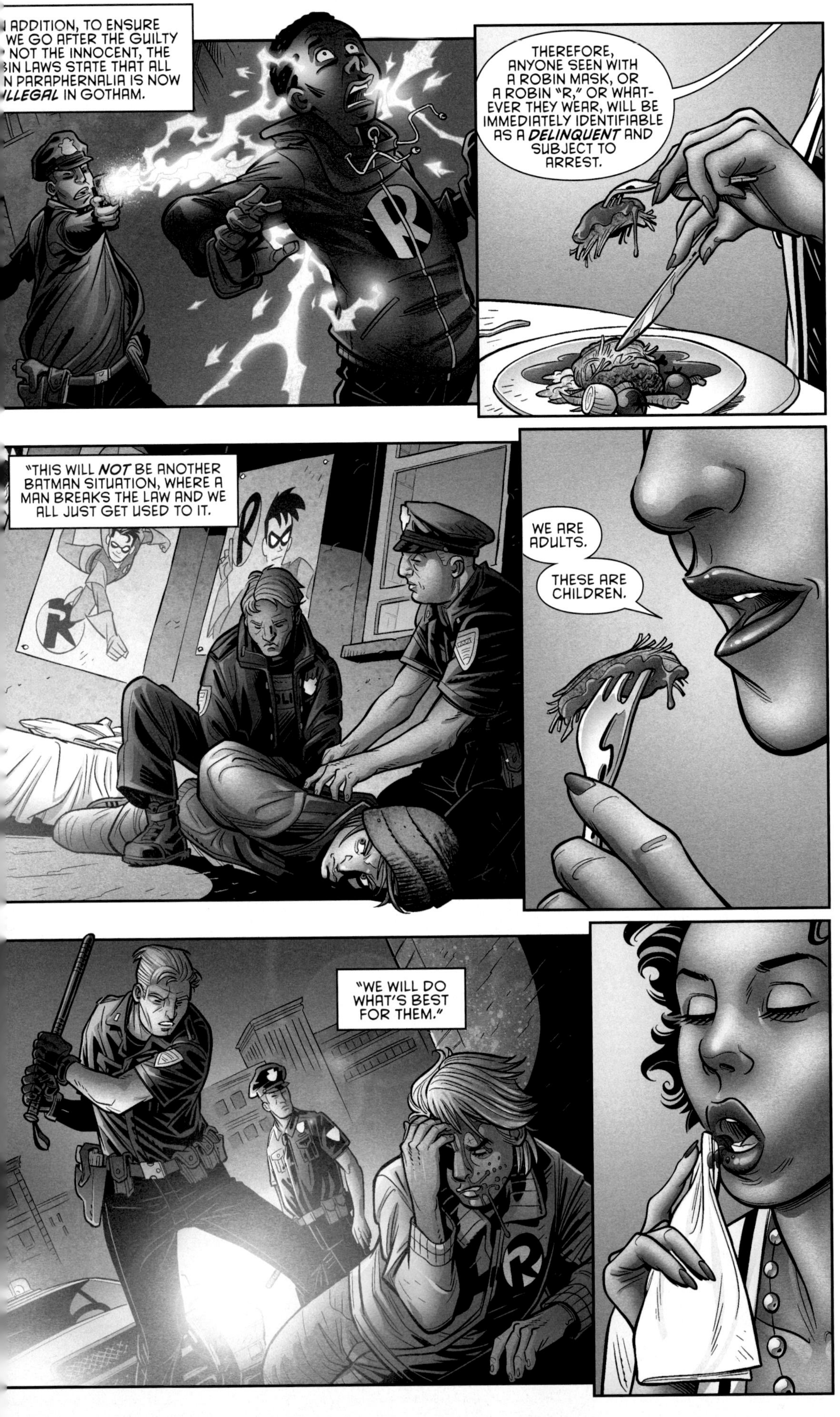

N ADDITION, TO ENSURE WE GO AFTER THE GUILTY NOT THE INNOCENT, THE BIN LAWS STATE THAT ALL N PARAPHERNALIA IS NOW ILLEGAL IN GOTHAM.
THEREFORE, ANYONE SEEN WITH A ROBIN MASK, OR A ROBIN "R," OR WHATEVER THEY WEAR, WILL BE IMMEDIATELY IDENTIFIABLE AS A DELINQUENT AND SUBJECT TO ARREST.
"THIS WILL NOT BE ANOTHER BATMAN SITUATION, WHERE A MAN BREAKS THE LAW AND WE ALL JUST GET USED TO IT.
WE ARE ADULTS.
THESE ARE CHILDREN.
"WE WILL DO WHAT'S BEST FOR THEM."

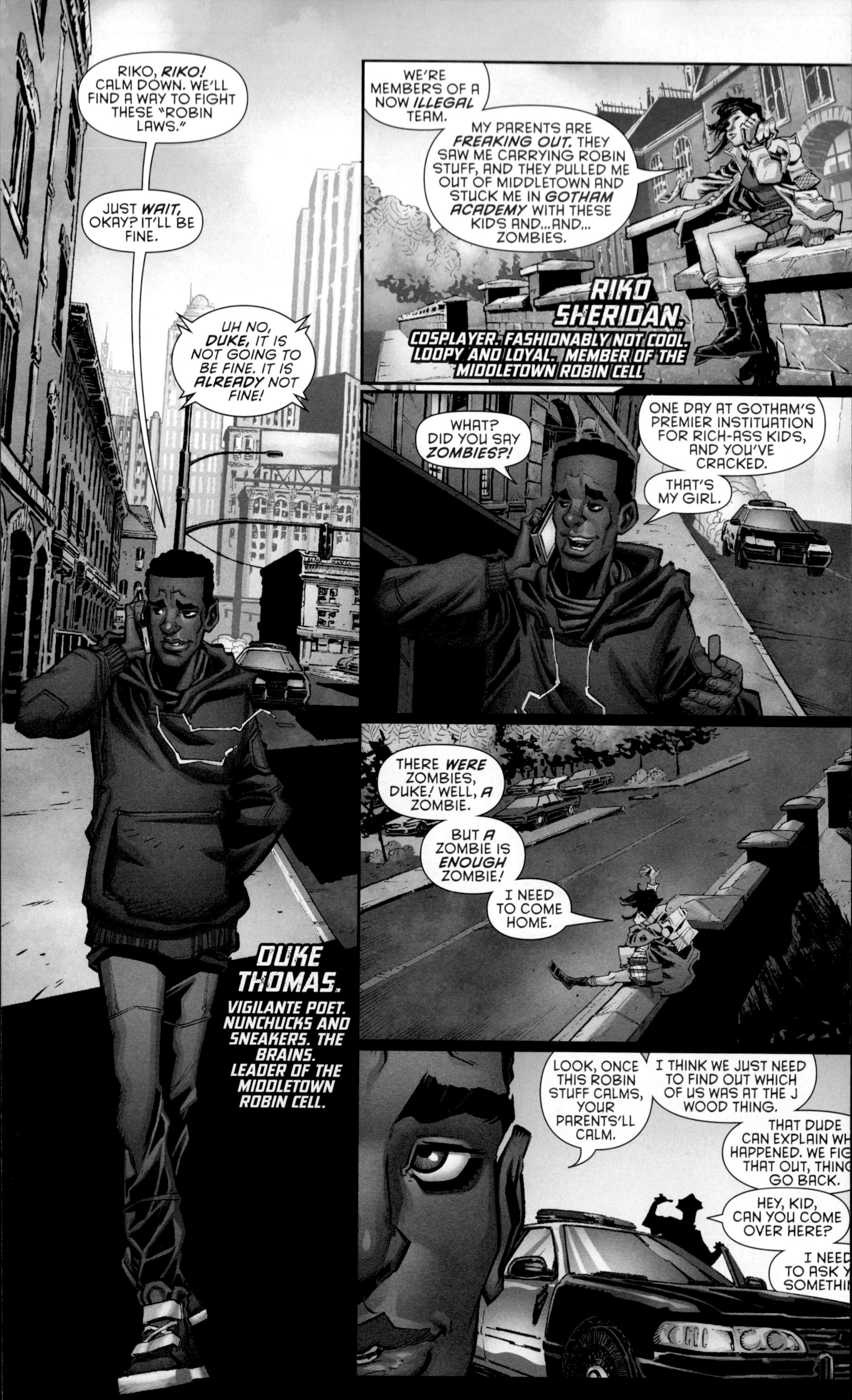

RIKO, *RIKO!* CALM DOWN. WE'LL FIND A WAY TO FIGHT THESE "ROBIN LAWS."
JUST *WAIT,* OKAY? IT'LL BE FINE.
UH NO, *DUKE,* IT IS NOT GOING TO BE FINE. IT IS *ALREADY* NOT FINE!
DUKE THOMAS.
VIGILANTE POET. NUNCHUCKS AND SNEAKERS. THE BRAINS. LEADER OF THE MIDDLETOWN ROBIN CELL.
WE'RE MEMBERS OF A NOW *ILLEGAL* TEAM.
MY PARENTS ARE *FREAKING OUT.* THEY SAW ME CARRYING ROBIN STUFF, AND THEY PULLED ME OUT OF MIDDLETOWN AND STUCK ME IN *GOTHAM ACADEMY* WITH THESE KIDS AND...AND... ZOMBIES.
RIKO SHERIDAN.
COSPLAYER. FASHIONABLY NOT COOL. LOOPY AND LOYAL. MEMBER OF THE MIDDLETOWN ROBIN CELL
WHAT? DID YOU SAY *ZOMBIES?!*
ONE DAY AT GOTHAM'S PREMIER INSTITUATION FOR RICH-ASS KIDS, AND YOU'VE CRACKED.
THAT'S MY GIRL.
THERE *WERE* ZOMBIES, DUKE! WELL, *A* ZOMBIE.
BUT *A* ZOMBIE IS *ENOUGH* ZOMBIE!
I NEED TO COME HOME.
LOOK, ONCE THIS ROBIN STUFF CALMS, YOUR PARENTS'LL CALM.
I THINK WE JUST NEED TO FIND OUT WHICH OF US WAS AT THE J WOOD THING.
HEY, KID, CAN YOU COME OVER HERE?

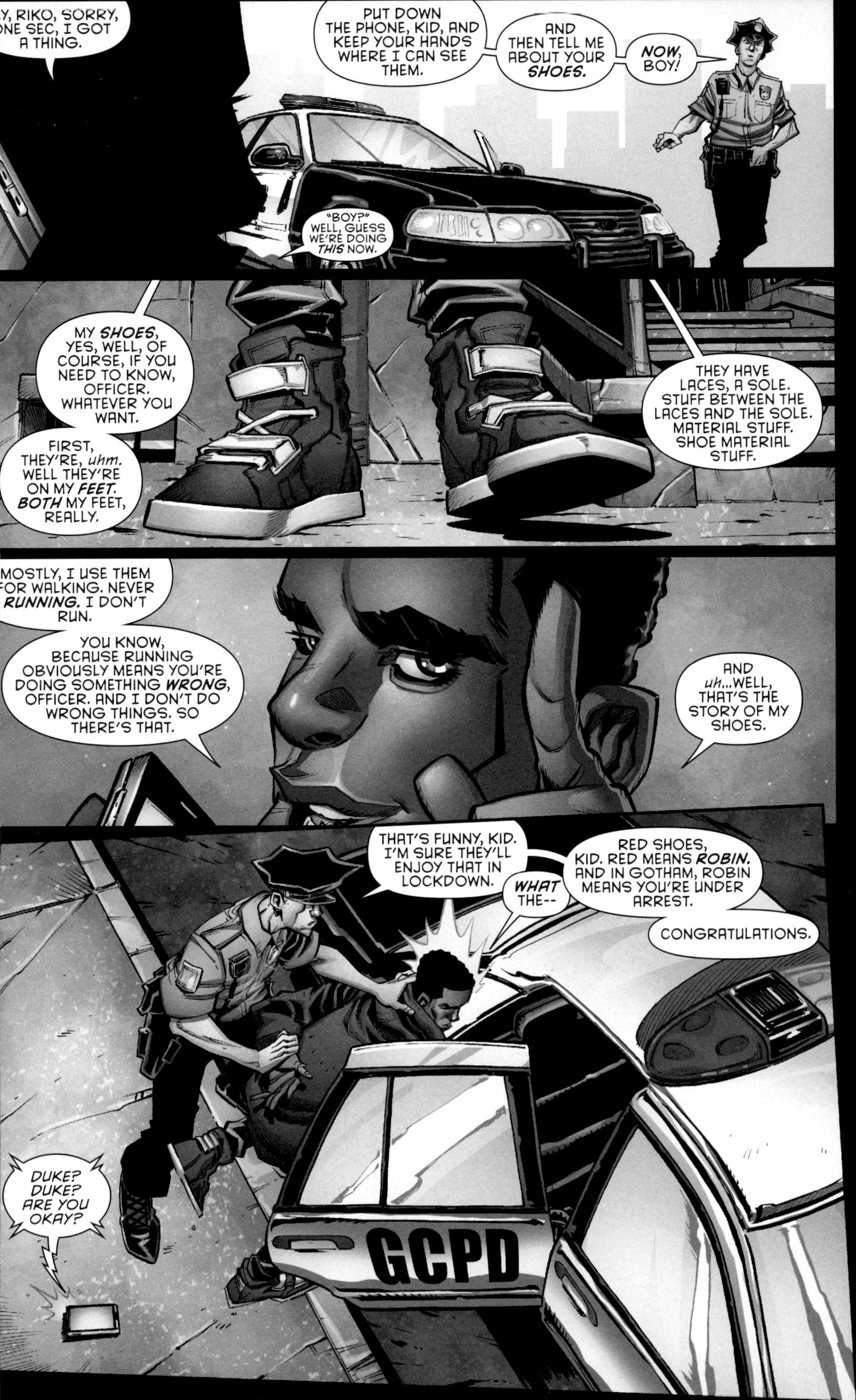
Y, RIKO, SORRY, ONE SEC, I GOT A THING.
PUT DOWN THE PHONE, KID, AND KEEP YOUR HANDS WHERE I CAN SEE THEM.
AND THEN TELL ME ABOUT YOUR SHOES.
NOW, BOY!
"BOY?" WELL, GUESS WE'RE DOING THIS NOW.
MY SHOES, YES, WELL, OF COURSE, IF YOU NEED TO KNOW, OFFICER. WHATEVER YOU WANT.
FIRST, THEY'RE, uhm. WELL THEY'RE ON MY FEET. BOTH MY FEET, REALLY.
THEY HAVE LACES, A SOLE. STUFF BETWEEN THE LACES AND THE SOLE. MATERIAL STUFF. SHOE MATERIAL STUFF.
MOSTLY, I USE THEM FOR WALKING. NEVER RUNNING. I DON'T RUN.
YOU KNOW, BECAUSE RUNNING OBVIOUSLY MEANS YOU'RE DOING SOMETHING WRONG, OFFICER. AND I DON'T DO WRONG THINGS. SO THERE'S THAT.
AND uh...WELL, THAT'S THE STORY OF MY SHOES.
THAT'S FUNNY, KID. I'M SURE THEY'LL ENJOY THAT IN LOCKDOWN.
WHAT THE--
RED SHOES, KID. RED MEANS ROBIN. AND IN GOTHAM, ROBIN MEANS YOU'RE UNDER ARREST.
CONGRATULATIONS.
DUKE? DUKE? ARE YOU OKAY?
GCPD

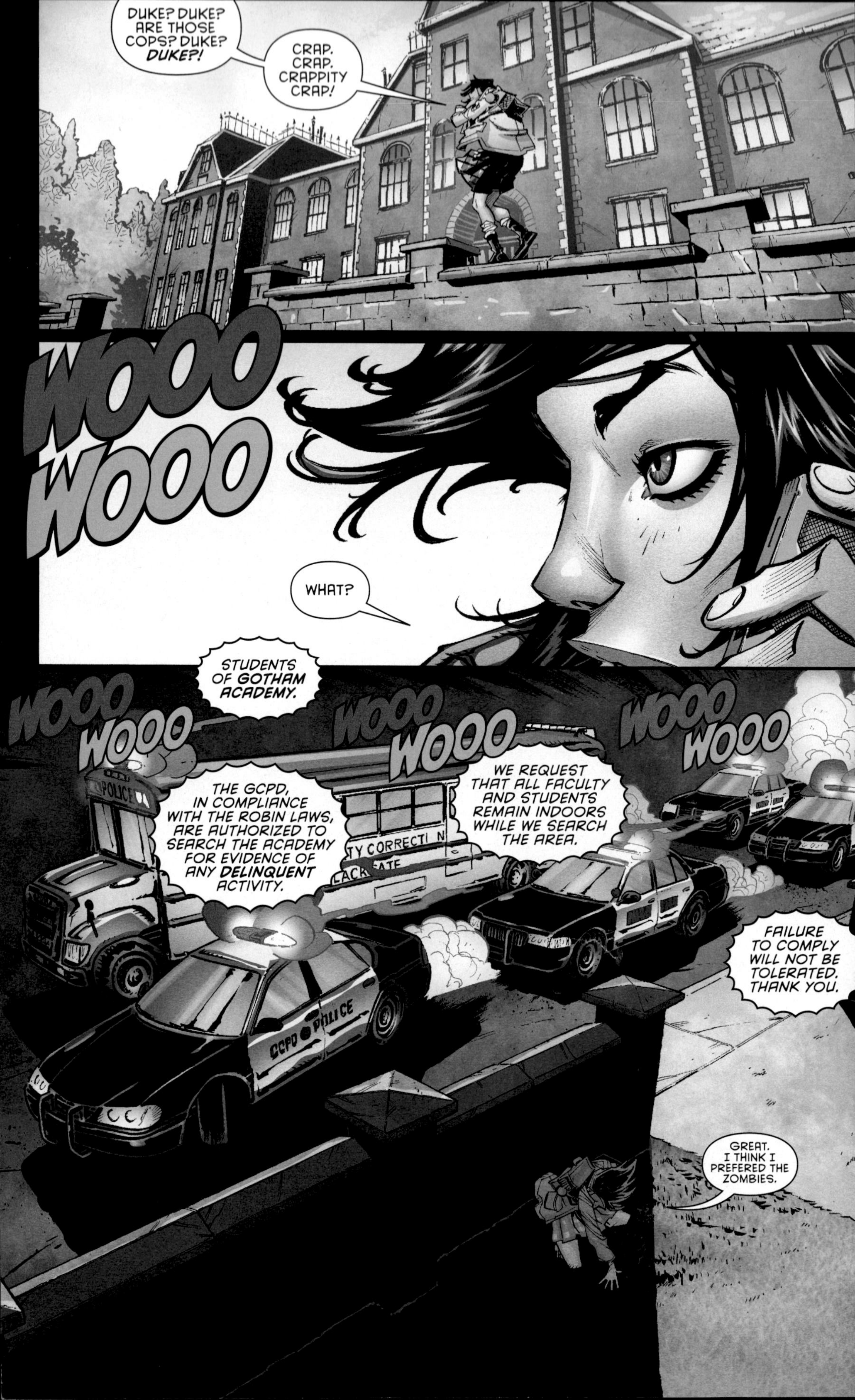
DUKE? DUKE? ARE THOSE COPS? DUKE? *DUKE?!*
CRAP. CRAP. CRAPPITY CRAP!
WOOO WOOO
WHAT?
STUDENTS OF *GOTHAM ACADEMY.*
WOOO WOOO
WOOO WOOO
WOOO WOOO
THE GCPD, IN COMPLIANCE WITH THE ROBIN LAWS, ARE AUTHORIZED TO SEARCH THE ACADEMY FOR EVIDENCE OF ANY *DELINQUENT* ACTIVITY.
WE REQUEST THAT ALL FACULTY AND STUDENTS REMAIN INDOORS WHILE WE SEARCH THE AREA.
FAILURE TO COMPLY WILL NOT BE TOLERATED. THANK YOU.
GCPD POLICE
GREAT. I THINK I PREFERED THE ZOMBIES.

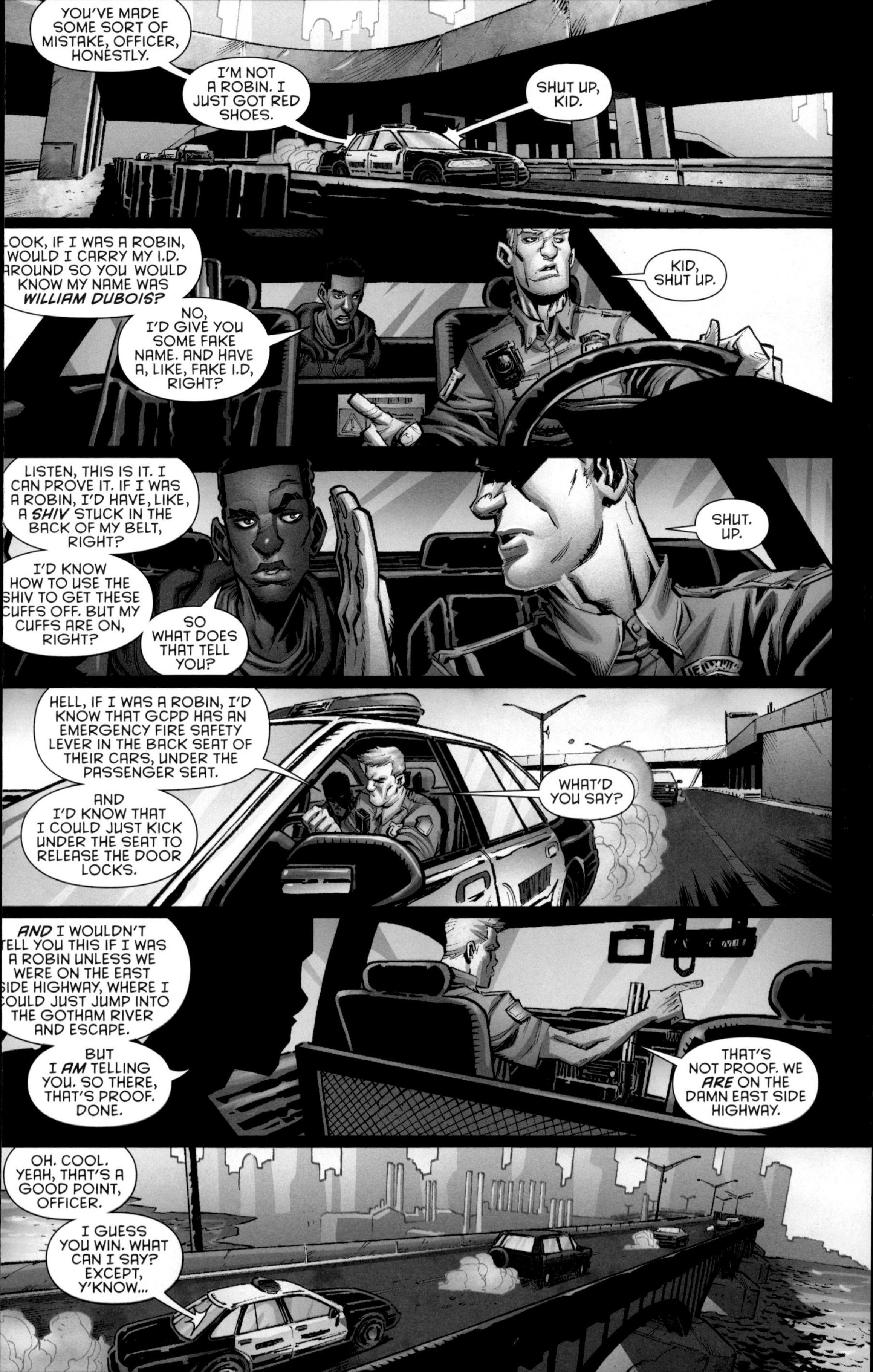
YOU'VE MADE SOME SORT OF MISTAKE, OFFICER, HONESTLY.
I'M NOT A ROBIN. I JUST GOT RED SHOES.
SHUT UP, KID.
LOOK, IF I WAS A ROBIN, WOULD I CARRY MY I.D. AROUND SO YOU WOULD KNOW MY NAME WAS WILLIAM DUBOIS?
NO, I'D GIVE YOU SOME FAKE NAME. AND HAVE A, LIKE, FAKE I.D, RIGHT?
KID, SHUT UP.
LISTEN, THIS IS IT. I CAN PROVE IT. IF I WAS A ROBIN, I'D HAVE, LIKE, A SHIV STUCK IN THE BACK OF MY BELT, RIGHT?
I'D KNOW HOW TO USE THE SHIV TO GET THESE CUFFS OFF. BUT MY CUFFS ARE ON, RIGHT?
SO WHAT DOES THAT TELL YOU?
SHUT. UP.
HELL, IF I WAS A ROBIN, I'D KNOW THAT GCPD HAS AN EMERGENCY FIRE SAFETY LEVER IN THE BACK SEAT OF THEIR CARS, UNDER THE PASSENGER SEAT.
AND I'D KNOW THAT I COULD JUST KICK UNDER THE SEAT TO RELEASE THE DOOR LOCKS.
WHAT'D YOU SAY?
AND I WOULDN'T TELL YOU THIS IF I WAS A ROBIN UNLESS WE WERE ON THE EAST SIDE HIGHWAY, WHERE I COULD JUST JUMP INTO THE GOTHAM RIVER AND ESCAPE.
BUT I AM TELLING YOU. SO THERE, THAT'S PROOF. DONE.
THAT'S NOT PROOF. WE ARE ON THE DAMN EAST SIDE HIGHWAY.
OH. COOL. YEAH, THAT'S A GOOD POINT, OFFICER.
I GUESS YOU WIN. WHAT CAN I SAY? EXCEPT, Y'KNOW...

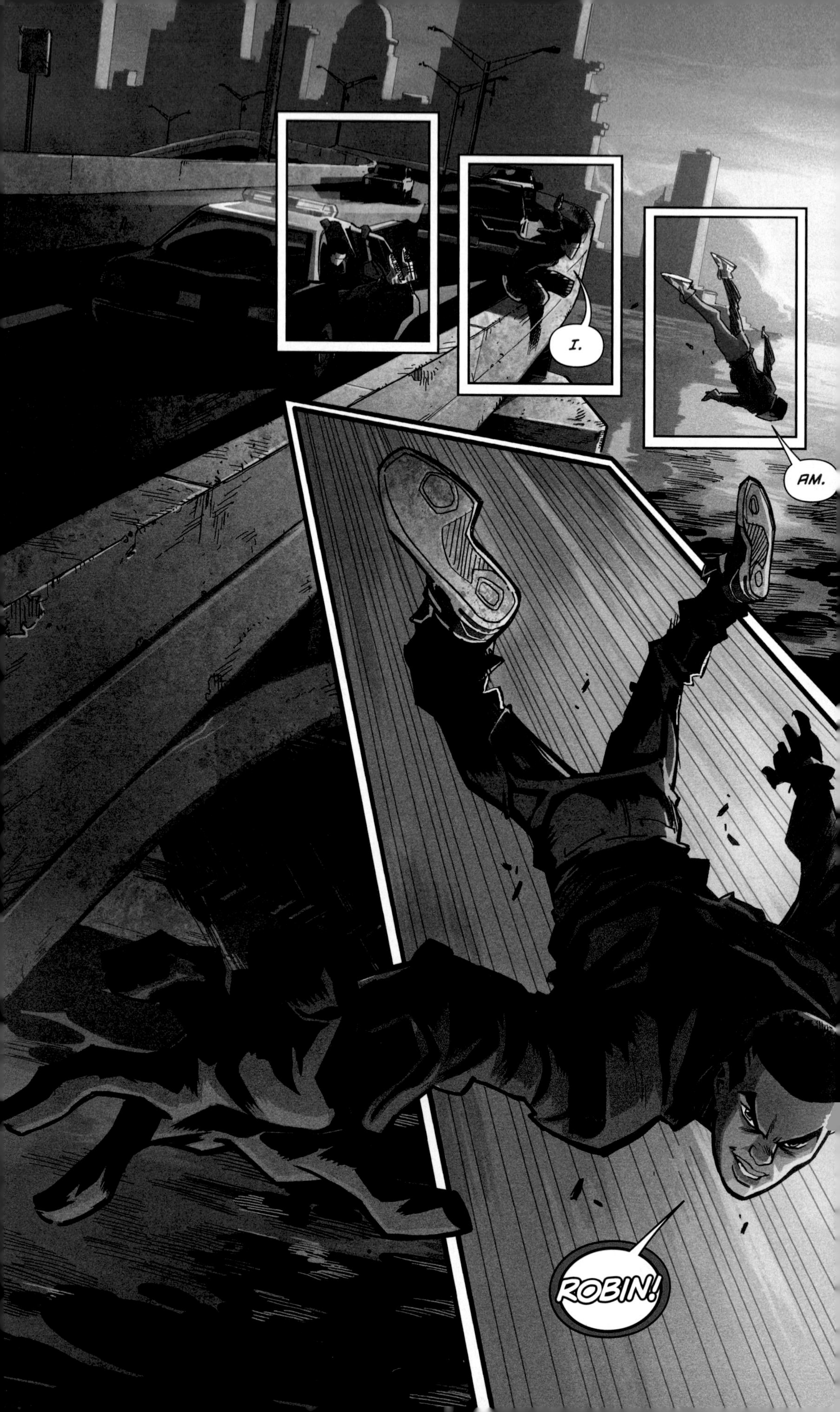
I.
AM.
ROBIN!

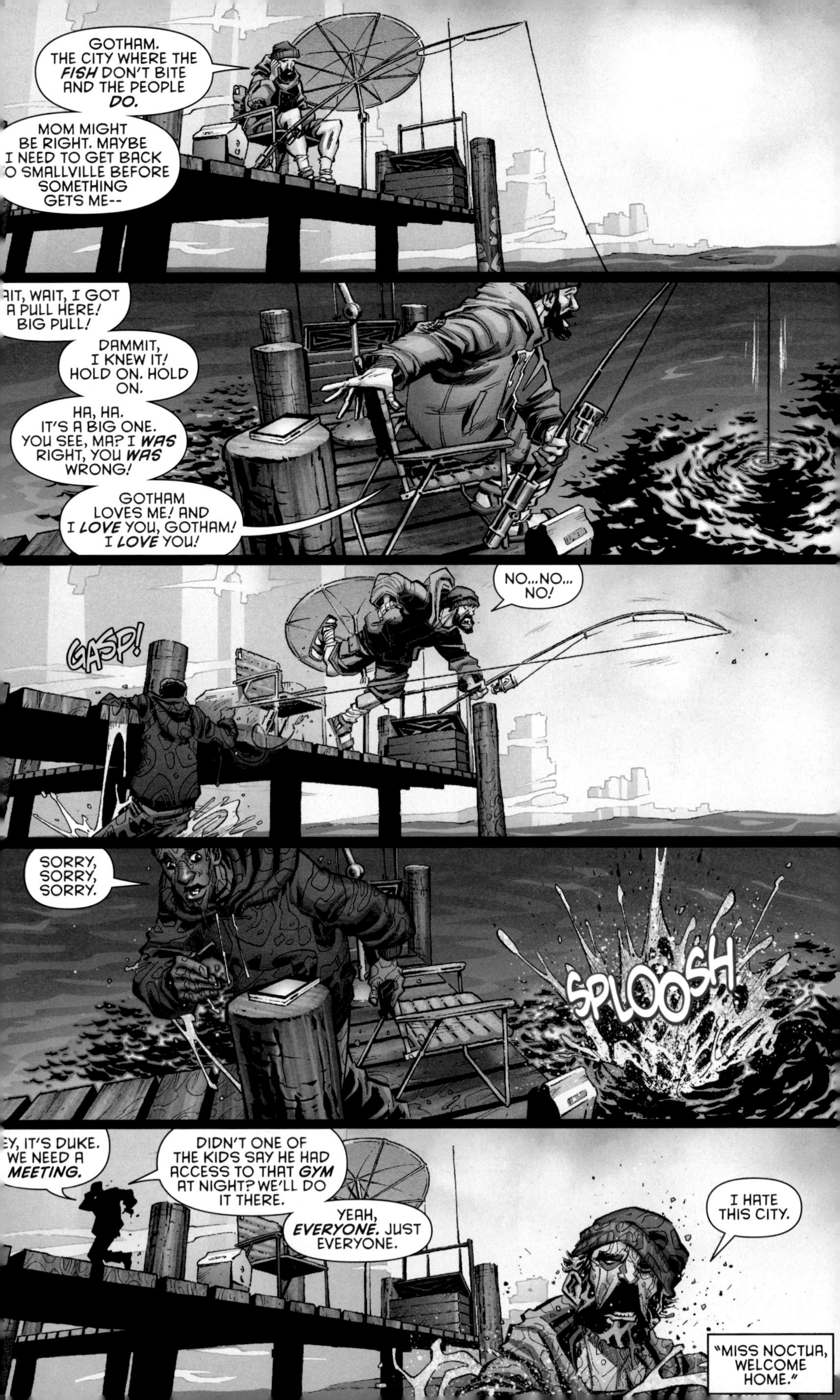
GOTHAM. THE CITY WHERE THE FISH DON'T BITE AND THE PEOPLE DO.
MOM MIGHT BE RIGHT. MAYBE I NEED TO GET BACK O SMALLVILLE BEFORE SOMETHING GETS ME--
AIT, WAIT, I GOT A PULL HERE! BIG PULL!
DAMMIT, I KNEW IT! HOLD ON. HOLD ON.
HA, HA. IT'S A BIG ONE. YOU SEE, MA? I WAS RIGHT, YOU WAS WRONG!
GOTHAM LOVES ME! AND I LOVE YOU, GOTHAM! I LOVE YOU!
NO...NO... NO!
GASP!
SORRY, SORRY, SORRY.
SPLOOSH
EY, IT'S DUKE. WE NEED A MEETING.
DIDN'T ONE OF THE KIDS SAY HE HAD ACCESS TO THAT GYM AT NIGHT? WE'LL DO IT THERE.
YEAH, EVERYONE. JUST EVERYONE.
I HATE THIS CITY.
"MISS NOCTUA, WELCOME HOME."

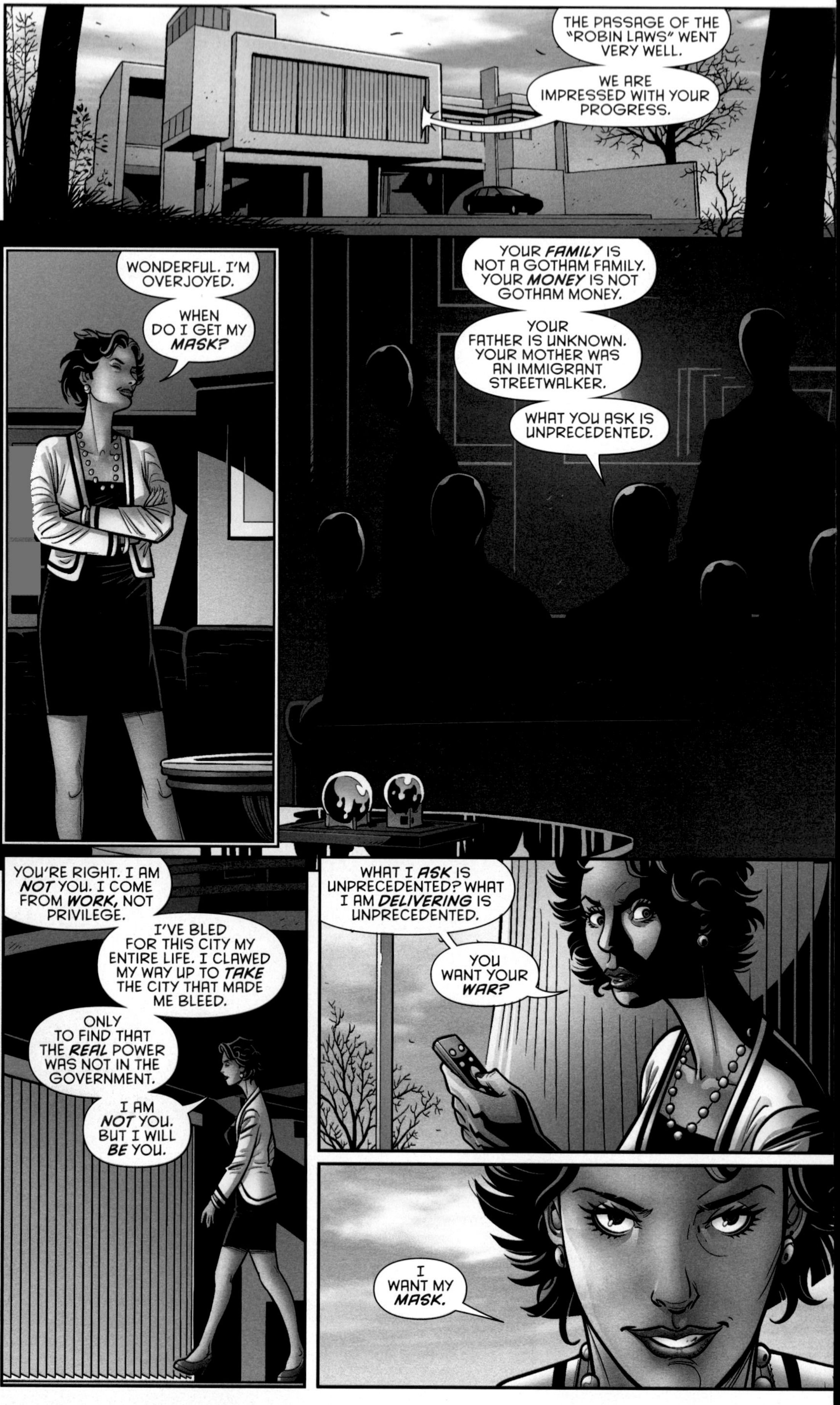

THE PASSAGE OF THE "ROBIN LAWS" WENT VERY WELL.
WE ARE IMPRESSED WITH YOUR PROGRESS.
WONDERFUL. I'M OVERJOYED.
WHEN DO I GET MY MASK?
YOUR FAMILY IS NOT A GOTHAM FAMILY. YOUR MONEY IS NOT GOTHAM MONEY.
YOUR FATHER IS UNKNOWN. YOUR MOTHER WAS AN IMMIGRANT STREETWALKER.
WHAT YOU ASK IS UNPRECEDENTED.
YOU'RE RIGHT. I AM NOT YOU. I COME FROM WORK, NOT PRIVILEGE.
I'VE BLED FOR THIS CITY MY ENTIRE LIFE. I CLAWED MY WAY UP TO TAKE THE CITY THAT MADE ME BLEED.
ONLY TO FIND THAT THE REAL POWER WAS NOT IN THE GOVERNMENT.
I AM NOT YOU. BUT I WILL BE YOU.
WHAT I ASK IS UNPRECEDENTED? WHAT I AM DELIVERING IS UNPRECEDENTED.
YOU WANT YOUR WAR?
I WANT MY MASK.

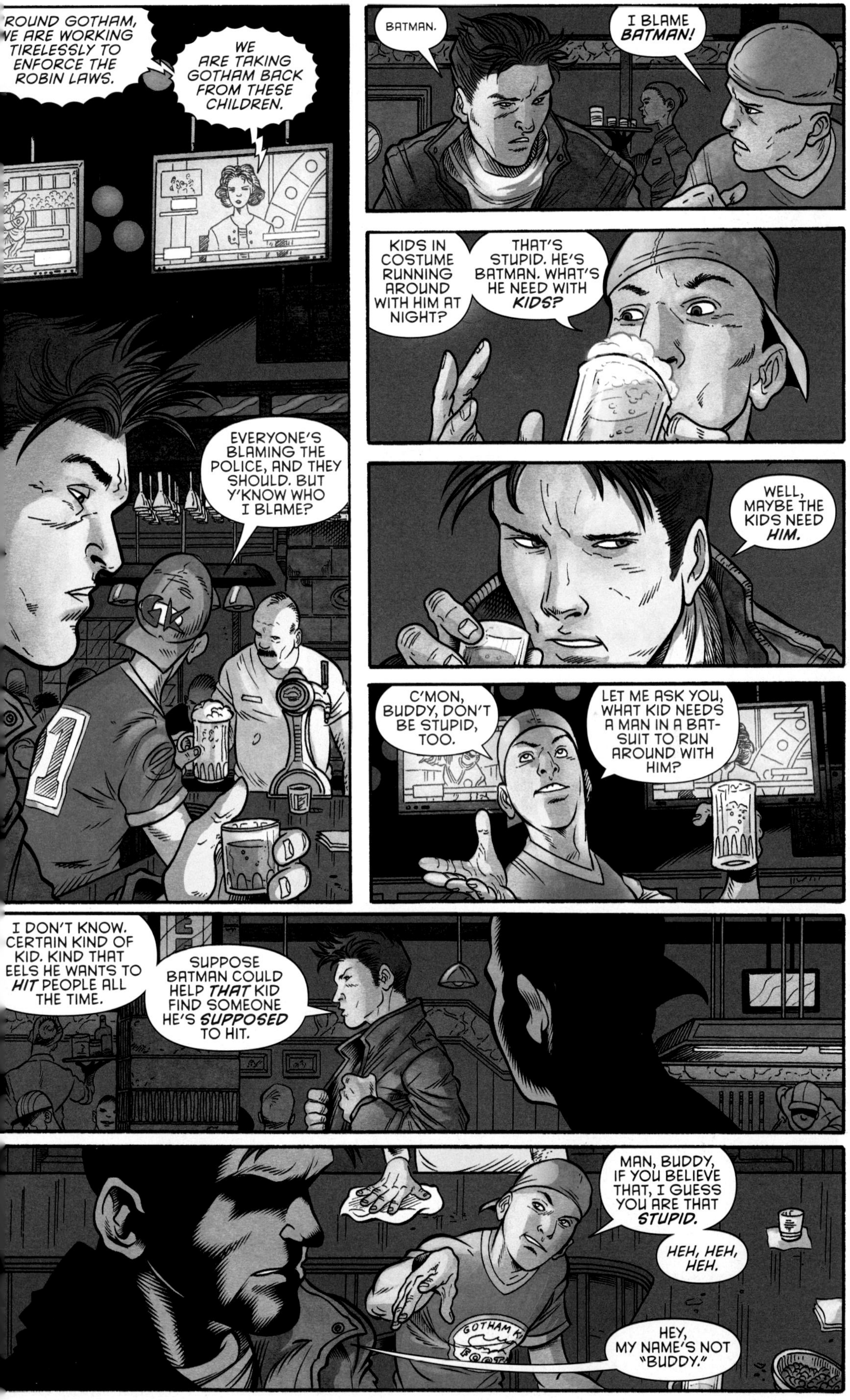
ROUND GOTHAM, VE ARE WORKING TIRELESSLY TO ENFORCE THE ROBIN LAWS.
WE ARE TAKING GOTHAM BACK FROM THESE CHILDREN.
EVERYONE'S BLAMING THE POLICE, AND THEY SHOULD. BUT Y'KNOW WHO I BLAME?
BATMAN.
I BLAME BATMAN!
KIDS IN COSTUME RUNNING AROUND WITH HIM AT NIGHT?
THAT'S STUPID. HE'S BATMAN. WHAT'S HE NEED WITH KIDS?
WELL, MAYBE THE KIDS NEED HIM.
C'MON, BUDDY, DON'T BE STUPID, TOO.
LET ME ASK YOU, WHAT KID NEEDS A MAN IN A BAT-SUIT TO RUN AROUND WITH HIM?
I DON'T KNOW. CERTAIN KIND OF KID. KIND THAT EELS HE WANTS TO HIT PEOPLE ALL THE TIME.
SUPPOSE BATMAN COULD HELP THAT KID FIND SOMEONE HE'S SUPPOSED TO HIT.
MAN, BUDDY, IF YOU BELIEVE THAT, I GUESS YOU ARE THAT STUPID.
HEH, HEH, HEH.
HEY, MY NAME'S NOT "BUDDY."

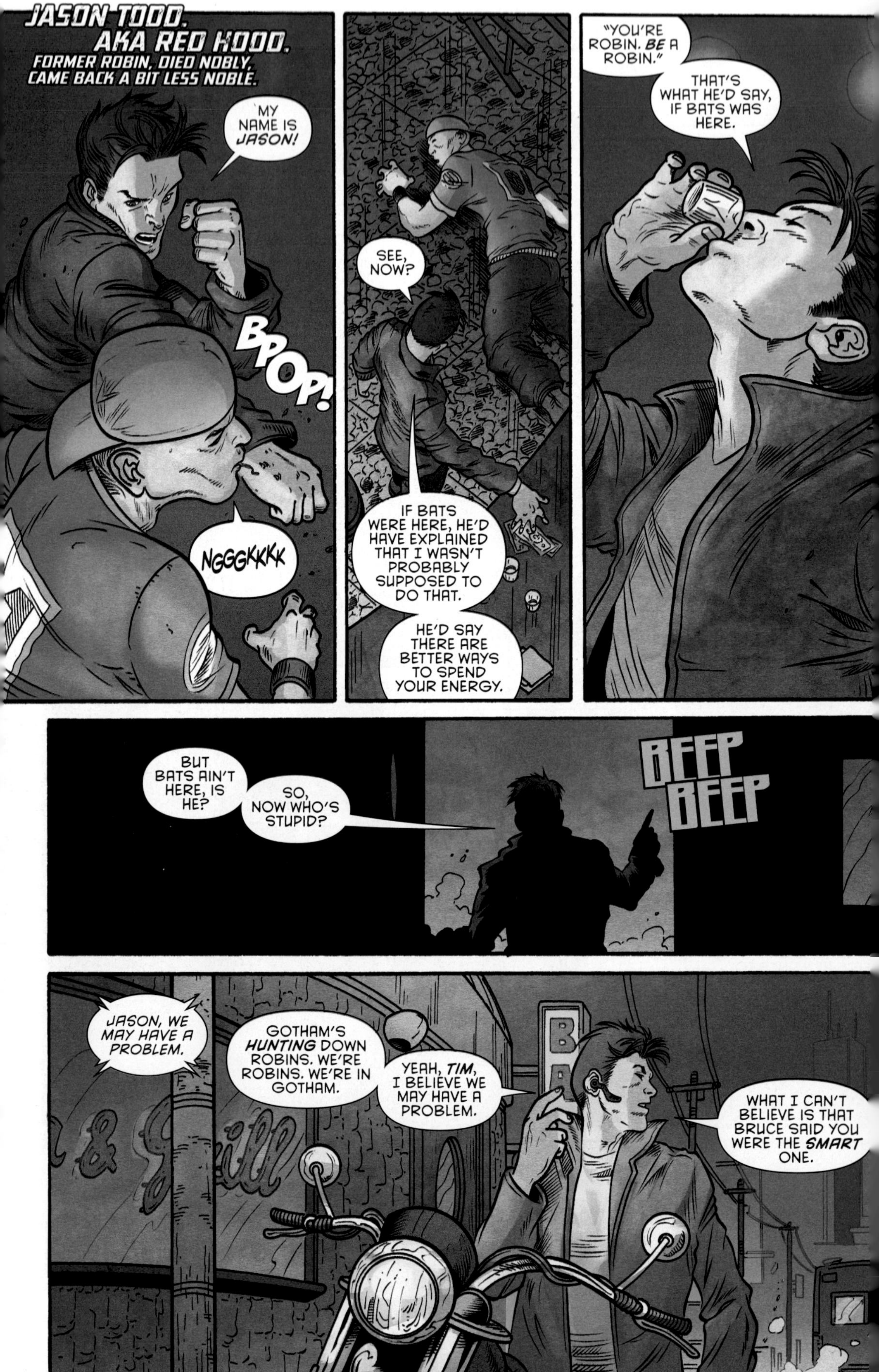
JASON TODD. AKA RED HOOD.
FORMER ROBIN, DIED NOBLY, CAME BACK A BIT LESS NOBLE.
MY NAME IS JASON!
BPOP!
NGGGKKKK
SEE, NOW?
IF BATS WERE HERE, HE'D HAVE EXPLAINED THAT I WASN'T PROBABLY SUPPOSED TO DO THAT.
HE'D SAY THERE ARE BETTER WAYS TO SPEND YOUR ENERGY.
"YOU'RE ROBIN. BE A ROBIN."
THAT'S WHAT HE'D SAY, IF BATS WAS HERE.
BUT BATS AIN'T HERE, IS HE?
SO, NOW WHO'S STUPID?
BEEP BEEP
JASON, WE MAY HAVE A PROBLEM.
GOTHAM'S HUNTING DOWN ROBINS. WE'RE ROBINS. WE'RE IN GOTHAM.
YEAH, TIM, I BELIEVE WE MAY HAVE A PROBLEM.
WHAT I CAN'T BELIEVE IS THAT BRUCE SAID YOU WERE THE SMART ONE.

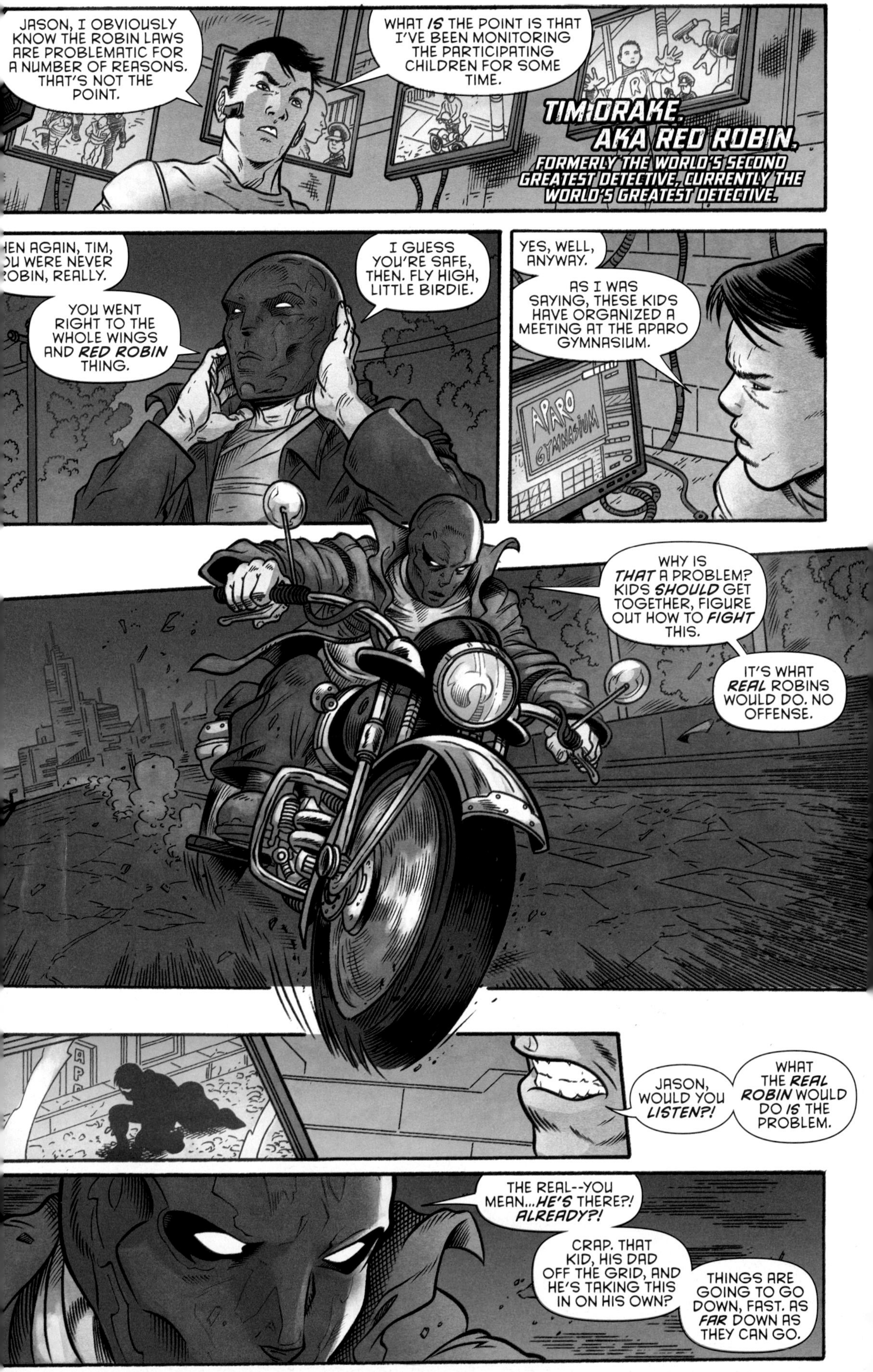
JASON, I OBVIOUSLY KNOW THE ROBIN LAWS ARE PROBLEMATIC FOR A NUMBER OF REASONS. THAT'S NOT THE POINT.
WHAT IS THE POINT IS THAT I'VE BEEN MONITORING THE PARTICIPATING CHILDREN FOR SOME TIME.
TIM DRAKE. AKA RED ROBIN.
FORMERLY THE WORLD'S SECOND GREATEST DETECTIVE, CURRENTLY THE WORLD'S GREATEST DETECTIVE.
HEN AGAIN, TIM, OU WERE NEVER OBIN, REALLY.
YOU WENT RIGHT TO THE WHOLE WINGS AND RED ROBIN THING.
I GUESS YOU'RE SAFE, THEN. FLY HIGH, LITTLE BIRDIE.
YES, WELL, ANYWAY.
AS I WAS SAYING, THESE KIDS HAVE ORGANIZED A MEETING AT THE APARO GYMNASIUM.
APARO GYMNASIUM
WHY IS THAT A PROBLEM? KIDS SHOULD GET TOGETHER, FIGURE OUT HOW TO FIGHT THIS.
IT'S WHAT REAL ROBINS WOULD DO. NO OFFENSE.
JASON, WOULD YOU LISTEN?!
WHAT THE REAL ROBIN WOULD DO IS THE PROBLEM.
THE REAL--YOU MEAN...HE'S THERE?! ALREADY?!
CRAP. THAT KID, HIS DAD OFF THE GRID, AND HE'S TAKING THIS IN ON HIS OWN?
THINGS ARE GOING TO GO DOWN, FAST. AS FAR DOWN AS THEY CAN GO.

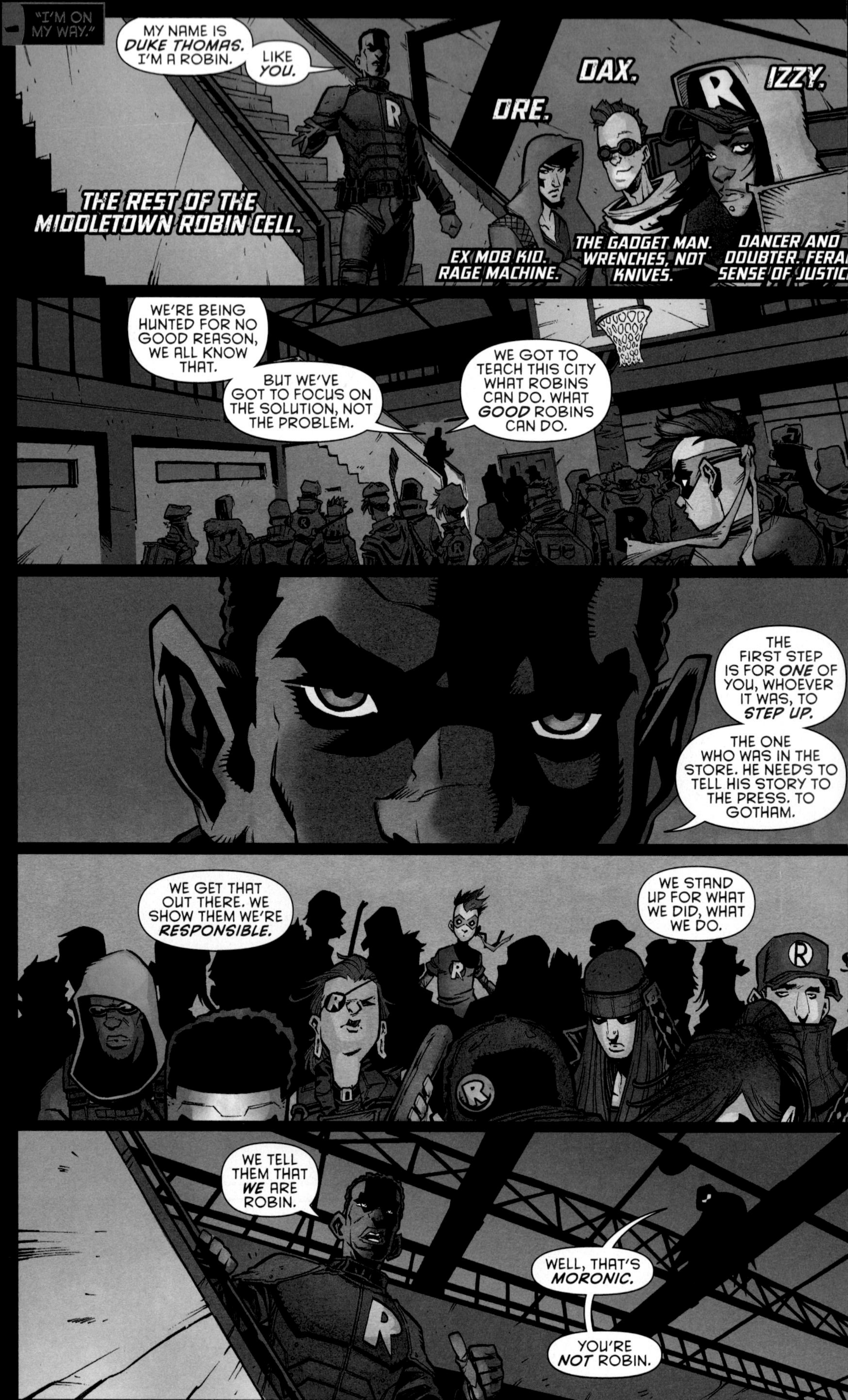
"I'M ON MY WAY."
MY NAME IS DUKE THOMAS. I'M A ROBIN.
LIKE YOU.
THE REST OF THE MIDDLETOWN ROBIN CELL.
DRE.
EX MOB KID. RAGE MACHINE.
DAX.
THE GADGET MAN. WRENCHES, NOT KNIVES.
IZZY.
DANCER AND DOUBTER. FERAL SENSE OF JUSTICE
WE'RE BEING HUNTED FOR NO GOOD REASON, WE ALL KNOW THAT.
BUT WE'VE GOT TO FOCUS ON THE SOLUTION, NOT THE PROBLEM.
WE GOT TO TEACH THIS CITY WHAT ROBINS CAN DO. WHAT GOOD ROBINS CAN DO.
THE FIRST STEP IS FOR ONE OF YOU, WHOEVER IT WAS, TO STEP UP.
THE ONE WHO WAS IN THE STORE. HE NEEDS TO TELL HIS STORY TO THE PRESS. TO GOTHAM.
WE GET THAT OUT THERE. WE SHOW THEM WE'RE RESPONSIBLE.
WE STAND UP FOR WHAT WE DID, WHAT WE DO.
WE TELL THEM THAT WE ARE ROBIN.
WELL, THAT'S MORONIC.
YOU'RE NOT ROBIN.

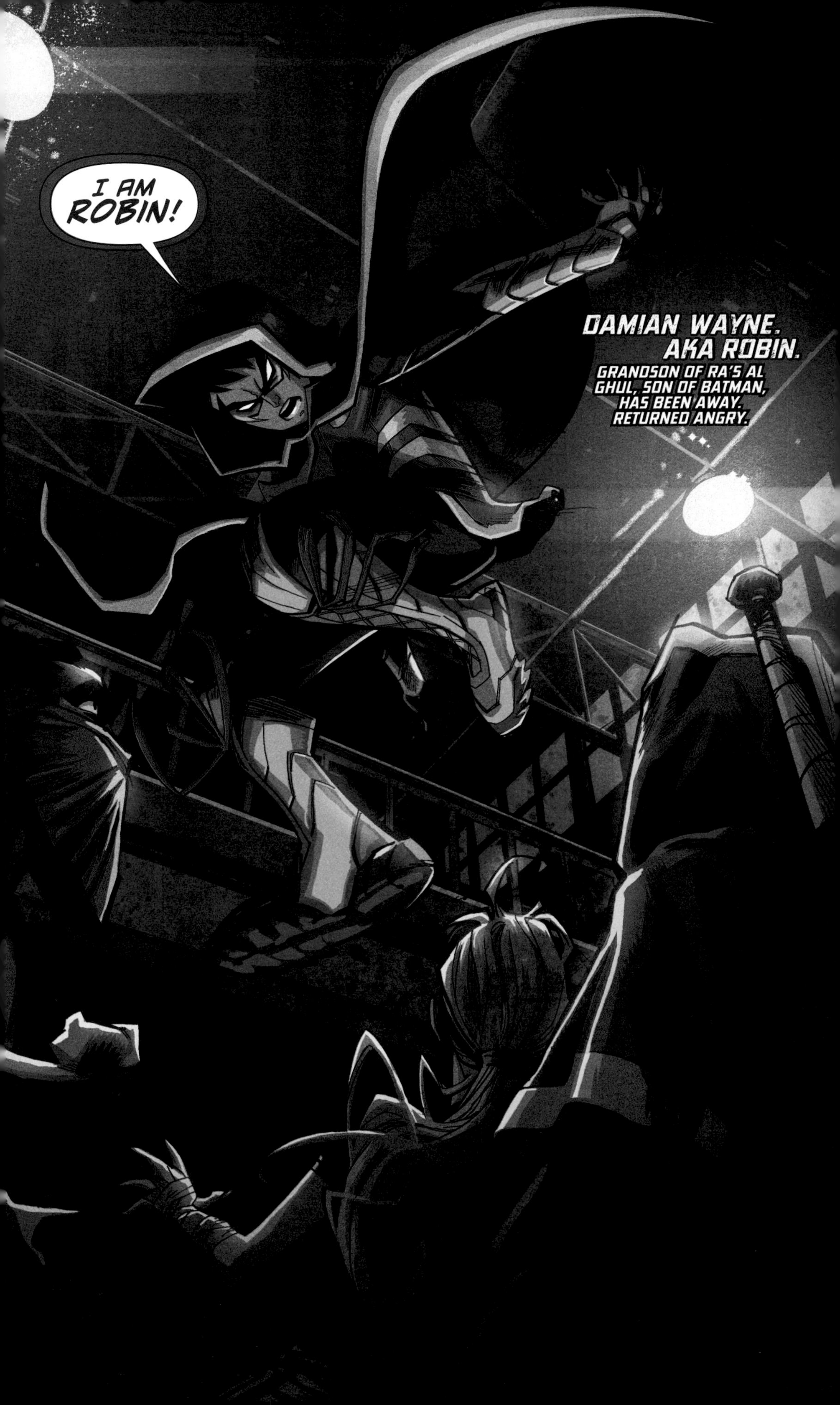
I AM ROBIN!
DAMIAN WAYNE. AKA ROBIN.
GRANDSON OF RA'S AL GHUL, SON OF BATMAN, HAS BEEN AWAY. RETURNED ANGRY.

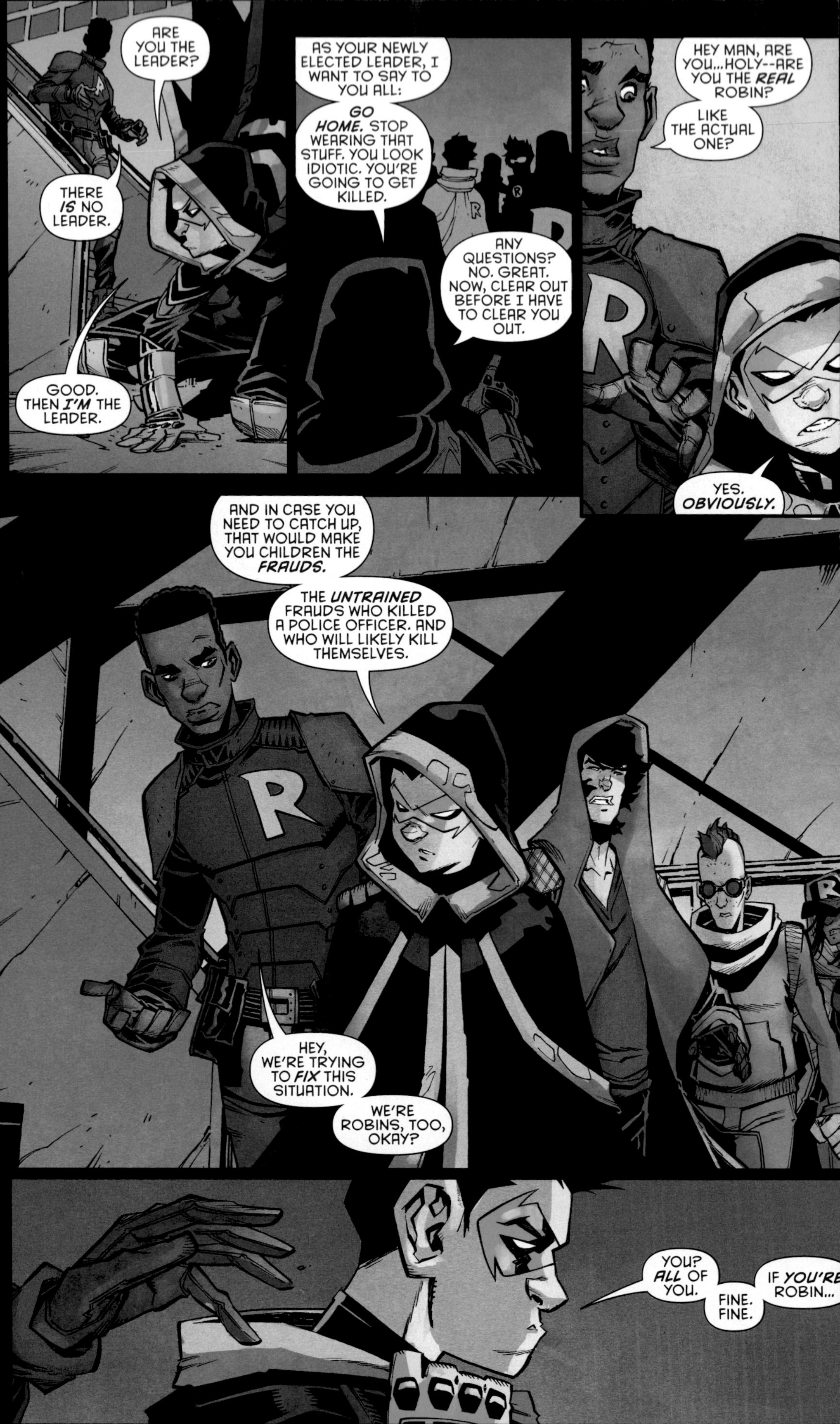
ARE YOU THE LEADER?
THERE *IS* NO LEADER.
GOOD. THEN *I'M* THE LEADER.
AS YOUR NEWLY ELECTED LEADER, I WANT TO SAY TO YOU ALL:
GO HOME. STOP WEARING THAT STUFF. YOU LOOK IDIOTIC. YOU'RE GOING TO GET KILLED.
ANY QUESTIONS? NO. GREAT. NOW, CLEAR OUT BEFORE I HAVE TO CLEAR YOU OUT.
HEY MAN, ARE YOU...HOLY--ARE YOU THE *REAL* ROBIN?
LIKE THE ACTUAL ONE?
YES. *OBVIOUSLY.*
AND IN CASE YOU NEED TO CATCH UP, THAT WOULD MAKE YOU CHILDREN THE *FRAUDS.*
THE *UNTRAINED* FRAUDS WHO KILLED A POLICE OFFICER. AND WHO WILL LIKELY KILL THEMSELVES.
HEY, WE'RE TRYING TO *FIX* THIS SITUATION.
WE'RE ROBINS, TOO, OKAY?
YOU? *ALL* OF YOU.
FINE. FINE.
IF *YOU'RE* ROBIN...

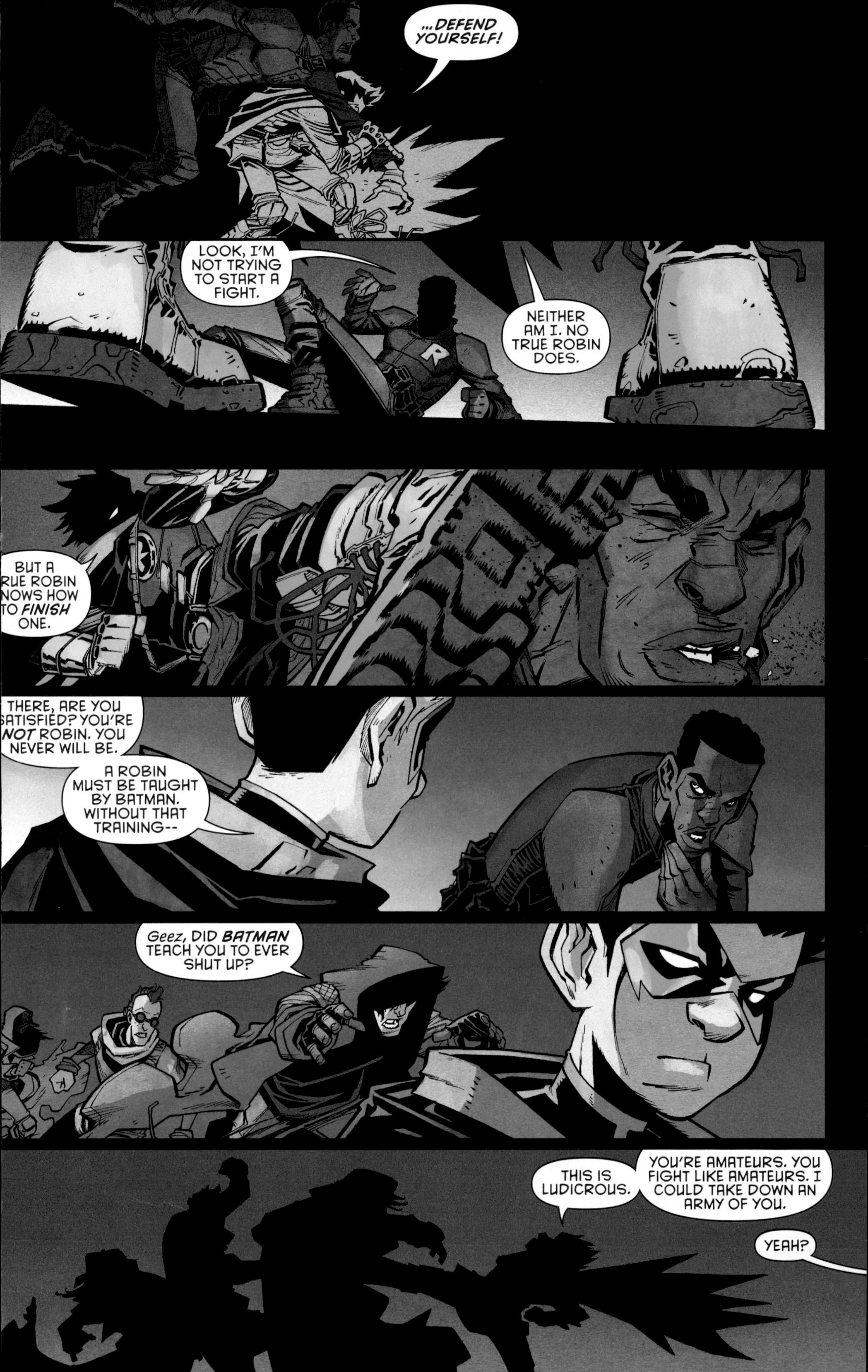
...DEFEND YOURSELF!
LOOK, I'M NOT TRYING TO START A FIGHT.
NEITHER AM I. NO TRUE ROBIN DOES.
BUT A TRUE ROBIN KNOWS HOW TO FINISH ONE.
THERE, ARE YOU SATISFIED? YOU'RE NOT ROBIN. YOU NEVER WILL BE.
A ROBIN MUST BE TAUGHT BY BATMAN. WITHOUT THAT TRAINING--
Geez, DID BATMAN TEACH YOU TO EVER SHUT UP?
THIS IS LUDICROUS.
YOU'RE AMATEURS. YOU FIGHT LIKE AMATEURS. I COULD TAKE DOWN AN ARMY OF YOU.
YEAH?

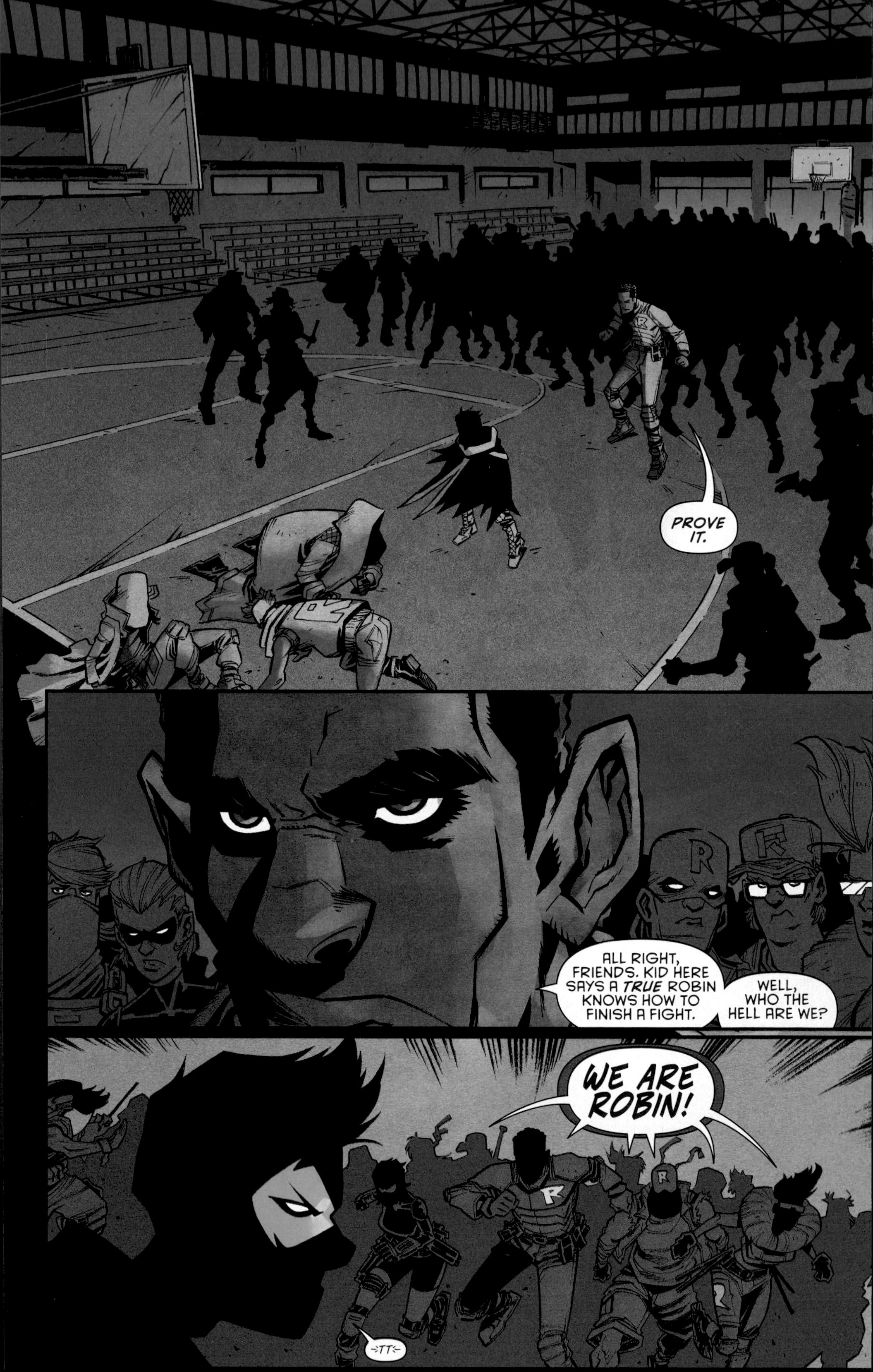
PROVE IT.
ALL RIGHT, FRIENDS. KID HERE SAYS A *TRUE* ROBIN KNOWS HOW TO FINISH A FIGHT.
WELL, WHO THE HELL ARE WE?
WE ARE ROBIN!
TT

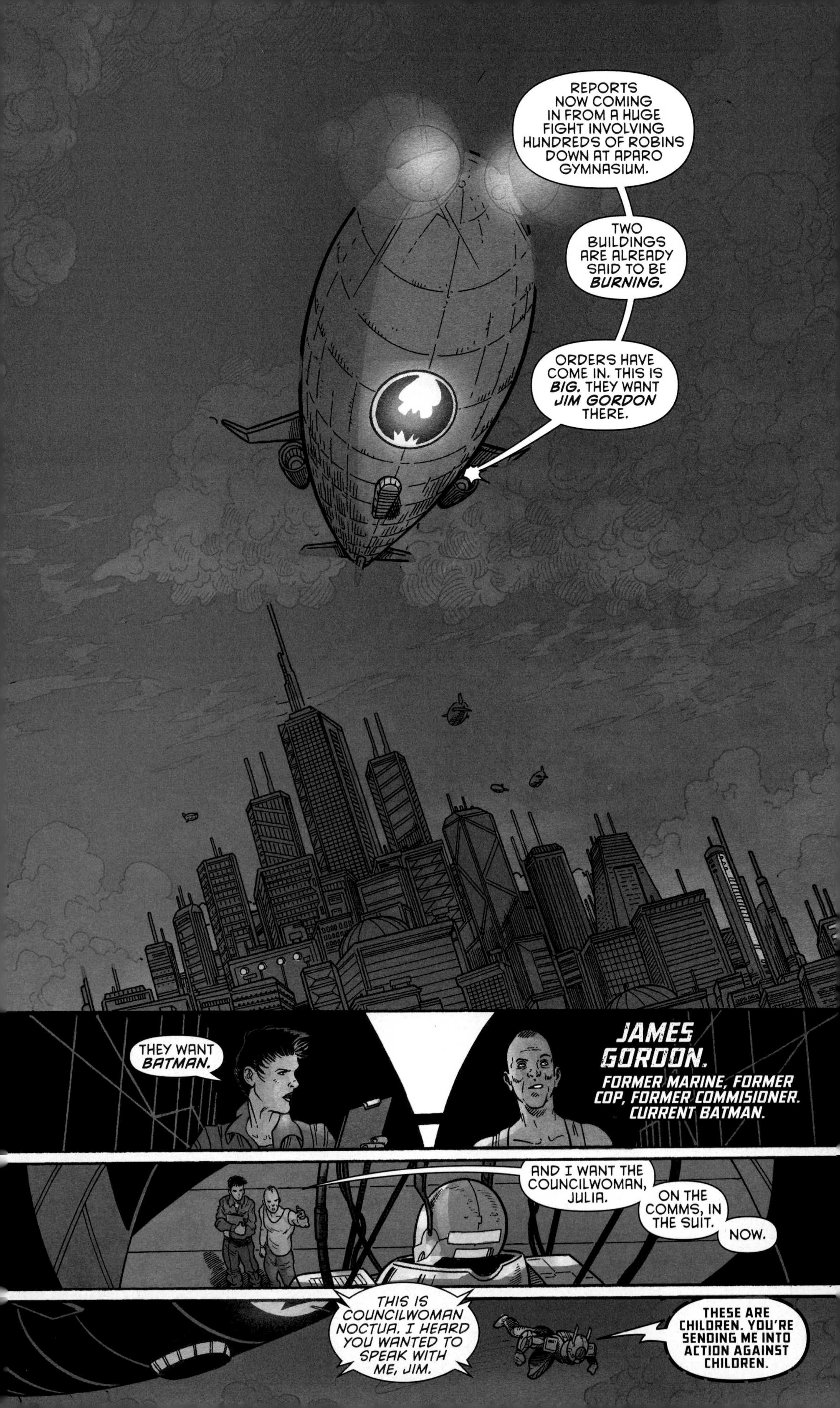
REPORTS NOW COMING IN FROM A HUGE FIGHT INVOLVING HUNDREDS OF ROBINS DOWN AT APARO GYMNASIUM.
TWO BUILDINGS ARE ALREADY SAID TO BE *BURNING.*
ORDERS HAVE COME IN. THIS IS *BIG.* THEY WANT *JIM GORDON* THERE.
THEY WANT *BATMAN.*
JAMES GORDON.
FORMER MARINE, FORMER COP, FORMER COMMISIONER. CURRENT BATMAN.
AND I WANT THE COUNCILWOMAN, JULIA.
ON THE COMMS, IN THE SUIT.
NOW.
THIS IS COUNCILWOMAN NOCTUA. I HEARD YOU WANTED TO SPEAK WITH ME, JIM.
THESE ARE CHILDREN. YOU'RE SENDING ME INTO ACTION AGAINST CHILDREN.

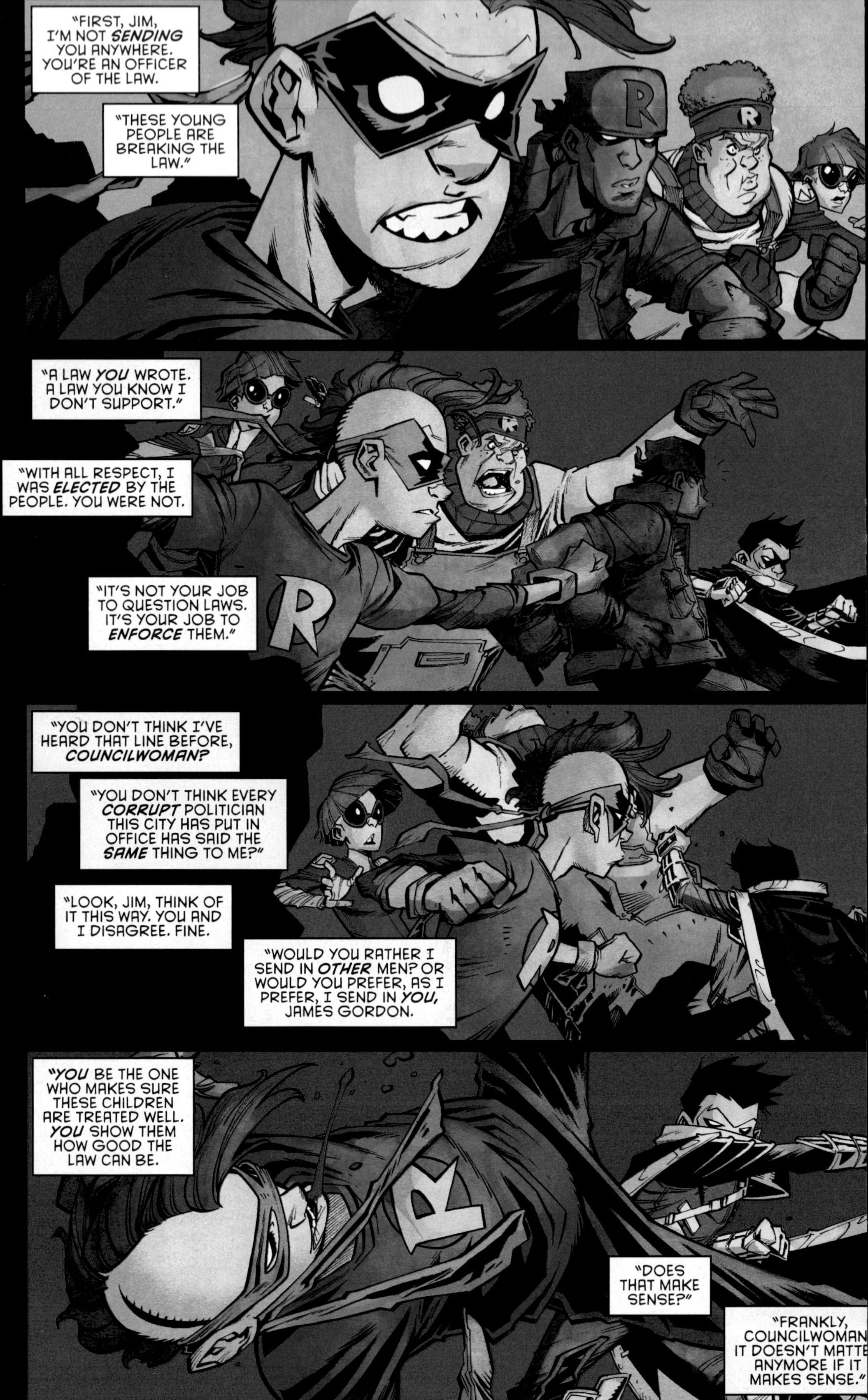
"FIRST, JIM, I'M NOT *SENDING* YOU ANYWHERE. YOU'RE AN OFFICER OF THE LAW.
"THESE YOUNG PEOPLE ARE BREAKING THE LAW."
"A LAW *YOU* WROTE. A LAW YOU KNOW I DON'T SUPPORT."
"WITH ALL RESPECT, I WAS *ELECTED* BY THE PEOPLE. YOU WERE NOT.
"IT'S NOT YOUR JOB TO QUESTION LAWS. IT'S YOUR JOB TO *ENFORCE* THEM."
"YOU DON'T THINK I'VE HEARD THAT LINE BEFORE, *COUNCILWOMAN?*
"YOU DON'T THINK EVERY *CORRUPT* POLITICIAN THIS CITY HAS PUT IN OFFICE HAS SAID THE *SAME* THING TO ME?"
"LOOK, JIM, THINK OF IT THIS WAY. YOU AND I DISAGREE. FINE.
"WOULD YOU RATHER I SEND IN *OTHER* MEN? OR WOULD YOU PREFER, AS I PREFER, I SEND IN *YOU,* JAMES GORDON.
"*YOU* BE THE ONE WHO MAKES SURE THESE CHILDREN ARE TREATED WELL. *YOU* SHOW THEM HOW GOOD THE LAW CAN BE.
"DOES THAT MAKE SENSE?"
"FRANKLY, COUNCILWOMAN IT DOESN'T MATTE ANYMORE IF IT MAKES SENSE."

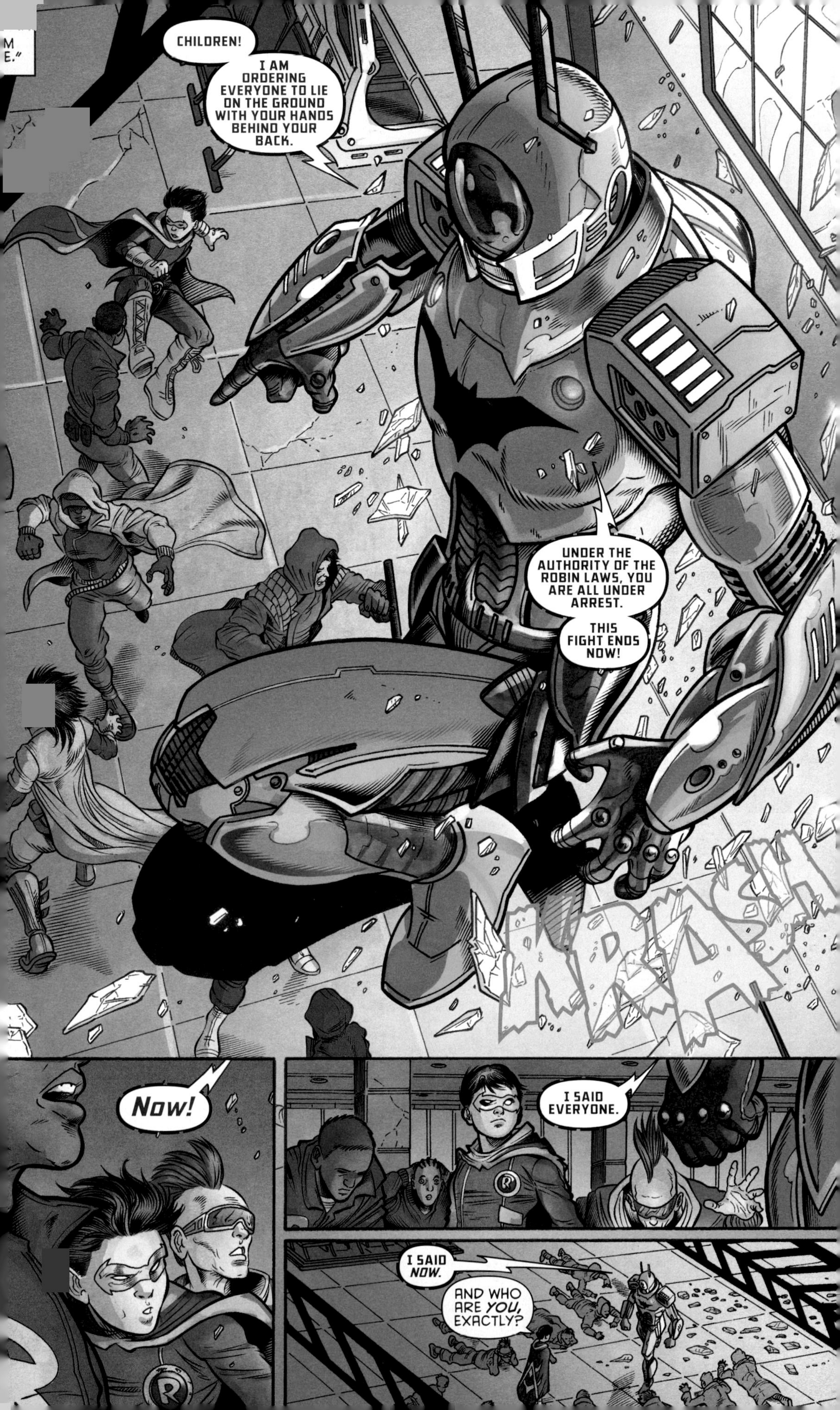
CHILDREN!
I AM ORDERING EVERYONE TO LIE ON THE GROUND WITH YOUR HANDS BEHIND YOUR BACK.
UNDER THE AUTHORITY OF THE ROBIN LAWS, YOU ARE ALL UNDER ARREST.
THIS FIGHT ENDS NOW!
KRASH
Now!
I SAID EVERYONE.
I SAID NOW.
AND WHO ARE YOU, EXACTLY?

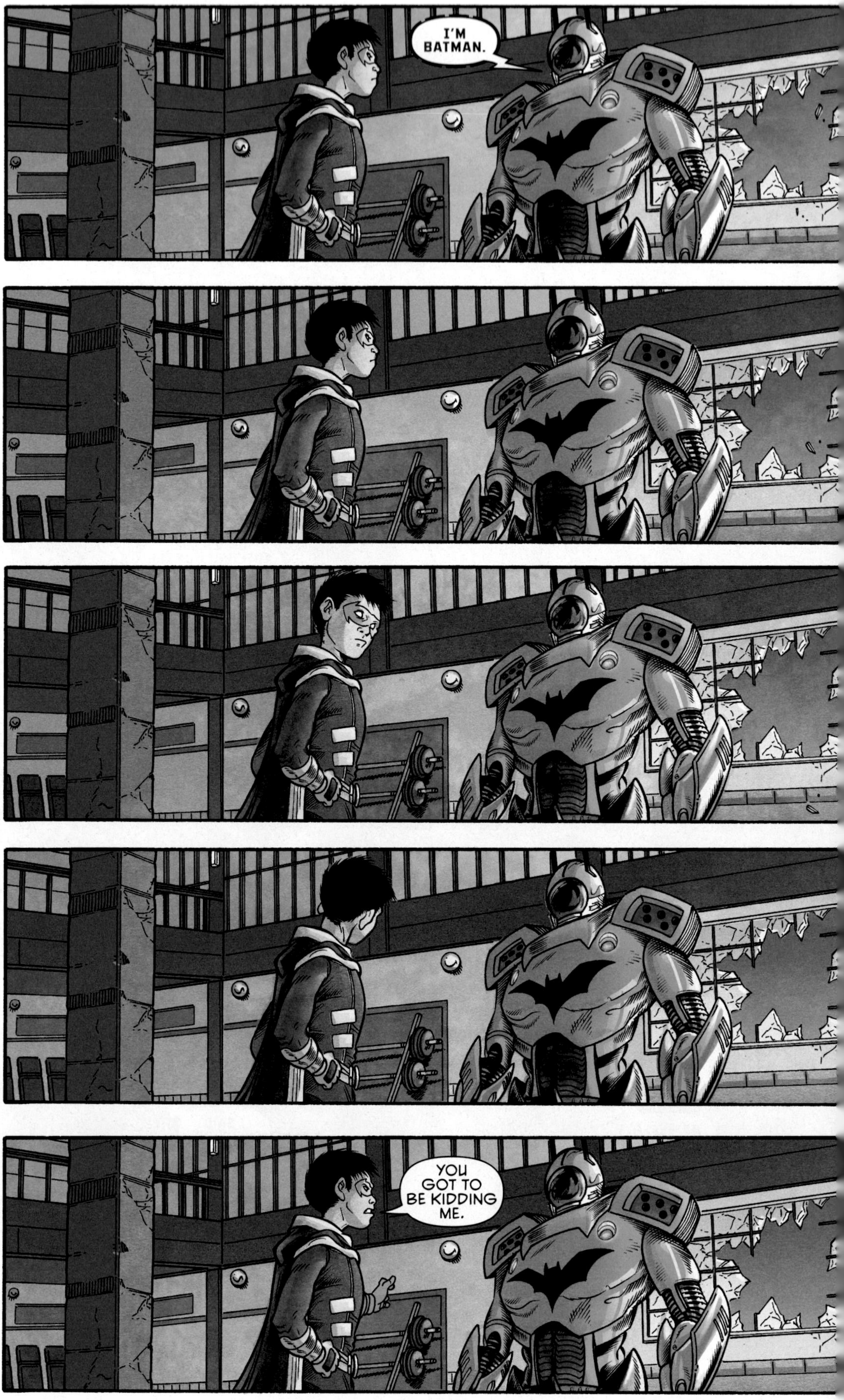
I'M BATMAN.
YOU GOT TO BE KIDDING ME.

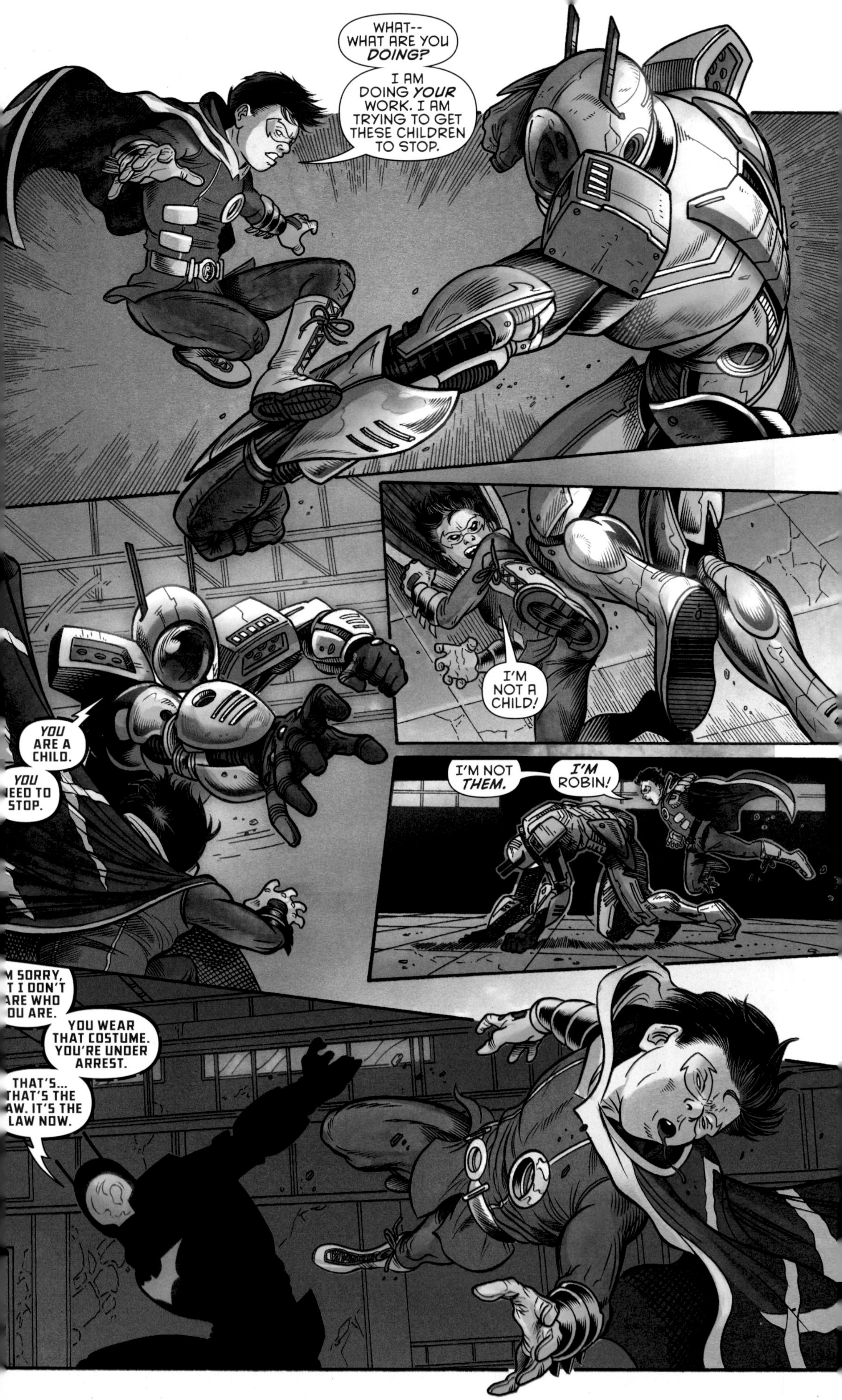

WHAT-- WHAT ARE YOU DOING?
I AM DOING YOUR WORK. I AM TRYING TO GET THESE CHILDREN TO STOP.
I'M NOT A CHILD!
YOU ARE A CHILD.
YOU NEED TO STOP.
I'M NOT THEM.
I'M ROBIN!
M SORRY, T I DON'T ARE WHO OU ARE.
YOU WEAR THAT COSTUME. YOU'RE UNDER ARREST.
THAT'S... THAT'S THE AW. IT'S THE LAW NOW.

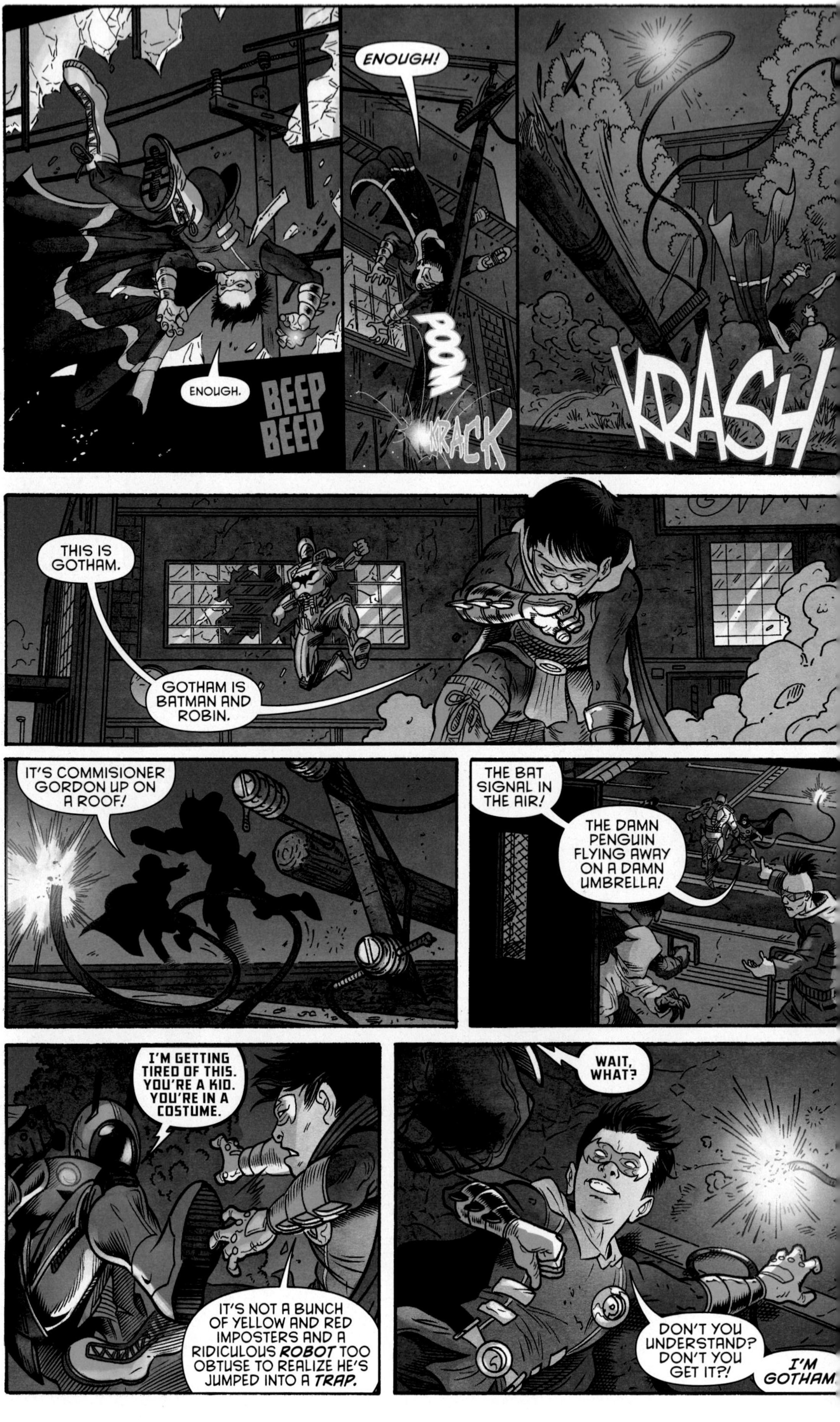
ENOUGH.
BEEP BEEP
ENOUGH!
POOM
KRACK
KRASH
THIS IS GOTHAM.
GOTHAM IS BATMAN AND ROBIN.
IT'S COMMISIONER GORDON UP ON A ROOF!
THE BAT SIGNAL IN THE AIR!
THE DAMN PENGUIN FLYING AWAY ON A DAMN UMBRELLA!
I'M GETTING TIRED OF THIS. YOU'RE A KID. YOU'RE IN A COSTUME.
IT'S NOT A BUNCH OF YELLOW AND RED IMPOSTERS AND A RIDICULOUS ROBOT TOO OBTUSE TO REALIZE HE'S JUMPED INTO A TRAP.
WAIT, WHAT?
DON'T YOU UNDERSTAND? DON'T YOU GET IT?!
I'M GOTHAM

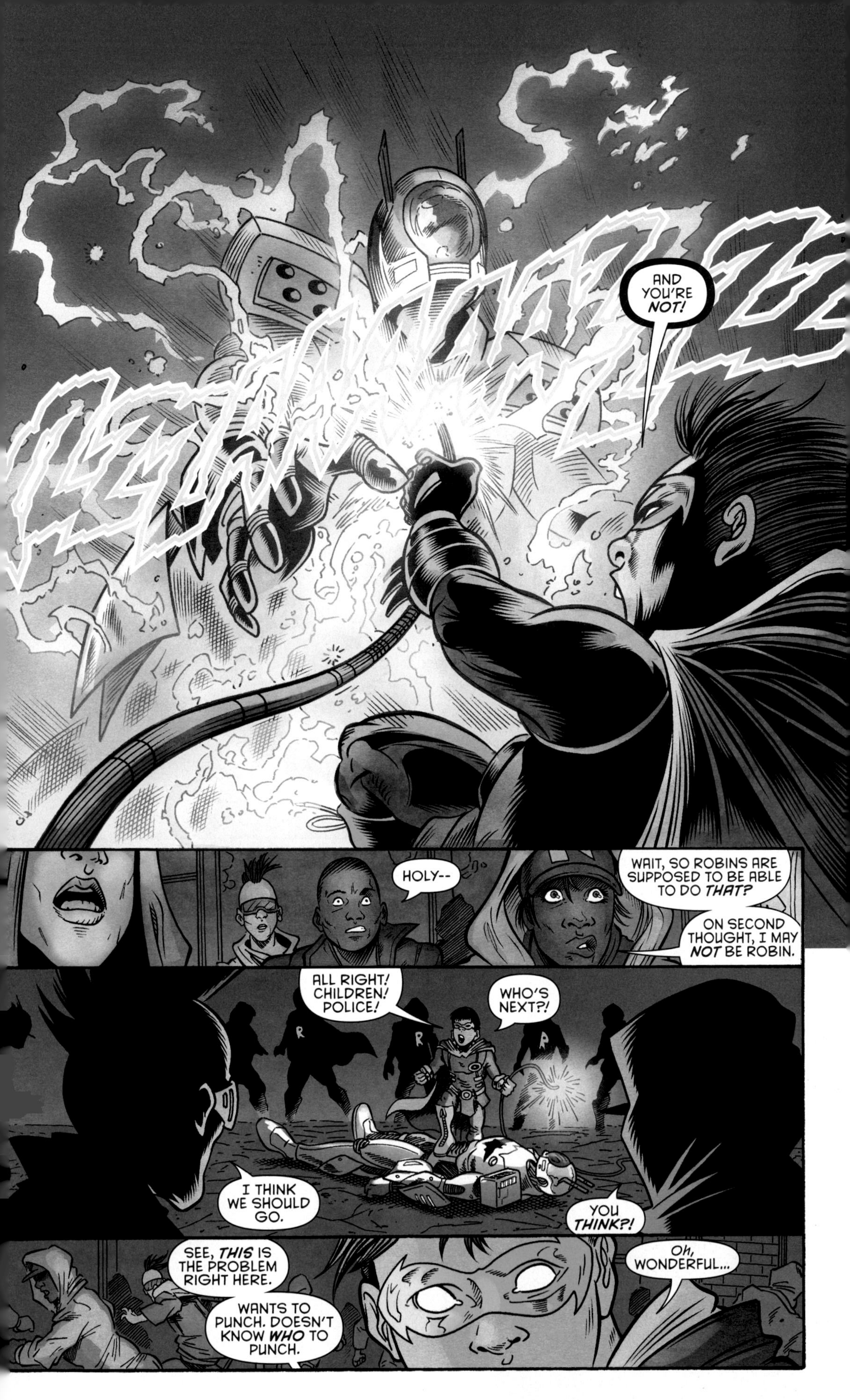
AND YOU'RE NOT!
HOLY--
WAIT, SO ROBINS ARE SUPPOSED TO BE ABLE TO DO THAT?
ON SECOND THOUGHT, I MAY NOT BE ROBIN.
ALL RIGHT! CHILDREN! POLICE!
WHO'S NEXT?!
I THINK WE SHOULD GO.
YOU THINK?!
SEE, THIS IS THE PROBLEM RIGHT HERE.
WANTS TO PUNCH. DOESN'T KNOW WHO TO PUNCH.
Oh, WONDERFUL...

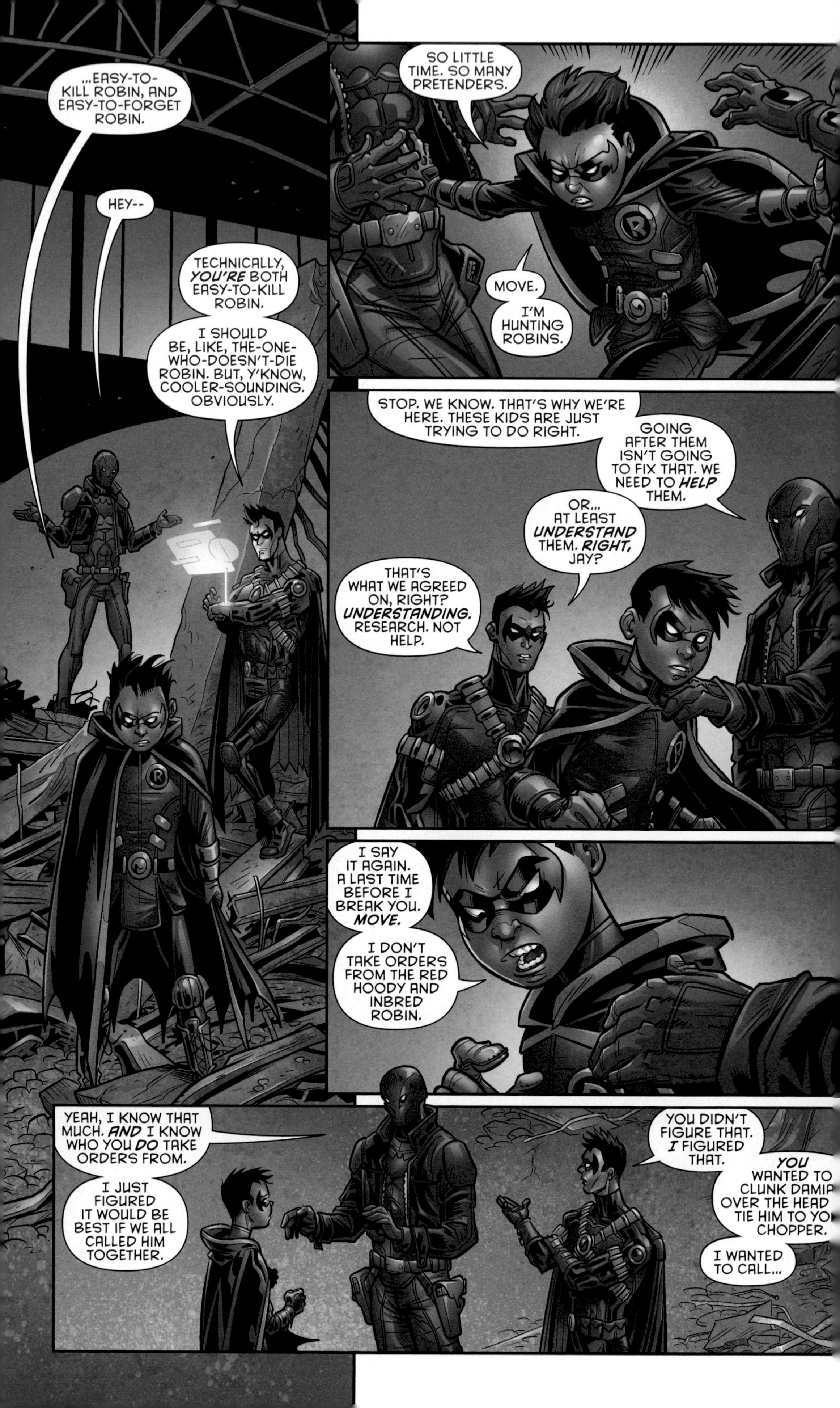
...EASY-TO-KILL ROBIN, AND EASY-TO-FORGET ROBIN.
HEY--
TECHNICALLY, *YOU'RE* BOTH EASY-TO-KILL ROBIN.
I SHOULD BE, LIKE, THE-ONE-WHO-DOESN'T-DIE ROBIN. BUT, Y'KNOW, COOLER-SOUNDING. OBVIOUSLY.
SO LITTLE TIME. SO MANY PRETENDERS.
MOVE.
I'M HUNTING ROBINS.
STOP. WE KNOW. THAT'S WHY WE'RE HERE. THESE KIDS ARE JUST TRYING TO DO RIGHT.
GOING AFTER THEM ISN'T GOING TO FIX THAT. WE NEED TO *HELP* THEM.
OR... AT LEAST *UNDERSTAND* THEM. *RIGHT,* JAY?
THAT'S WHAT WE AGREED ON, RIGHT? *UNDERSTANDING.* RESEARCH. NOT HELP.
I SAY IT AGAIN. A LAST TIME BEFORE I BREAK YOU. *MOVE.*
I DON'T TAKE ORDERS FROM THE RED HOODY AND INBRED ROBIN.
YEAH, I KNOW THAT MUCH. *AND* I KNOW WHO YOU *DO* TAKE ORDERS FROM.
I JUST FIGURED IT WOULD BE BEST IF WE ALL CALLED HIM TOGETHER.
YOU DIDN'T FIGURE THAT. *I* FIGURED THAT.
YOU WANTED TO CLUNK DAMIP OVER THE HEAD TIE HIM TO YO CHOPPER.
I WANTED TO CALL...

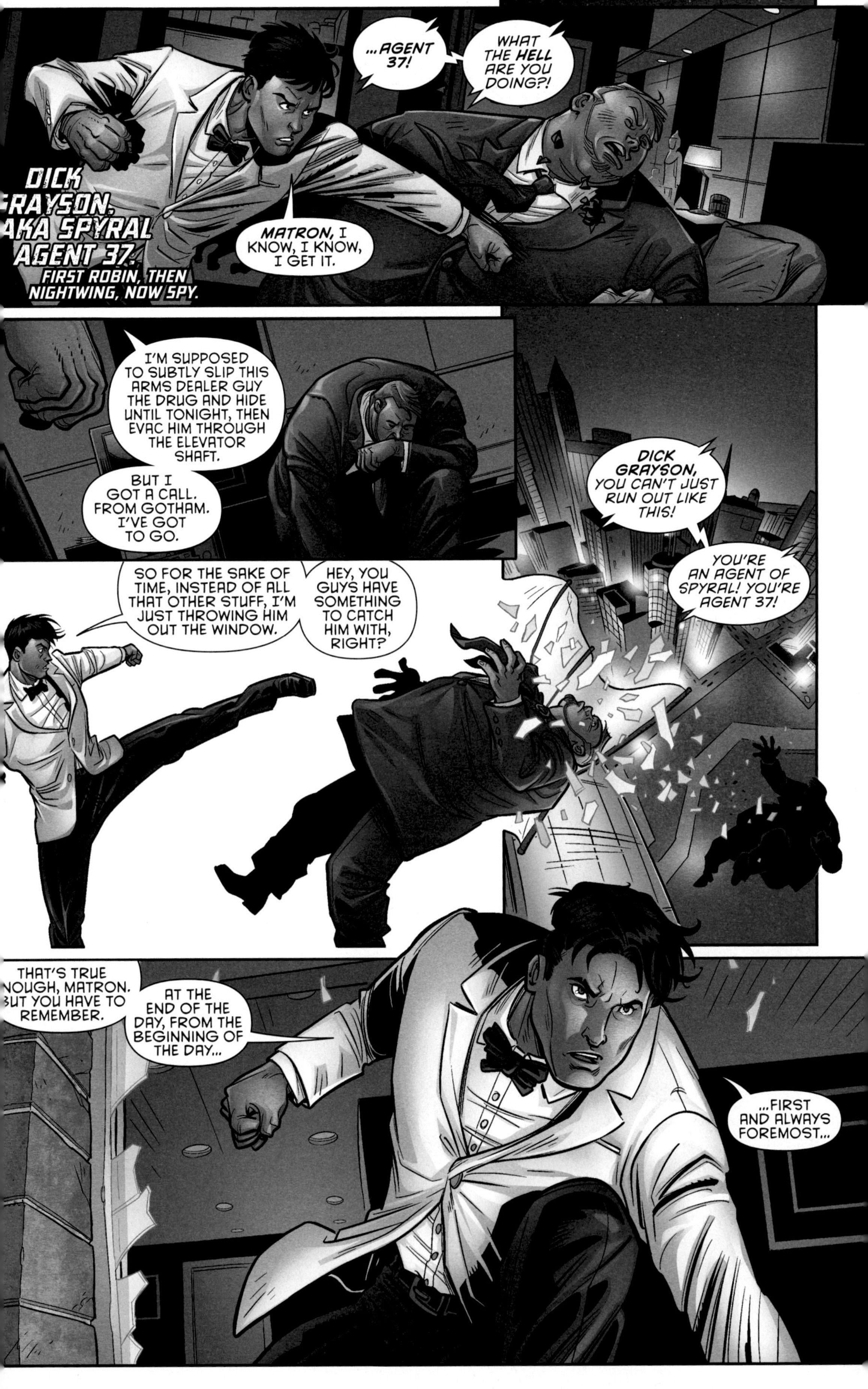
DICK GRAYSON. AKA SPYRAL AGENT 37.
FIRST ROBIN, THEN NIGHTWING, NOW SPY.
...AGENT 37!
WHAT THE HELL ARE YOU DOING?!
MATRON, I KNOW, I KNOW, I GET IT.
I'M SUPPOSED TO SUBTLY SLIP THIS ARMS DEALER GUY THE DRUG AND HIDE UNTIL TONIGHT, THEN EVAC HIM THROUGH THE ELEVATOR SHAFT.
BUT I GOT A CALL. FROM GOTHAM. I'VE GOT TO GO.
DICK GRAYSON, YOU CAN'T JUST RUN OUT LIKE THIS!
YOU'RE AN AGENT OF SPYRAL! YOU'RE AGENT 37!
SO FOR THE SAKE OF TIME, INSTEAD OF ALL THAT OTHER STUFF, I'M JUST THROWING HIM OUT THE WINDOW.
HEY, YOU GUYS HAVE SOMETHING TO CATCH HIM WITH, RIGHT?
THAT'S TRUE NOUGH, MATRON. BUT YOU HAVE TO REMEMBER.
AT THE END OF THE DAY, FROM THE BEGINNING OF THE DAY...
...FIRST AND ALWAYS FOREMOST...

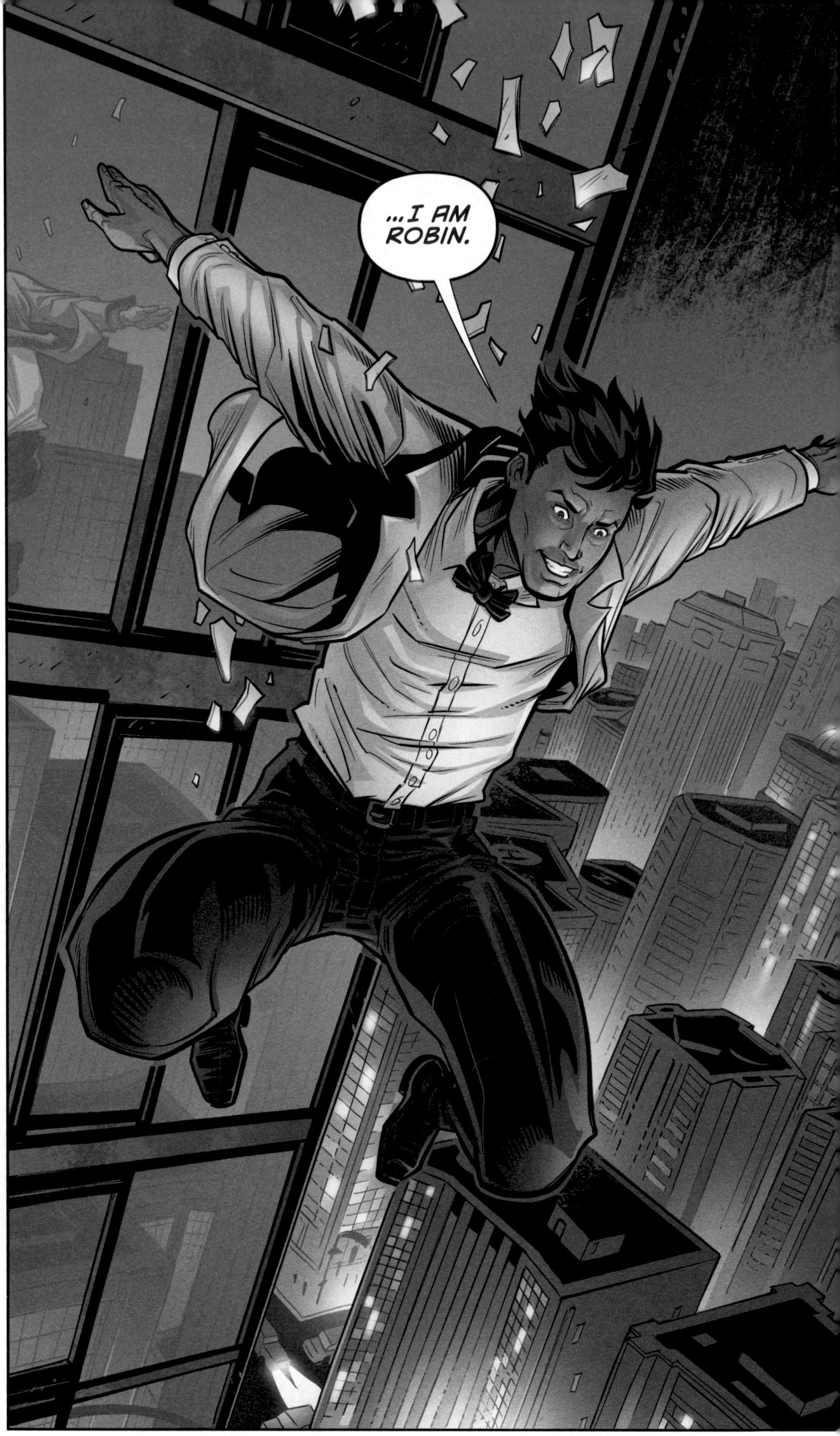
...I AM ROBIN.

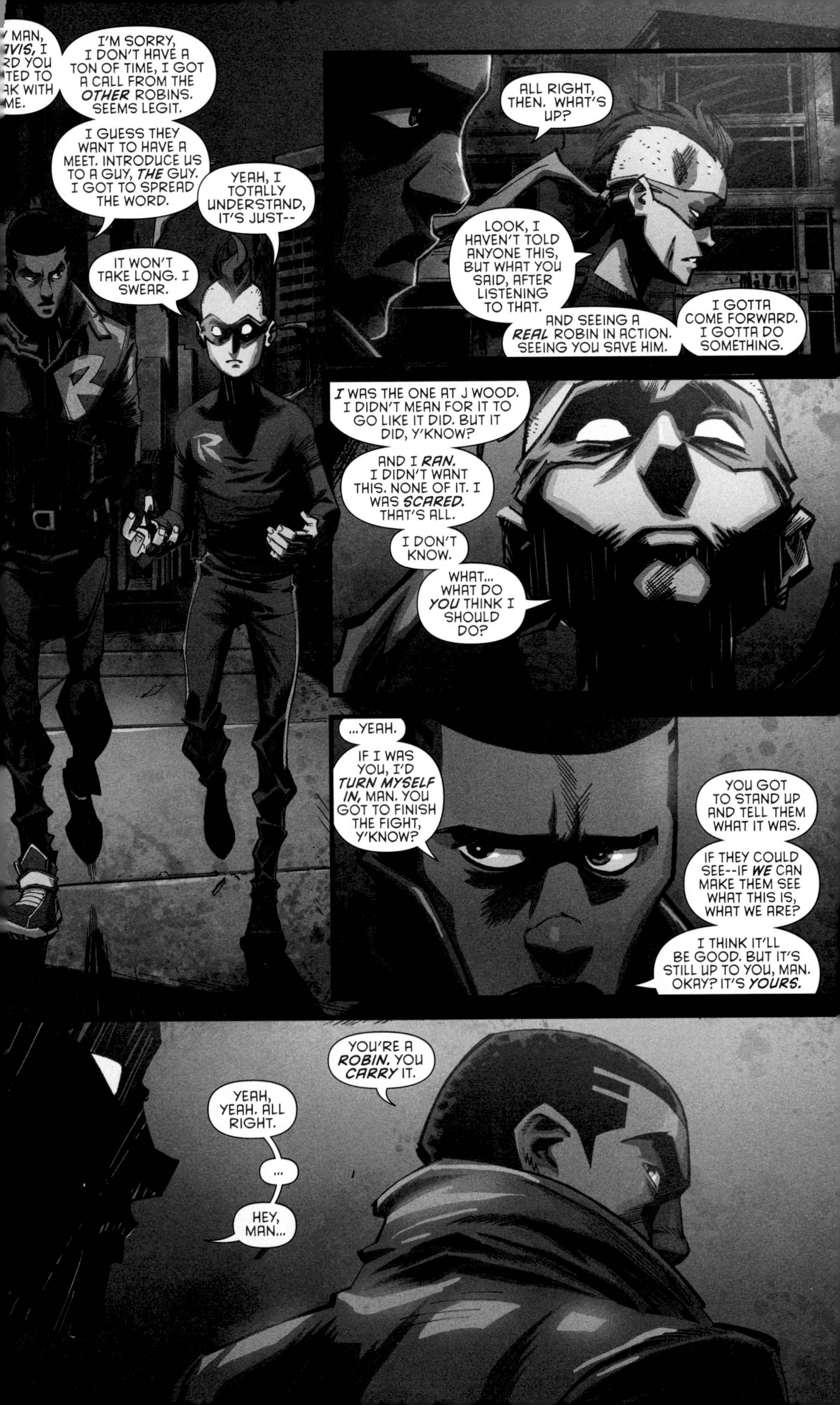

MAN, VIS, I RD YOU TED TO AK WITH ME.
I'M SORRY, I DON'T HAVE A TON OF TIME, I GOT A CALL FROM THE *OTHER* ROBINS. SEEMS LEGIT.
I GUESS THEY WANT TO HAVE A MEET. INTRODUCE US TO A GUY, *THE* GUY. I GOT TO SPREAD THE WORD.
YEAH, I TOTALLY UNDERSTAND, IT'S JUST--
IT WON'T TAKE LONG. I SWEAR.
ALL RIGHT, THEN. WHAT'S UP?
LOOK, I HAVEN'T TOLD ANYONE THIS, BUT WHAT YOU SAID, AFTER LISTENING TO THAT.
AND SEEING A *REAL* ROBIN IN ACTION. SEEING YOU SAVE HIM.
I GOTTA COME FORWARD. I GOTTA DO SOMETHING.
I WAS THE ONE AT J WOOD. I DIDN'T MEAN FOR IT TO GO LIKE IT DID. BUT IT DID, Y'KNOW?
AND I *RAN.* I DIDN'T WANT THIS. NONE OF IT. I WAS *SCARED.* THAT'S ALL.
I DON'T KNOW.
WHAT... WHAT DO *YOU* THINK I SHOULD DO?
...YEAH.
IF I WAS YOU, I'D *TURN MYSELF IN,* MAN. YOU GOT TO FINISH THE FIGHT, Y'KNOW?
YOU GOT TO STAND UP AND TELL THEM WHAT IT WAS.
IF THEY COULD SEE--IF *WE* CAN MAKE THEM SEE WHAT THIS IS, WHAT WE ARE?
I THINK IT'LL BE GOOD. BUT IT'S STILL UP TO YOU, MAN. OKAY? IT'S *YOURS.*
YOU'RE A *ROBIN.* YOU *CARRY* IT.
YEAH, YEAH. ALL RIGHT.
...
HEY, MAN...

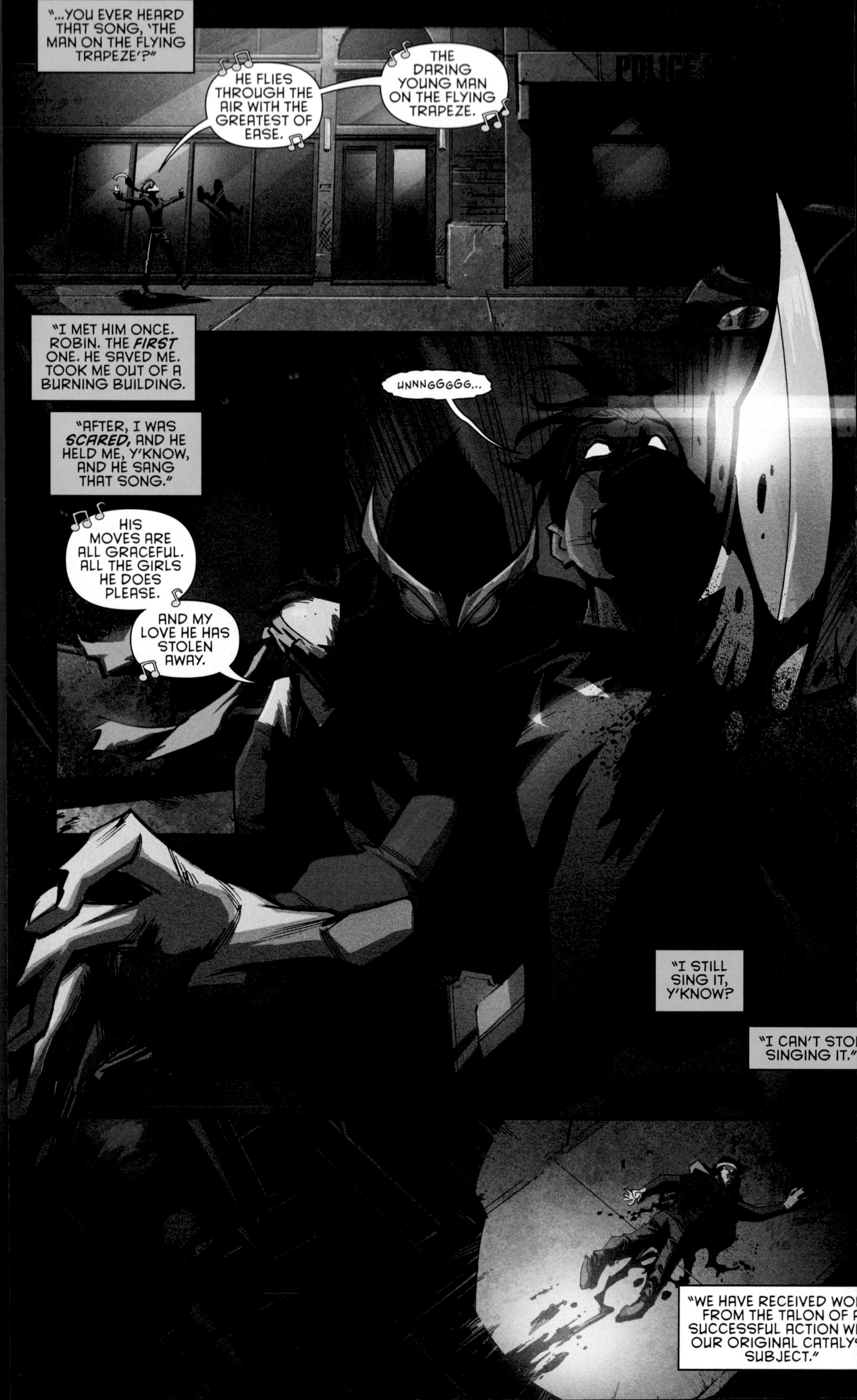
"...YOU EVER HEARD THAT SONG, 'THE MAN ON THE FLYING TRAPEZE'?"
HE FLIES THROUGH THE AIR WITH THE GREATEST OF EASE.
THE DARING YOUNG MAN ON THE FLYING TRAPEZE.
"I MET HIM ONCE. ROBIN. THE *FIRST* ONE. HE SAVED ME. TOOK ME OUT OF A BURNING BUILDING.
"AFTER, I WAS *SCARED,* AND HE HELD ME, Y'KNOW, AND HE SANG THAT SONG."
UNNNGGGGG...
HIS MOVES ARE ALL GRACEFUL. ALL THE GIRLS HE DOES PLEASE.
AND MY LOVE HE HAS STOLEN AWAY.
"I STILL SING IT, Y'KNOW?
"I CAN'T STO SINGING IT."
"WE HAVE RECEIVED WO FROM THE TALON OF SUCCESSFUL ACTION WI OUR ORIGINAL CATALY SUBJECT."

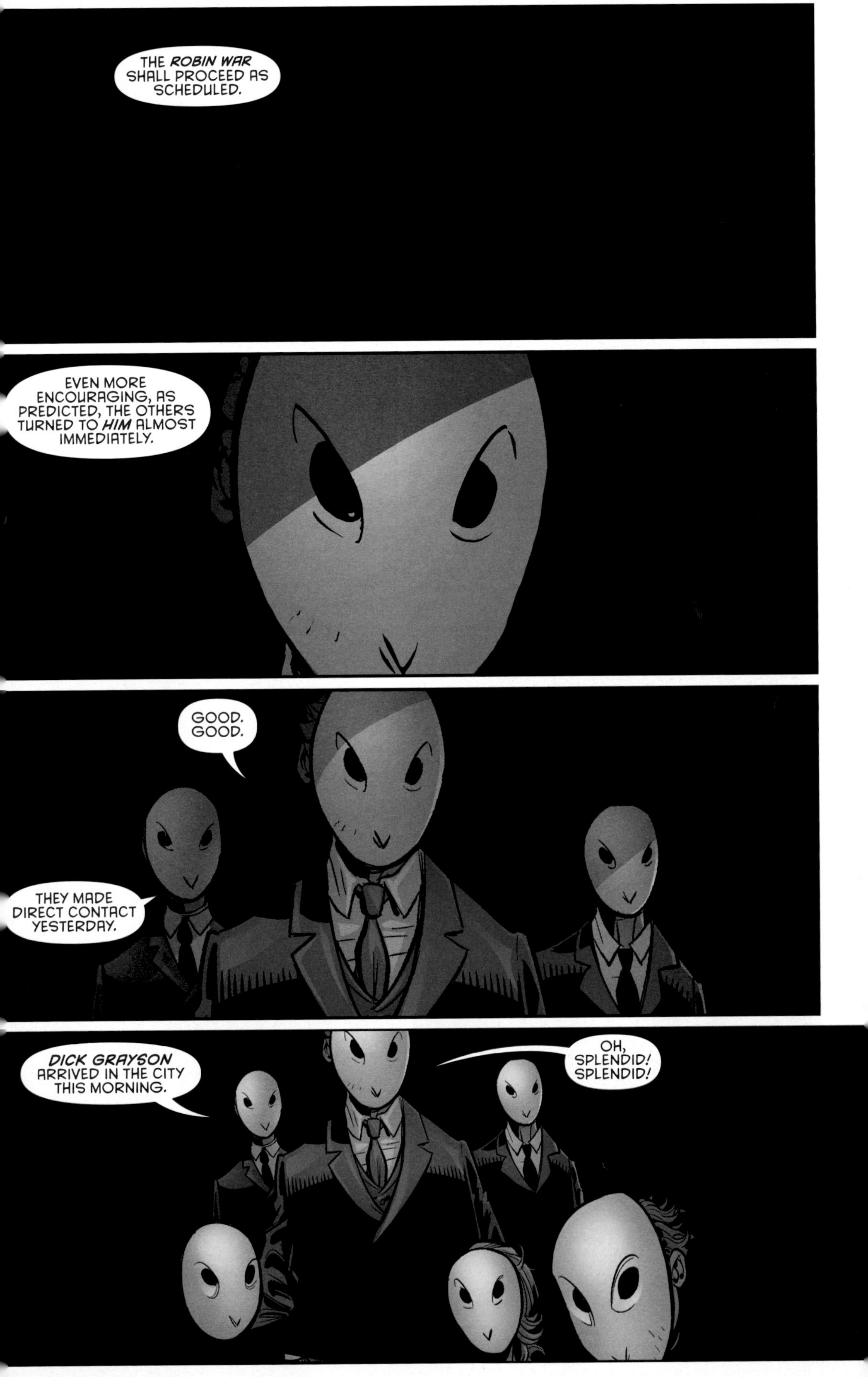
THE *ROBIN WAR* SHALL PROCEED AS SCHEDULED.
EVEN MORE ENCOURAGING, AS PREDICTED, THE OTHERS TURNED TO *HIM* ALMOST IMMEDIATELY.
GOOD. GOOD.
THEY MADE DIRECT CONTACT YESTERDAY.
DICK GRAYSON ARRIVED IN THE CITY THIS MORNING.
OH, SPLENDID! SPLENDID!

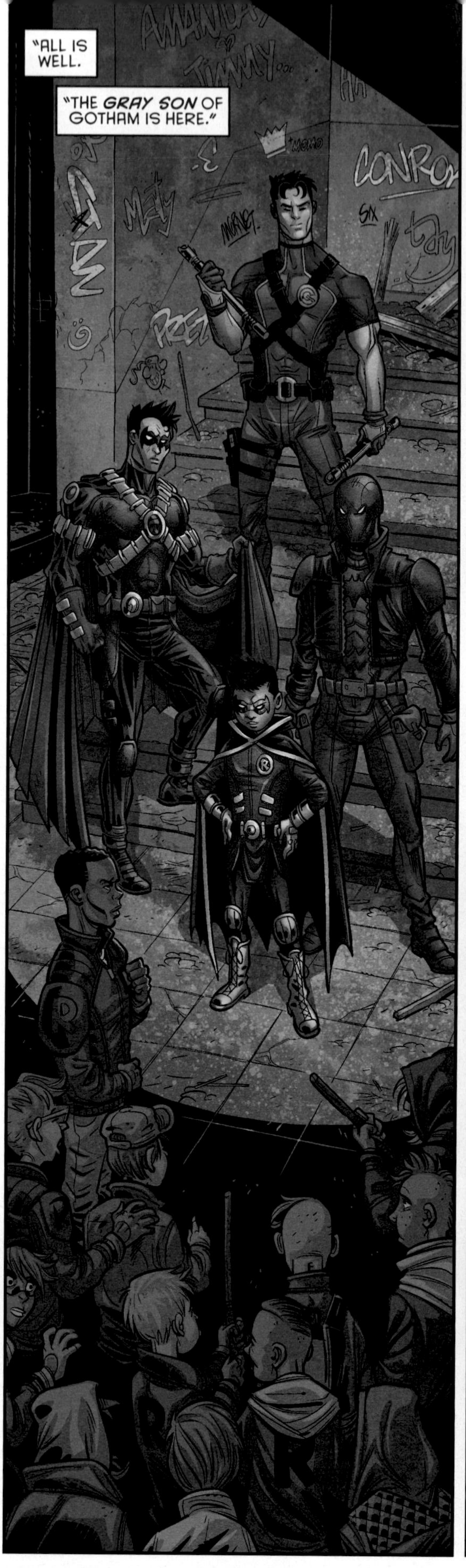
"ALL IS WELL.
"THE GRAY SON OF GOTHAM IS HERE."

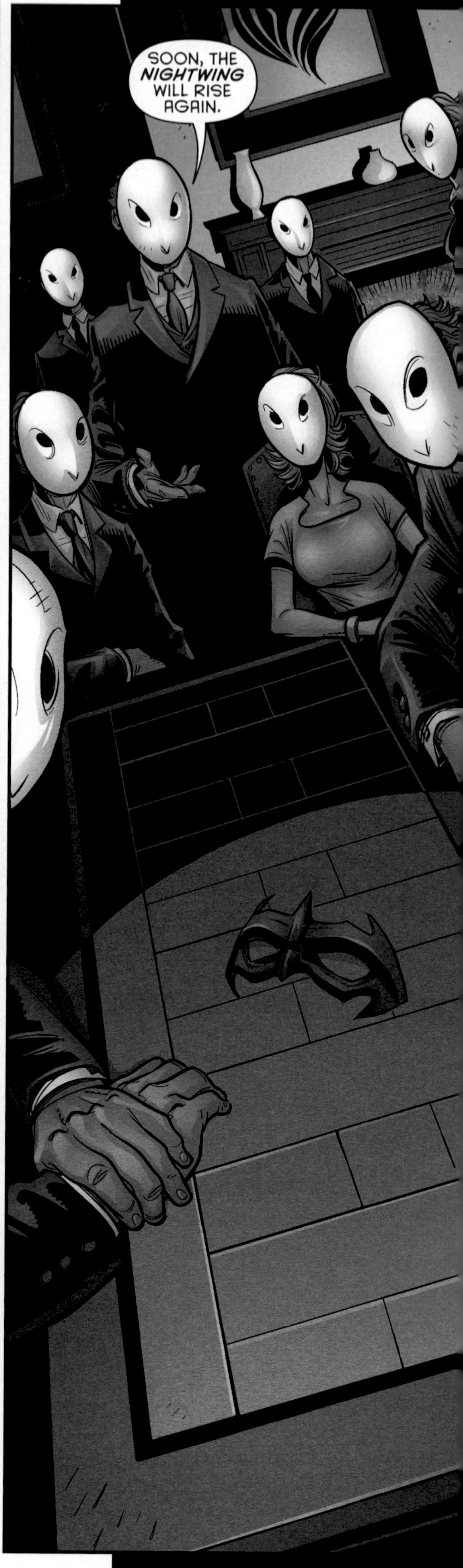
SOON, THE NIGHTWING WILL RISE AGAIN.

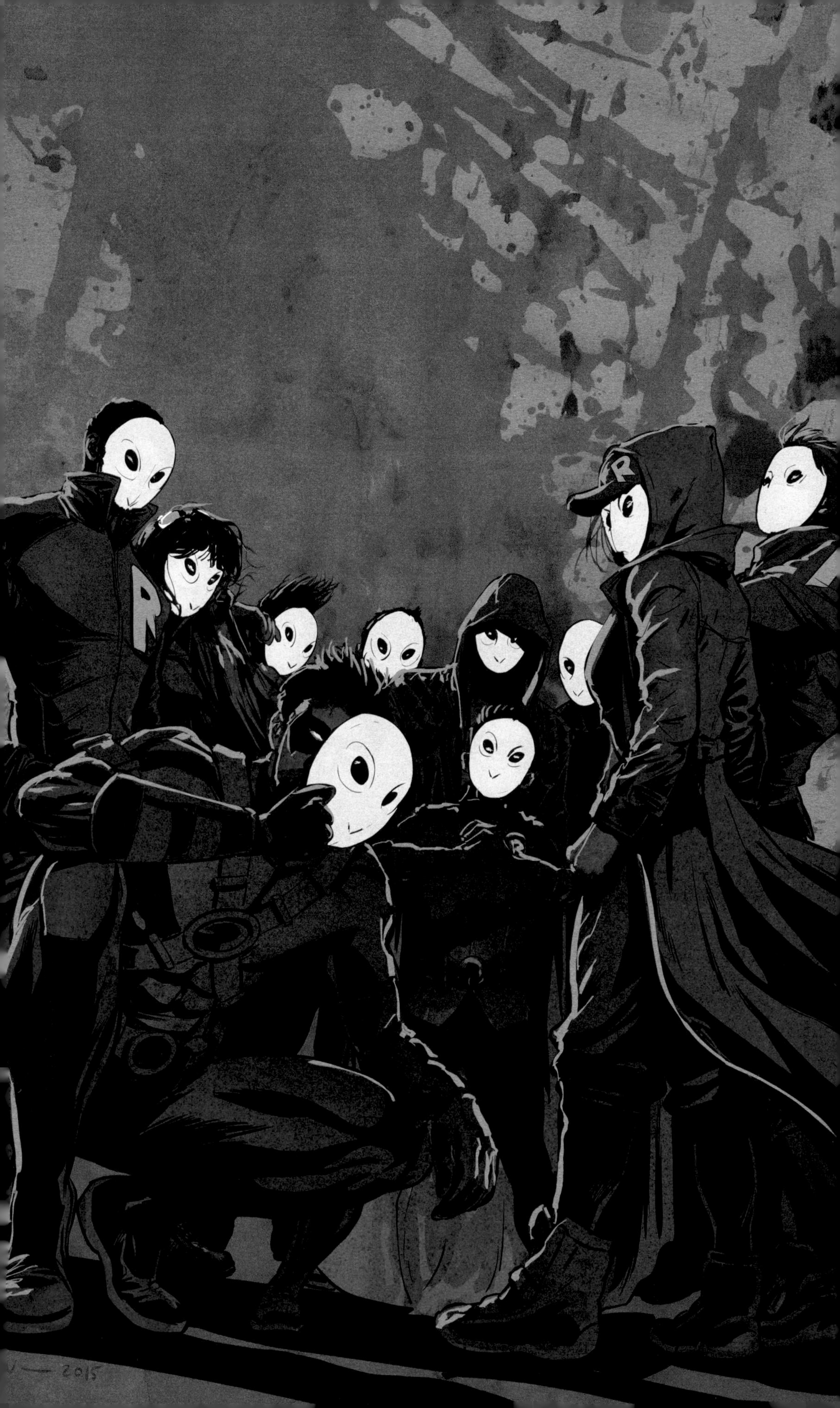

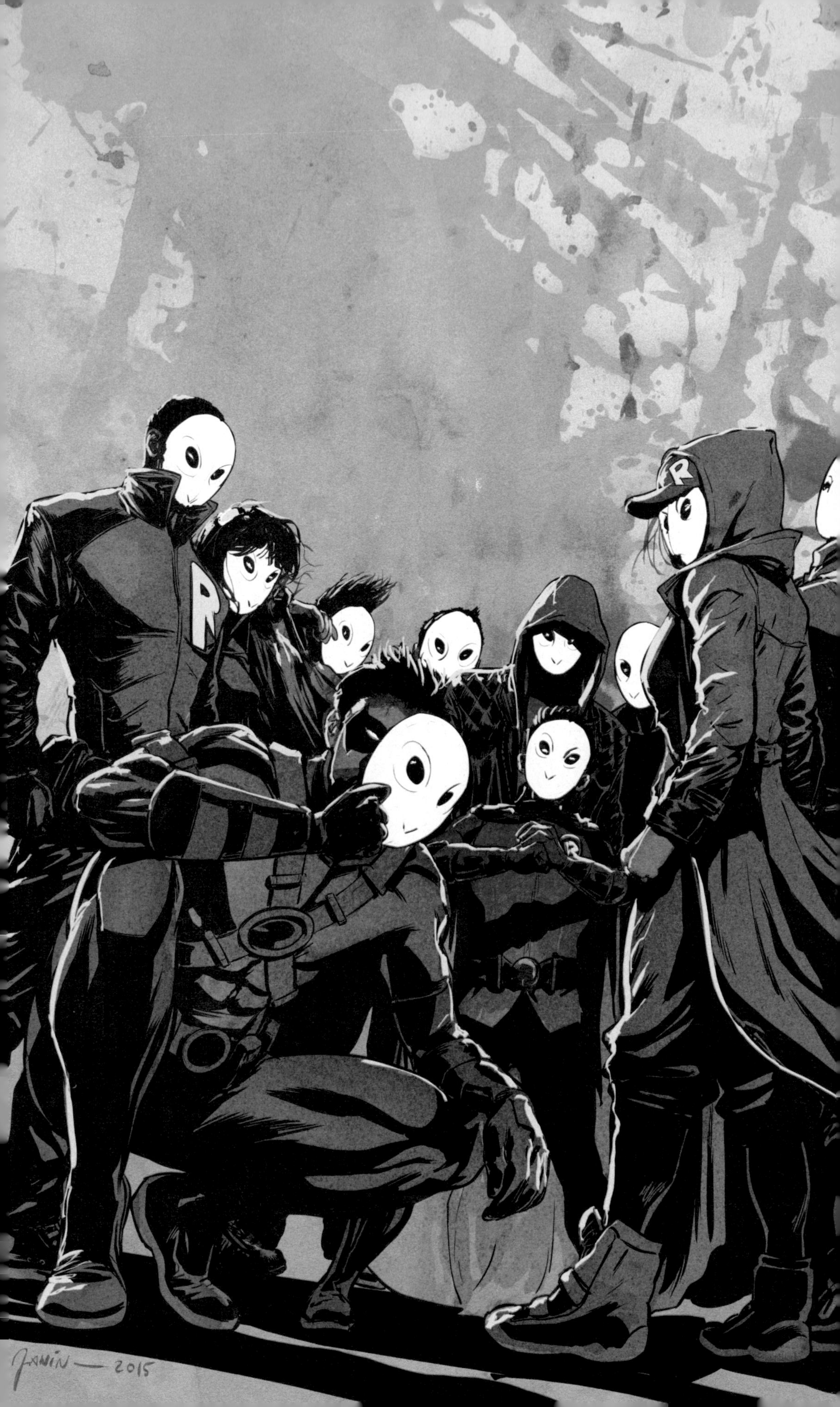
Janin — 2015

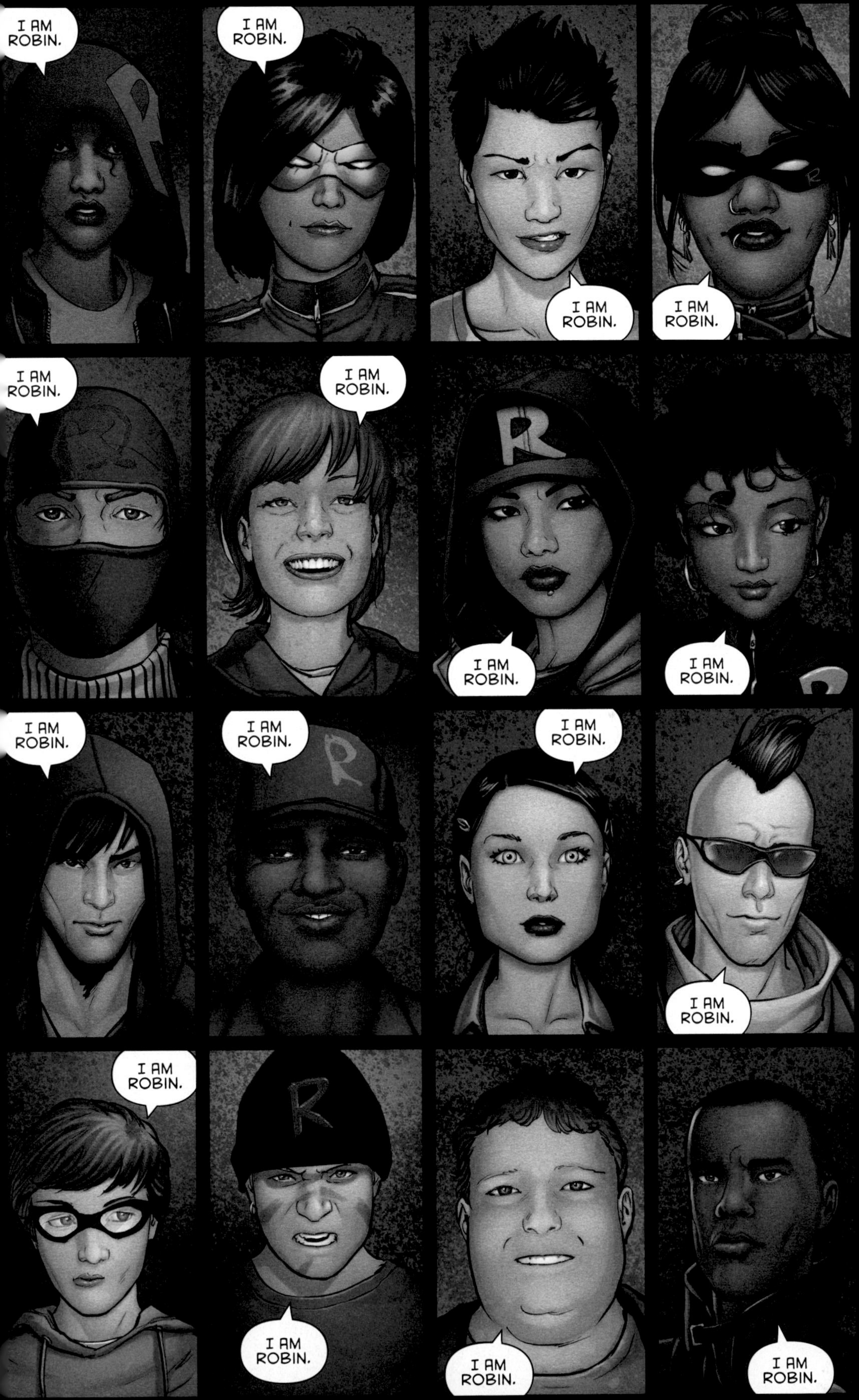
I AM ROBIN.
I AM ROBIN.
I AM ROBIN.
I AM ROBIN.
I AM ROBIN.
I AM ROBIN.
I AM ROBIN.
I AM ROBIN.
I AM ROBIN.
I AM ROBIN.
I AM ROBIN.
I AM ROBIN.
I AM ROBIN.
I AM ROBIN.
I AM ROBIN.
I AM ROBIN.

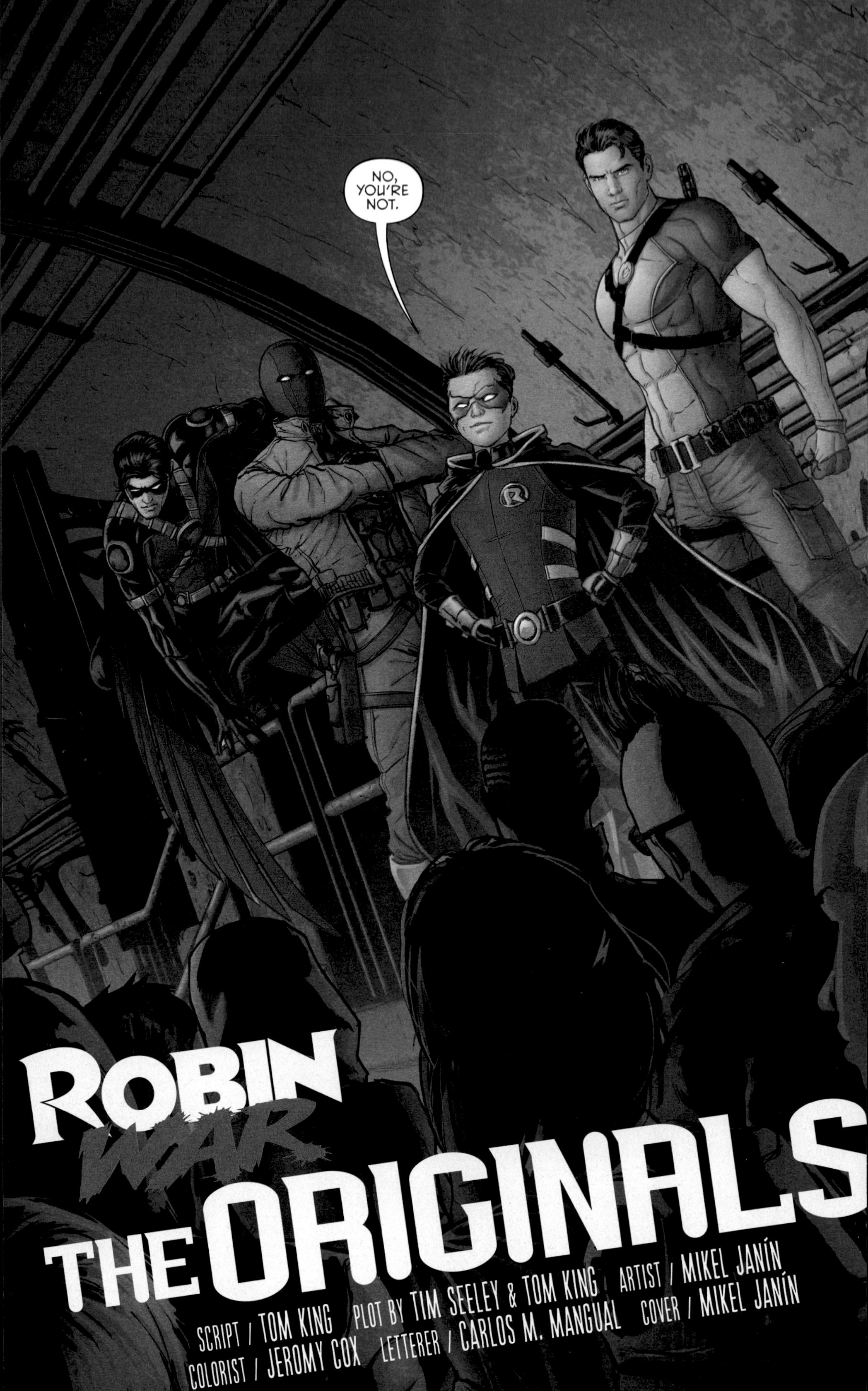
NO, YOU'RE NOT.
ROBIN WAR
THE ORIGINALS
SCRIPT / TOM KING PLOT BY TIM SEELEY & TOM KING ARTIST / MIKEL JANÍN
COLORIST / JEROMY COX LETTERER / CARLOS M. MANGUAL COVER / MIKEL JANÍN

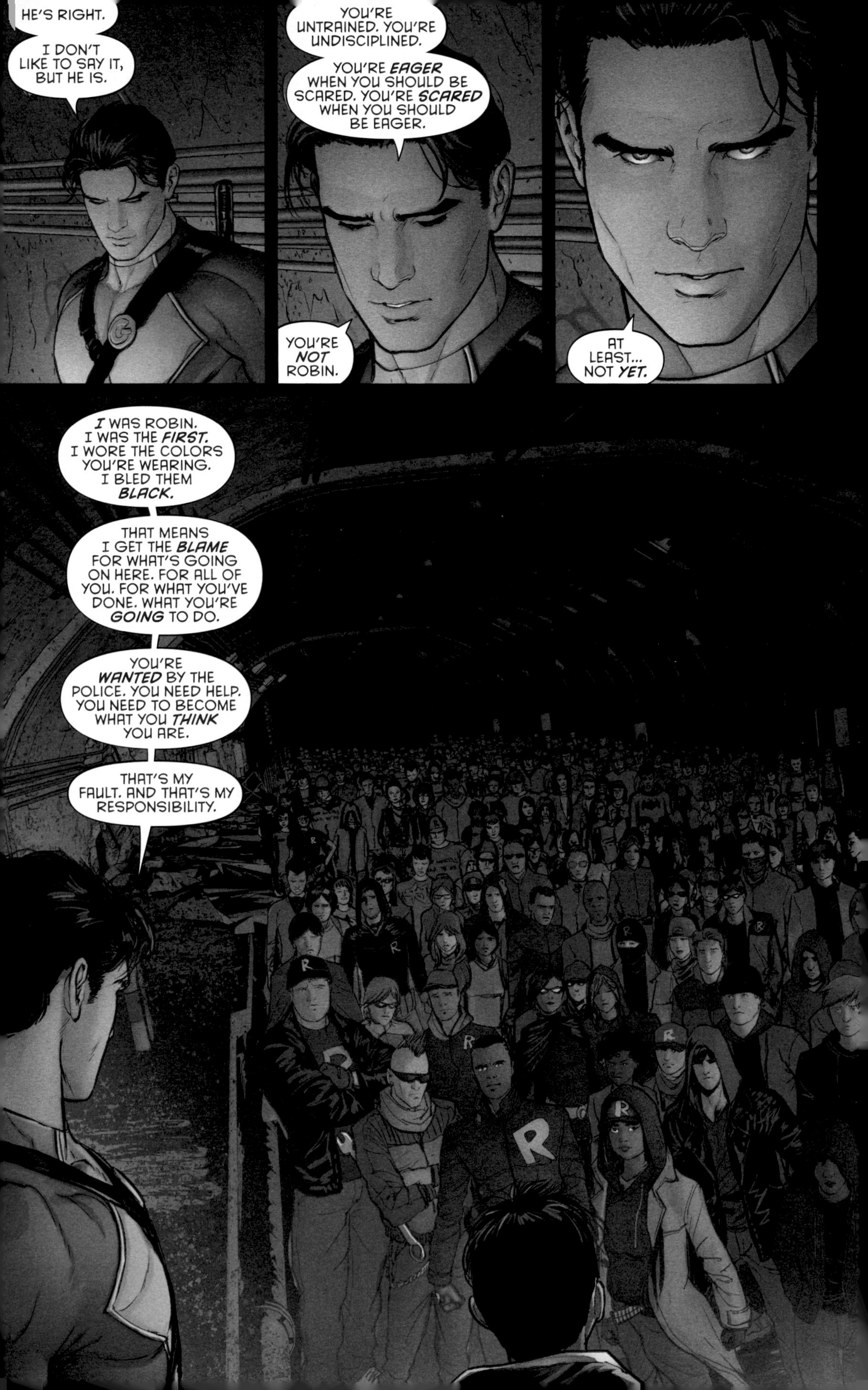
HE'S RIGHT.
I DON'T LIKE TO SAY IT, BUT HE IS.
YOU'RE UNTRAINED. YOU'RE UNDISCIPLINED.
YOU'RE EAGER WHEN YOU SHOULD BE SCARED. YOU'RE SCARED WHEN YOU SHOULD BE EAGER.
YOU'RE NOT ROBIN.
AT LEAST... NOT YET.
I WAS ROBIN. I WAS THE FIRST. I WORE THE COLORS YOU'RE WEARING. I BLED THEM BLACK.
THAT MEANS I GET THE BLAME FOR WHAT'S GOING ON HERE. FOR ALL OF YOU. FOR WHAT YOU'VE DONE. WHAT YOU'RE GOING TO DO.
YOU'RE WANTED BY THE POLICE. YOU NEED HELP. YOU NEED TO BECOME WHAT YOU THINK YOU ARE.
THAT'S MY FAULT. AND THAT'S MY RESPONSIBILITY.

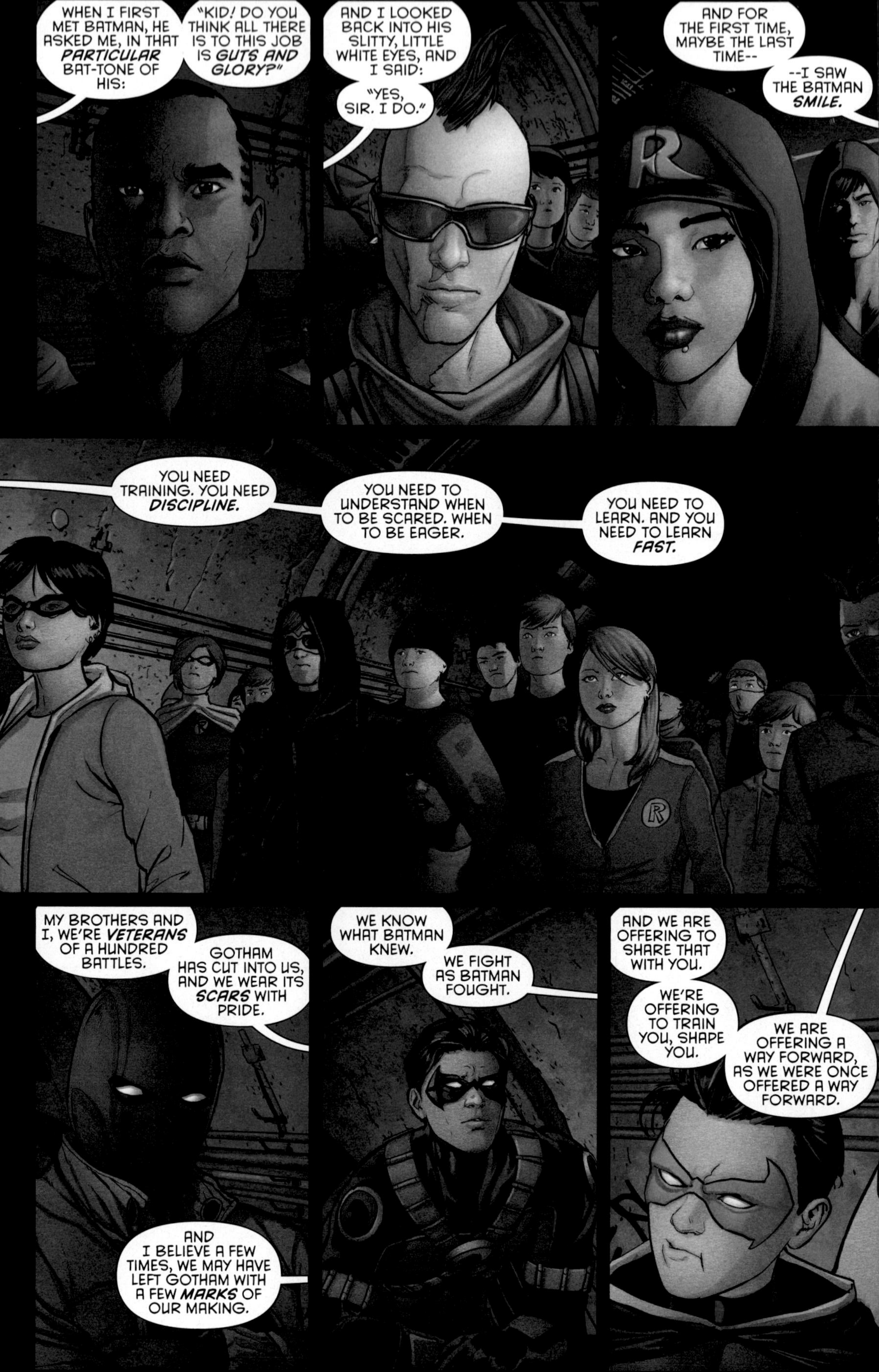
WHEN I FIRST MET BATMAN, HE ASKED ME, IN THAT PARTICULAR BAT-TONE OF HIS:
"KID! DO YOU THINK ALL THERE IS TO THIS JOB IS GUTS AND GLORY?"
AND I LOOKED BACK INTO HIS SLITTY, LITTLE WHITE EYES, AND I SAID:
"YES, SIR. I DO."
AND FOR THE FIRST TIME, MAYBE THE LAST TIME--
--I SAW THE BATMAN SMILE.
YOU NEED TRAINING. YOU NEED DISCIPLINE.
YOU NEED TO UNDERSTAND WHEN TO BE SCARED. WHEN TO BE EAGER.
YOU NEED TO LEARN. AND YOU NEED TO LEARN FAST.
MY BROTHERS AND I, WE'RE VETERANS OF A HUNDRED BATTLES.
GOTHAM HAS CUT INTO US, AND WE WEAR ITS SCARS WITH PRIDE.
AND I BELIEVE A FEW TIMES, WE MAY HAVE LEFT GOTHAM WITH A FEW MARKS OF OUR MAKING.
WE KNOW WHAT BATMAN KNEW.
WE FIGHT AS BATMAN FOUGHT.
AND WE ARE OFFERING TO SHARE THAT WITH YOU.
WE'RE OFFERING TO TRAIN YOU, SHAPE YOU.
WE ARE OFFERING A WAY FORWARD, AS WE WERE ONCE OFFERED A WAY FORWARD.

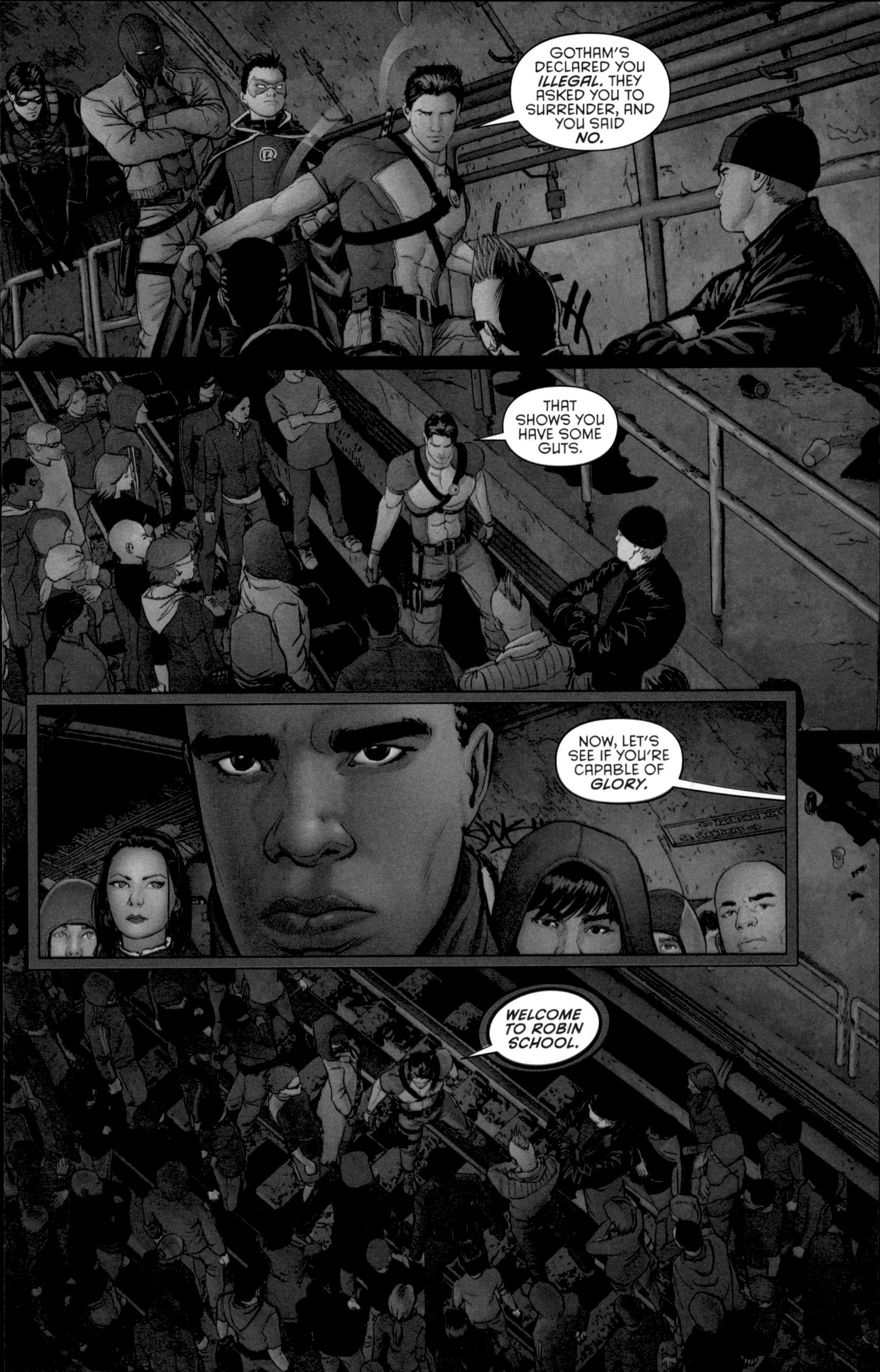
GOTHAM'S DECLARED YOU ILLEGAL. THEY ASKED YOU TO SURRENDER, AND YOU SAID NO.
THAT SHOWS YOU HAVE SOME GUTS.
NOW, LET'S SEE IF YOU'RE CAPABLE OF GLORY.
WELCOME TO ROBIN SCHOOL.

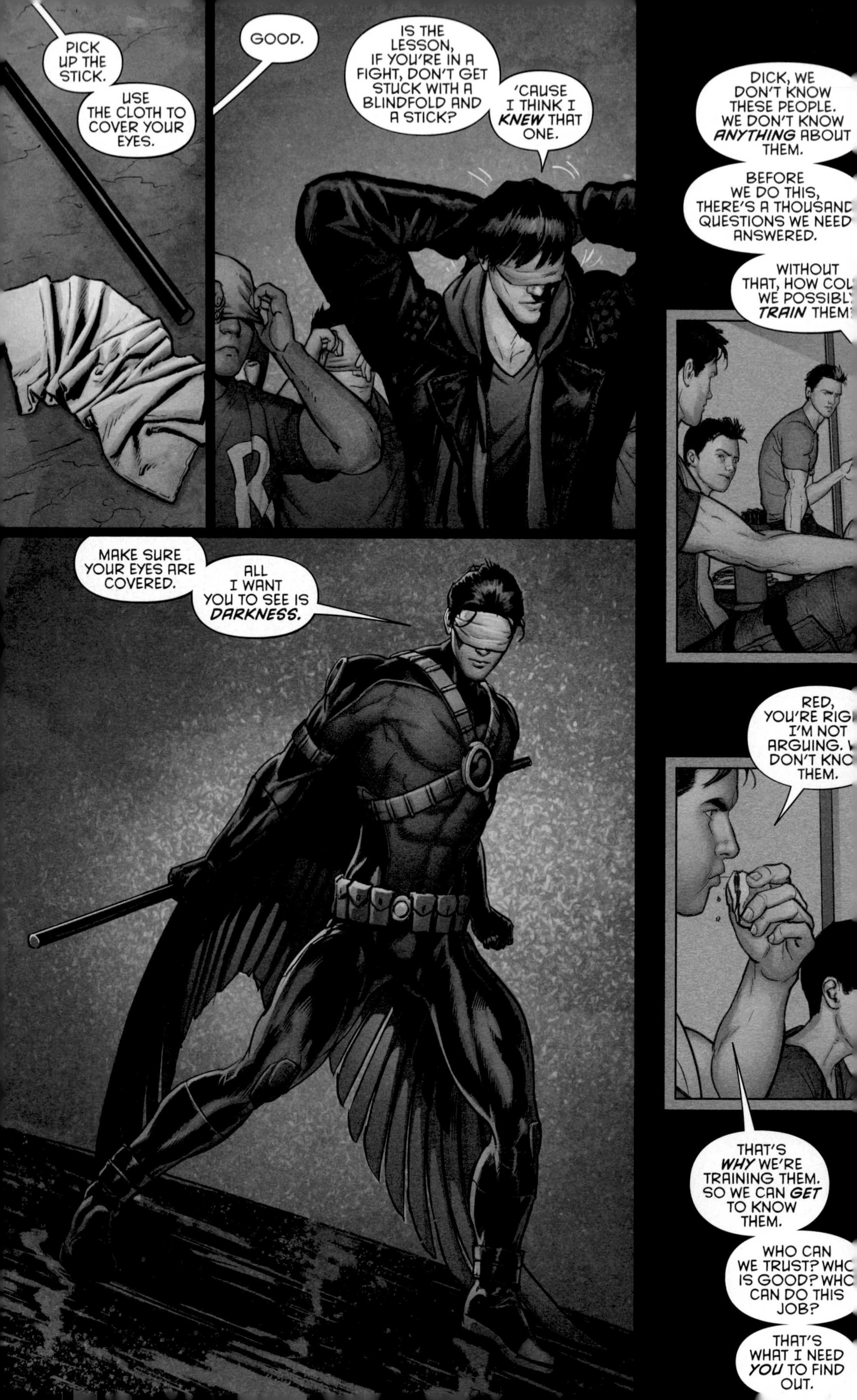
PICK UP THE STICK.
USE THE CLOTH TO COVER YOUR EYES.
GOOD.
IS THE LESSON, IF YOU'RE IN A FIGHT, DON'T GET STUCK WITH A BLINDFOLD AND A STICK?
'CAUSE I THINK I KNEW THAT ONE.
DICK, WE DON'T KNOW THESE PEOPLE. WE DON'T KNOW ANYTHING ABOUT THEM.
BEFORE WE DO THIS, THERE'S A THOUSAND QUESTIONS WE NEED ANSWERED.
WITHOUT THAT, HOW CO WE POSSIBL TRAIN THEM
MAKE SURE YOUR EYES ARE COVERED.
ALL I WANT YOU TO SEE IS DARKNESS.
RED, YOU'RE RIG I'M NOT ARGUING. DON'T KNO THEM.
THAT'S WHY WE'RE TRAINING THEM. SO WE CAN GET TO KNOW THEM.
WHO CAN WE TRUST? WHO IS GOOD? WHO CAN DO THIS JOB?
THAT'S WHAT I NEED YOU TO FIND OUT.

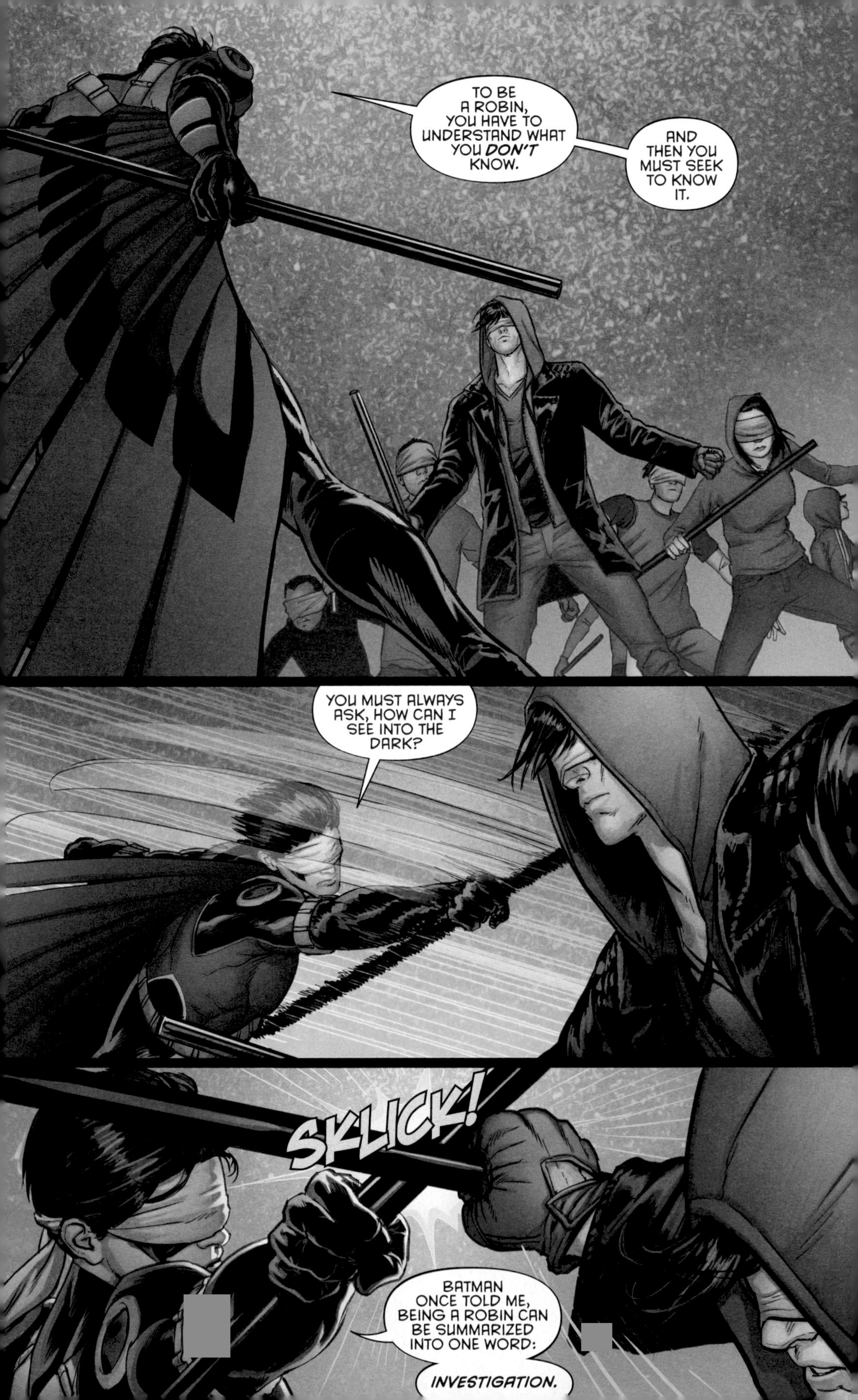
TO BE A ROBIN, YOU HAVE TO UNDERSTAND WHAT YOU *DON'T* KNOW.
AND THEN YOU MUST SEEK TO KNOW IT.
YOU MUST ALWAYS ASK, HOW CAN I SEE INTO THE DARK?
SKLICK!
BATMAN ONCE TOLD ME, BEING A ROBIN CAN BE SUMMARIZED INTO ONE WORD:
INVESTIGATION.

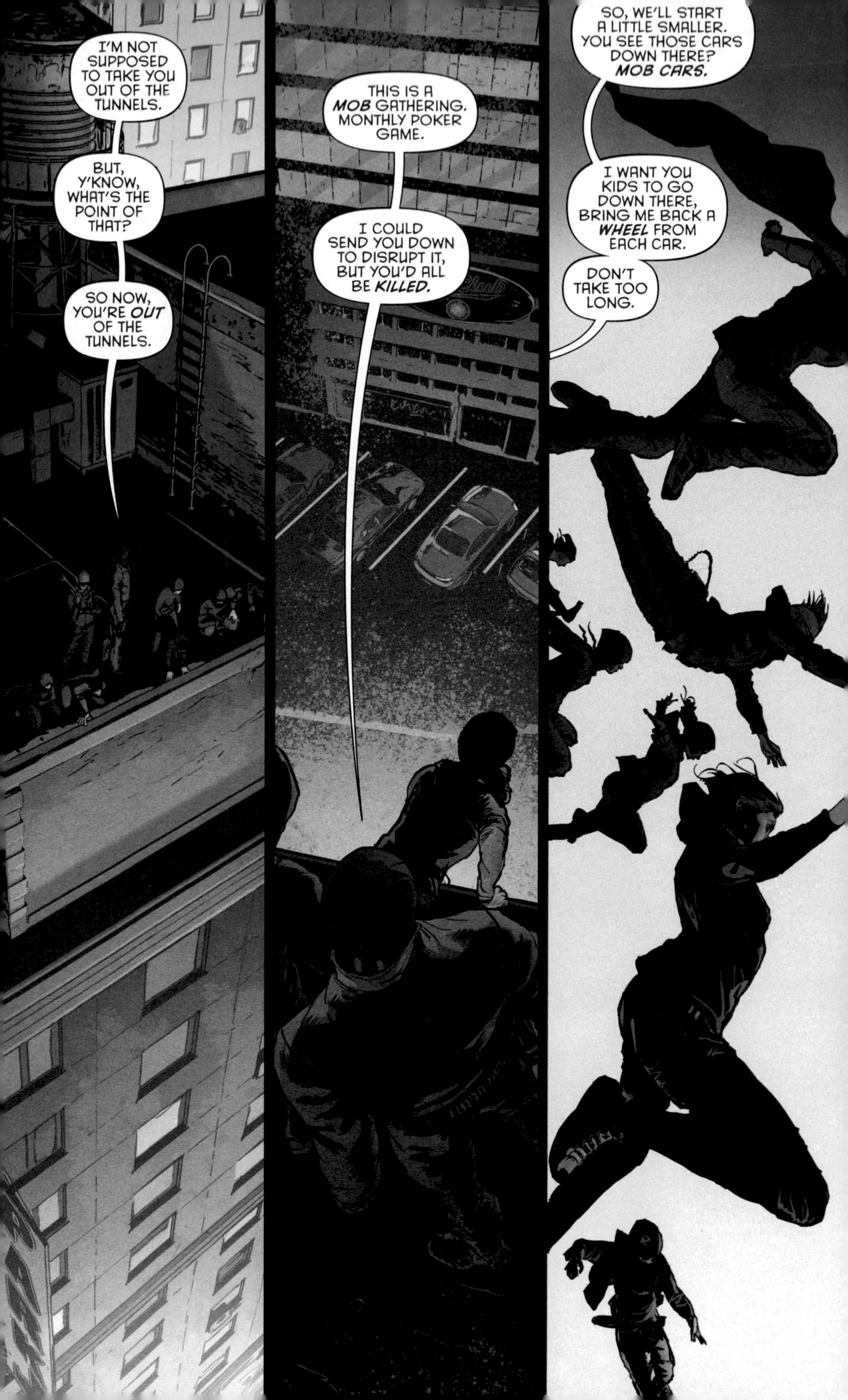
I'M NOT SUPPOSED TO TAKE YOU OUT OF THE TUNNELS.
BUT, Y'KNOW, WHAT'S THE POINT OF THAT?
SO NOW, YOU'RE *OUT* OF THE TUNNELS.
THIS IS A *MOB* GATHERING. MONTHLY POKER GAME.
I COULD SEND YOU DOWN TO DISRUPT IT, BUT YOU'D ALL BE *KILLED.*
SO, WE'LL START A LITTLE SMALLER. YOU SEE THOSE CARS DOWN THERE? *MOB CARS.*
I WANT YOU KIDS TO GO DOWN THERE, BRING ME BACK A *WHEEL* FROM EACH CAR.
DON'T TAKE TOO LONG.

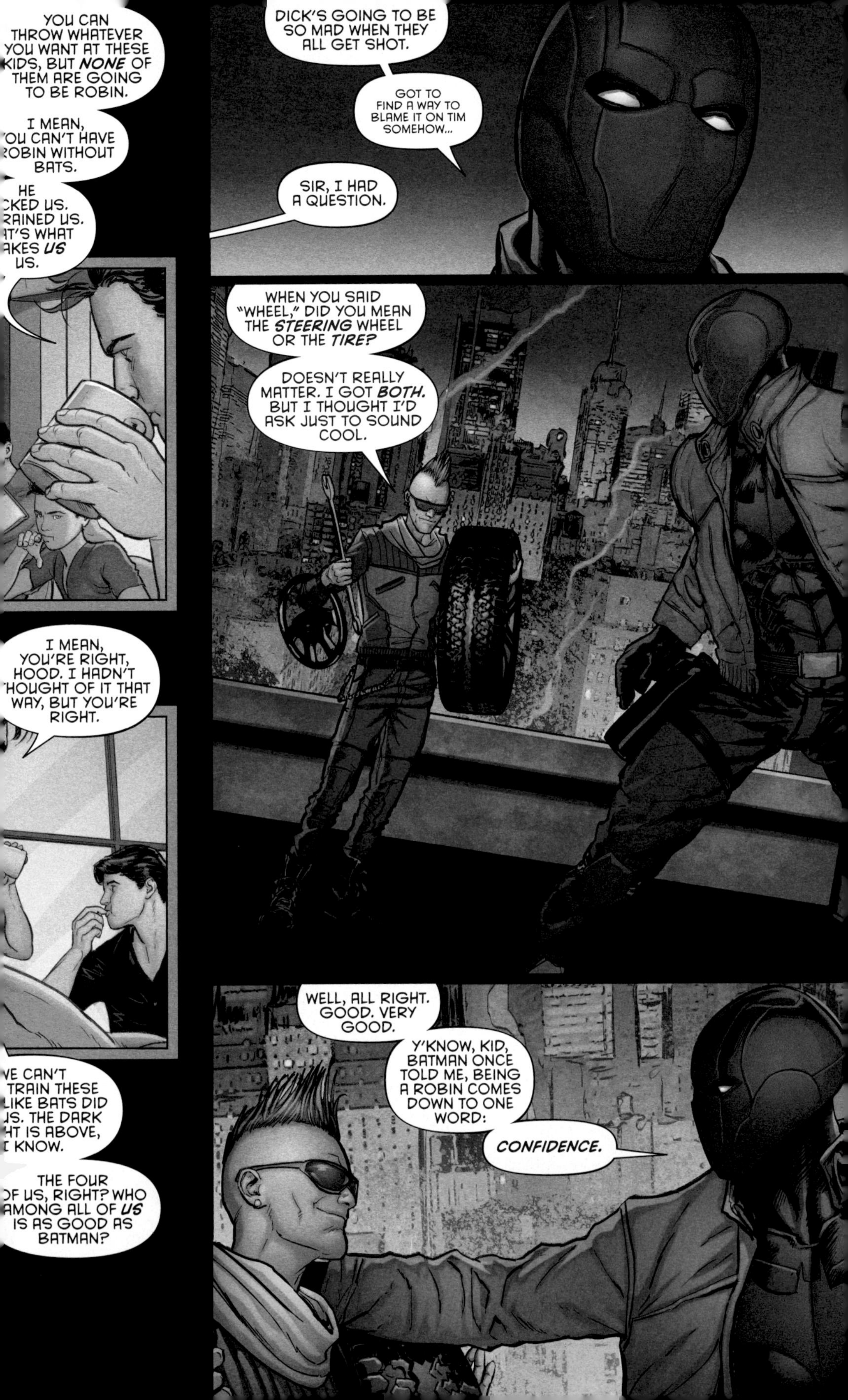

YOU CAN THROW WHATEVER YOU WANT AT THESE KIDS, BUT NONE OF THEM ARE GOING TO BE ROBIN.
I MEAN, OU CAN'T HAVE OBIN WITHOUT BATS.
HE CKED US. RAINED US. T'S WHAT AKES US US.
I MEAN, YOU'RE RIGHT, HOOD. I HADN'T HOUGHT OF IT THAT WAY, BUT YOU'RE RIGHT.
VE CAN'T TRAIN THESE LIKE BATS DID US. THE DARK HT IS ABOVE, I KNOW.
THE FOUR OF US, RIGHT? WHO AMONG ALL OF US IS AS GOOD AS BATMAN?
DICK'S GOING TO BE SO MAD WHEN THEY ALL GET SHOT.
GOT TO FIND A WAY TO BLAME IT ON TIM SOMEHOW...
SIR, I HAD A QUESTION.
WHEN YOU SAID "WHEEL," DID YOU MEAN THE STEERING WHEEL OR THE TIRE?
DOESN'T REALLY MATTER. I GOT BOTH. BUT I THOUGHT I'D ASK JUST TO SOUND COOL.
WELL, ALL RIGHT. GOOD. VERY GOOD.
Y'KNOW, KID, BATMAN ONCE TOLD ME, BEING A ROBIN COMES DOWN TO ONE WORD:
CONFIDENCE.

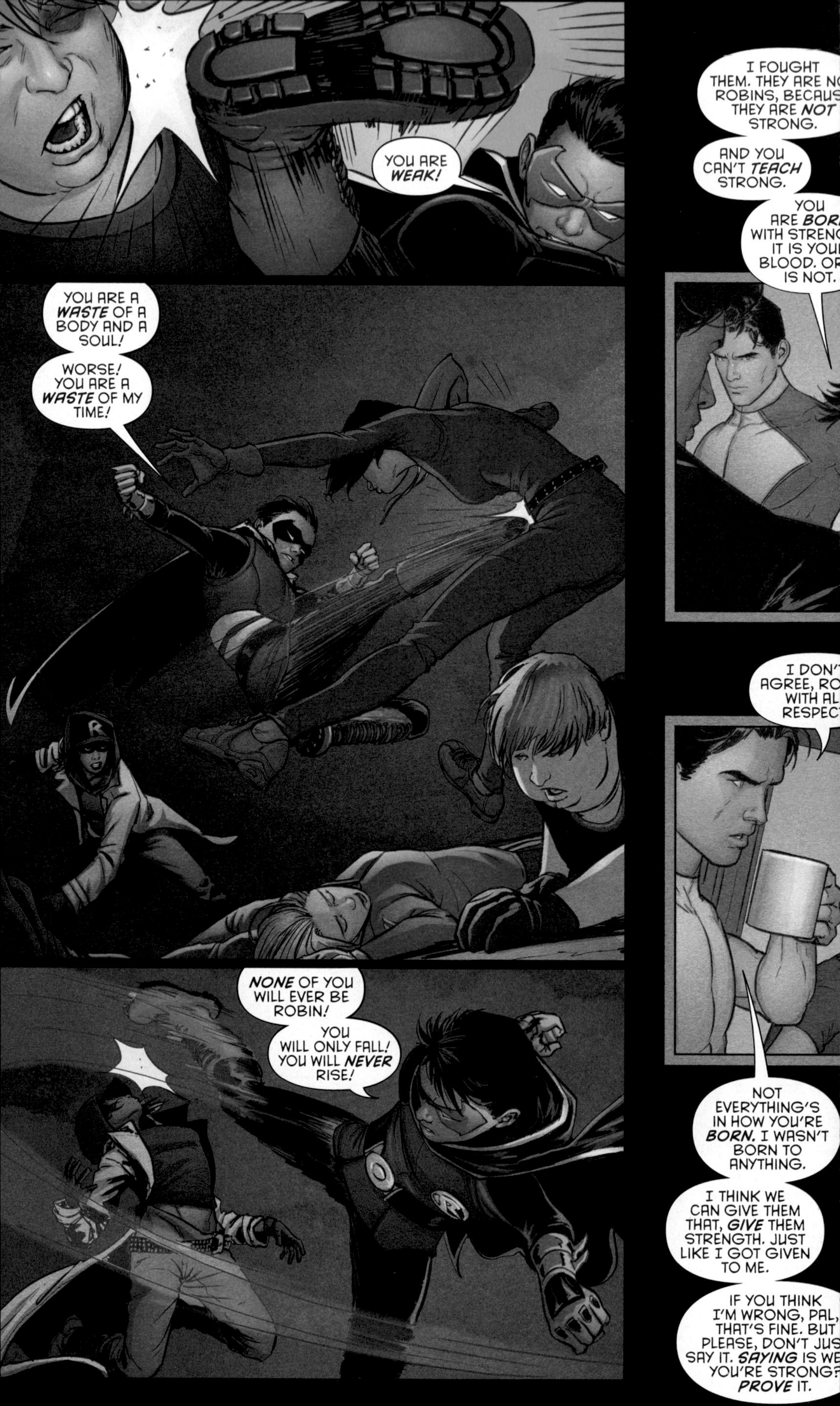
YOU ARE WEAK!
YOU ARE A WASTE OF A BODY AND A SOUL!
WORSE! YOU ARE A WASTE OF MY TIME!
NONE OF YOU WILL EVER BE ROBIN!
YOU WILL ONLY FALL! YOU WILL NEVER RISE!
I FOUGHT THEM. THEY ARE NO ROBINS, BECAUS THEY ARE NOT STRONG.
AND YOU CAN'T TEACH STRONG.
YOU ARE BOR WITH STRENG IT IS YOU BLOOD. OR IS NOT.
I DON' AGREE, RO WITH AL RESPEC
NOT EVERYTHING'S IN HOW YOU'RE BORN. I WASN'T BORN TO ANYTHING.
I THINK WE CAN GIVE THEM THAT, GIVE THEM STRENGTH. JUST LIKE I GOT GIVEN TO ME.
IF YOU THINK I'M WRONG, PAL, THAT'S FINE. BUT PLEASE, DON'T JUS SAY IT. SAYING IS WE YOU'RE STRONG? PROVE IT.

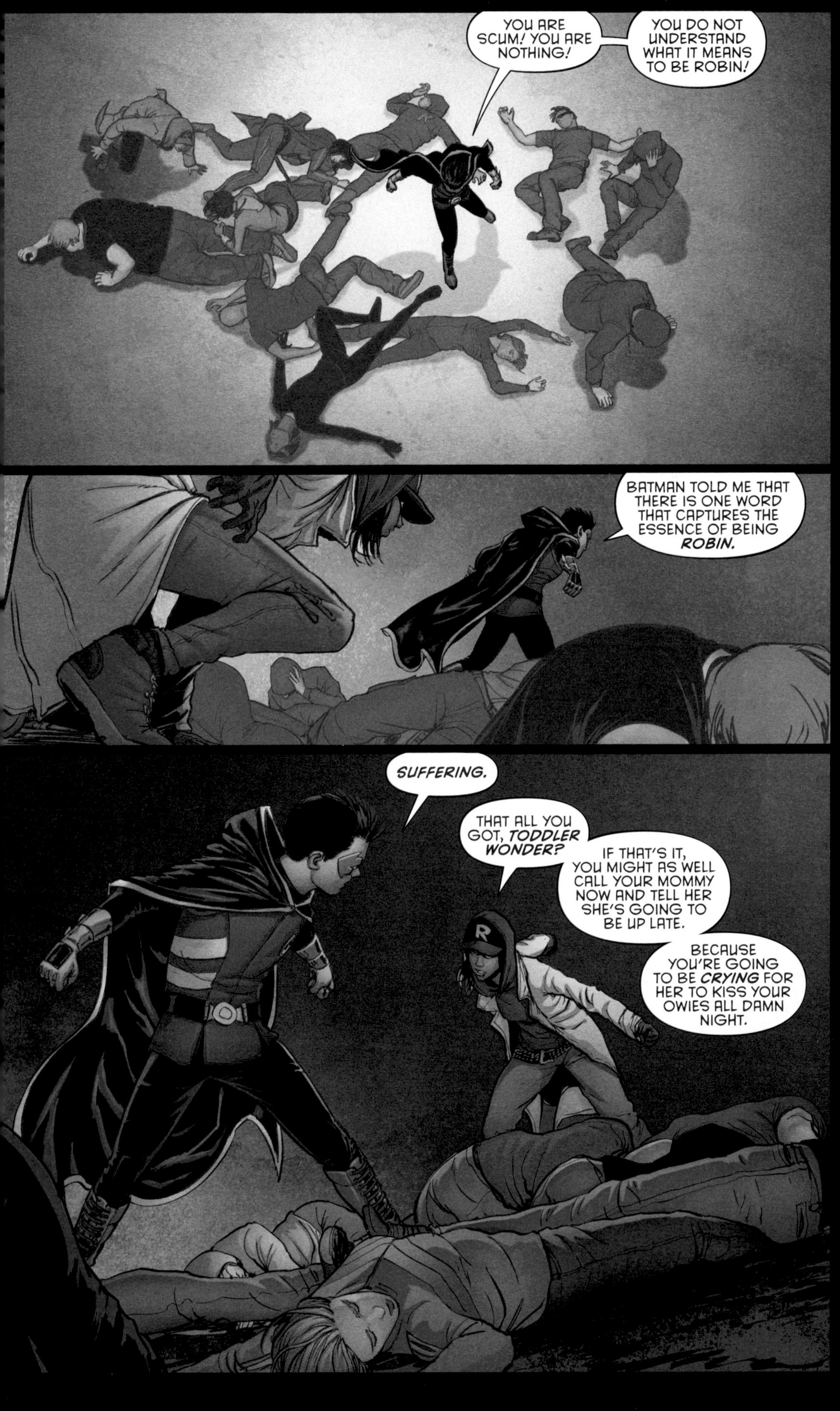
YOU ARE SCUM! YOU ARE NOTHING!
YOU DO NOT UNDERSTAND WHAT IT MEANS TO BE ROBIN!
BATMAN TOLD ME THAT THERE IS ONE WORD THAT CAPTURES THE ESSENCE OF BEING *ROBIN.*
SUFFERING.
THAT ALL YOU GOT, *TODDLER WONDER?*
IF THAT'S IT, YOU MIGHT AS WELL CALL YOUR MOMMY NOW AND TELL HER SHE'S GOING TO BE UP LATE.
BECAUSE YOU'RE GOING TO BE *CRYING* FOR HER TO KISS YOUR OWIES ALL DAMN NIGHT.

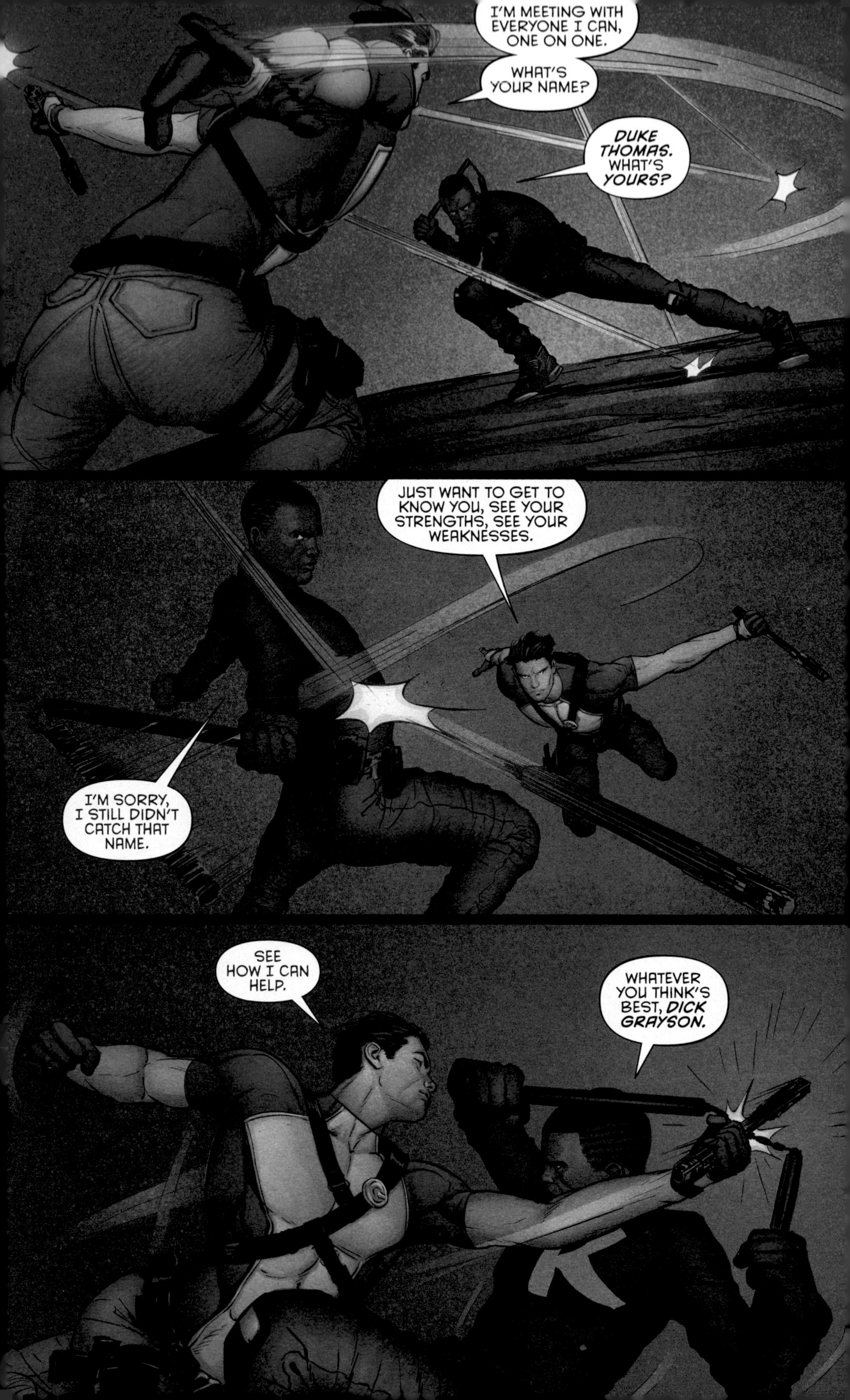

I'M MEETING WITH EVERYONE I CAN, ONE ON ONE.
WHAT'S YOUR NAME?
DUKE THOMAS. WHAT'S *YOURS?*
JUST WANT TO GET TO KNOW YOU, SEE YOUR STRENGTHS, SEE YOUR WEAKNESSES.
I'M SORRY, I STILL DIDN'T CATCH THAT NAME.
SEE HOW I CAN HELP.
WHATEVER YOU THINK'S BEST, *DICK GRAYSON.*

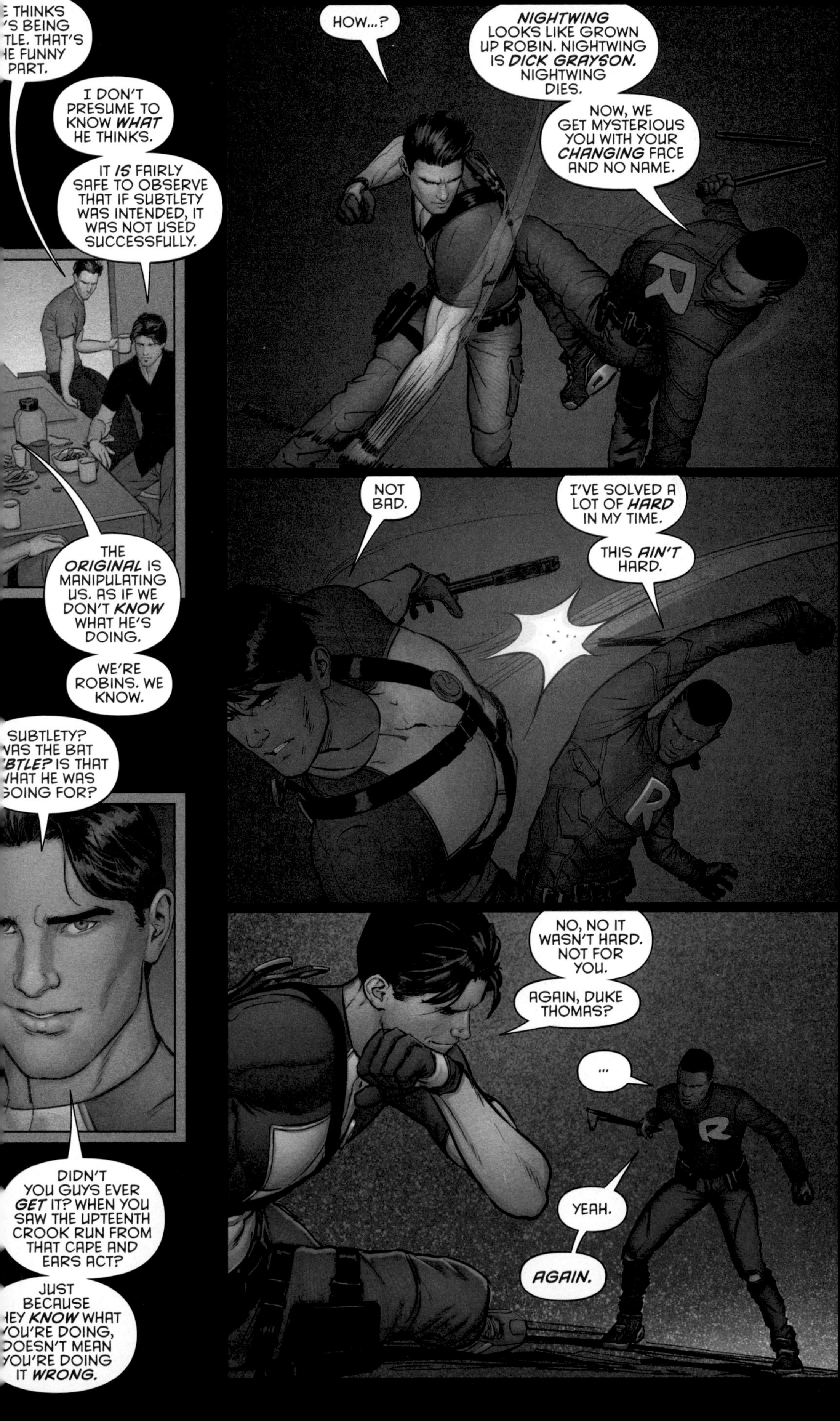

E THINKS 'S BEING TLE. THAT'S HE FUNNY PART.
I DON'T PRESUME TO KNOW WHAT HE THINKS.
IT IS FAIRLY SAFE TO OBSERVE THAT IF SUBTLETY WAS INTENDED, IT WAS NOT USED SUCCESSFULLY.
THE ORIGINAL IS MANIPULATING US. AS IF WE DON'T KNOW WHAT HE'S DOING.
WE'RE ROBINS. WE KNOW.
SUBTLETY? VAS THE BAT BTLE? IS THAT VHAT HE WAS GOING FOR?
DIDN'T YOU GUYS EVER GET IT? WHEN YOU SAW THE UPTEENTH CROOK RUN FROM THAT CAPE AND EARS ACT?
JUST BECAUSE HEY KNOW WHAT YOU'RE DOING, DOESN'T MEAN YOU'RE DOING IT WRONG.
HOW...?
NIGHTWING LOOKS LIKE GROWN UP ROBIN. NIGHTWING IS DICK GRAYSON. NIGHTWING DIES.
NOW, WE GET MYSTERIOUS YOU WITH YOUR CHANGING FACE AND NO NAME.
NOT BAD.
I'VE SOLVED A LOT OF HARD IN MY TIME.
THIS AIN'T HARD.
NO, NO IT WASN'T HARD. NOT FOR YOU.
AGAIN, DUKE THOMAS?
...
YEAH.
AGAIN.

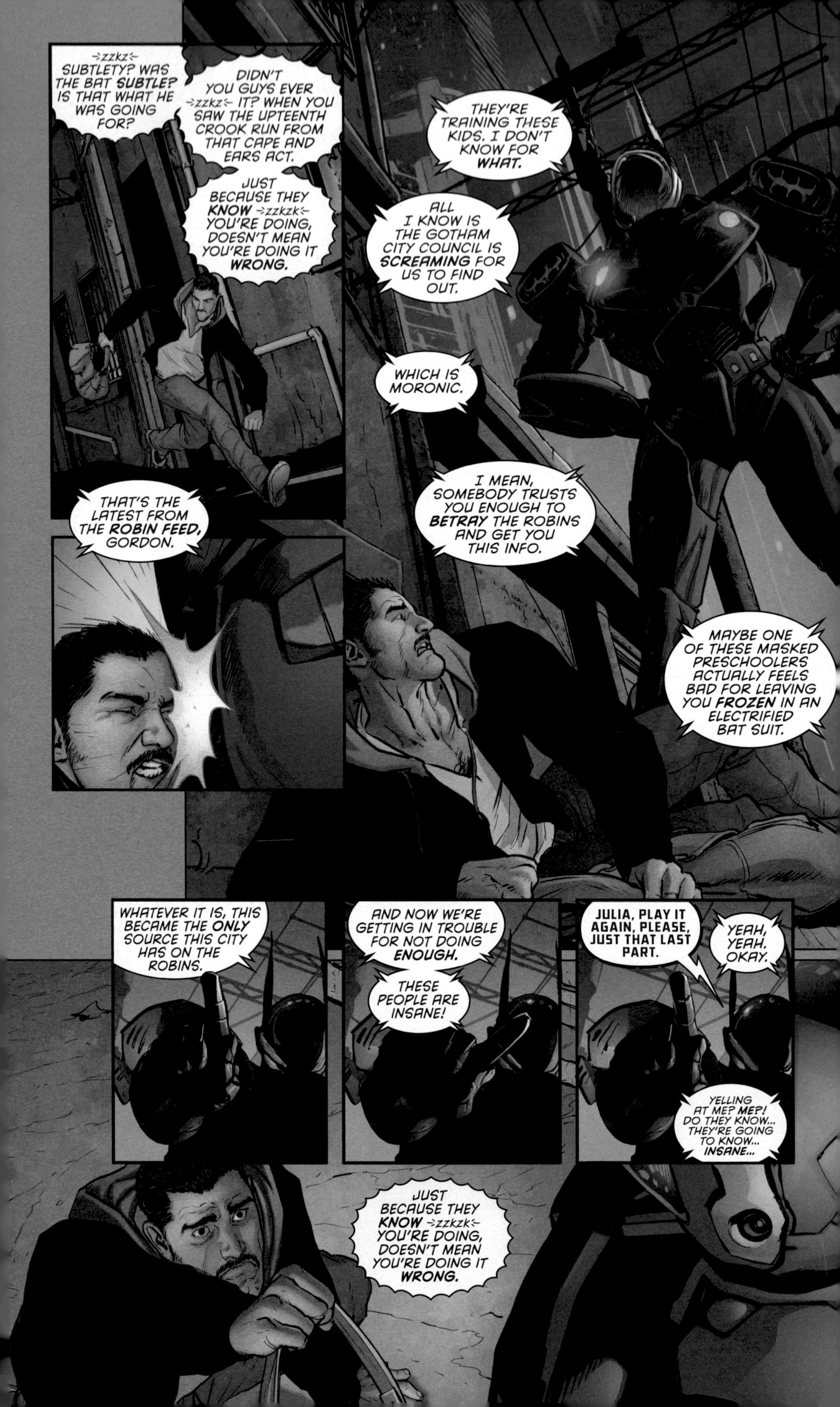

-zzkz- SUBTLETY? WAS THE BAT SUBTLE? IS THAT WHAT HE WAS GOING FOR?
DIDN'T YOU GUYS EVER -zzkz- IT? WHEN YOU SAW THE UPTEENTH CROOK RUN FROM THAT CAPE AND EARS ACT.
JUST BECAUSE THEY KNOW -zzkzk- YOU'RE DOING, DOESN'T MEAN YOU'RE DOING IT WRONG.
THAT'S THE LATEST FROM THE ROBIN FEED, GORDON.
THEY'RE TRAINING THESE KIDS. I DON'T KNOW FOR WHAT.
ALL I KNOW IS THE GOTHAM CITY COUNCIL IS SCREAMING FOR US TO FIND OUT.
WHICH IS MORONIC.
I MEAN, SOMEBODY TRUSTS YOU ENOUGH TO BETRAY THE ROBINS AND GET YOU THIS INFO.
MAYBE ONE OF THESE MASKED PRESCHOOLERS ACTUALLY FEELS BAD FOR LEAVING YOU FROZEN IN AN ELECTRIFIED BAT SUIT.
WHATEVER IT IS, THIS BECAME THE ONLY SOURCE THIS CITY HAS ON THE ROBINS.
AND NOW WE'RE GETTING IN TROUBLE FOR NOT DOING ENOUGH.
THESE PEOPLE ARE INSANE!
JULIA, PLAY IT AGAIN, PLEASE, JUST THAT LAST PART.
YEAH, YEAH. OKAY.
YELLING AT ME? ME?! DO THEY KNOW... THEY'RE GOING TO KNOW... INSANE...
JUST BECAUSE THEY KNOW -zzkzk- YOU'RE DOING, DOESN'T MEAN YOU'RE DOING IT WRONG.

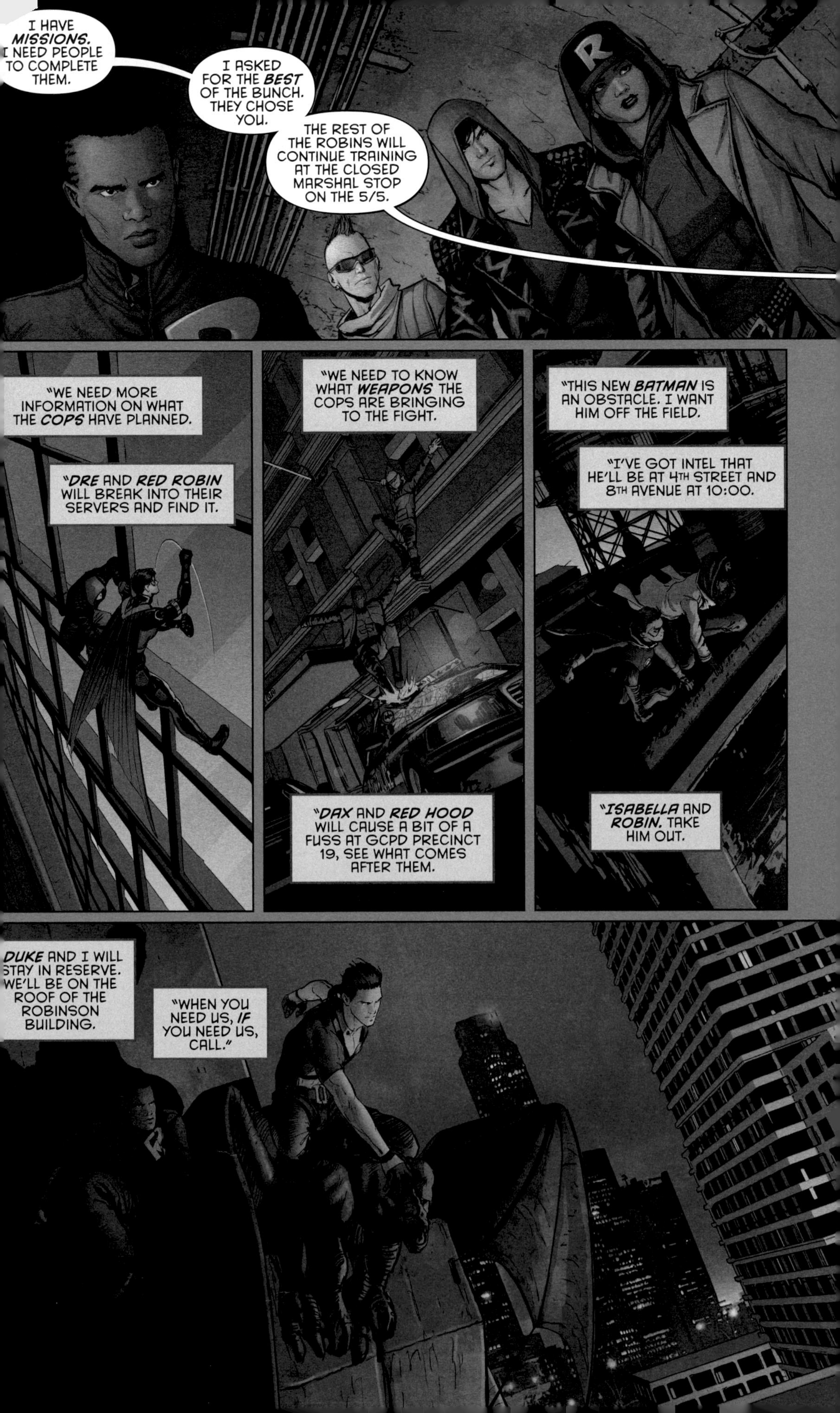

I HAVE MISSIONS. I NEED PEOPLE TO COMPLETE THEM.
I ASKED FOR THE BEST OF THE BUNCH. THEY CHOSE YOU.
THE REST OF THE ROBINS WILL CONTINUE TRAINING AT THE CLOSED MARSHAL STOP ON THE 5/5.
"WE NEED MORE INFORMATION ON WHAT THE COPS HAVE PLANNED.
"DRE AND RED ROBIN WILL BREAK INTO THEIR SERVERS AND FIND IT.
"WE NEED TO KNOW WHAT WEAPONS THE COPS ARE BRINGING TO THE FIGHT.
"DAX AND RED HOOD WILL CAUSE A BIT OF A FUSS AT GCPD PRECINCT 19, SEE WHAT COMES AFTER THEM.
"THIS NEW BATMAN IS AN OBSTACLE. I WANT HIM OFF THE FIELD.
"I'VE GOT INTEL THAT HE'LL BE AT 4TH STREET AND 8TH AVENUE AT 10:00.
"ISABELLA AND ROBIN. TAKE HIM OUT.
DUKE AND I WILL STAY IN RESERVE. WE'LL BE ON THE ROOF OF THE ROBINSON BUILDING.
"WHEN YOU NEED US, IF YOU NEED US, CALL."

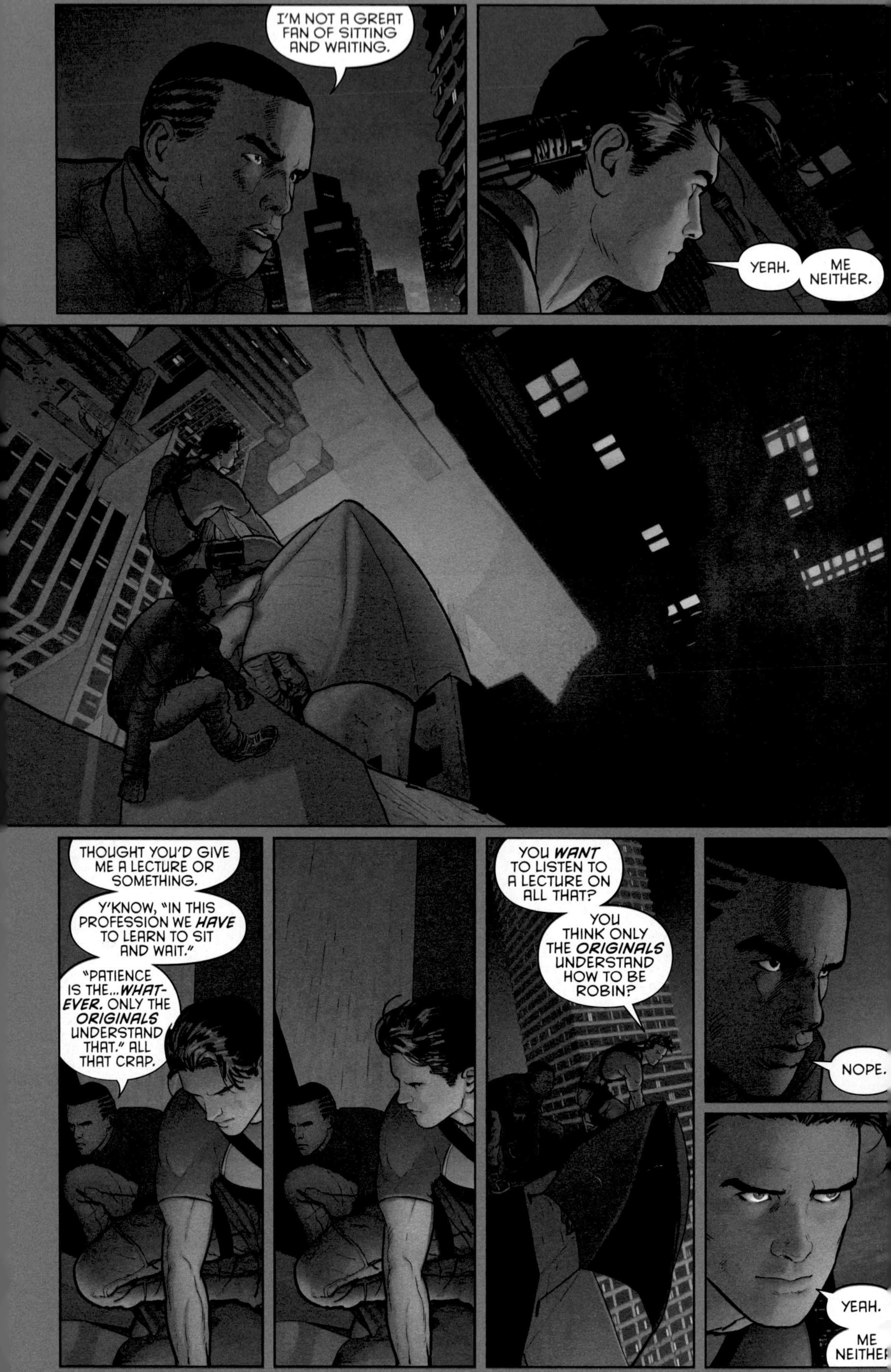

I'M NOT A GREAT FAN OF SITTING AND WAITING.
YEAH.
ME NEITHER.
THOUGHT YOU'D GIVE ME A LECTURE OR SOMETHING.
Y'KNOW, "IN THIS PROFESSION WE *HAVE* TO LEARN TO SIT AND WAIT."
"PATIENCE IS THE...*WHAT-EVER.* ONLY THE *ORIGINALS* UNDERSTAND THAT." ALL THAT CRAP.
YOU *WANT* TO LISTEN TO A LECTURE ON ALL THAT?
YOU THINK ONLY THE *ORIGINALS* UNDERSTAND HOW TO BE ROBIN?
NOPE.
YEAH.

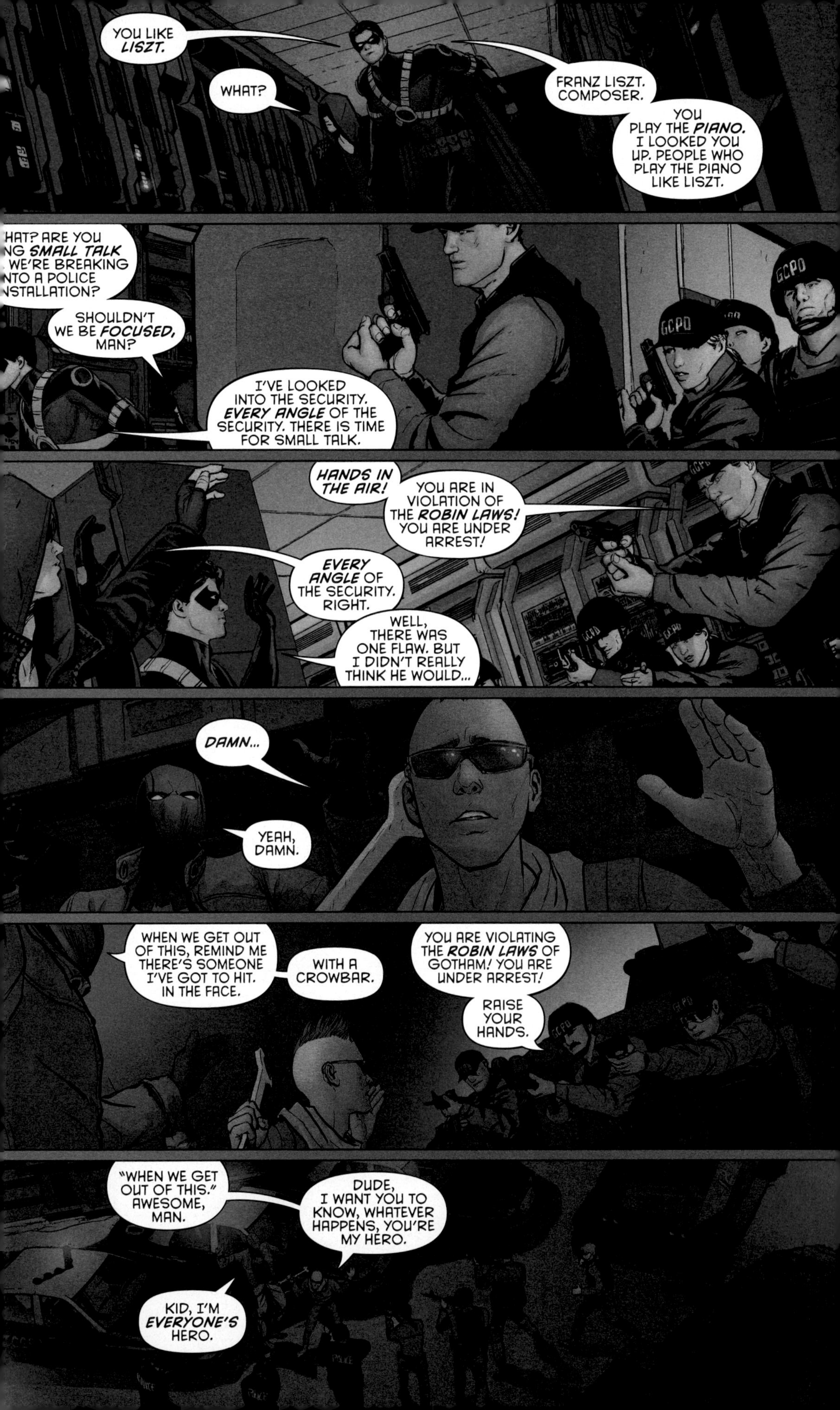
YOU LIKE LISZT.
WHAT?
FRANZ LISZT. COMPOSER.
YOU PLAY THE PIANO. I LOOKED YOU UP. PEOPLE WHO PLAY THE PIANO LIKE LISZT.
HAT? ARE YOU NG SMALL TALK WE'RE BREAKING NTO A POLICE NSTALLATION?
SHOULDN'T WE BE FOCUSED, MAN?
I'VE LOOKED INTO THE SECURITY. EVERY ANGLE OF THE SECURITY. THERE IS TIME FOR SMALL TALK.
GCPD
HANDS IN THE AIR!
YOU ARE IN VIOLATION OF THE ROBIN LAWS! YOU ARE UNDER ARREST!
EVERY ANGLE OF THE SECURITY. RIGHT.
WELL, THERE WAS ONE FLAW. BUT I DIDN'T REALLY THINK HE WOULD...
DAMN...
YEAH, DAMN.
WHEN WE GET OUT OF THIS, REMIND ME THERE'S SOMEONE I'VE GOT TO HIT. IN THE FACE.
WITH A CROWBAR.
YOU ARE VIOLATING THE ROBIN LAWS OF GOTHAM! YOU ARE UNDER ARREST!
RAISE YOUR HANDS.
"WHEN WE GET OUT OF THIS." AWESOME, MAN.
DUDE, I WANT YOU TO KNOW, WHATEVER HAPPENS, YOU'RE MY HERO.
KID, I'M EVERYONE'S HERO.

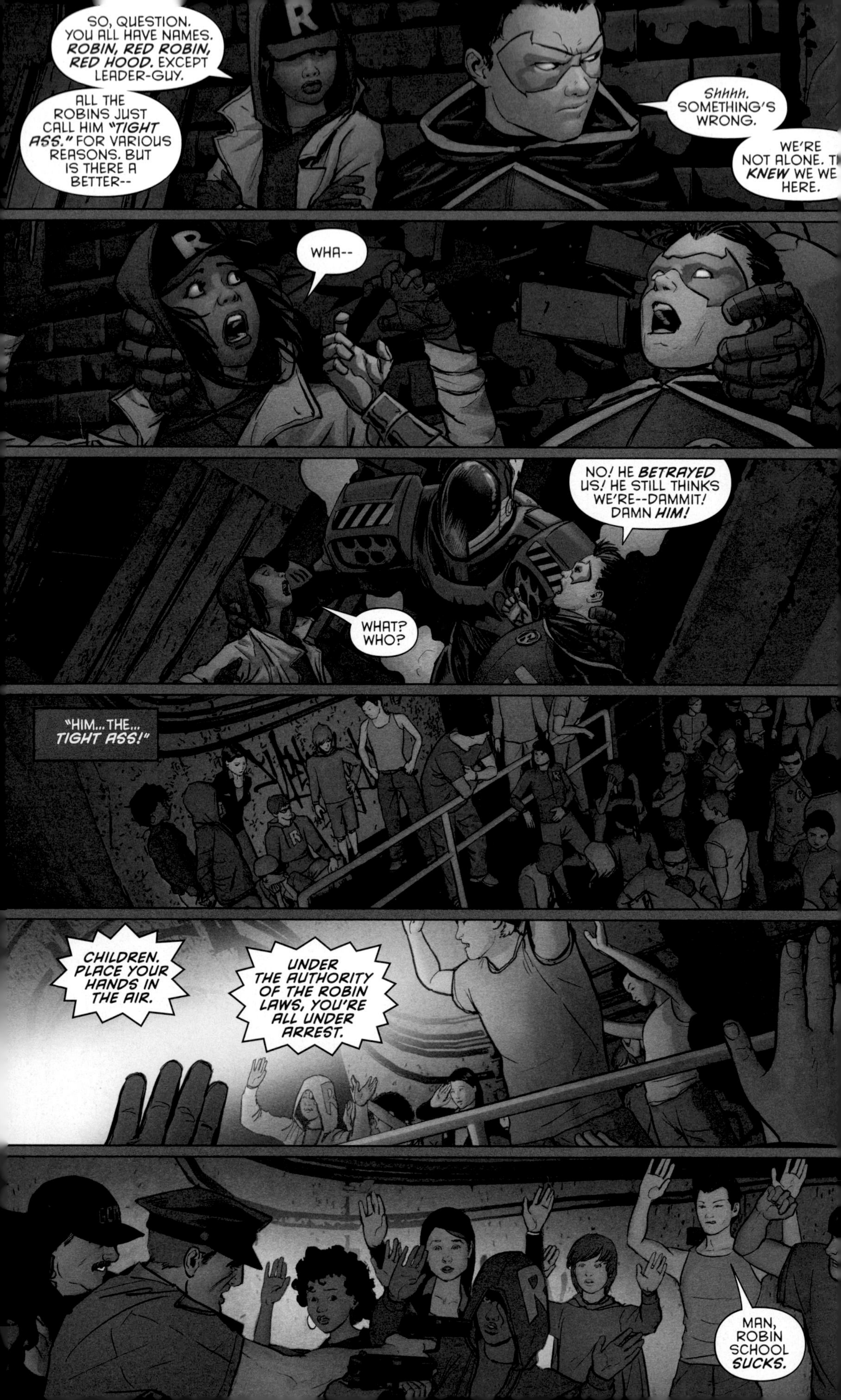
SO, QUESTION. YOU ALL HAVE NAMES. ROBIN, RED ROBIN, RED HOOD. EXCEPT LEADER-GUY.
ALL THE ROBINS JUST CALL HIM "TIGHT ASS." FOR VARIOUS REASONS. BUT IS THERE A BETTER--
Shhhh. SOMETHING'S WRONG.
WE'RE NOT ALONE. T KNEW WE WE HERE.
WHA--
NO! HE BETRAYED US! HE STILL THINKS WE'RE--DAMMIT! DAMN HIM!
WHAT? WHO?
"HIM... THE... TIGHT ASS!"
CHILDREN. PLACE YOUR HANDS IN THE AIR.
UNDER THE AUTHORITY OF THE ROBIN LAWS, YOU'RE ALL UNDER ARREST.
MAN, ROBIN SCHOOL SUCKS.

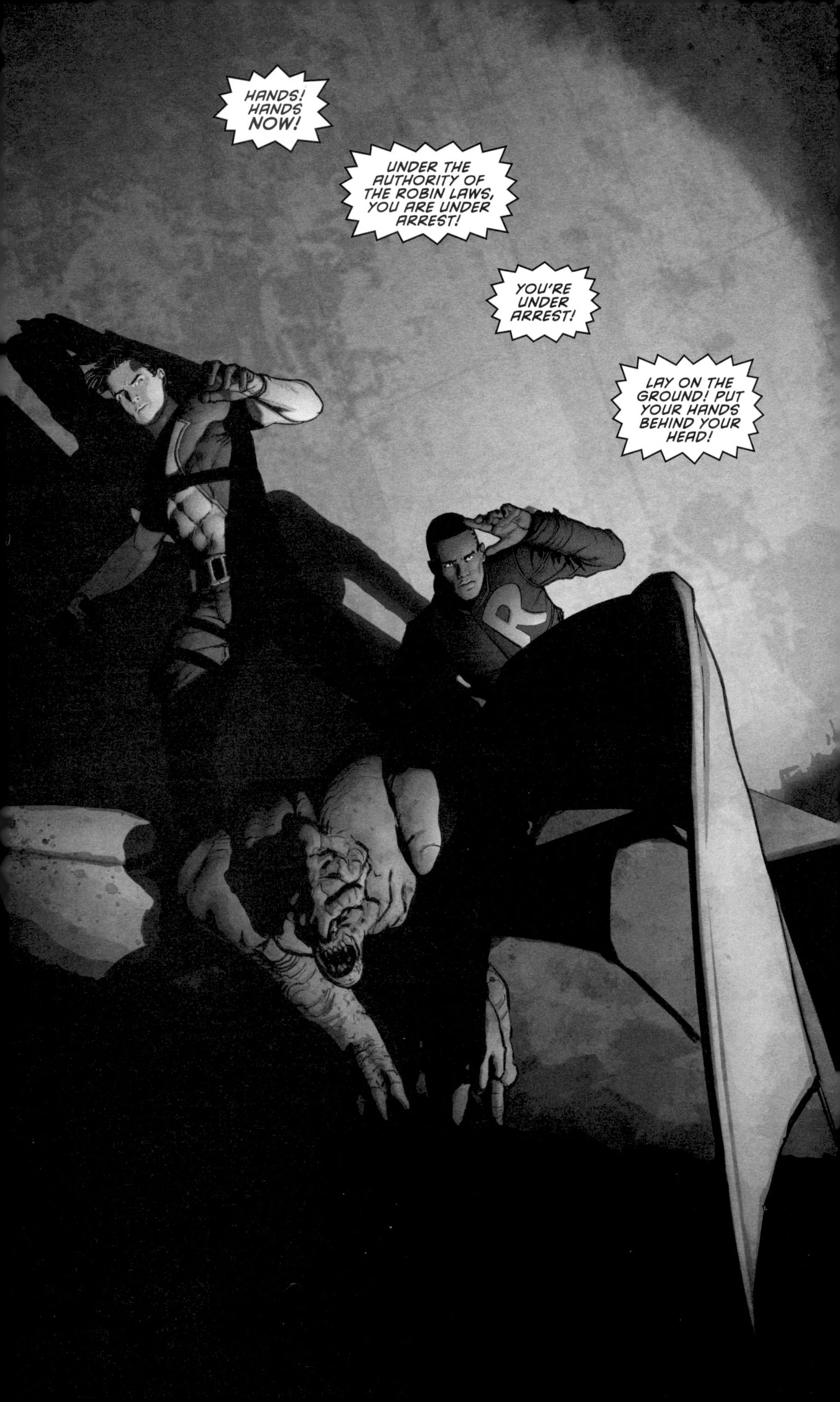
HANDS! HANDS NOW!
UNDER THE AUTHORITY OF THE ROBIN LAWS, YOU ARE UNDER ARREST!
YOU'RE UNDER ARREST!
LAY ON THE GROUND! PUT YOUR HANDS BEHIND YOUR HEAD!

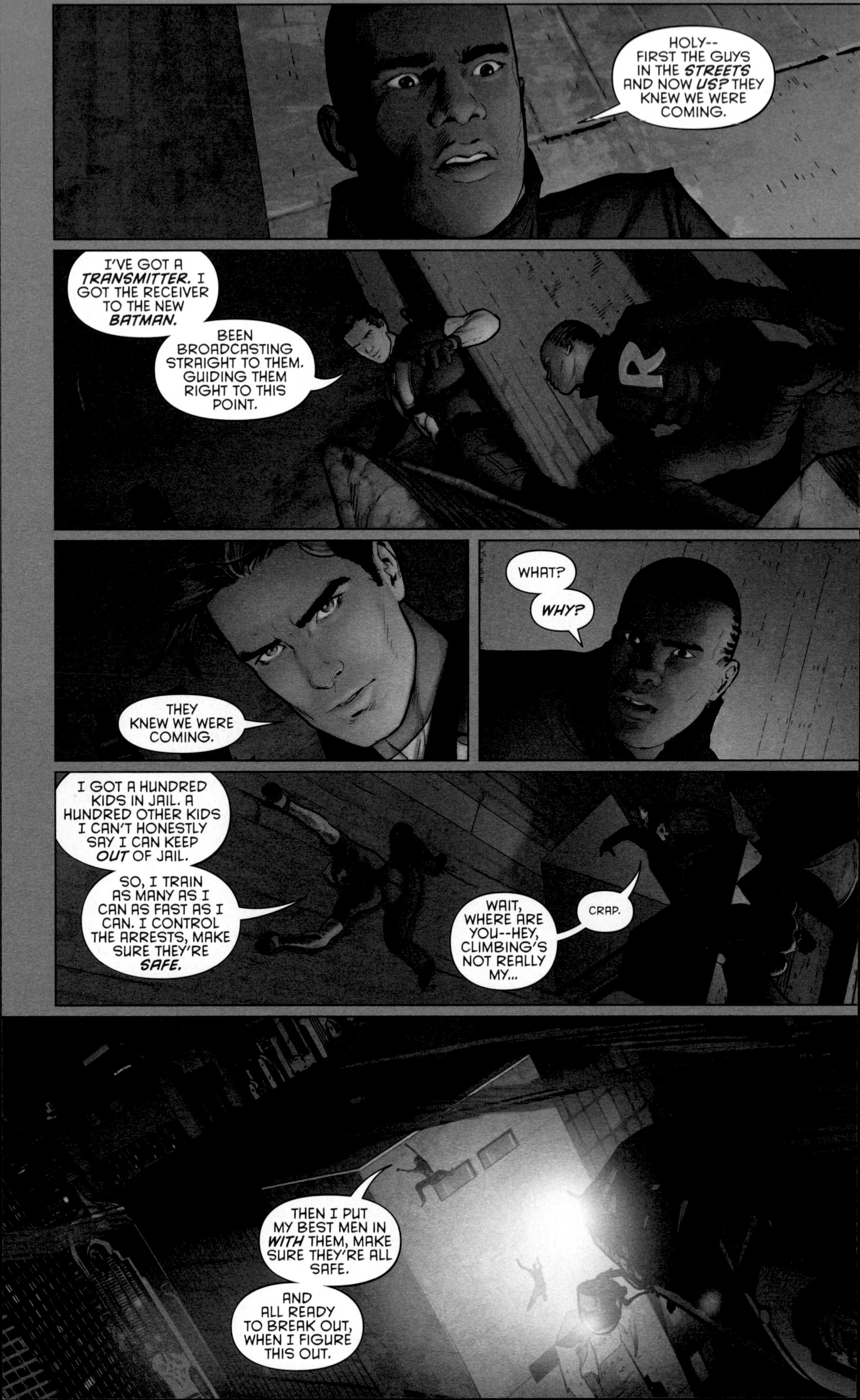

HOLY-- FIRST THE GUYS IN THE *STREETS* AND NOW *US?* THEY KNEW WE WERE COMING.
I'VE GOT A *TRANSMITTER.* I GOT THE RECEIVER TO THE NEW *BATMAN.*
BEEN BROADCASTING STRAIGHT TO THEM. GUIDING THEM RIGHT TO THIS POINT.
THEY KNEW WE WERE COMING.
WHAT?
WHY?
I GOT A HUNDRED KIDS IN JAIL. A HUNDRED OTHER KIDS I CAN'T HONESTLY SAY I CAN KEEP *OUT* OF JAIL.
SO, I TRAIN AS MANY AS I CAN AS FAST AS I CAN. I CONTROL THE ARRESTS, MAKE SURE THEY'RE *SAFE.*
WAIT, WHERE ARE YOU--HEY, CLIMBING'S NOT REALLY MY...
CRAP.
THEN I PUT MY BEST MEN IN *WITH* THEM, MAKE SURE THEY'RE ALL SAFE.
AND ALL READY TO BREAK OUT, WHEN I FIGURE THIS OUT.

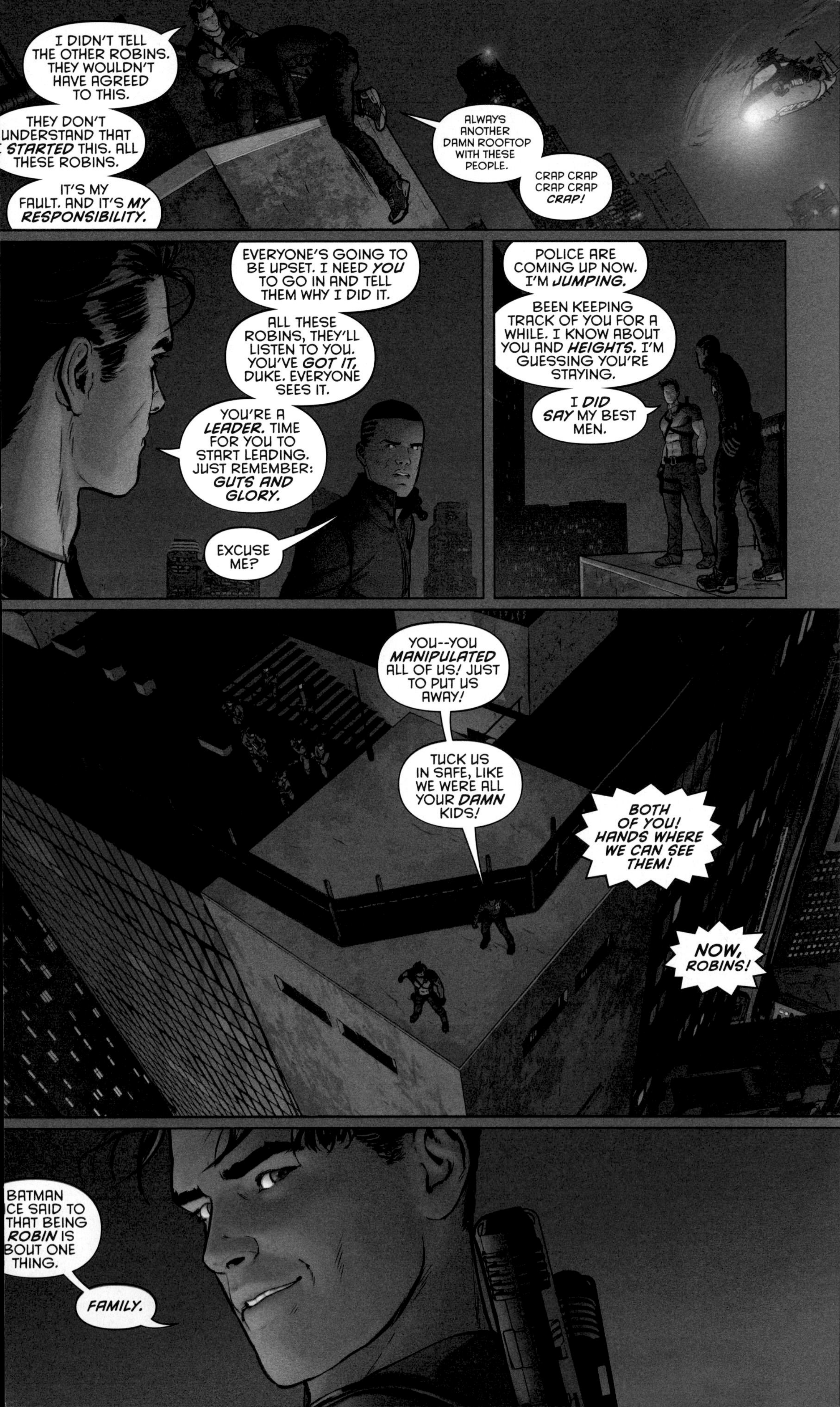

I DIDN'T TELL THE OTHER ROBINS. THEY WOULDN'T HAVE AGREED TO THIS.
THEY DON'T UNDERSTAND THAT I STARTED THIS. ALL THESE ROBINS.
IT'S MY FAULT. AND IT'S MY RESPONSIBILITY.
ALWAYS ANOTHER DAMN ROOFTOP WITH THESE PEOPLE.
CRAP CRAP CRAP CRAP CRAP!
EVERYONE'S GOING TO BE UPSET. I NEED YOU TO GO IN AND TELL THEM WHY I DID IT.
ALL THESE ROBINS, THEY'LL LISTEN TO YOU. YOU'VE GOT IT, DUKE. EVERYONE SEES IT.
YOU'RE A LEADER. TIME FOR YOU TO START LEADING. JUST REMEMBER: GUTS AND GLORY.
EXCUSE ME?
POLICE ARE COMING UP NOW. I'M JUMPING.
BEEN KEEPING TRACK OF YOU FOR A WHILE. I KNOW ABOUT YOU AND HEIGHTS. I'M GUESSING YOU'RE STAYING.
I DID SAY MY BEST MEN.
YOU--YOU MANIPULATED ALL OF US! JUST TO PUT US AWAY!
TUCK US IN SAFE, LIKE WE WERE ALL YOUR DAMN KIDS!
BOTH OF YOU! HANDS WHERE WE CAN SEE THEM!
NOW, ROBINS!
BATMAN ICE SAID TO THAT BEING ROBIN IS BOUT ONE THING.
FAMILY.

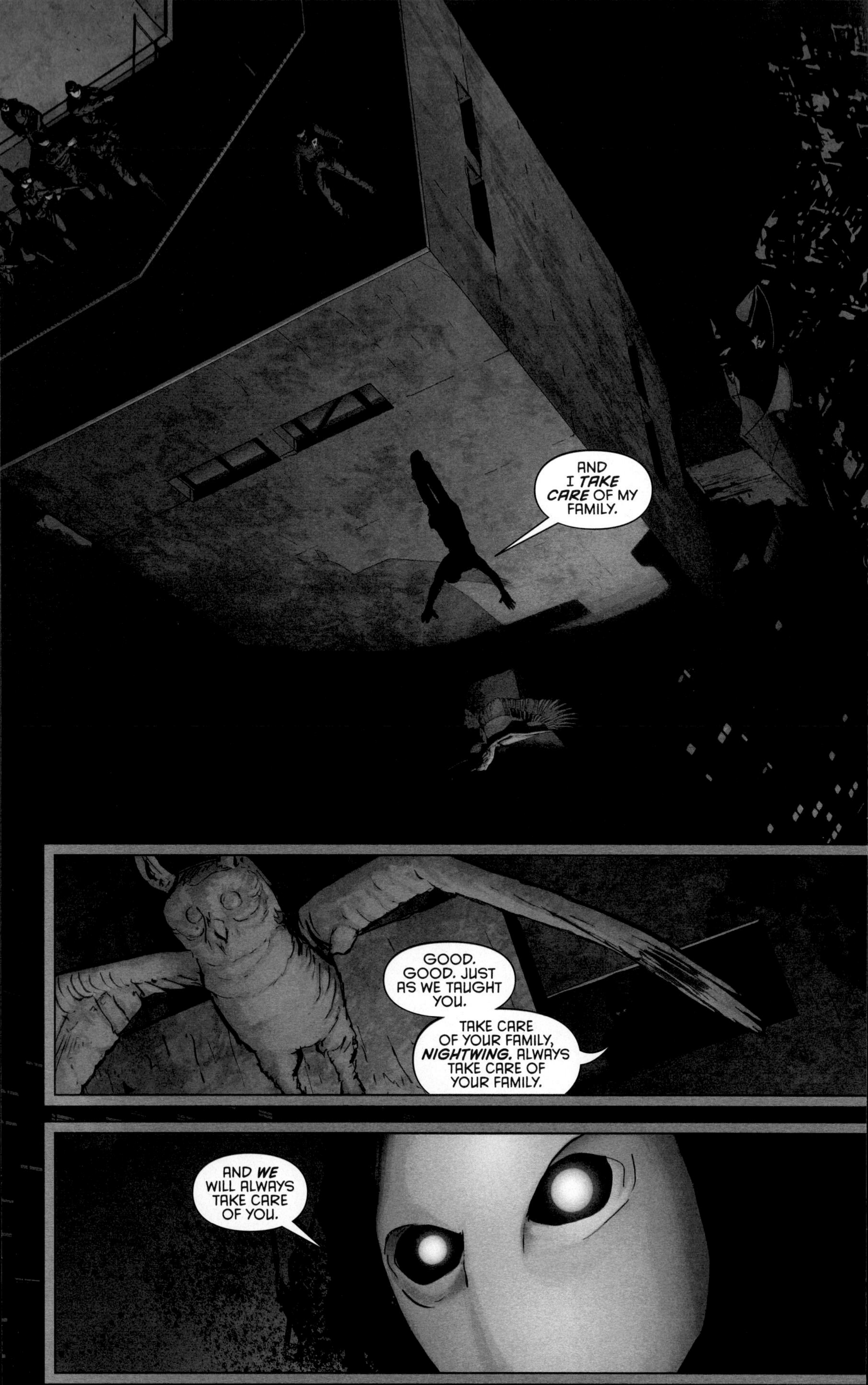
AND I TAKE CARE OF MY FAMILY.
GOOD. GOOD. JUST AS WE TAUGHT YOU.
TAKE CARE OF YOUR FAMILY, NIGHTWING. ALWAYS TAKE CARE OF YOUR FAMILY.
AND WE WILL ALWAYS TAKE CARE OF YOU.

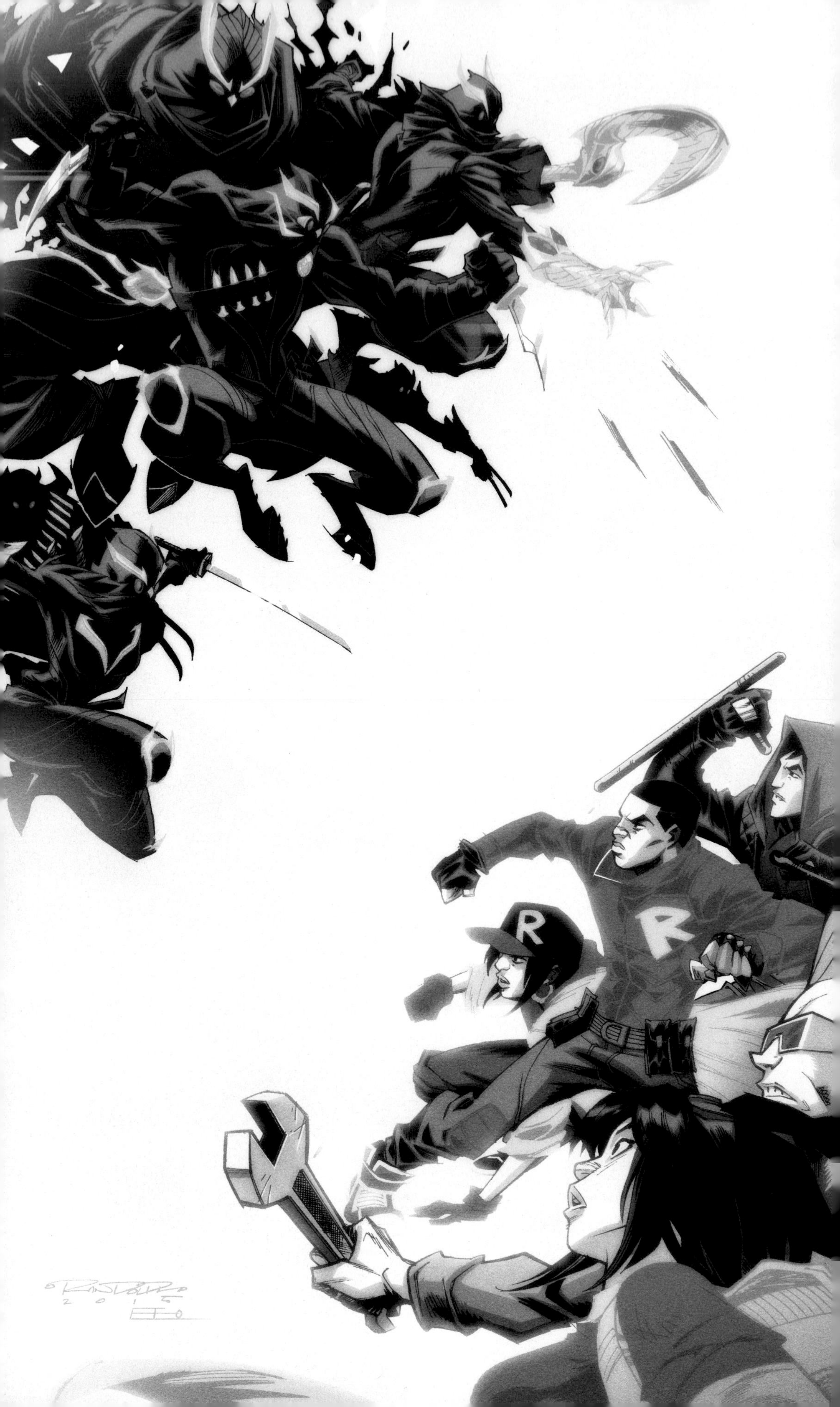

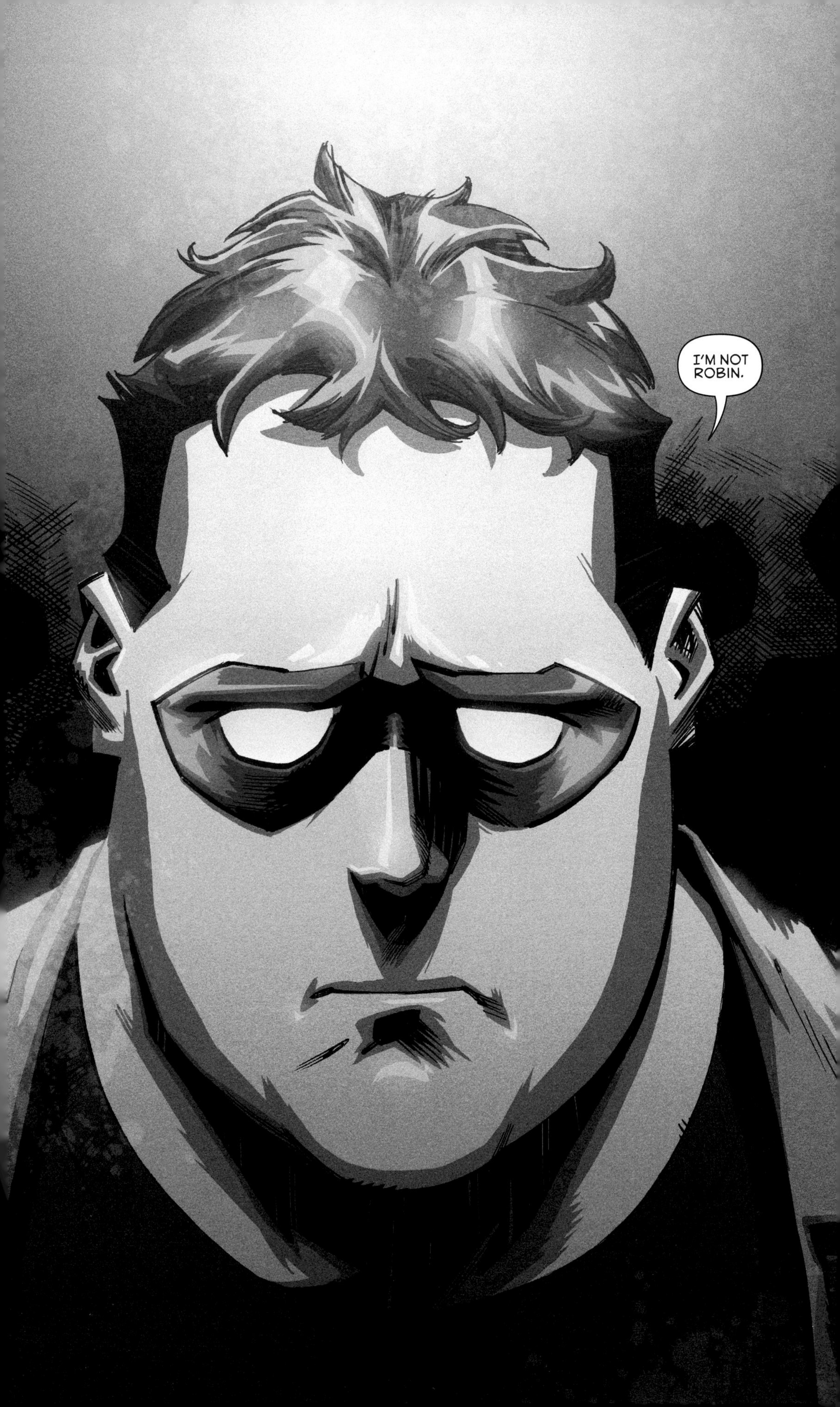
I'M NOT ROBIN.

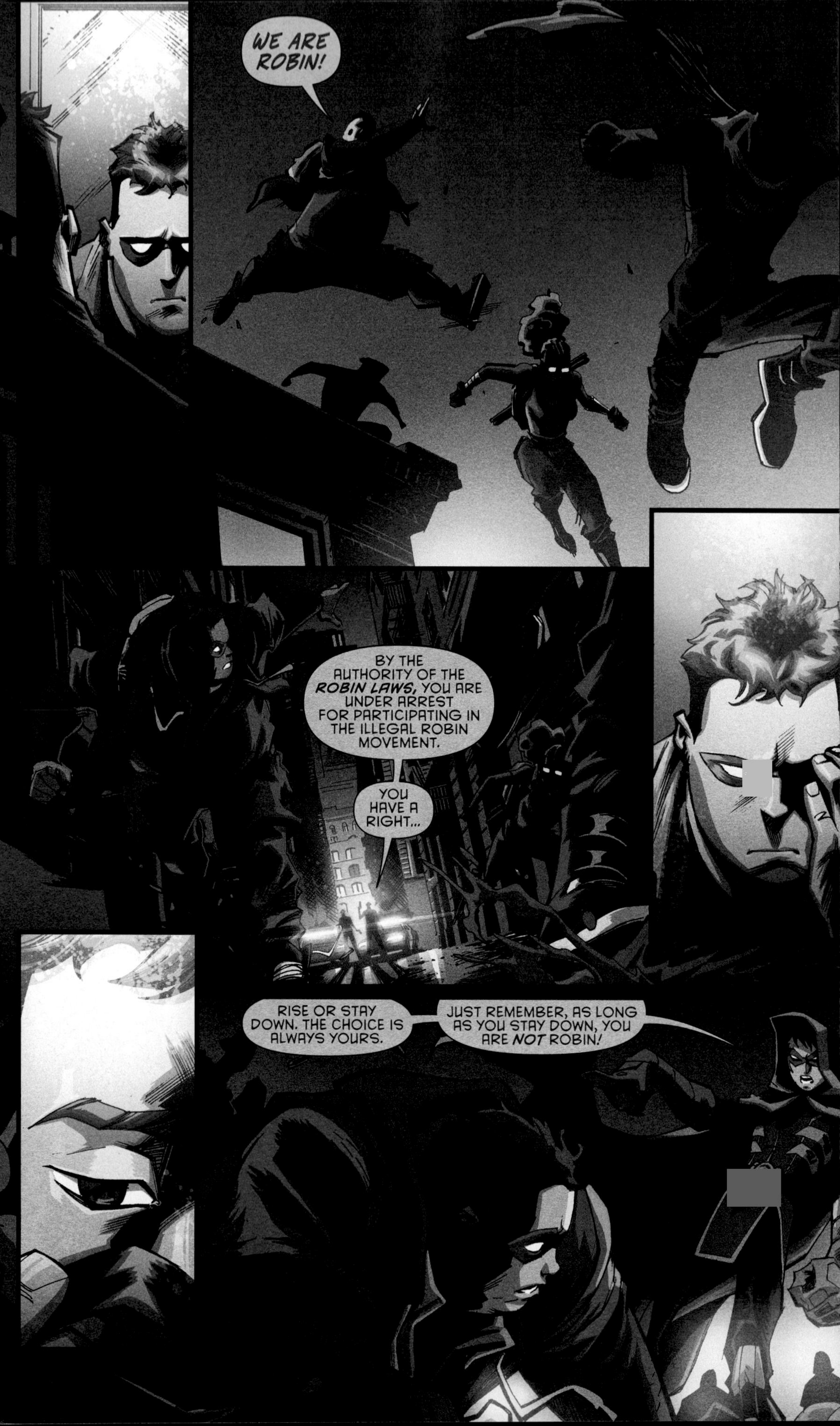
WE ARE ROBIN!
BY THE AUTHORITY OF THE ROBIN LAWS, YOU ARE UNDER ARREST FOR PARTICIPATING IN THE ILLEGAL ROBIN MOVEMENT.
YOU HAVE A RIGHT...
RISE OR STAY DOWN. THE CHOICE IS ALWAYS YOURS.
JUST REMEMBER, AS LONG AS YOU STAY DOWN, YOU ARE NOT ROBIN!

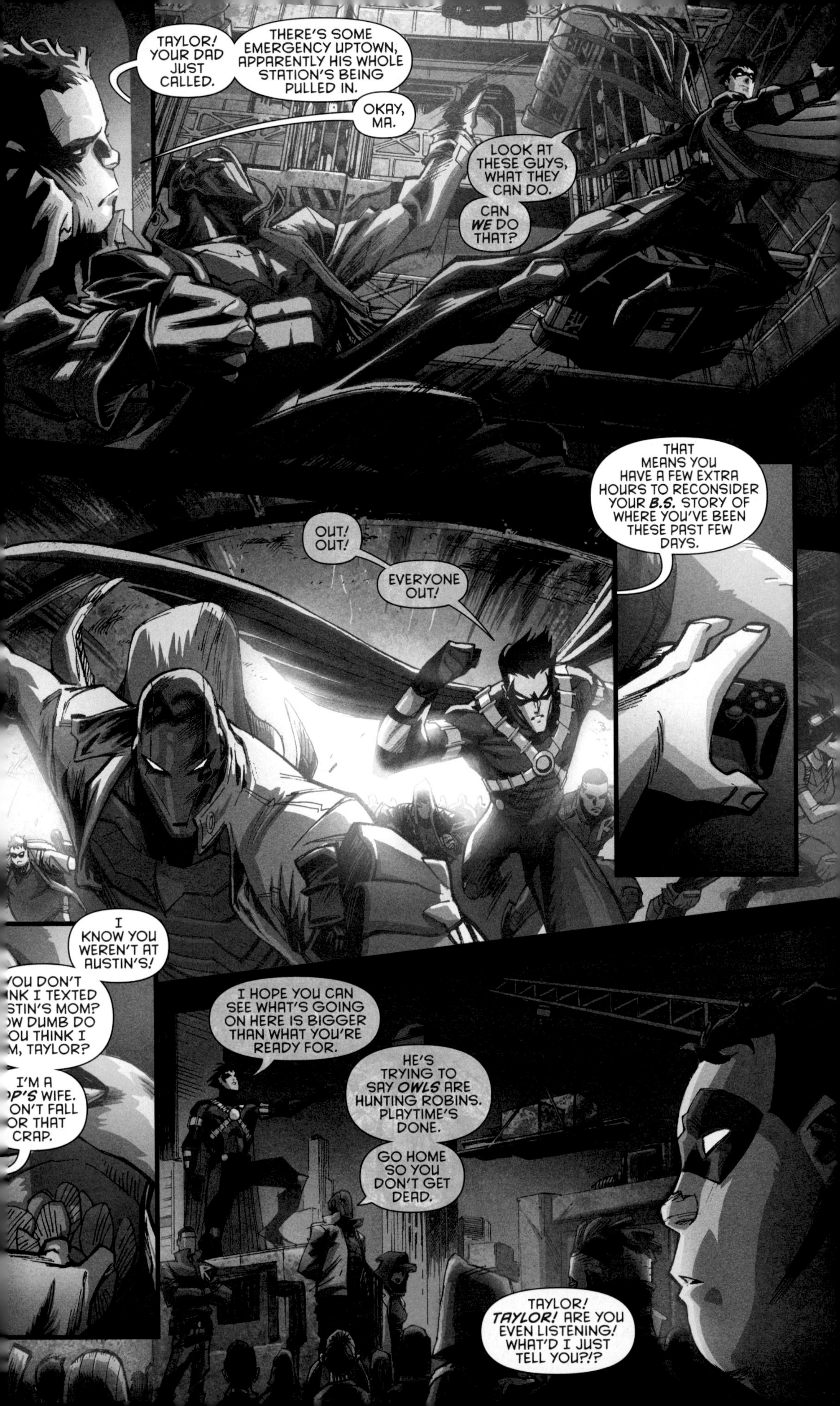

TAYLOR! YOUR DAD JUST CALLED.
THERE'S SOME EMERGENCY UPTOWN, APPARENTLY HIS WHOLE STATION'S BEING PULLED IN.
OKAY, MA.
LOOK AT THESE GUYS, WHAT THEY CAN DO.
CAN WE DO THAT?
THAT MEANS YOU HAVE A FEW EXTRA HOURS TO RECONSIDER YOUR B.S. STORY OF WHERE YOU'VE BEEN THESE PAST FEW DAYS.
OUT! OUT!
EVERYONE OUT!
I KNOW YOU WEREN'T AT AUSTIN'S!
I HOPE YOU CAN SEE WHAT'S GOING ON HERE IS BIGGER THAN WHAT YOU'RE READY FOR.
HE'S TRYING TO SAY OWLS ARE HUNTING ROBINS. PLAYTIME'S DONE.
GO HOME SO YOU DON'T GET DEAD.
TAYLOR! TAYLOR! ARE YOU EVEN LISTENING! WHAT'D I JUST TELL YOU?!?

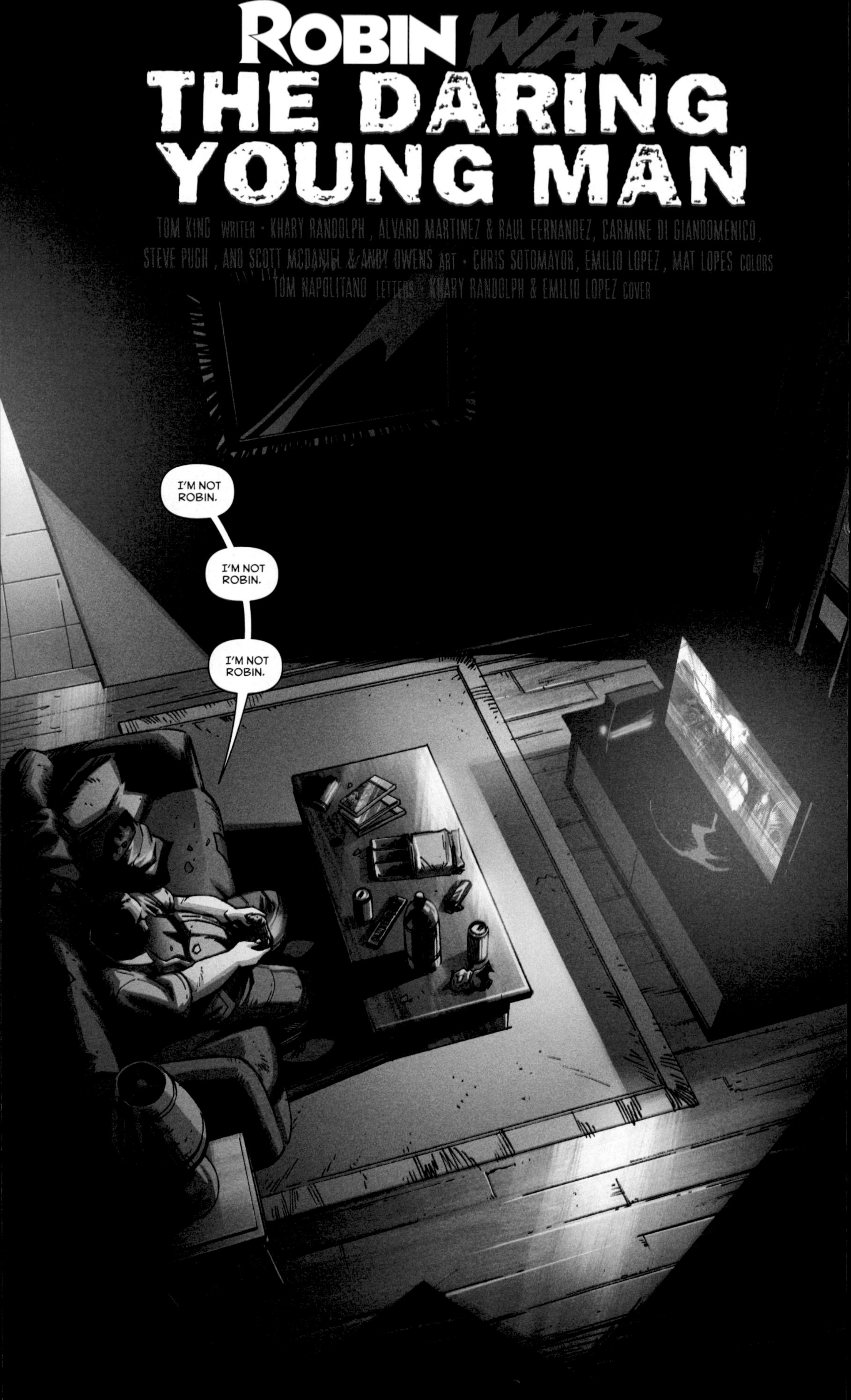
ROBIN WAR
THE DARING YOUNG MAN
TOM KING WRITER · KHARY RANDOLPH, ALVARO MARTINEZ & RAUL FERNANDEZ, CARMINE DI GIANDOMENICO, STEVE PUGH, AND SCOTT MCDANIEL & ANDY OWENS ART · CHRIS SOTOMAYOR, EMILIO LOPEZ, MAT LOPES COLORS
TOM NAPOLITANO LETTERS · KHARY RANDOLPH & EMILIO LOPEZ COVER
I'M NOT ROBIN.
I'M NOT ROBIN.
I'M NOT ROBIN.

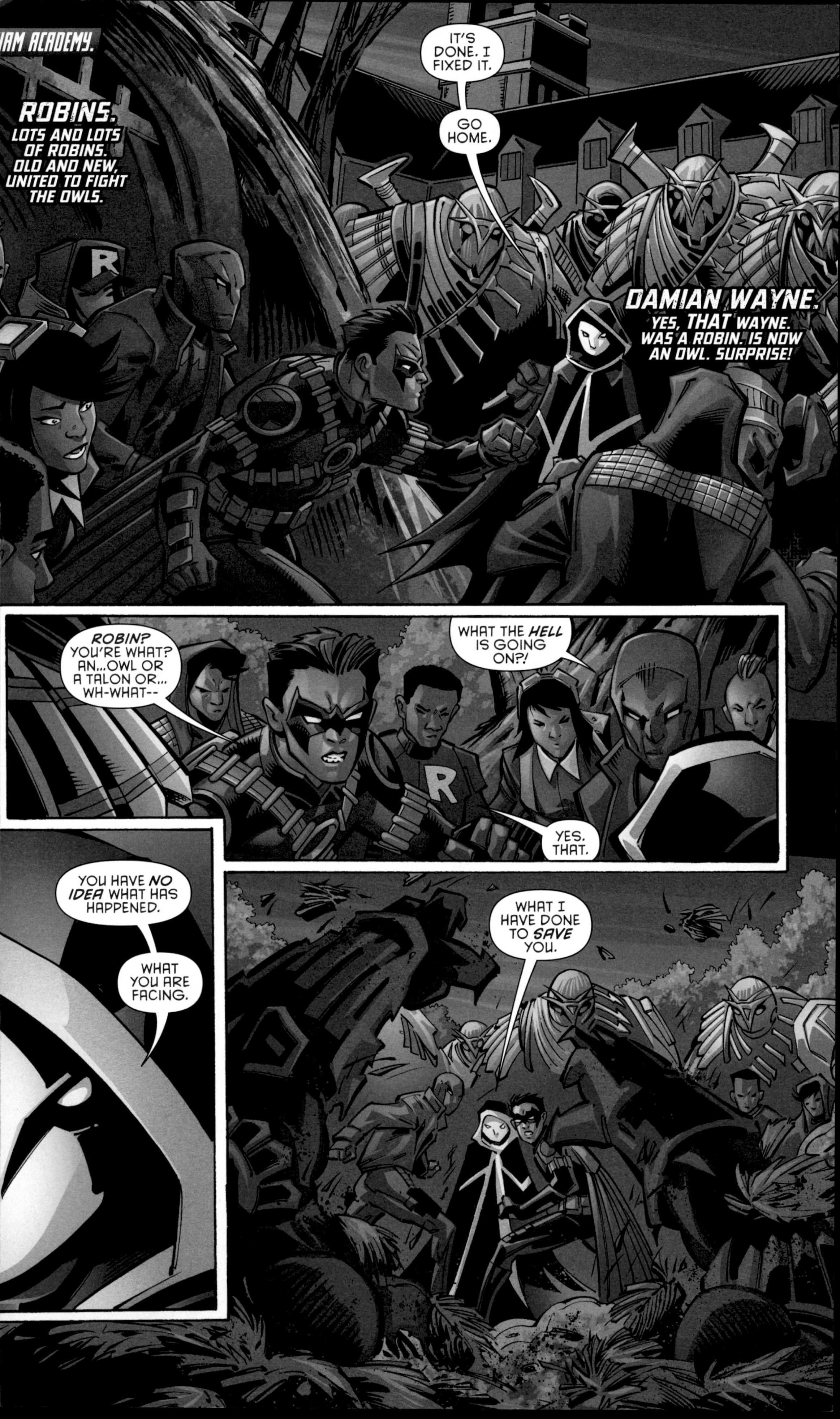

...IAM ACADEMY.
ROBINS.
LOTS AND LOTS OF ROBINS. OLD AND NEW, UNITED TO FIGHT THE OWLS.
IT'S DONE. I FIXED IT.
GO HOME.
DAMIAN WAYNE.
YES, THAT WAYNE. WAS A ROBIN. IS NOW AN OWL. SURPRISE!
ROBIN? YOU'RE WHAT? AN...OWL OR A TALON OR... WH-WHAT--
WHAT THE HELL IS GOING ON?!
YES. THAT.
YOU HAVE NO IDEA WHAT HAS HAPPENED.
WHAT YOU ARE FACING.
WHAT I HAVE DONE TO SAVE YOU.

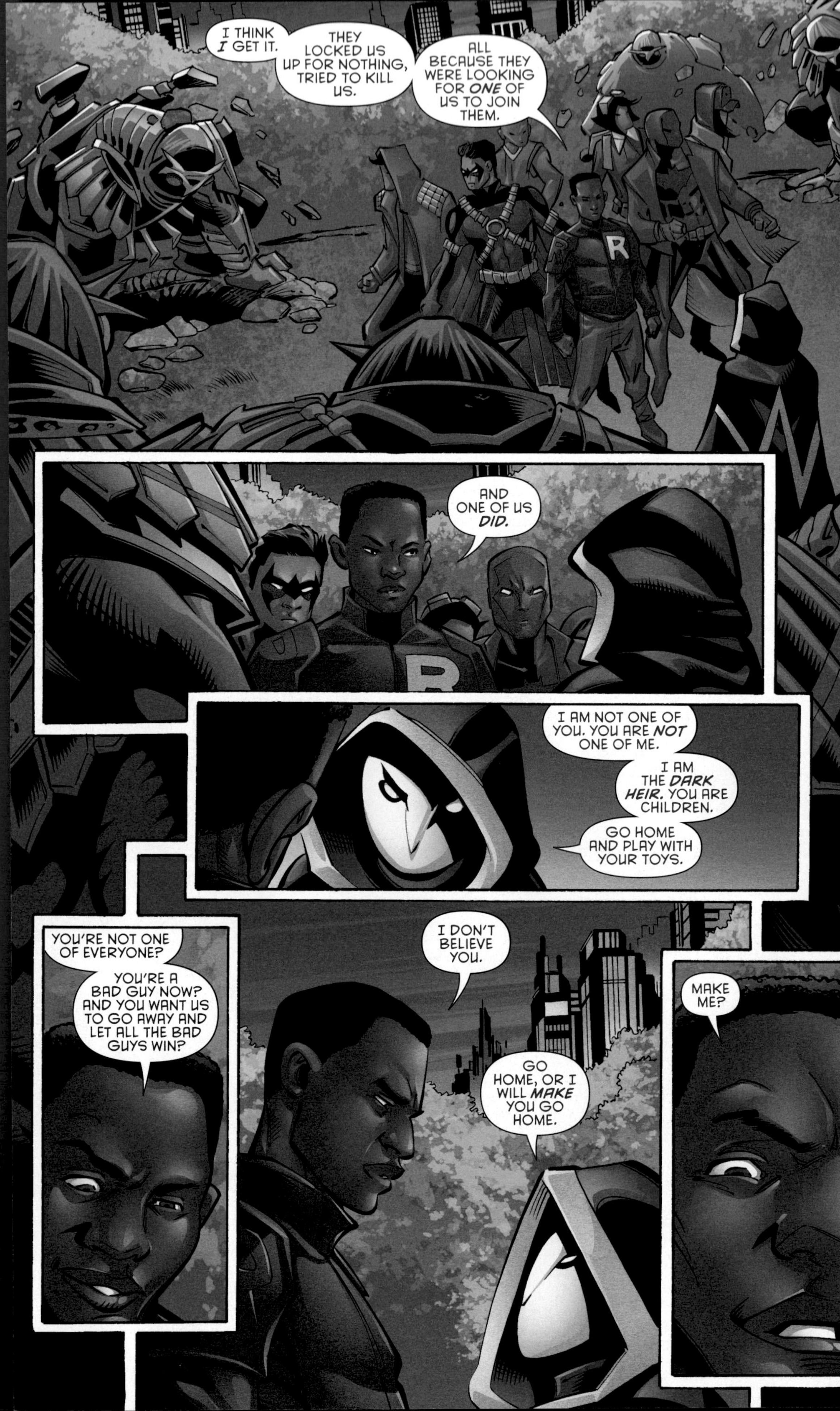
I THINK *I* GET IT.
THEY LOCKED US UP FOR NOTHING, TRIED TO KILL US.
ALL BECAUSE THEY WERE LOOKING FOR *ONE* OF US TO JOIN THEM.
AND ONE OF US *DID.*
I AM NOT ONE OF YOU. YOU ARE *NOT* ONE OF ME.
I AM THE *DARK HEIR.* YOU ARE CHILDREN.
GO HOME AND PLAY WITH YOUR TOYS.
YOU'RE NOT ONE OF EVERYONE?
YOU'RE A BAD GUY NOW? AND YOU WANT US TO GO AWAY AND LET ALL THE BAD GUYS WIN?
I DON'T BELIEVE YOU.
GO HOME, OR I WILL *MAKE* YOU GO HOME.
MAKE ME?

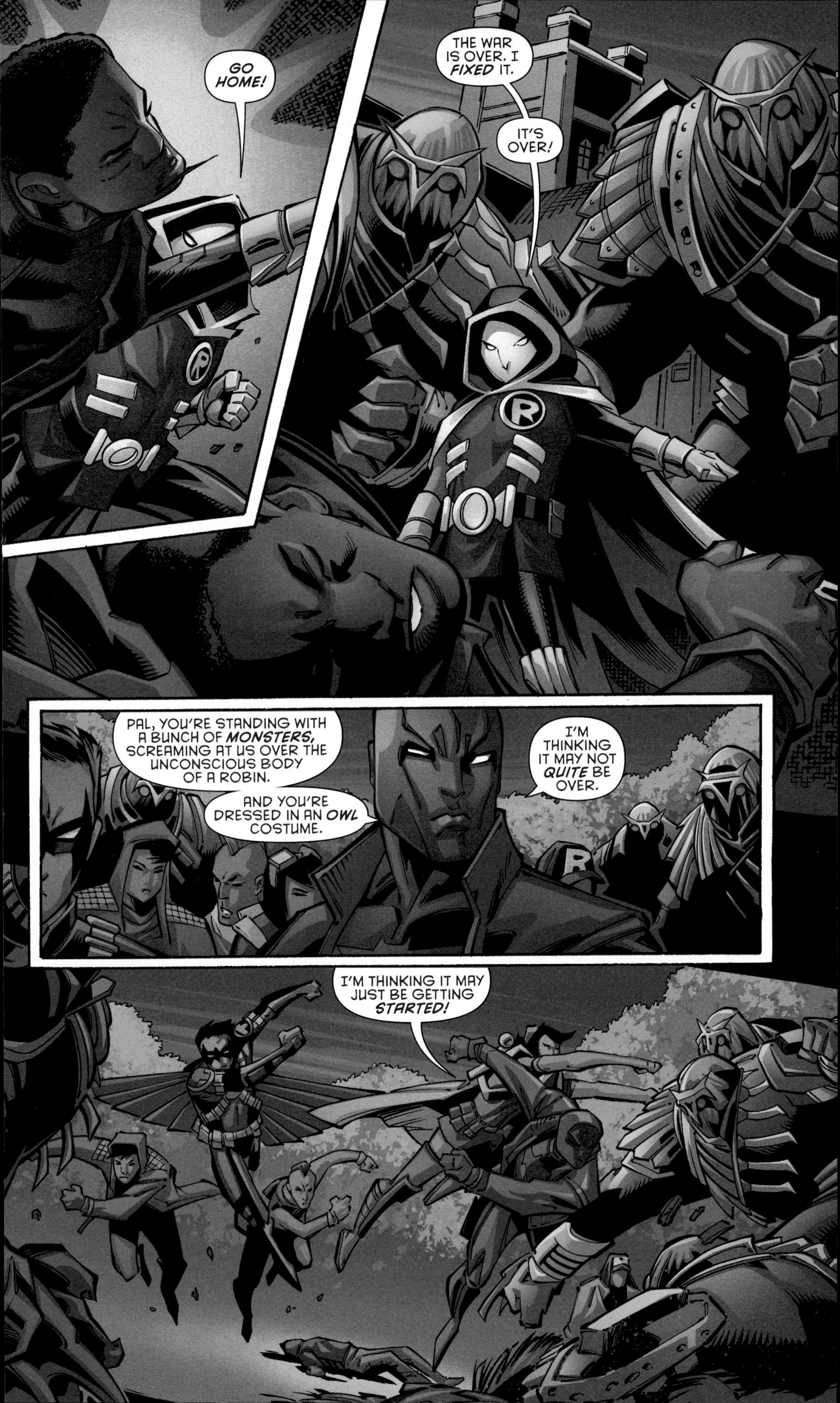

GO HOME!
THE WAR IS OVER. I FIXED IT.
IT'S OVER!
PAL, YOU'RE STANDING WITH A BUNCH OF MONSTERS, SCREAMING AT US OVER THE UNCONSCIOUS BODY OF A ROBIN.
AND YOU'RE DRESSED IN AN OWL COSTUME.
I'M THINKING IT MAY NOT QUITE BE OVER.
I'M THINKING IT MAY JUST BE GETTING STARTED!

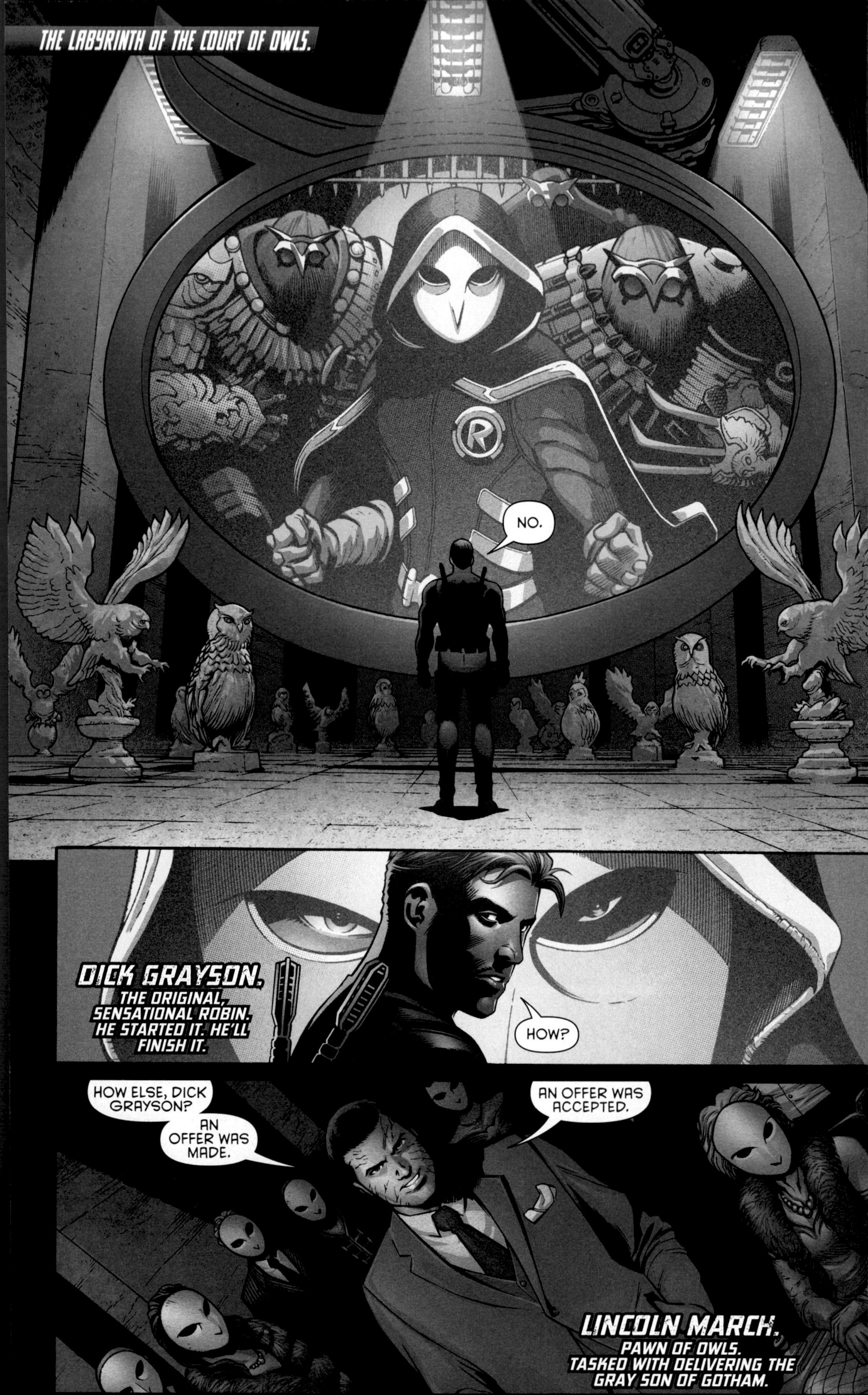
THE LABYRINTH OF THE COURT OF OWLS.
NO.
DICK GRAYSON.
THE ORIGINAL, SENSATIONAL ROBIN. HE STARTED IT. HE'LL FINISH IT.
HOW?
HOW ELSE, DICK GRAYSON?
AN OFFER WAS MADE.
AN OFFER WAS ACCEPTED.
LINCOLN MARCH.
PAWN OF OWLS. TASKED WITH DELIVERING THE GRAY SON OF GOTHAM.

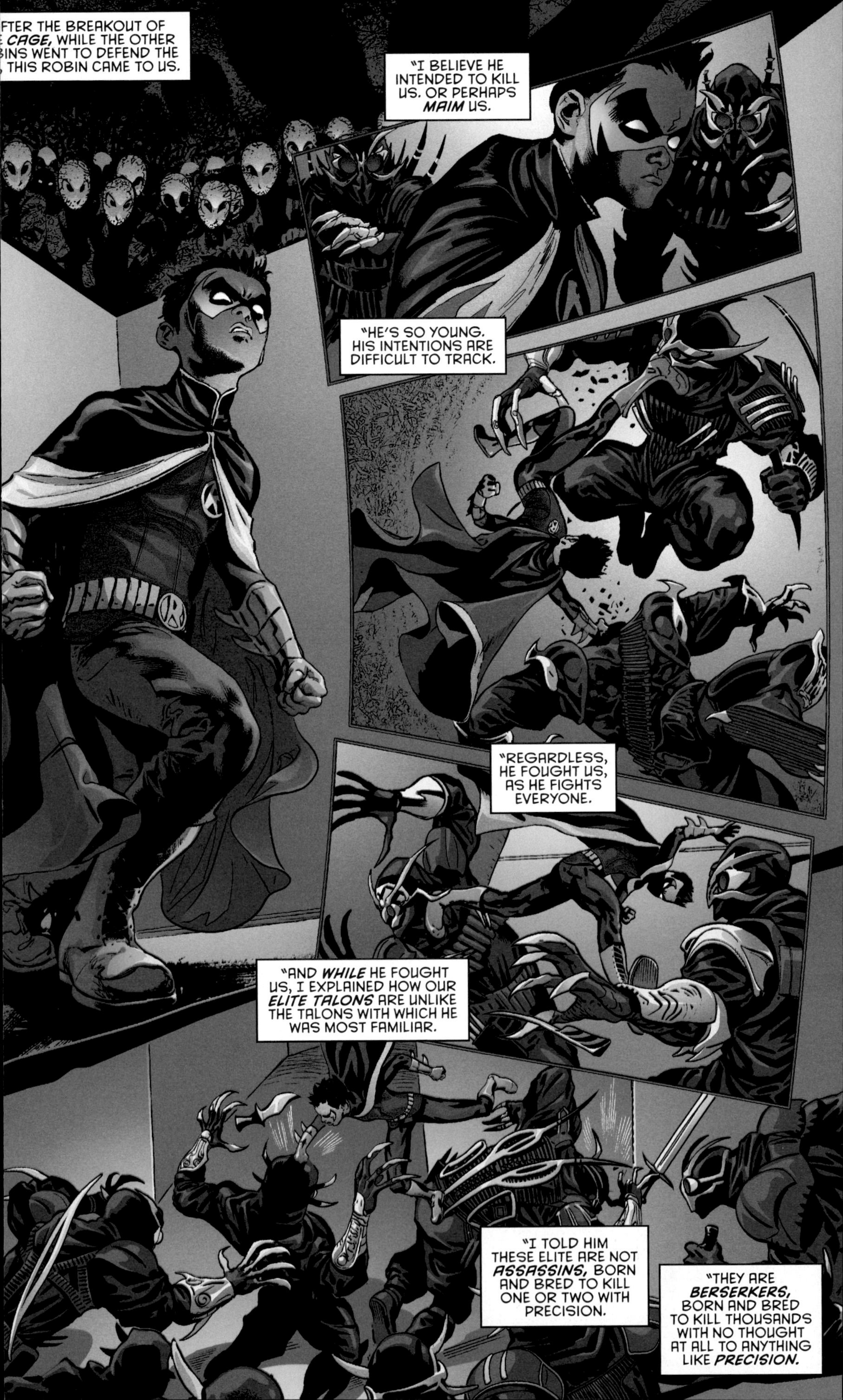

FTER THE BREAKOUT OF CAGE, WHILE THE OTHER BINS WENT TO DEFEND THE , THIS ROBIN CAME TO US.
"I BELIEVE HE INTENDED TO KILL US. OR PERHAPS MAIM US.
"HE'S SO YOUNG. HIS INTENTIONS ARE DIFFICULT TO TRACK.
"REGARDLESS, HE FOUGHT US, AS HE FIGHTS EVERYONE.
"AND WHILE HE FOUGHT US, I EXPLAINED HOW OUR ELITE TALONS ARE UNLIKE THE TALONS WITH WHICH HE WAS MOST FAMILIAR.
"I TOLD HIM THESE ELITE ARE NOT ASSASSINS, BORN AND BRED TO KILL ONE OR TWO WITH PRECISION.
"THEY ARE BERSERKERS, BORN AND BRED TO KILL THOUSANDS WITH NO THOUGHT AT ALL TO ANYTHING LIKE PRECISION.

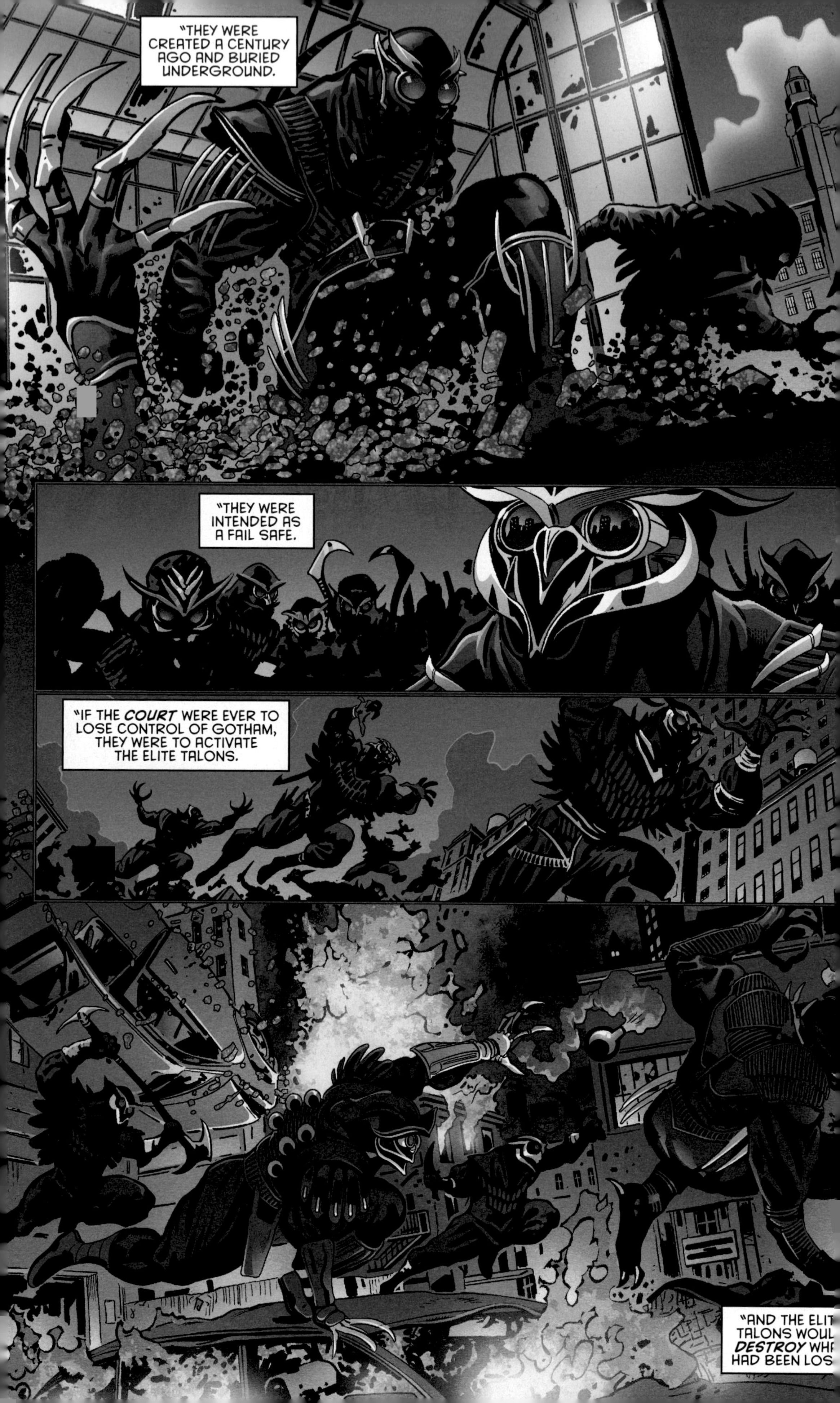
"THEY WERE CREATED A CENTURY AGO AND BURIED UNDERGROUND.
"THEY WERE INTENDED AS A FAIL SAFE.
"IF THE *COURT* WERE EVER TO LOSE CONTROL OF GOTHAM, THEY WERE TO ACTIVATE THE ELITE TALONS.
"AND THE ELIT TALONS WOUL *DESTROY* WHI HAD BEEN LOS

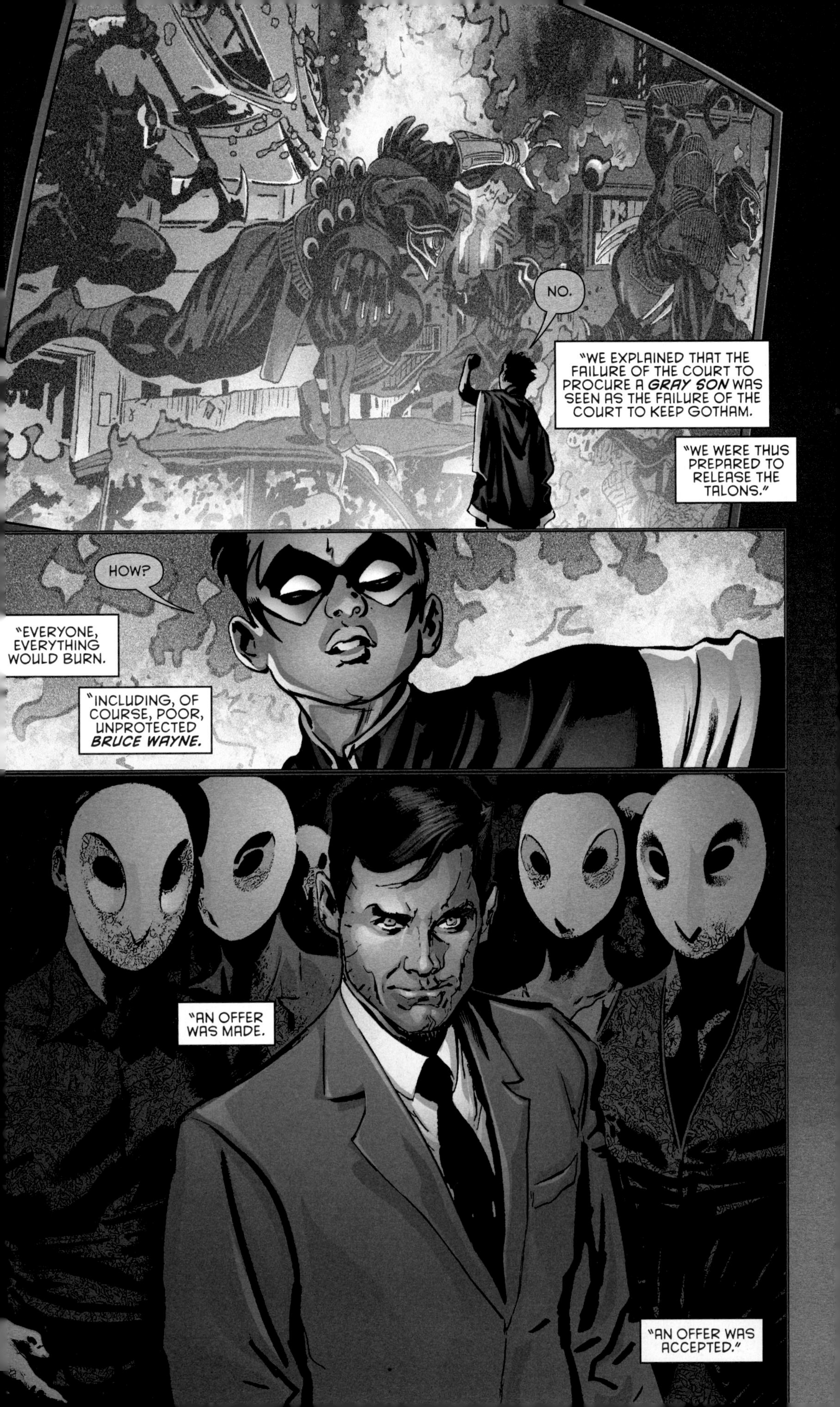

NO.
"WE EXPLAINED THAT THE FAILURE OF THE COURT TO PROCURE A GRAY SON WAS SEEN AS THE FAILURE OF THE COURT TO KEEP GOTHAM.
"WE WERE THUS PREPARED TO RELEASE THE TALONS."
HOW?
"EVERYONE, EVERYTHING WOULD BURN.
"INCLUDING, OF COURSE, POOR, UNPROTECTED BRUCE WAYNE.
"AN OFFER WAS MADE.
"AN OFFER WAS ACCEPTED."

Taylor, something's happening at the academy.

Brit's there, said there's a bunch of Robins. And monsters or something.

Oh, SHUT UP.

Brit says sirens in the area.

Looks like Robins fighting monsters.

Whole school tearing up.

Getting my police scanner out.

SHUT UP.

THE COPS'LL HANDLE IT.

A big ass brawl now.

Brit can see from her window.

What are those things?

Should we do something? We should do something.

We can't do anything. They said to go home.

Cops definitely coming.

Brit says she can hear the cops.

Dude, those things are going to kill people.

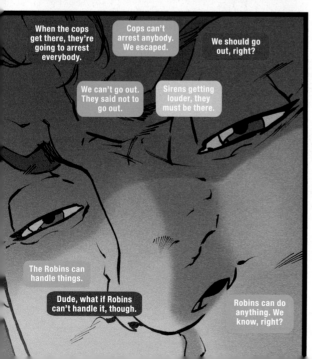

When the cops get there, they're going to arrest everybody.

Cops can't arrest anybody. We escaped.

We should go out, right?

We can't go out. They said not to go out.

Sirens getting louder, they must be there.

The Robins can handle things.

Dude, what if Robins can't handle it, though.

Robins can do anything. We know, right?

We we Robir

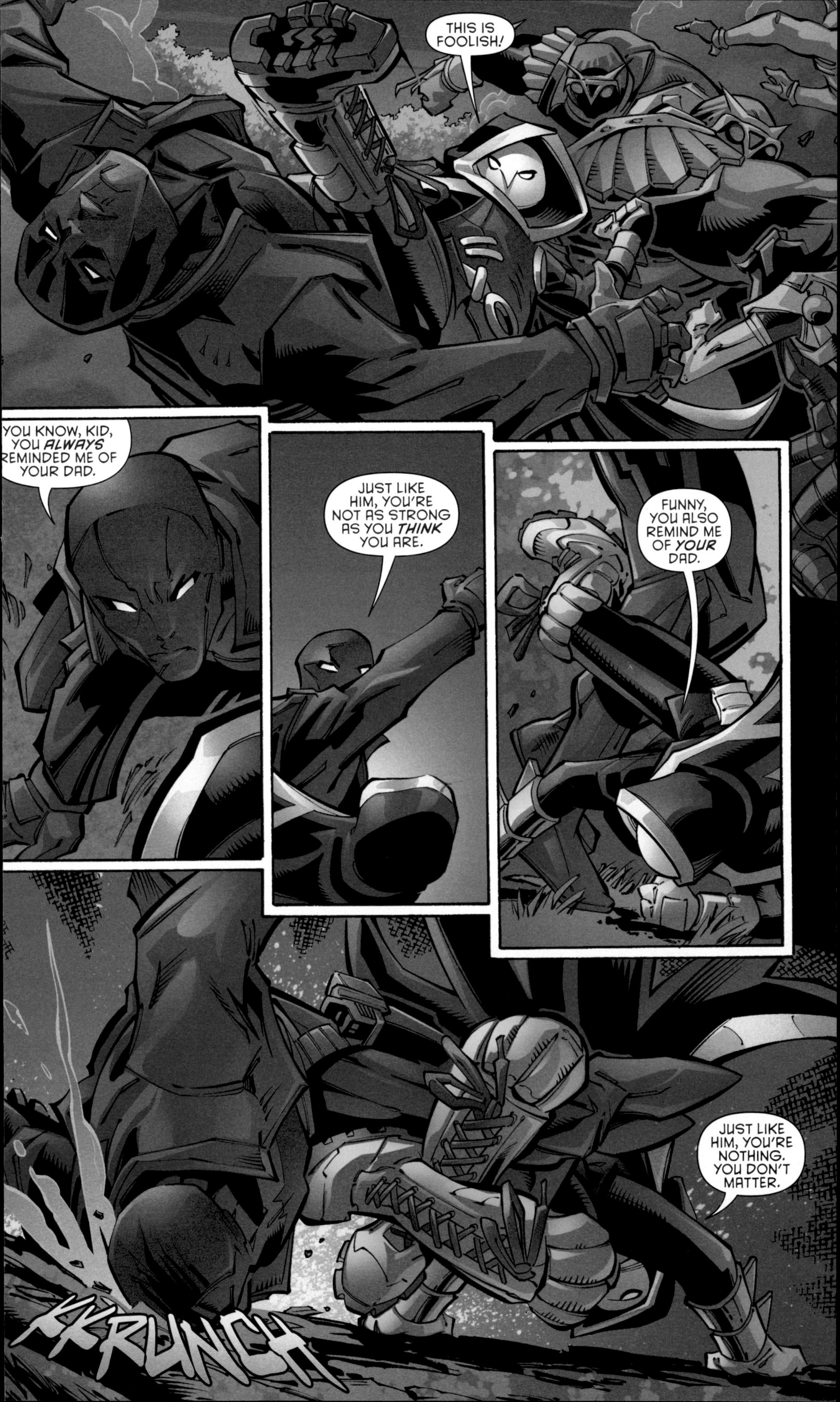

THIS IS FOOLISH!
YOU KNOW, KID, YOU ALWAYS REMINDED ME OF YOUR DAD.
JUST LIKE HIM, YOU'RE NOT AS STRONG AS YOU THINK YOU ARE.
FUNNY, YOU ALSO REMIND ME OF YOUR DAD.
JUST LIKE HIM, YOU'RE NOTHING. YOU DON'T MATTER.
KKRUNCH

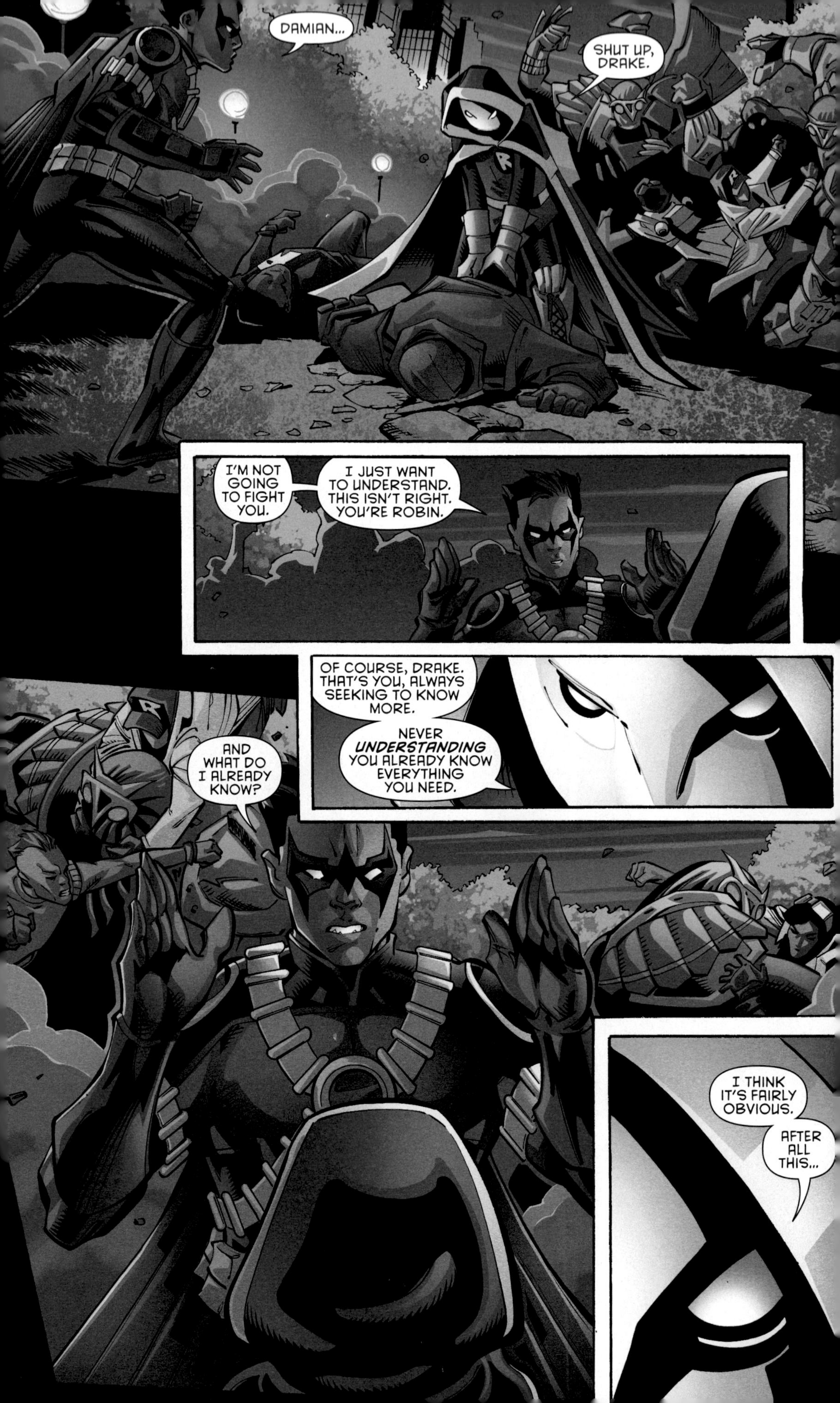

DAMIAN...
SHUT UP, DRAKE.
I'M NOT GOING TO FIGHT YOU.
I JUST WANT TO UNDERSTAND. THIS ISN'T RIGHT. YOU'RE ROBIN.
OF COURSE, DRAKE. THAT'S YOU, ALWAYS SEEKING TO KNOW MORE.
NEVER *UNDERSTANDING* YOU ALREADY KNOW EVERYTHING YOU NEED.
AND WHAT DO I ALREADY KNOW?
I THINK IT'S FAIRLY OBVIOUS.
AFTER ALL THIS...

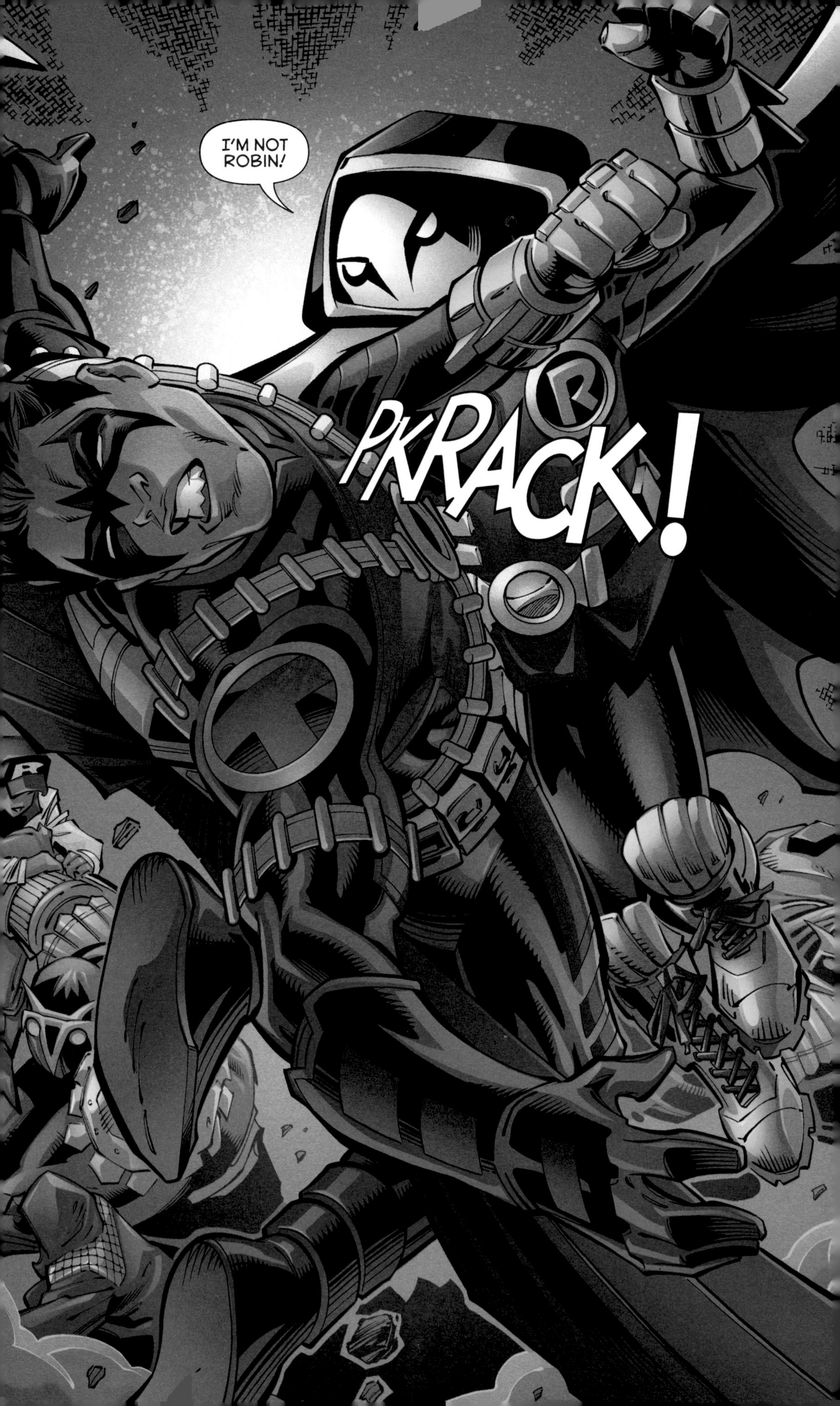
I'M NOT ROBIN!
PKRACK!

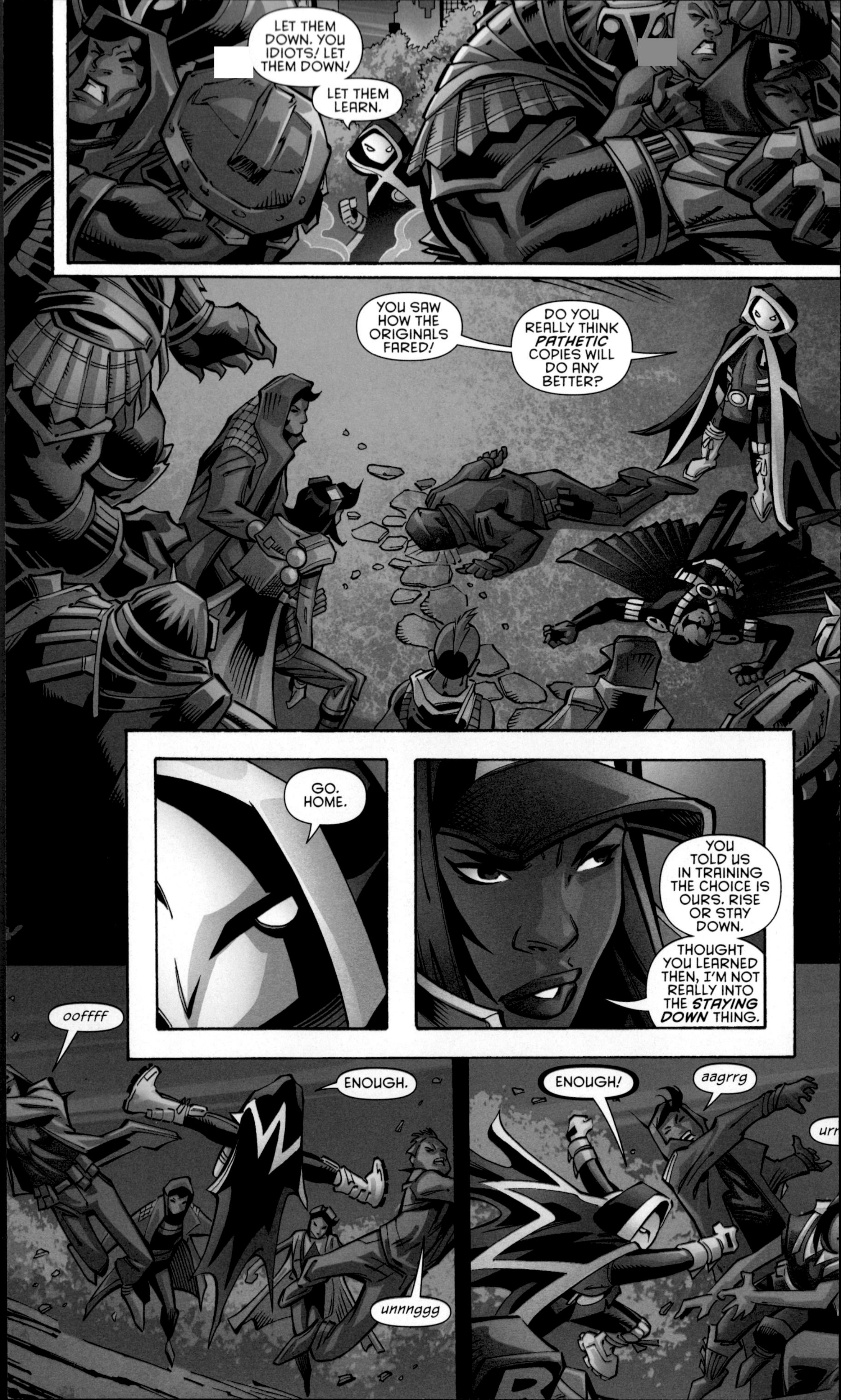
LET THEM DOWN. YOU IDIOTS! LET THEM DOWN!
LET THEM LEARN.
YOU SAW HOW THE ORIGINALS FARED!
DO YOU REALLY THINK PATHETIC COPIES WILL DO ANY BETTER?
GO. HOME.
YOU TOLD US IN TRAINING THE CHOICE IS OURS. RISE OR STAY DOWN.
THOUGHT YOU LEARNED THEN, I'M NOT REALLY INTO THE STAYING DOWN THING.
oofffff
ENOUGH.
unnnggg
ENOUGH!
aagrrg

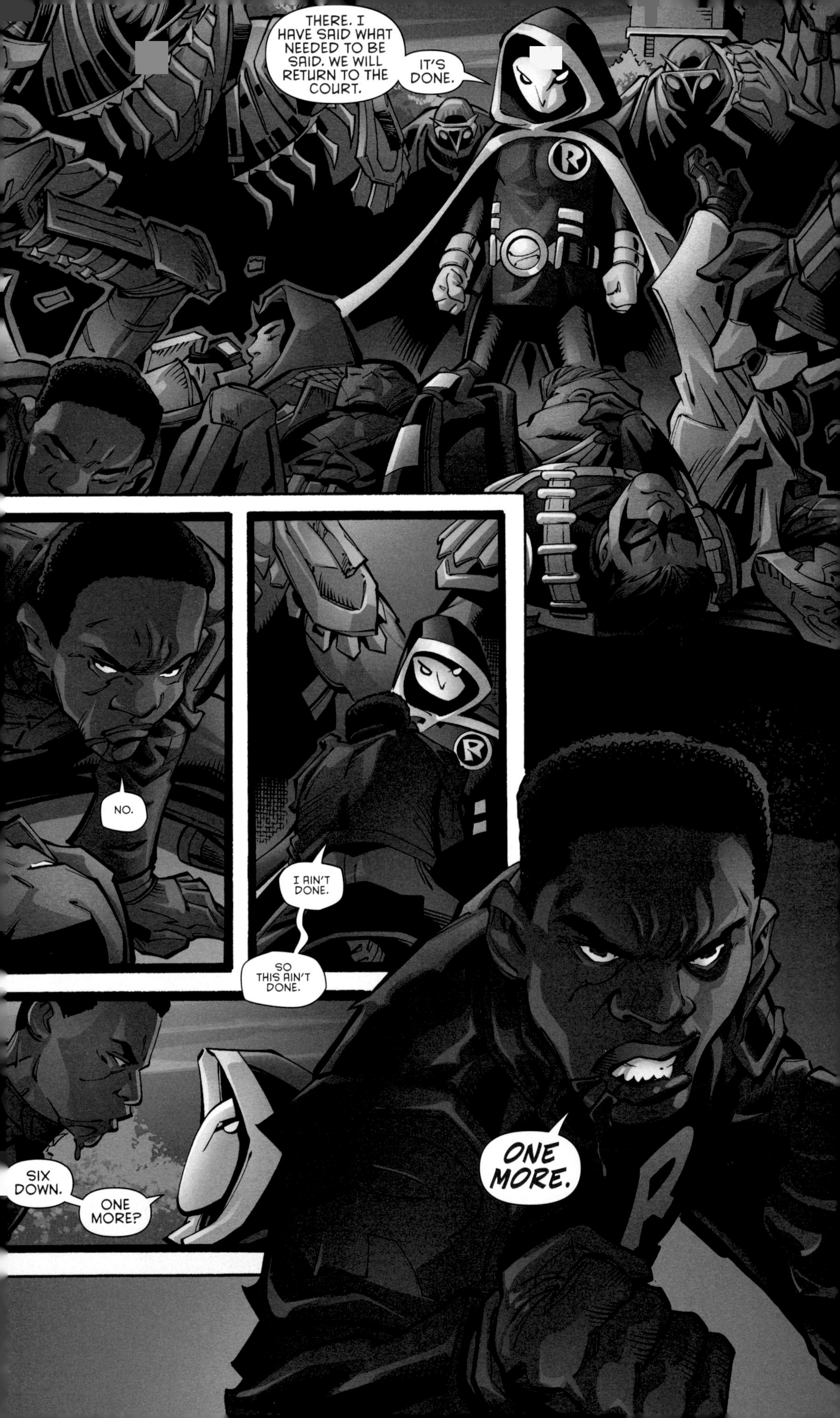
THERE. I HAVE SAID WHAT NEEDED TO BE SAID. WE WILL RETURN TO THE COURT.
IT'S DONE.
NO.
I AIN'T DONE.
SO THIS AIN'T DONE.
SIX DOWN.
ONE MORE?
ONE MORE.

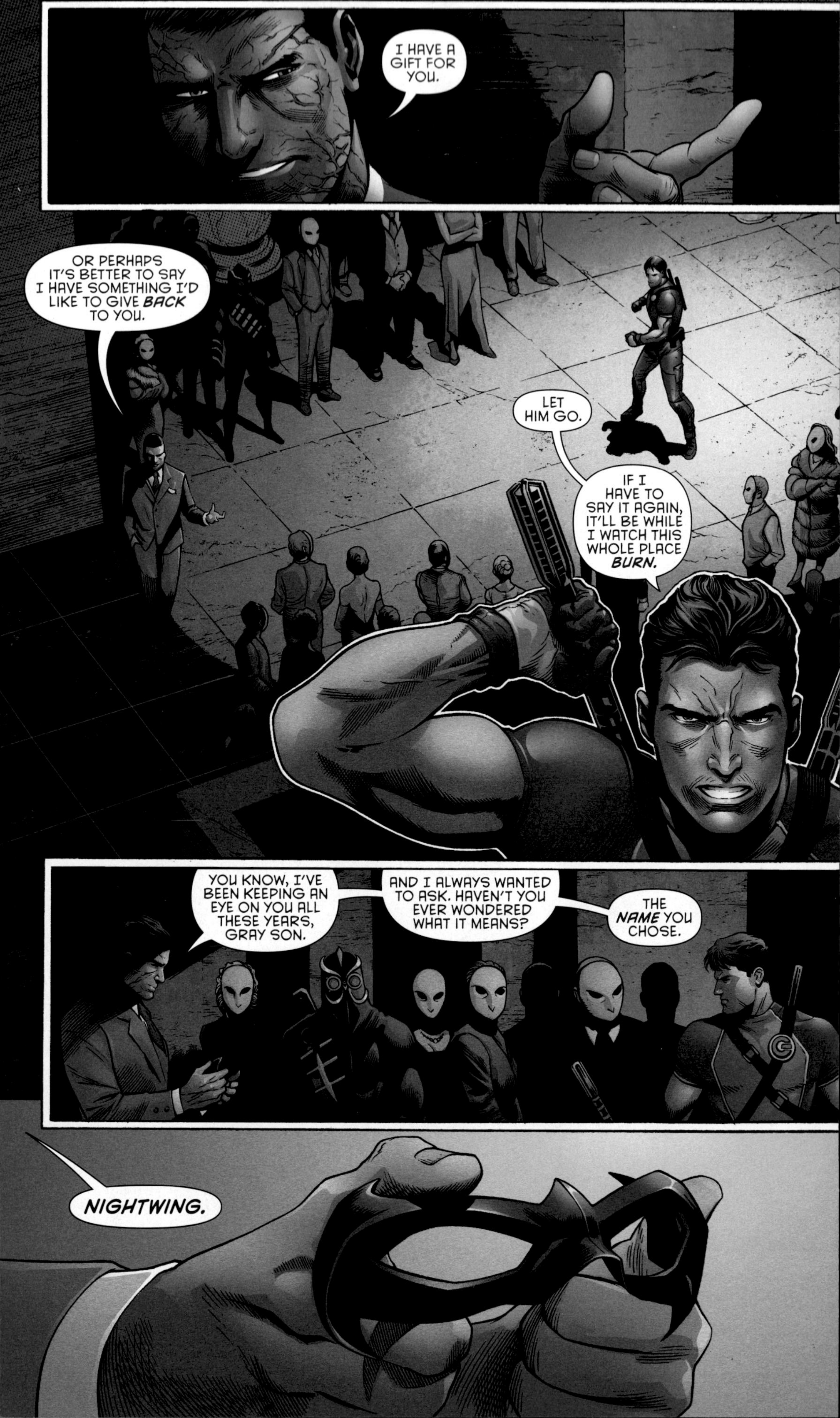
I HAVE A GIFT FOR YOU.
OR PERHAPS IT'S BETTER TO SAY I HAVE SOMETHING I'D LIKE TO GIVE *BACK* TO YOU.
LET HIM GO.
IF I HAVE TO SAY IT AGAIN, IT'LL BE WHILE I WATCH THIS WHOLE PLACE *BURN.*
YOU KNOW, I'VE BEEN KEEPING AN EYE ON YOU ALL THESE YEARS, GRAY SON.
AND I ALWAYS WANTED TO ASK. HAVEN'T YOU EVER WONDERED WHAT IT MEANS?
THE *NAME* YOU CHOSE.
NIGHTWING.

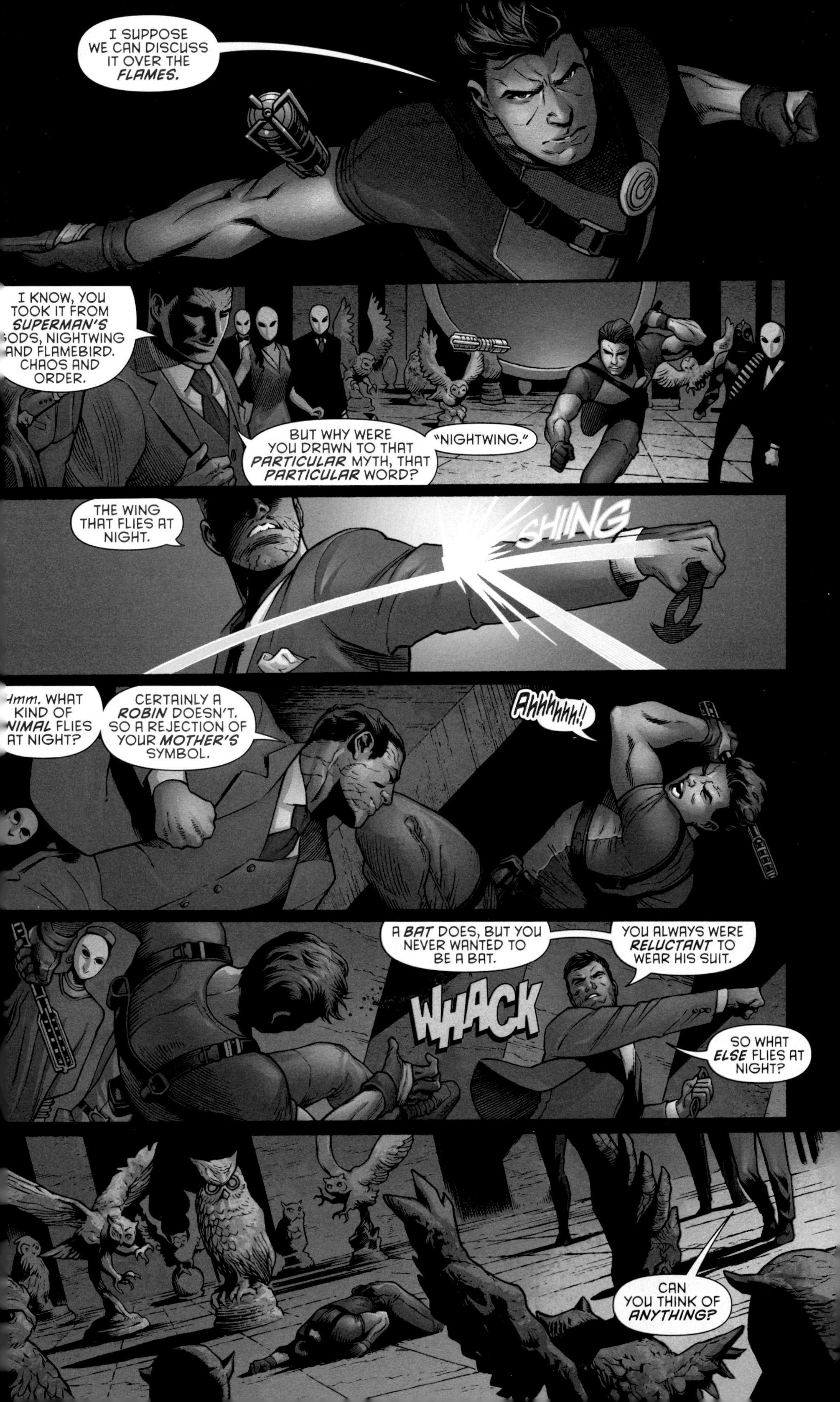

I SUPPOSE WE CAN DISCUSS IT OVER THE *FLAMES.*
I KNOW, YOU TOOK IT FROM *SUPERMAN'S* GODS, NIGHTWING AND FLAMEBIRD. CHAOS AND ORDER.
BUT WHY WERE YOU DRAWN TO THAT *PARTICULAR* MYTH, THAT *PARTICULAR* WORD?
"NIGHTWING."
THE WING THAT FLIES AT NIGHT.
SHIING
mm. WHAT KIND OF NIMAL FLIES AT NIGHT?
CERTAINLY A *ROBIN* DOESN'T. SO A REJECTION OF YOUR *MOTHER'S* SYMBOL.
Ahhhhhh!!
A *BAT* DOES, BUT YOU NEVER WANTED TO BE A BAT.
YOU ALWAYS WERE *RELUCTANT* TO WEAR HIS SUIT.
WHACK
SO WHAT *ELSE* FLIES AT NIGHT?
CAN YOU THINK OF *ANYTHING?*

The cops are there.

I've got it on my police scanner now.

Cops arriving at Gotham Academy.

Dude, they're going to get slaughtered.

WOOO WOOOO

WOOO WOOOO

WOOO WOOOO WO

We have to do something. There's no Robins there to fight.

What we going to do?

Getting stuff coming in on the scanner now... oh man...

Cops started fighting. It's war, man. It's war.

AAAAA!

SURREN PUT D YOUR-- ALL DO

Should we do something? They told us to stay home?

What do we do???????

RISE OR ST DOWN

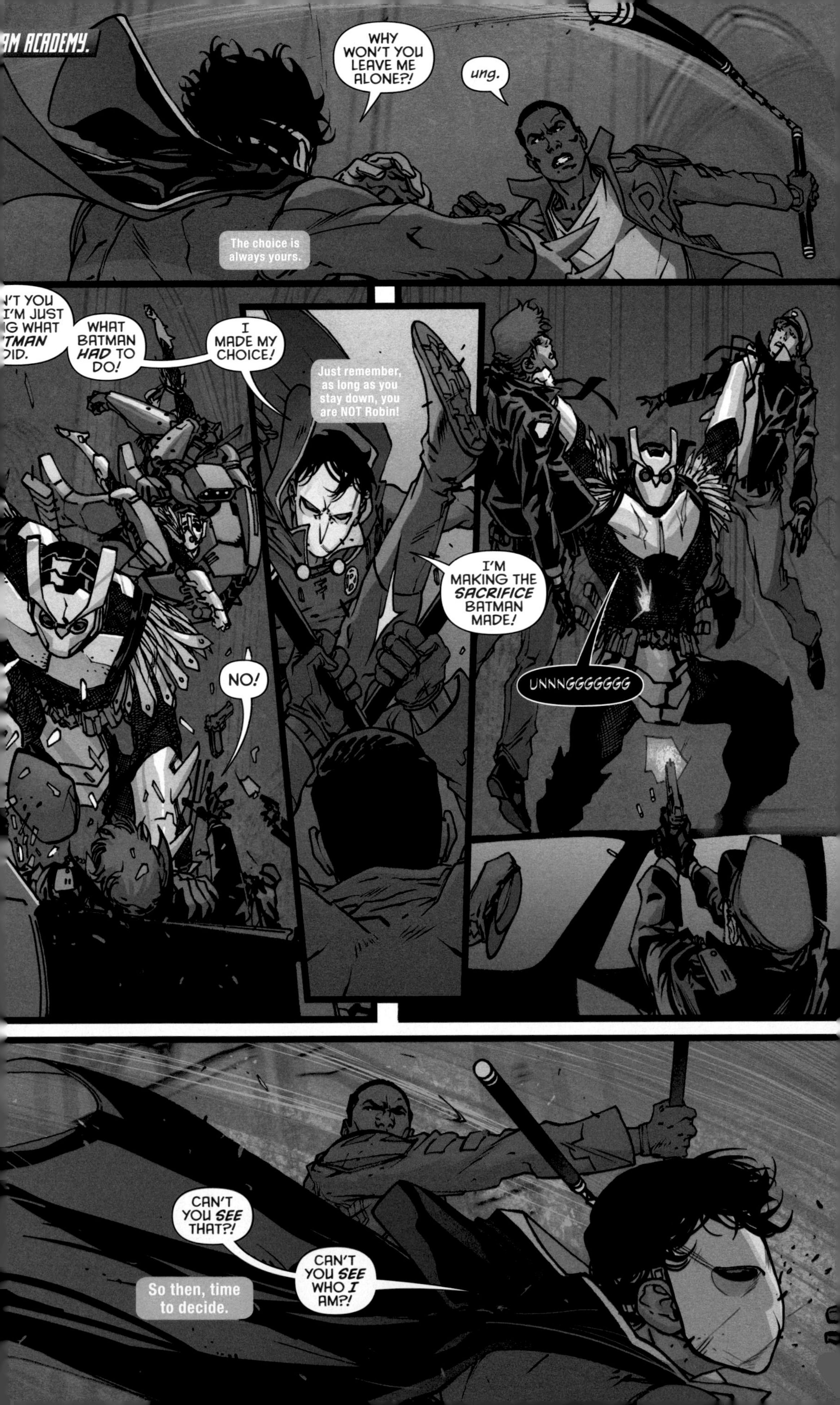

AM ACADEMY.
WHY WON'T YOU LEAVE ME ALONE?!
ung.
The choice is always yours.
'T YOU I'M JUST G WHAT TMAN DID.
WHAT BATMAN HAD TO DO!
I MADE MY CHOICE!
Just remember, as long as you stay down, you are NOT Robin!
I'M MAKING THE SACRIFICE BATMAN MADE!
NO!
UNNNGGGGGGG
CAN'T YOU SEE THAT?!
CAN'T YOU SEE WHO I AM?!
So then, time to decide.

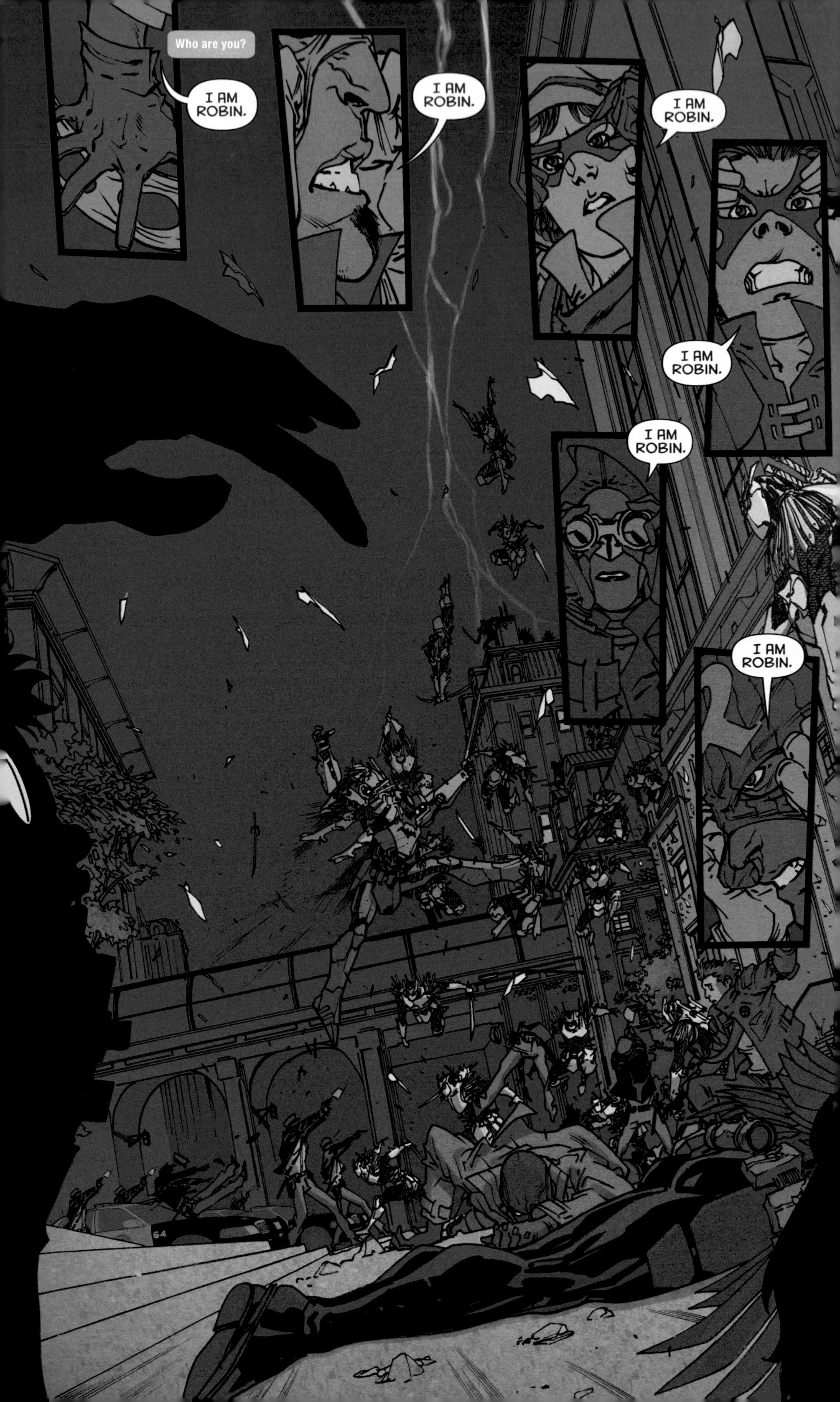
Who are you?
I AM ROBIN.
I AM ROBIN.
I AM ROBIN.
I AM ROBIN.
I AM ROBIN.
I AM ROBIN.

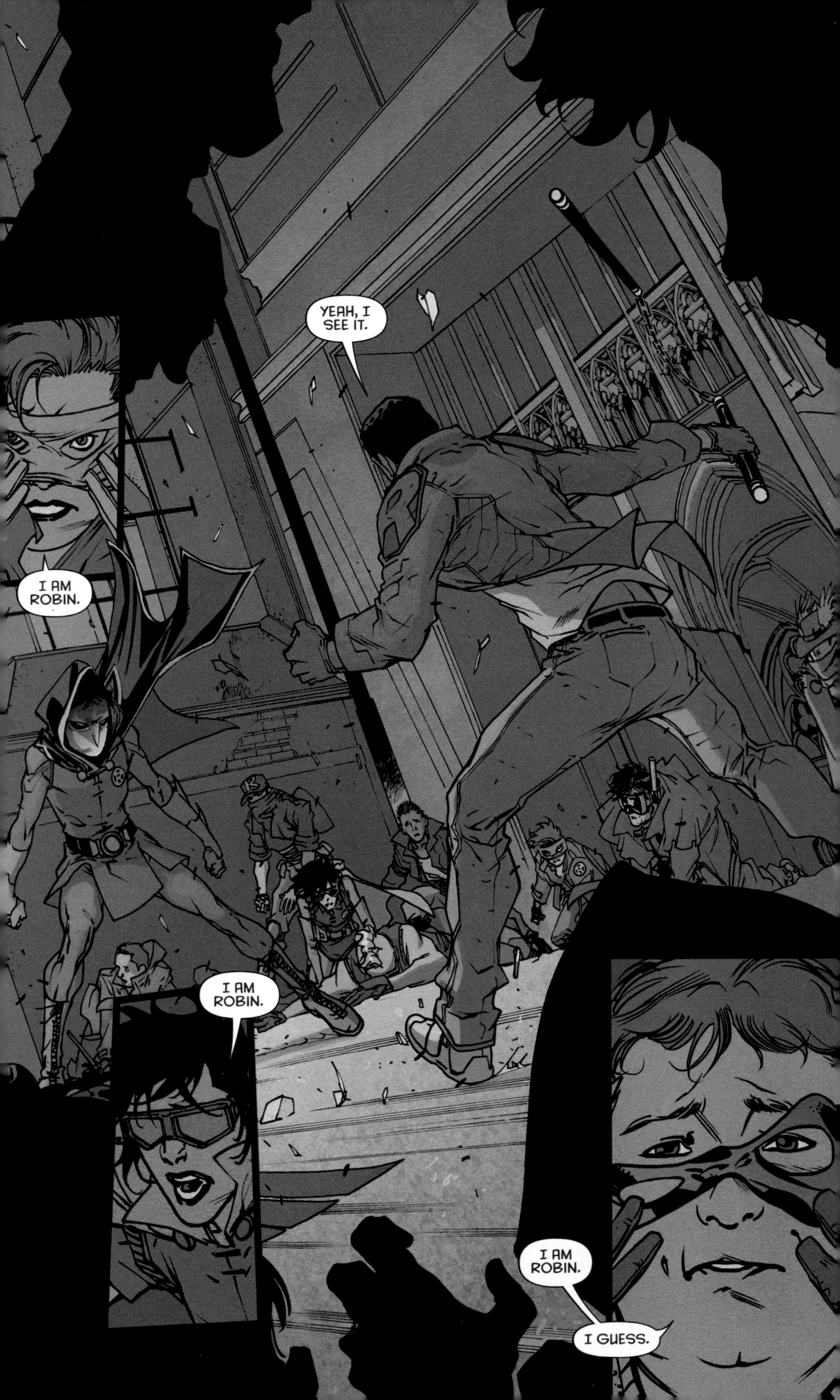
YEAH, I SEE IT.
I AM ROBIN.
I AM ROBIN.
I AM ROBIN.
I GUESS.

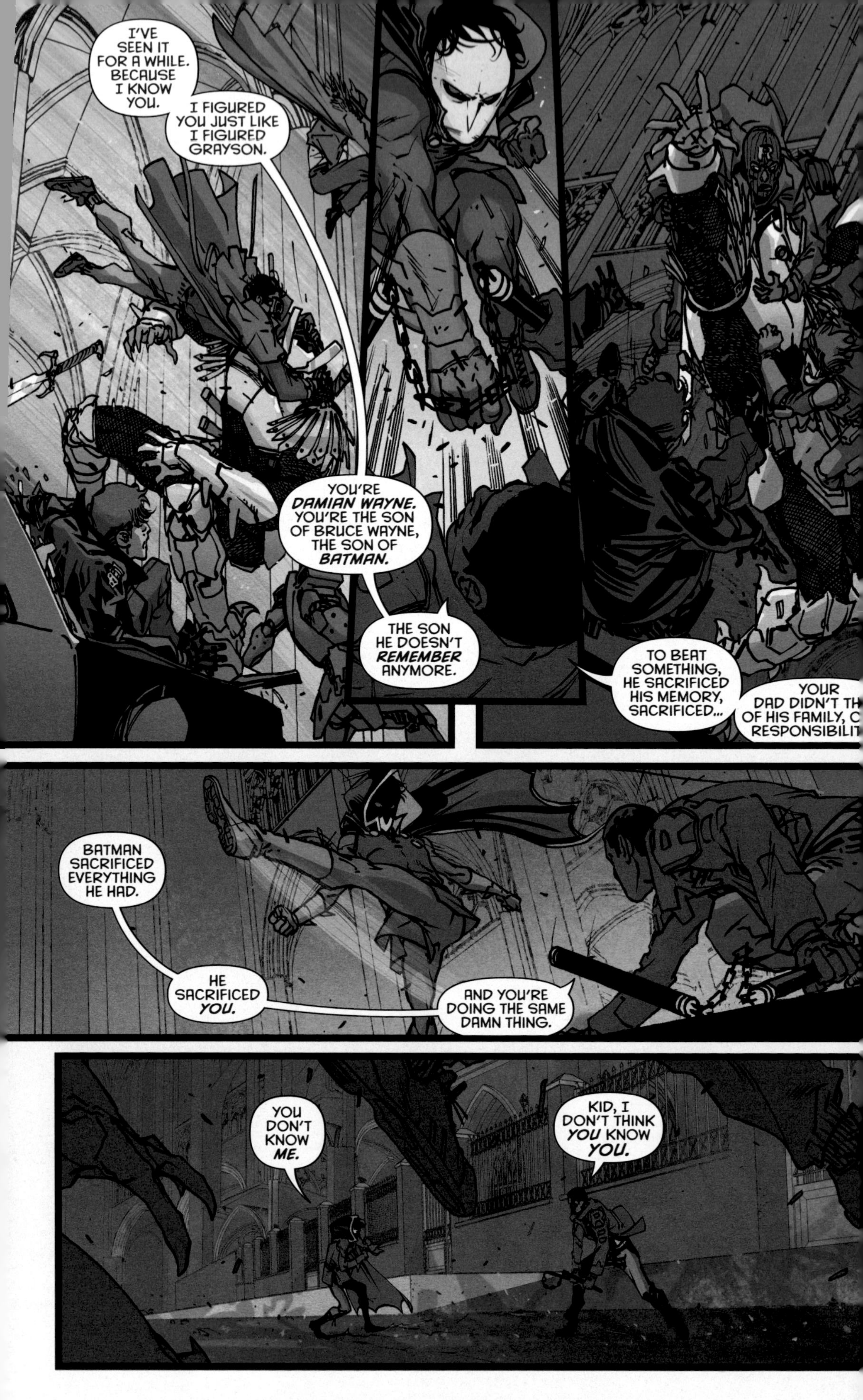

I'VE SEEN IT FOR A WHILE. BECAUSE I KNOW YOU.
I FIGURED YOU JUST LIKE I FIGURED GRAYSON.
YOU'RE DAMIAN WAYNE. YOU'RE THE SON OF BRUCE WAYNE, THE SON OF BATMAN.
THE SON HE DOESN'T REMEMBER ANYMORE.
TO BEAT SOMETHING, HE SACRIFICED HIS MEMORY, SACRIFICED...
YOUR DAD DIDN'T TH OF HIS FAMILY, C RESPONSIBILIT
BATMAN SACRIFICED EVERYTHING HE HAD.
HE SACRIFICED YOU.
AND YOU'RE DOING THE SAME DAMN THING.
YOU DON'T KNOW ME.
KID, I DON'T THINK YOU KNOW YOU.

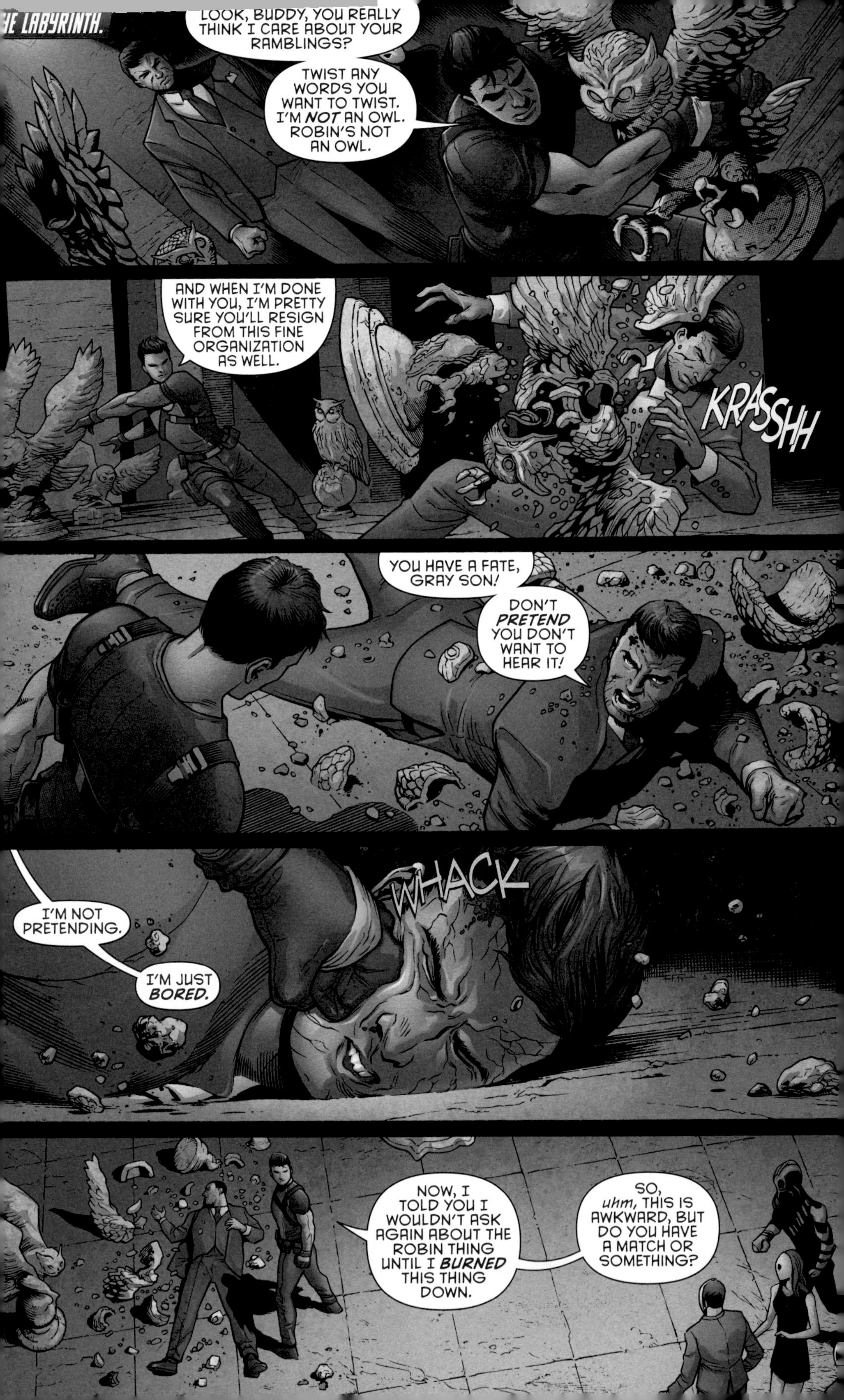
...E LABYRINTH.
LOOK, BUDDY, YOU REALLY THINK I CARE ABOUT YOUR RAMBLINGS?
TWIST ANY WORDS YOU WANT TO TWIST. I'M *NOT* AN OWL. ROBIN'S NOT AN OWL.
AND WHEN I'M DONE WITH YOU, I'M PRETTY SURE YOU'LL RESIGN FROM THIS FINE ORGANIZATION AS WELL.
KRASSHH
YOU HAVE A FATE, GRAY SON!
DON'T *PRETEND* YOU DON'T WANT TO HEAR IT!
WHACK
I'M NOT PRETENDING.
I'M JUST *BORED.*
NOW, I TOLD YOU I WOULDN'T ASK AGAIN ABOUT THE ROBIN THING UNTIL I *BURNED* THIS THING DOWN.
SO, *uhm,* THIS IS AWKWARD, BUT DO YOU HAVE A MATCH OR SOMETHING?

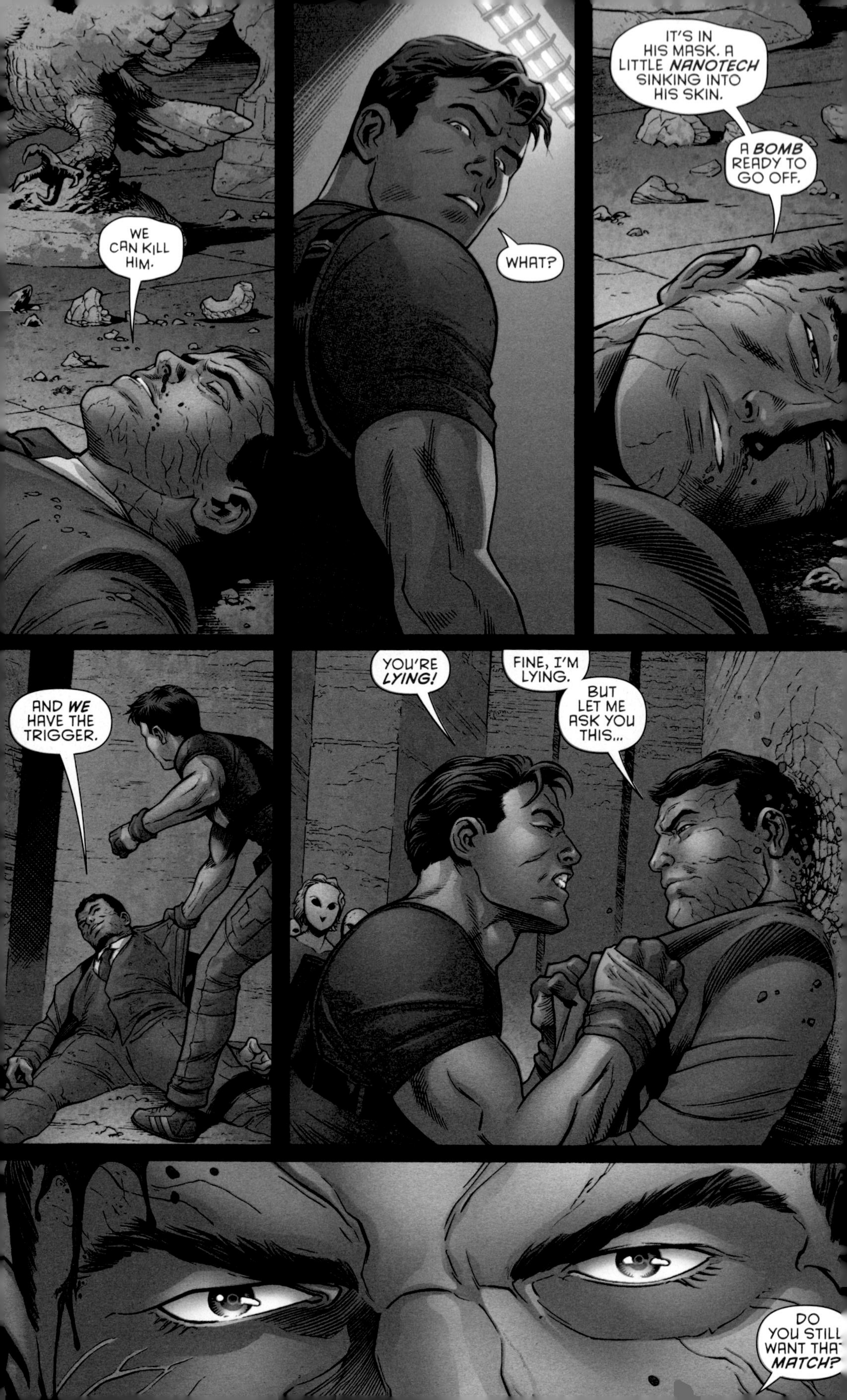
WE CAN KILL HIM.
WHAT?
IT'S IN HIS MASK. A LITTLE NANOTECH SINKING INTO HIS SKIN.
A BOMB READY TO GO OFF.
AND WE HAVE THE TRIGGER.
YOU'RE LYING!
FINE, I'M LYING.
BUT LET ME ASK YOU THIS...
DO YOU STILL WANT THA MATCH?

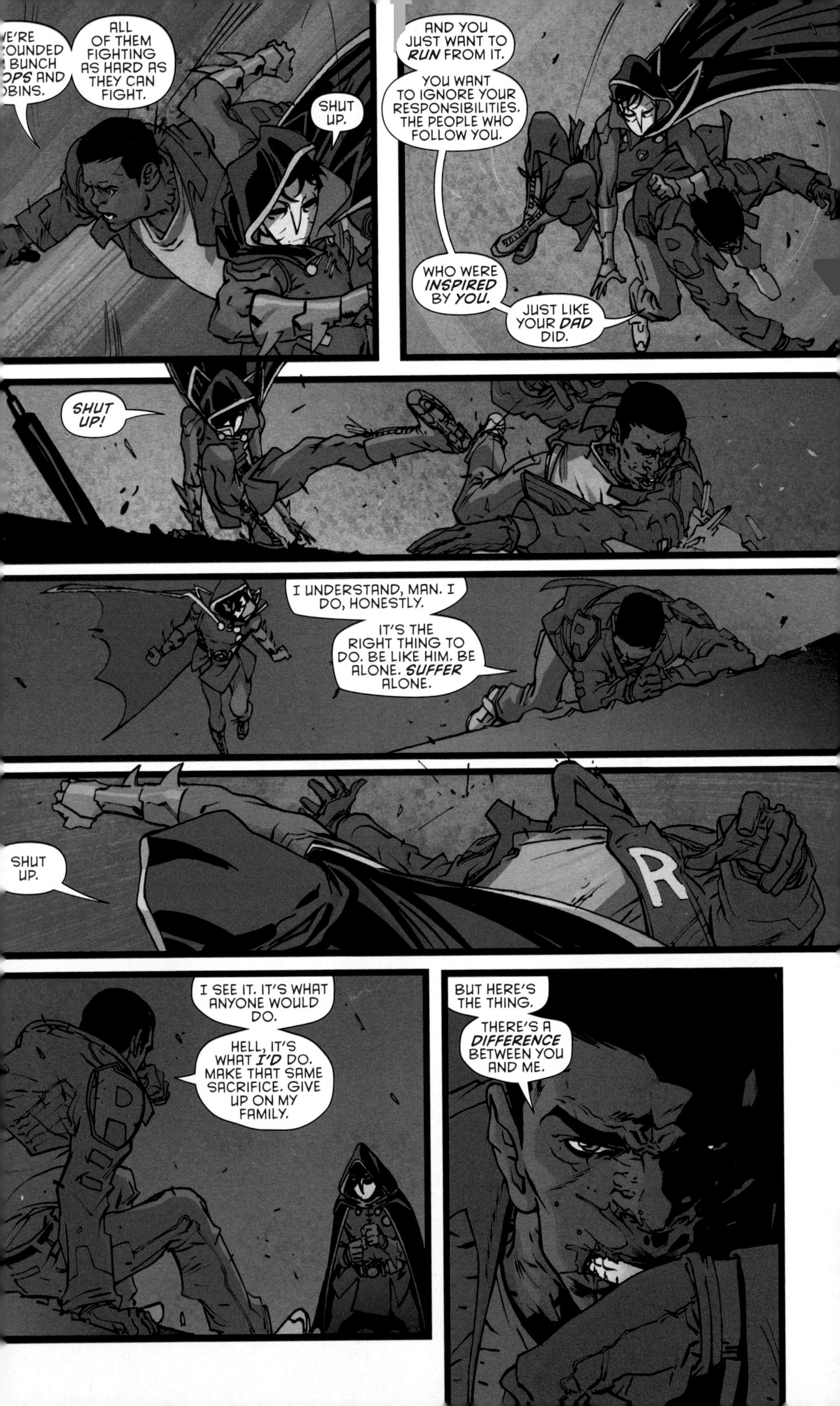

...E'RE ...OUNDED ...BUNCH ...OPS AND ...OBINS.
ALL OF THEM FIGHTING AS HARD AS THEY CAN FIGHT.
SHUT UP.
AND YOU JUST WANT TO RUN FROM IT.
YOU WANT TO IGNORE YOUR RESPONSIBILITIES. THE PEOPLE WHO FOLLOW YOU.
WHO WERE INSPIRED BY YOU.
JUST LIKE YOUR DAD DID.
SHUT UP!
I UNDERSTAND, MAN. I DO, HONESTLY.
IT'S THE RIGHT THING TO DO. BE LIKE HIM. BE ALONE. SUFFER ALONE.
SHUT UP.
R
I SEE IT. IT'S WHAT ANYONE WOULD DO.
HELL, IT'S WHAT I'D DO. MAKE THAT SAME SACRIFICE. GIVE UP ON MY FAMILY.
BUT HERE'S THE THING.
THERE'S A DIFFERENCE BETWEEN YOU AND ME.

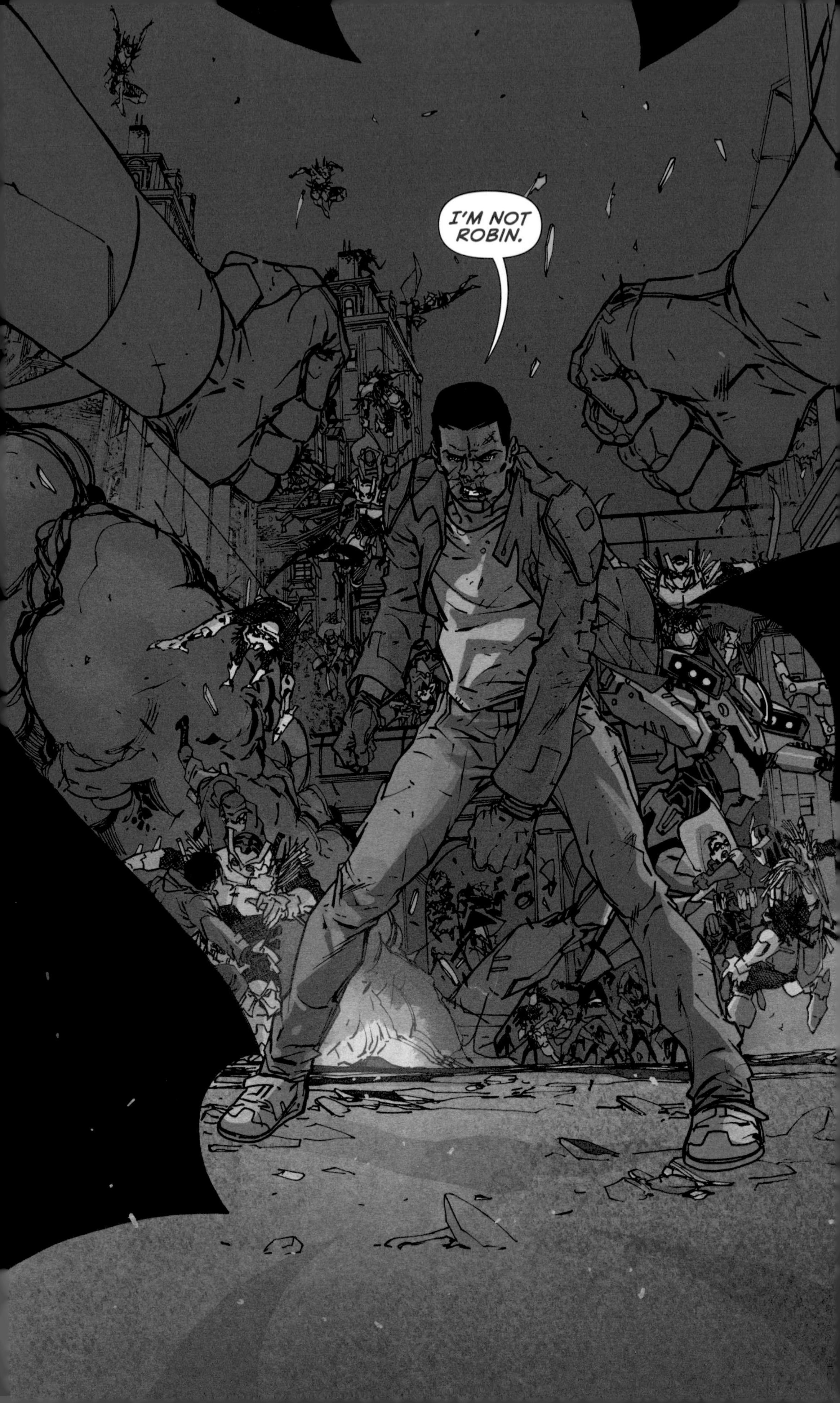
I'M NOT ROBIN.

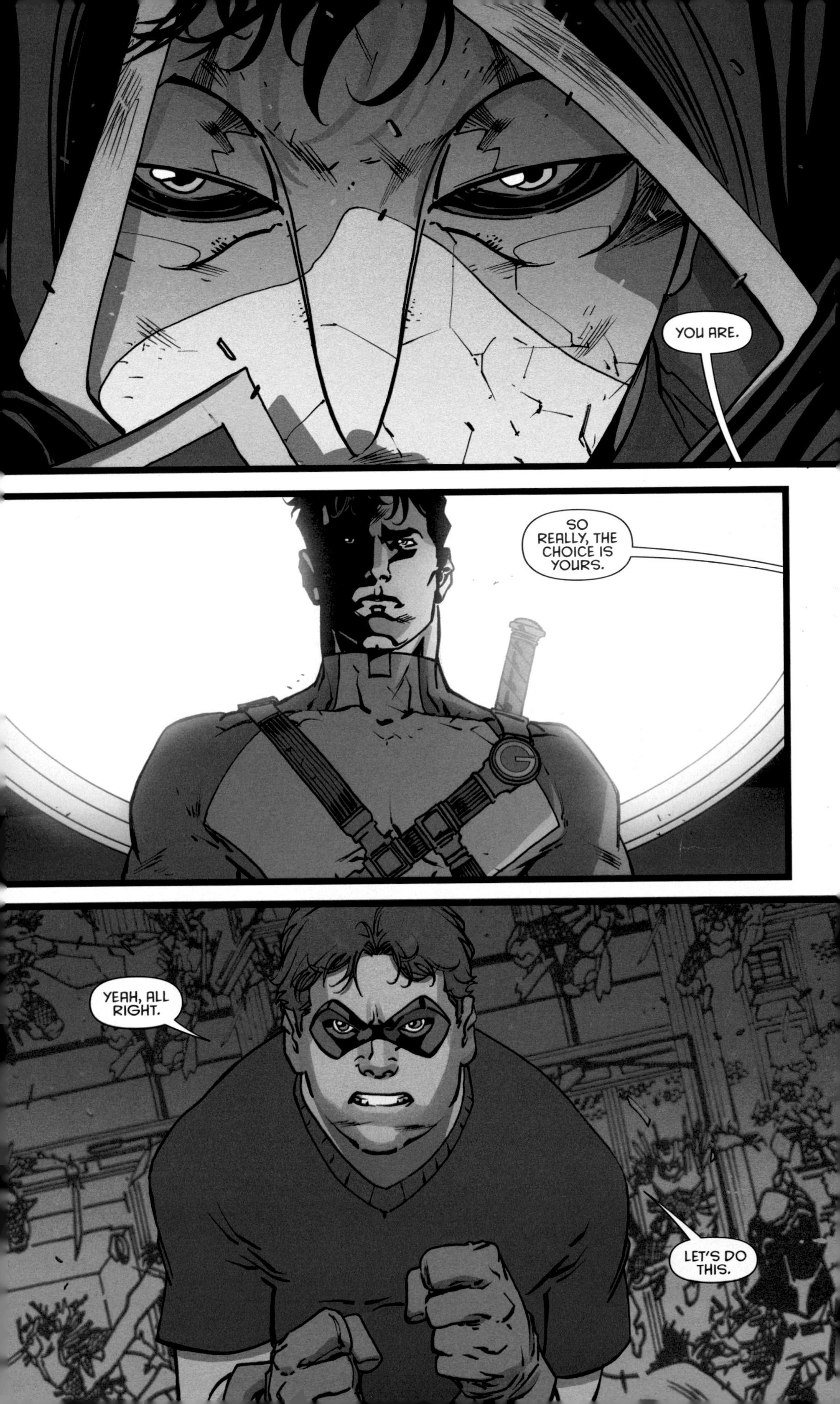
YOU ARE.
SO REALLY, THE CHOICE IS YOURS.
YEAH, ALL RIGHT.
LET'S DO THIS.

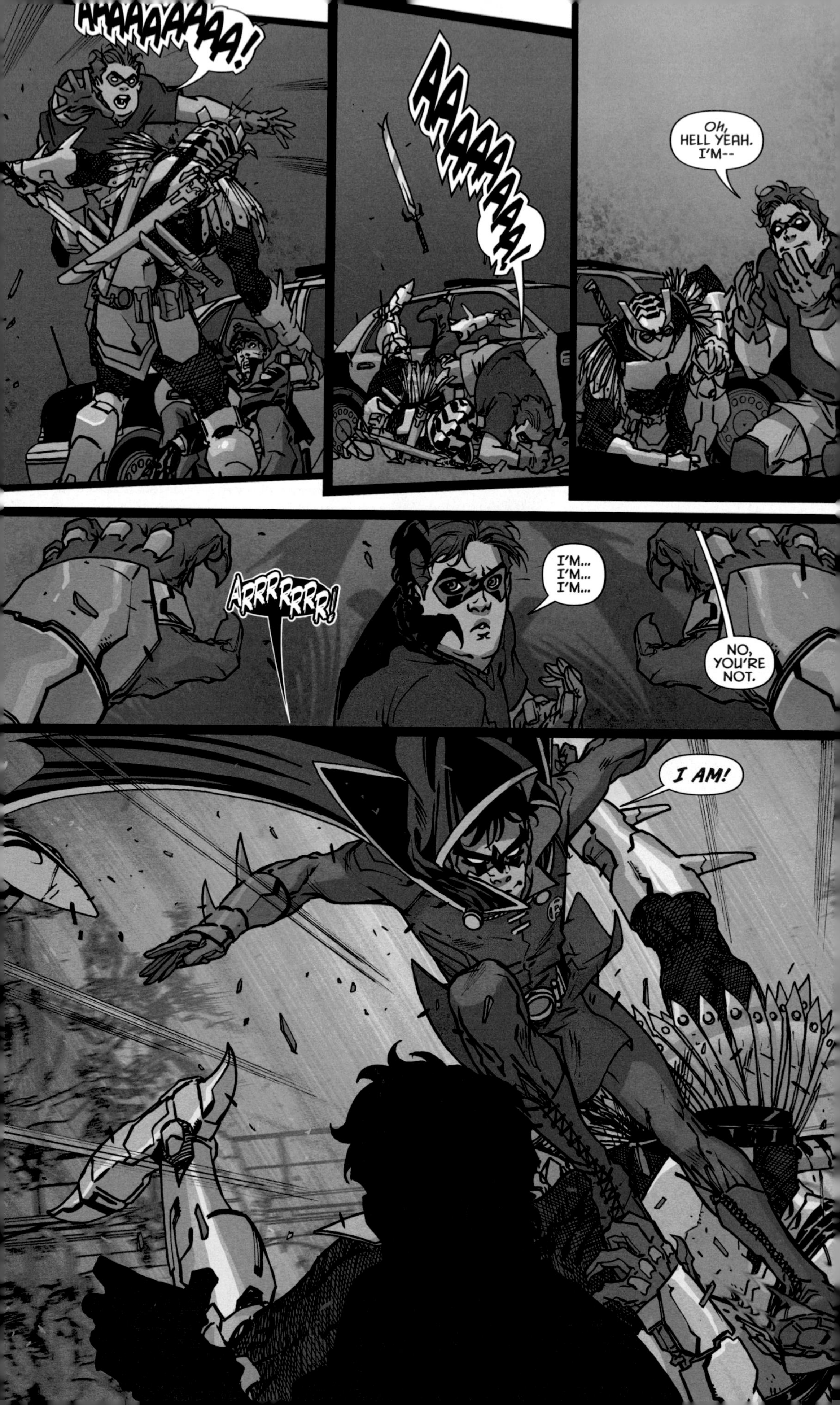
AAAAAAAAAA!
AAAAAAAAAA!
Oh, HELL YEAH. I'M--
ARRRRRRR!
I'M... I'M... I'M...
NO, YOU'RE NOT.
I AM!

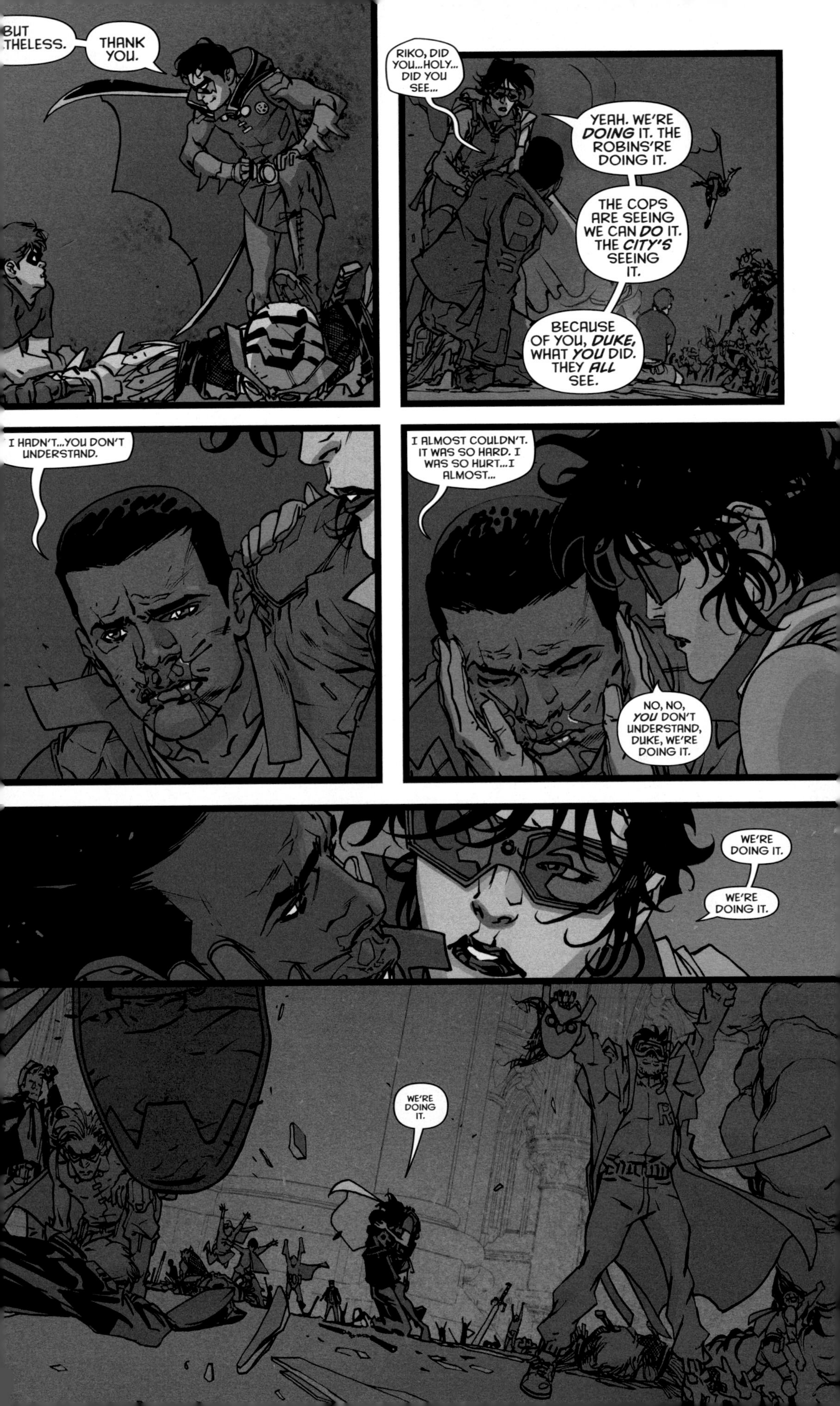

BUT
..THELESS.
THANK YOU.
RIKO, DID YOU...HOLY... DID YOU SEE...
YEAH. WE'RE DOING IT. THE ROBINS'RE DOING IT.
THE COPS ARE SEEING WE CAN DO IT. THE CITY'S SEEING IT.
BECAUSE OF YOU, DUKE, WHAT YOU DID. THEY ALL SEE.
I HADN'T...YOU DON'T UNDERSTAND.
I ALMOST COULDN'T. IT WAS SO HARD. I WAS SO HURT...I ALMOST...
NO, NO, YOU DON'T UNDERSTAND, DUKE, WE'RE DOING IT.
WE'RE DOING IT.
WE'RE DOING IT.
WE'RE DOING IT.

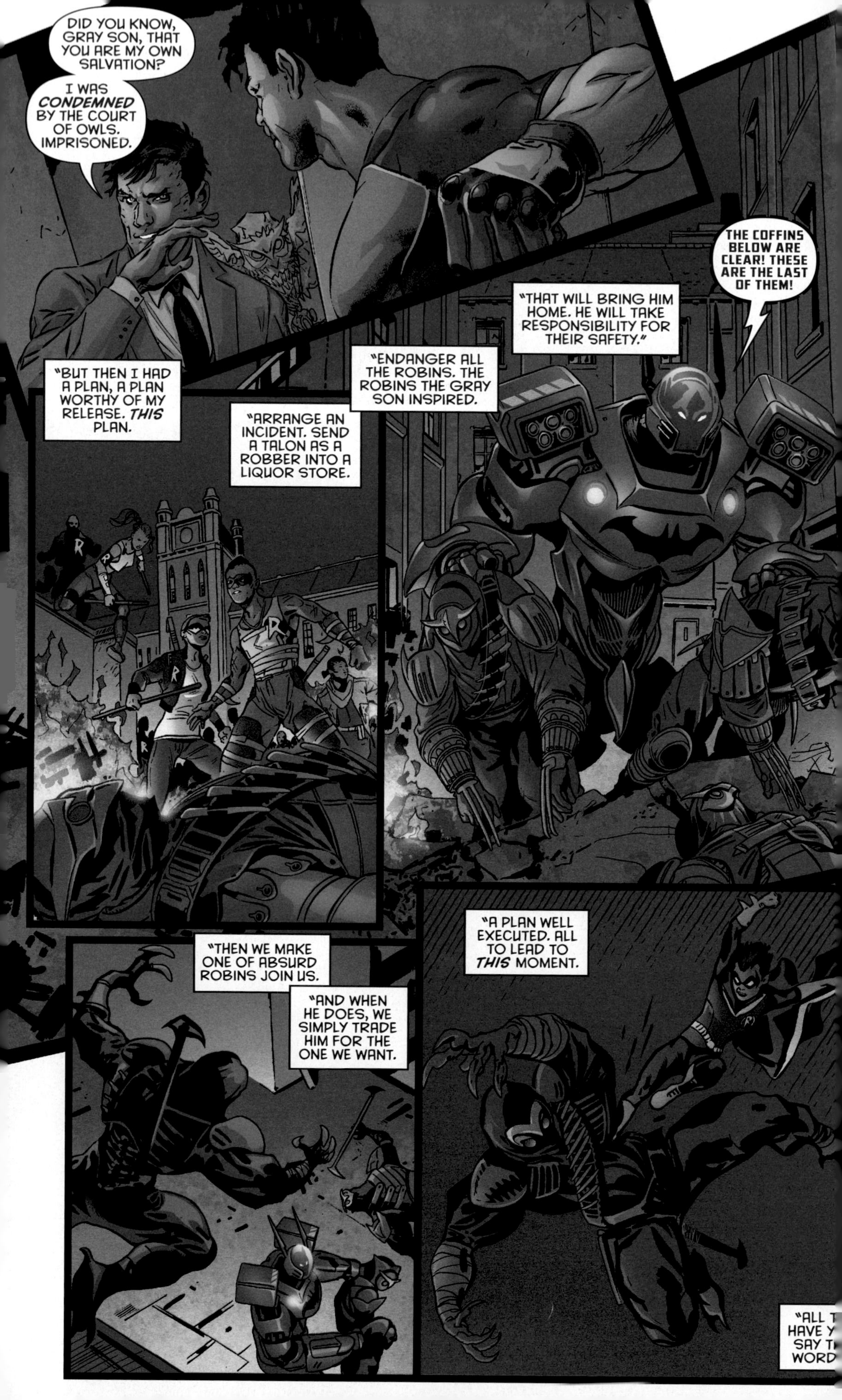
DID YOU KNOW, GRAY SON, THAT YOU ARE MY OWN SALVATION?
I WAS CONDEMNED BY THE COURT OF OWLS. IMPRISONED.
THE COFFINS BELOW ARE CLEAR! THESE ARE THE LAST OF THEM!
"THAT WILL BRING HIM HOME. HE WILL TAKE RESPONSIBILITY FOR THEIR SAFETY."
"BUT THEN I HAD A PLAN, A PLAN WORTHY OF MY RELEASE. THIS PLAN.
"ARRANGE AN INCIDENT. SEND A TALON AS A ROBBER INTO A LIQUOR STORE.
"ENDANGER ALL THE ROBINS. THE ROBINS THE GRAY SON INSPIRED.
"THEN WE MAKE ONE OF ABSURD ROBINS JOIN US.
"AND WHEN HE DOES, WE SIMPLY TRADE HIM FOR THE ONE WE WANT.
"A PLAN WELL EXECUTED. ALL TO LEAD TO THIS MOMENT.

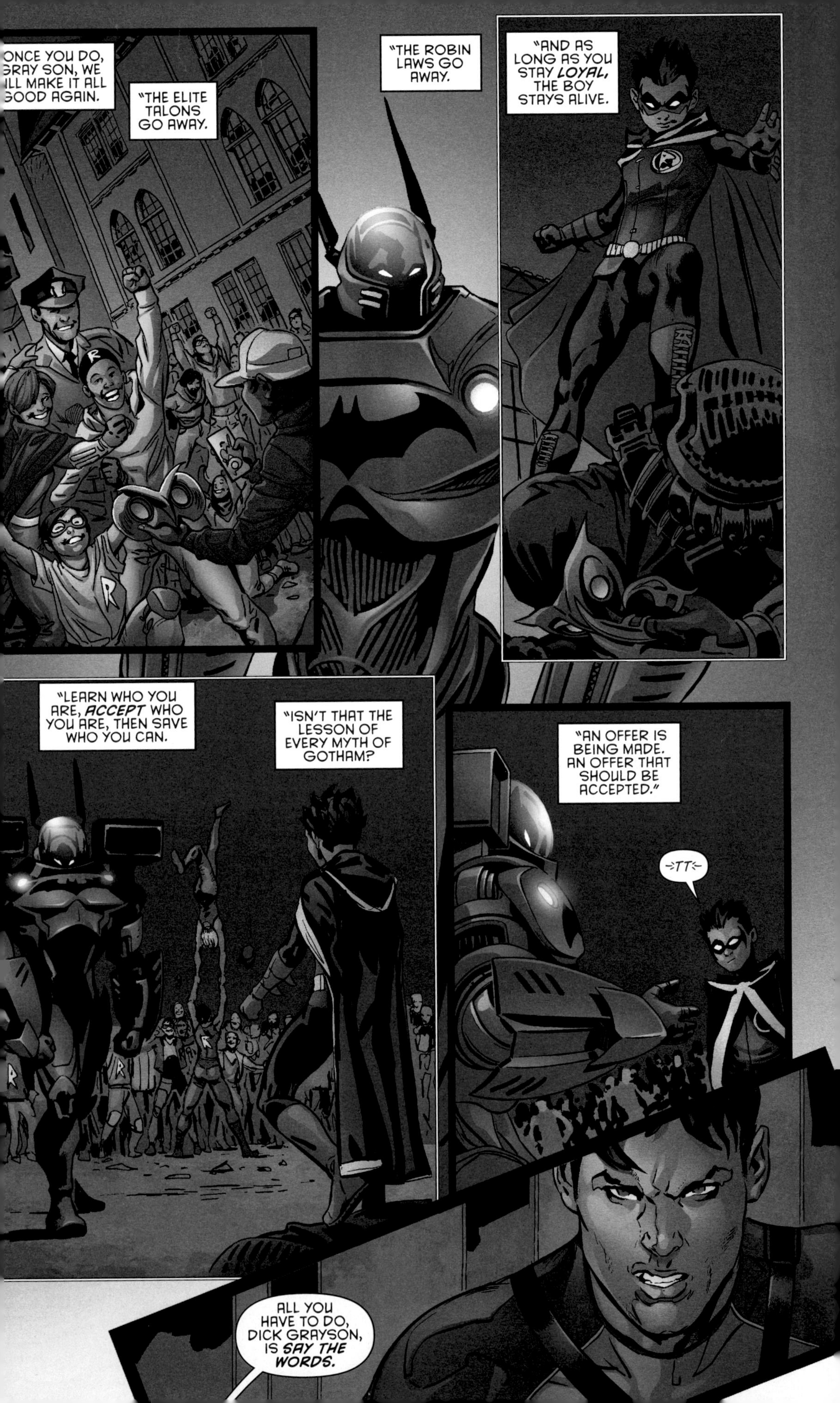
ONCE YOU DO, GRAY SON, WE ILL MAKE IT ALL GOOD AGAIN.
"THE ELITE TALONS GO AWAY.
"THE ROBIN LAWS GO AWAY.
"AND AS LONG AS YOU STAY LOYAL, THE BOY STAYS ALIVE.
"LEARN WHO YOU ARE, ACCEPT WHO YOU ARE, THEN SAVE WHO YOU CAN.
"ISN'T THAT THE LESSON OF EVERY MYTH OF GOTHAM?
"AN OFFER IS BEING MADE. AN OFFER THAT SHOULD BE ACCEPTED."
TT
ALL YOU HAVE TO DO, DICK GRAYSON, IS SAY THE WORDS.

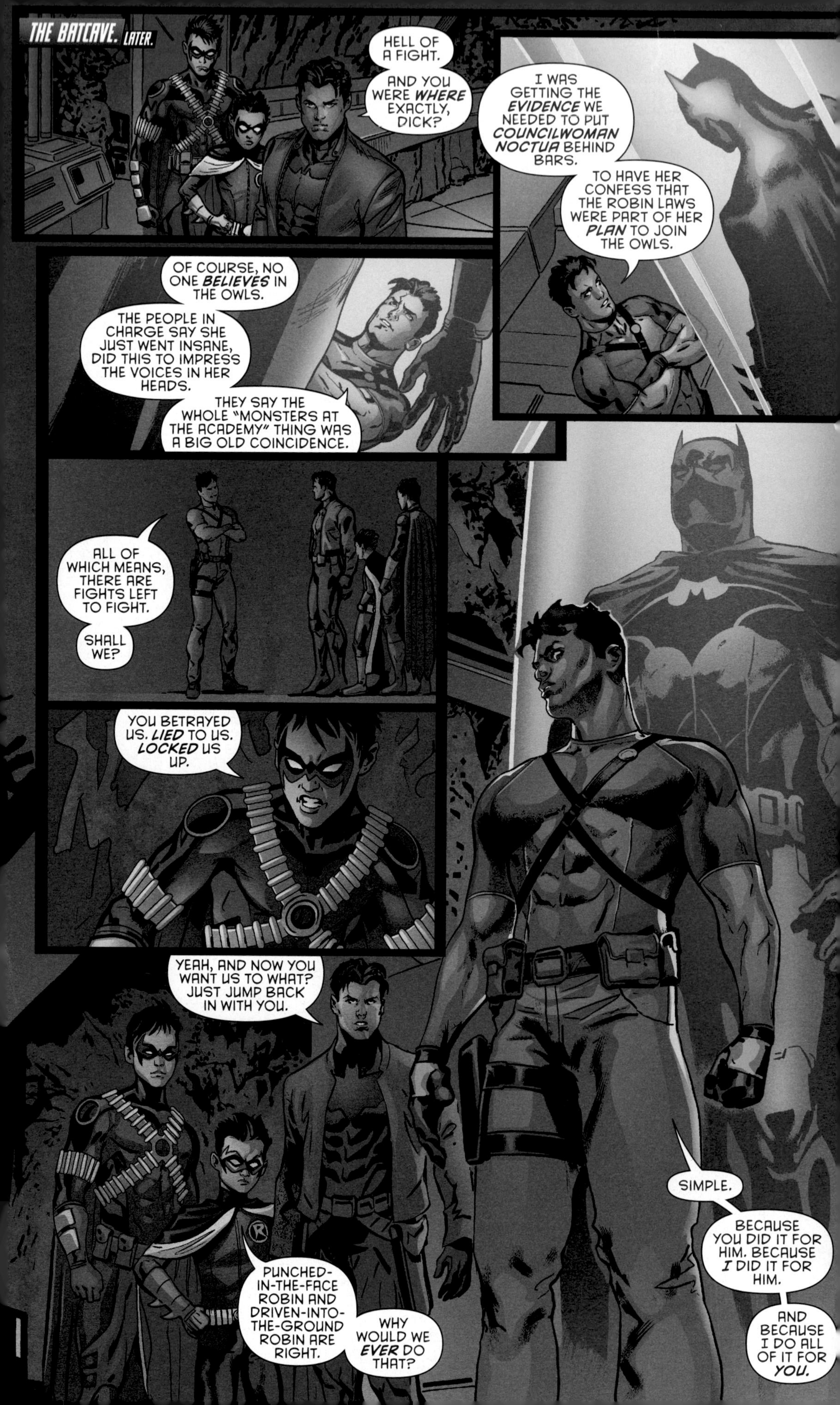

THE BATCAVE. LATER.
HELL OF A FIGHT.
AND YOU WERE WHERE EXACTLY, DICK?
I WAS GETTING THE EVIDENCE WE NEEDED TO PUT COUNCILWOMAN NOCTUA BEHIND BARS.
TO HAVE HER CONFESS THAT THE ROBIN LAWS WERE PART OF HER PLAN TO JOIN THE OWLS.
OF COURSE, NO ONE BELIEVES IN THE OWLS.
THE PEOPLE IN CHARGE SAY SHE JUST WENT INSANE, DID THIS TO IMPRESS THE VOICES IN HER HEADS.
THEY SAY THE WHOLE "MONSTERS AT THE ACADEMY" THING WAS A BIG OLD COINCIDENCE.
ALL OF WHICH MEANS, THERE ARE FIGHTS LEFT TO FIGHT.
SHALL WE?
YOU BETRAYED US. LIED TO US. LOCKED US UP.
YEAH, AND NOW YOU WANT US TO WHAT? JUST JUMP BACK IN WITH YOU.
PUNCHED-IN-THE-FACE ROBIN AND DRIVEN-INTO-THE-GROUND ROBIN ARE RIGHT.
WHY WOULD WE EVER DO THAT?
SIMPLE.
BECAUSE YOU DID IT FOR HIM. BECAUSE I DID IT FOR HIM.
AND BECAUSE I DO ALL OF IT FOR YOU.

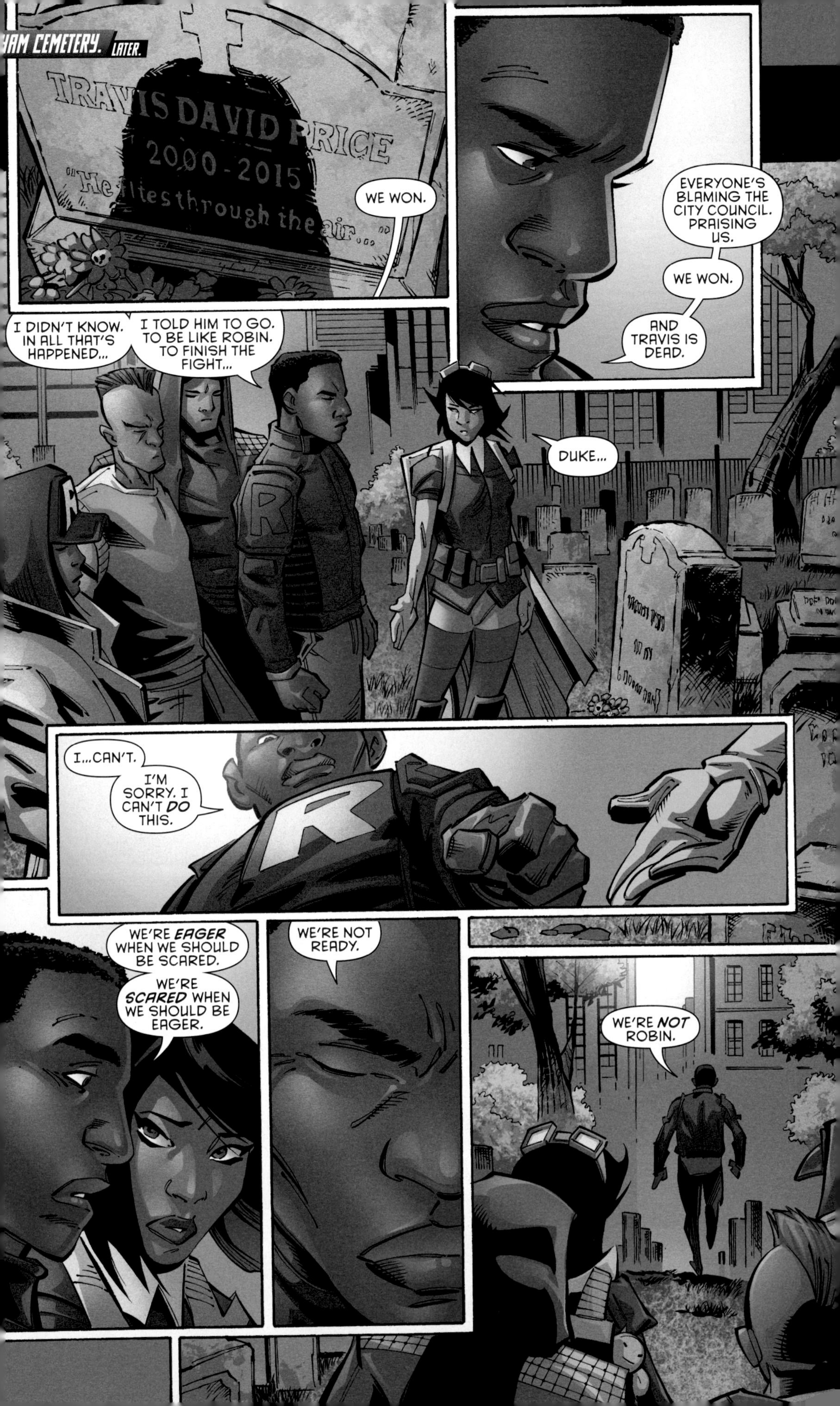

HAM CEMETERY. LATER.
TRAVIS DAVID PRICE
2000-2015
"He flies through the air..."
WE WON.
EVERYONE'S BLAMING THE CITY COUNCIL. PRAISING US.
WE WON.
AND TRAVIS IS DEAD.
I DIDN'T KNOW. IN ALL THAT'S HAPPENED...
I TOLD HIM TO GO. TO BE LIKE ROBIN. TO FINISH THE FIGHT...
DUKE...
I...CAN'T.
I'M SORRY. I CAN'T DO THIS.
WE'RE EAGER WHEN WE SHOULD BE SCARED.
WE'RE SCARED WHEN WE SHOULD BE EAGER.
WE'RE NOT READY.
WE'RE NOT ROBIN.

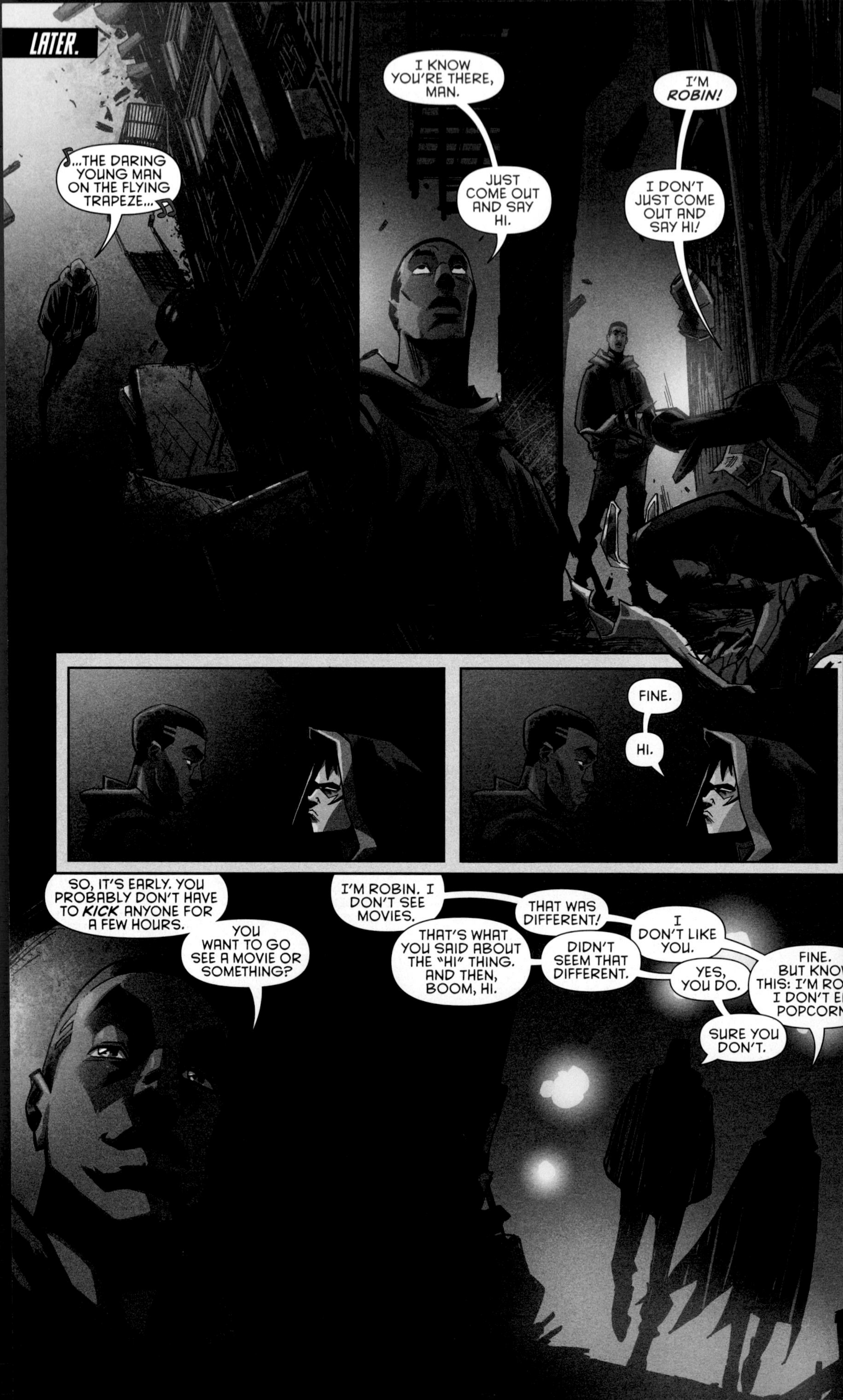
LATER.
...THE DARING YOUNG MAN ON THE FLYING TRAPEZE...
I KNOW YOU'RE THERE, MAN.
JUST COME OUT AND SAY HI.
I'M ROBIN!
I DON'T JUST COME OUT AND SAY HI!
FINE.
HI.
SO, IT'S EARLY. YOU PROBABLY DON'T HAVE TO KICK ANYONE FOR A FEW HOURS.
YOU WANT TO GO SEE A MOVIE OR SOMETHING?
I'M ROBIN. I DON'T SEE MOVIES.
THAT'S WHAT YOU SAID ABOUT THE "HI" THING. AND THEN, BOOM, HI.
THAT WAS DIFFERENT!
DIDN'T SEEM THAT DIFFERENT.
I DON'T LIKE YOU.
YES, YOU DO.
SURE YOU DON'T.

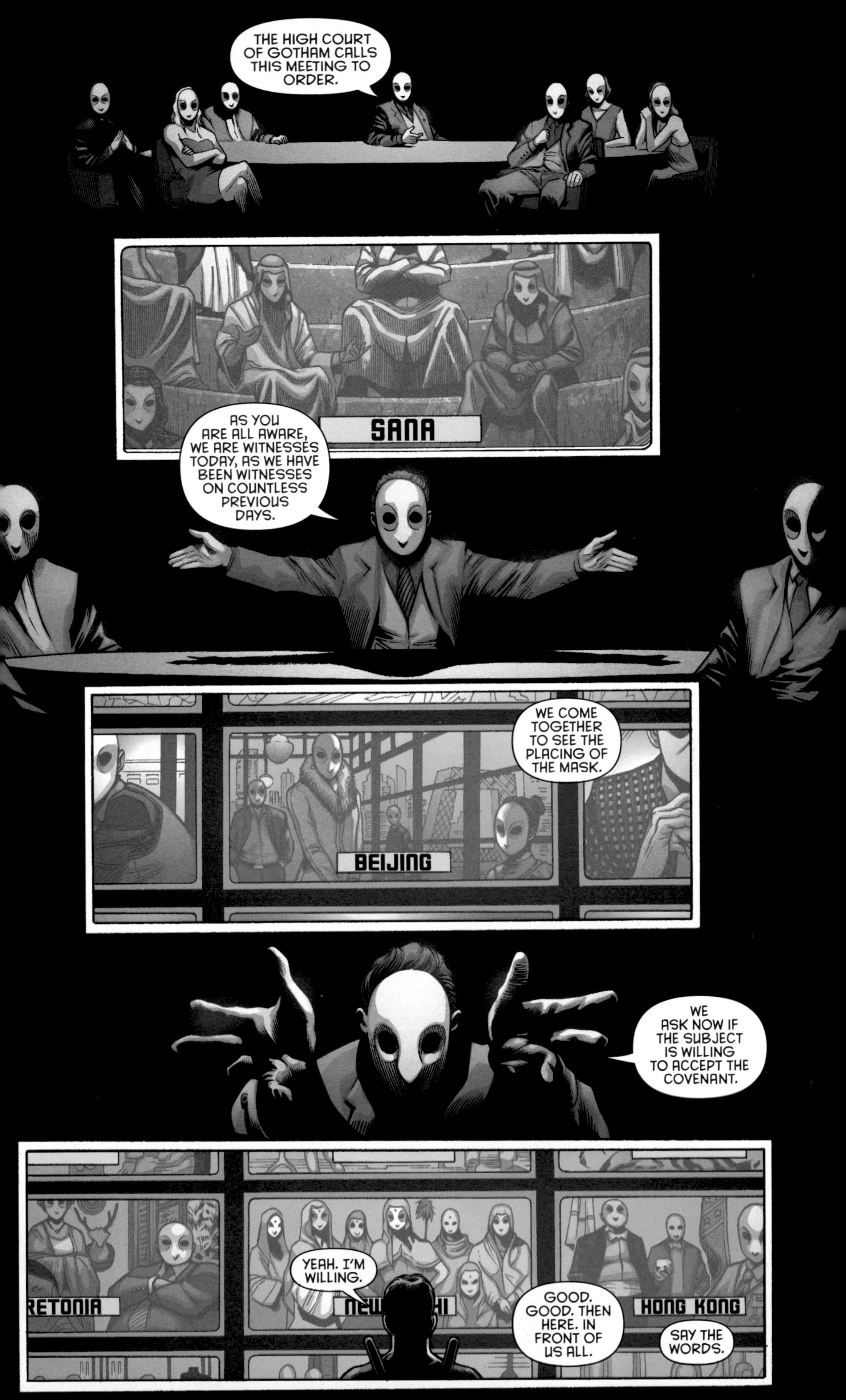
THE HIGH COURT OF GOTHAM CALLS THIS MEETING TO ORDER.
SANA
AS YOU ARE ALL AWARE, WE ARE WITNESSES TODAY, AS WE HAVE BEEN WITNESSES ON COUNTLESS PREVIOUS DAYS.
WE COME TOGETHER TO SEE THE PLACING OF THE MASK.
BEIJING
WE ASK NOW IF THE SUBJECT IS WILLING TO ACCEPT THE COVENANT.
RETONIA
YEAH. I'M WILLING.
HONG KONG
GOOD. GOOD. THEN HERE. IN FRONT OF US ALL.
SAY THE WORDS.

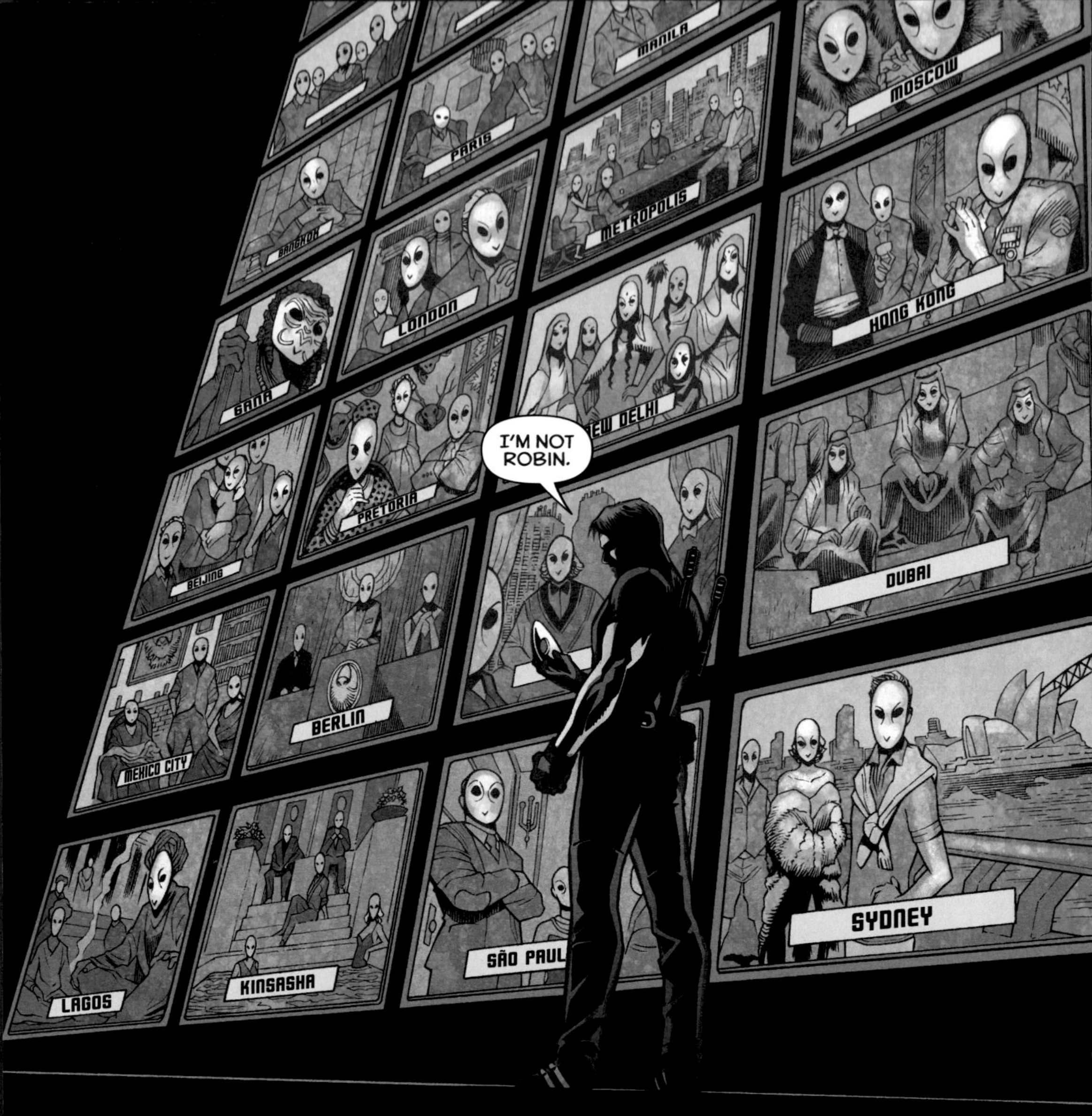
I'M NOT ROBIN.
MANILA
MOSCOW
PARIS
METROPOLIS
BANGKOK
LONDON
HONG KONG
SANA
EW DELHI
PRETORIA
BEIJING
DUBAI
BERLIN
MEXICO CITY
SYDNEY
LAGOS
KINSASHA
SÃO PAUL

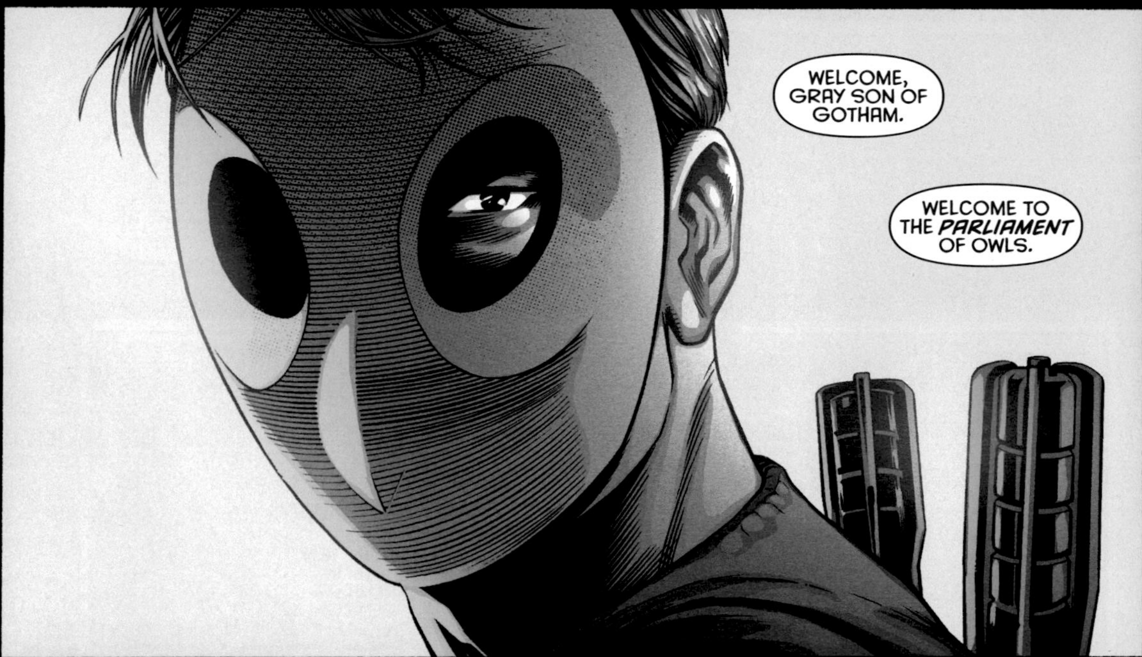
WELCOME, GRAY SON OF GOTHAM.
WELCOME TO THE *PARLIAMENT* OF OWLS.

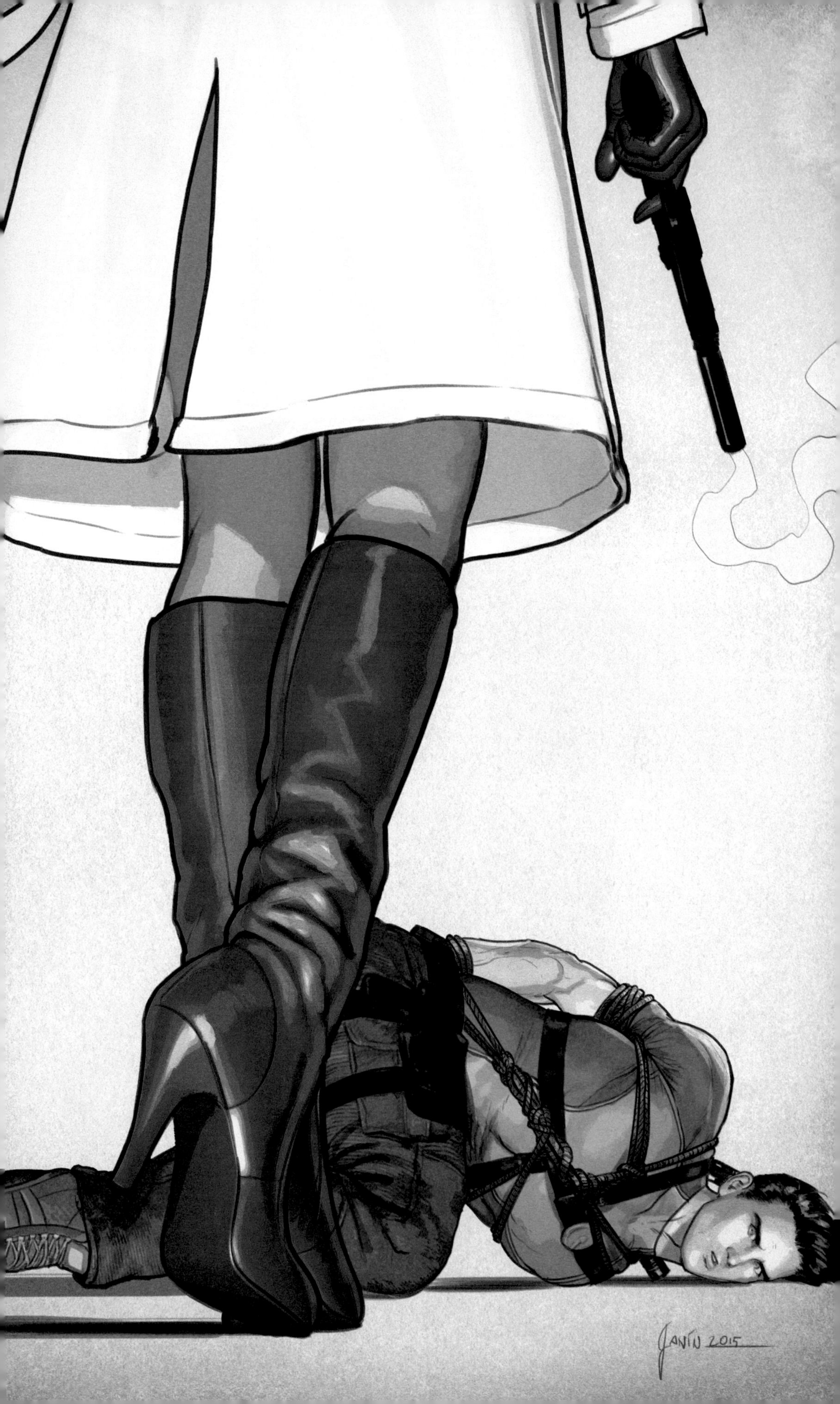
JANÍN 2015

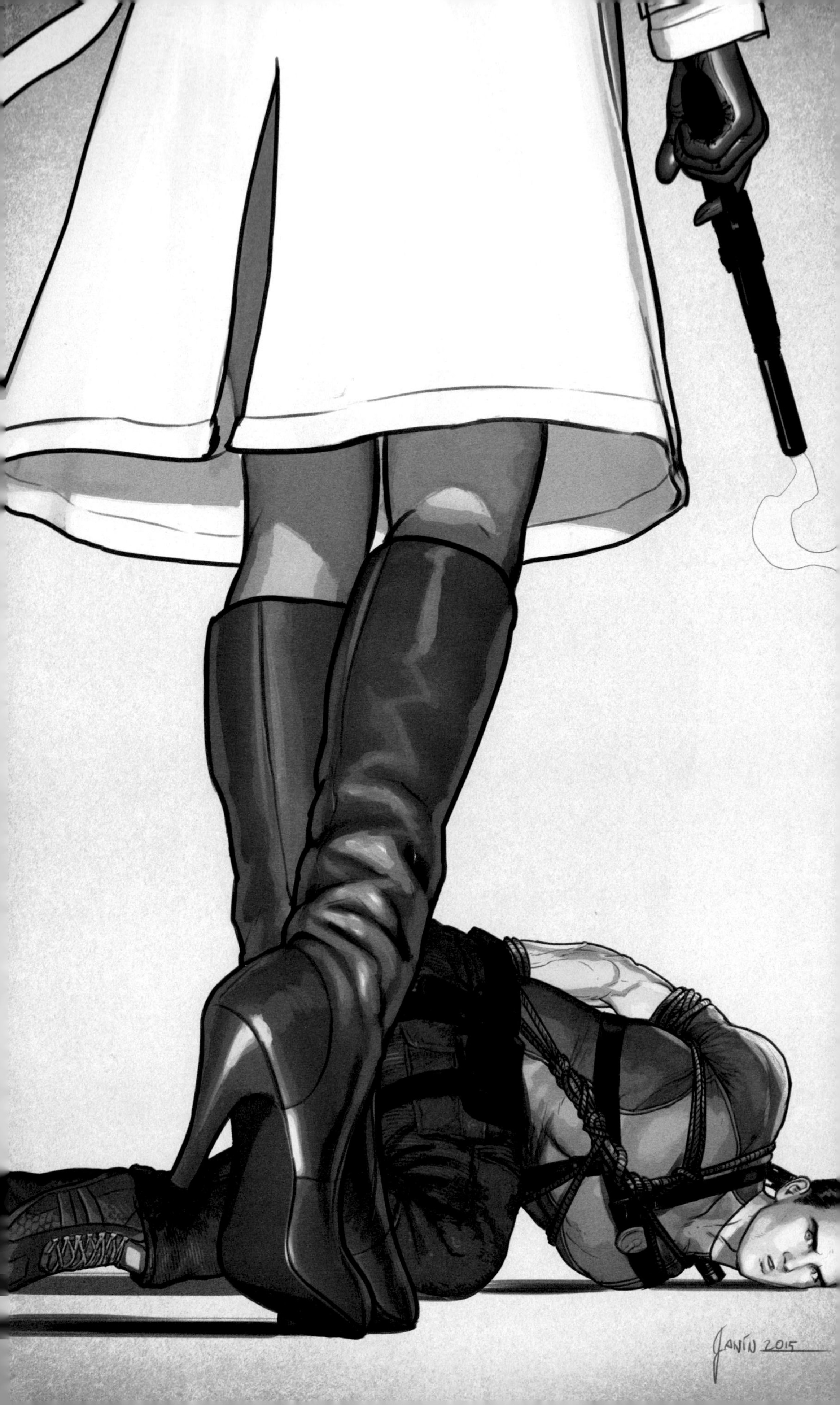
JANÍN 2015

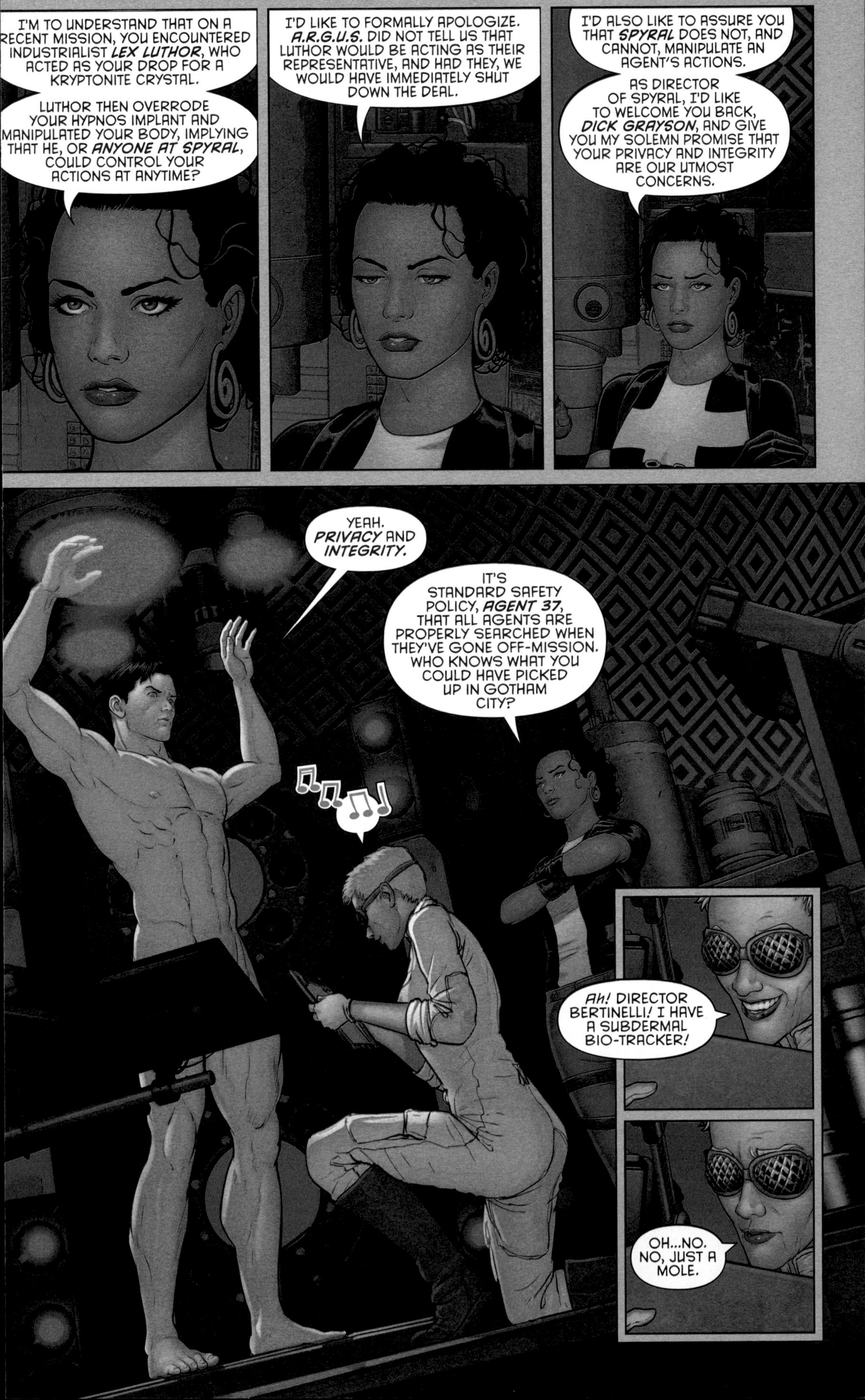
I'M TO UNDERSTAND THAT ON A RECENT MISSION, YOU ENCOUNTERED INDUSTRIALIST LEX LUTHOR, WHO ACTED AS YOUR DROP FOR A KRYPTONITE CRYSTAL.
LUTHOR THEN OVERRODE YOUR HYPNOS IMPLANT AND MANIPULATED YOUR BODY, IMPLYING THAT HE, OR ANYONE AT SPYRAL, COULD CONTROL YOUR ACTIONS AT ANYTIME?
I'D LIKE TO FORMALLY APOLOGIZE. A.R.G.U.S. DID NOT TELL US THAT LUTHOR WOULD BE ACTING AS THEIR REPRESENTATIVE, AND HAD THEY, WE WOULD HAVE IMMEDIATELY SHUT DOWN THE DEAL.
I'D ALSO LIKE TO ASSURE YOU THAT SPYRAL DOES NOT, AND CANNOT, MANIPULATE AN AGENT'S ACTIONS.
AS DIRECTOR OF SPYRAL, I'D LIKE TO WELCOME YOU BACK, DICK GRAYSON, AND GIVE YOU MY SOLEMN PROMISE THAT YOUR PRIVACY AND INTEGRITY ARE OUR UTMOST CONCERNS.
YEAH. PRIVACY AND INTEGRITY.
IT'S STANDARD SAFETY POLICY, AGENT 37, THAT ALL AGENTS ARE PROPERLY SEARCHED WHEN THEY'VE GONE OFF-MISSION. WHO KNOWS WHAT YOU COULD HAVE PICKED UP IN GOTHAM CITY?
Ah! DIRECTOR BERTINELLI! I HAVE A SUBDERMAL BIO-TRACKER!
OH...NO. NO, JUST A MOLE.

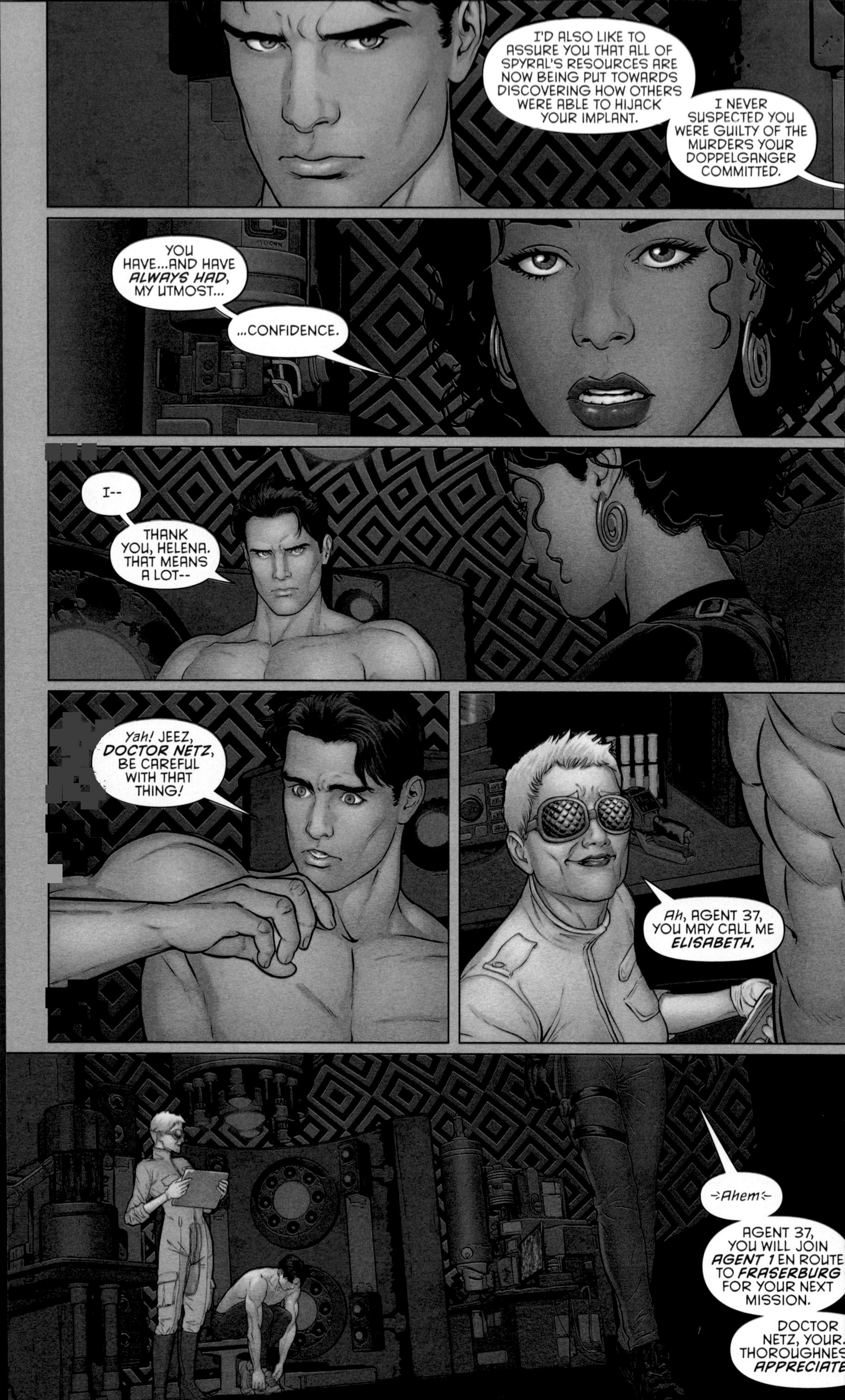

I'D ALSO LIKE TO ASSURE YOU THAT ALL OF SPYRAL'S RESOURCES ARE NOW BEING PUT TOWARDS DISCOVERING HOW OTHERS WERE ABLE TO HIJACK YOUR IMPLANT.
I NEVER SUSPECTED YOU WERE GUILTY OF THE MURDERS YOUR DOPPELGANGER COMMITTED.
YOU HAVE...AND HAVE ALWAYS HAD, MY UTMOST...
...CONFIDENCE.
I--
THANK YOU, HELENA. THAT MEANS A LOT--
Yah! JEEZ, DOCTOR NETZ, BE CAREFUL WITH THAT THING!
Ah, AGENT 37, YOU MAY CALL ME ELISABETH.
Ahem
AGENT 37, YOU WILL JOIN AGENT 1 EN ROUTE TO FRASERBURG FOR YOUR NEXT MISSION.
DOCTOR NETZ, YOUR THOROUGHNES APPRECIATE

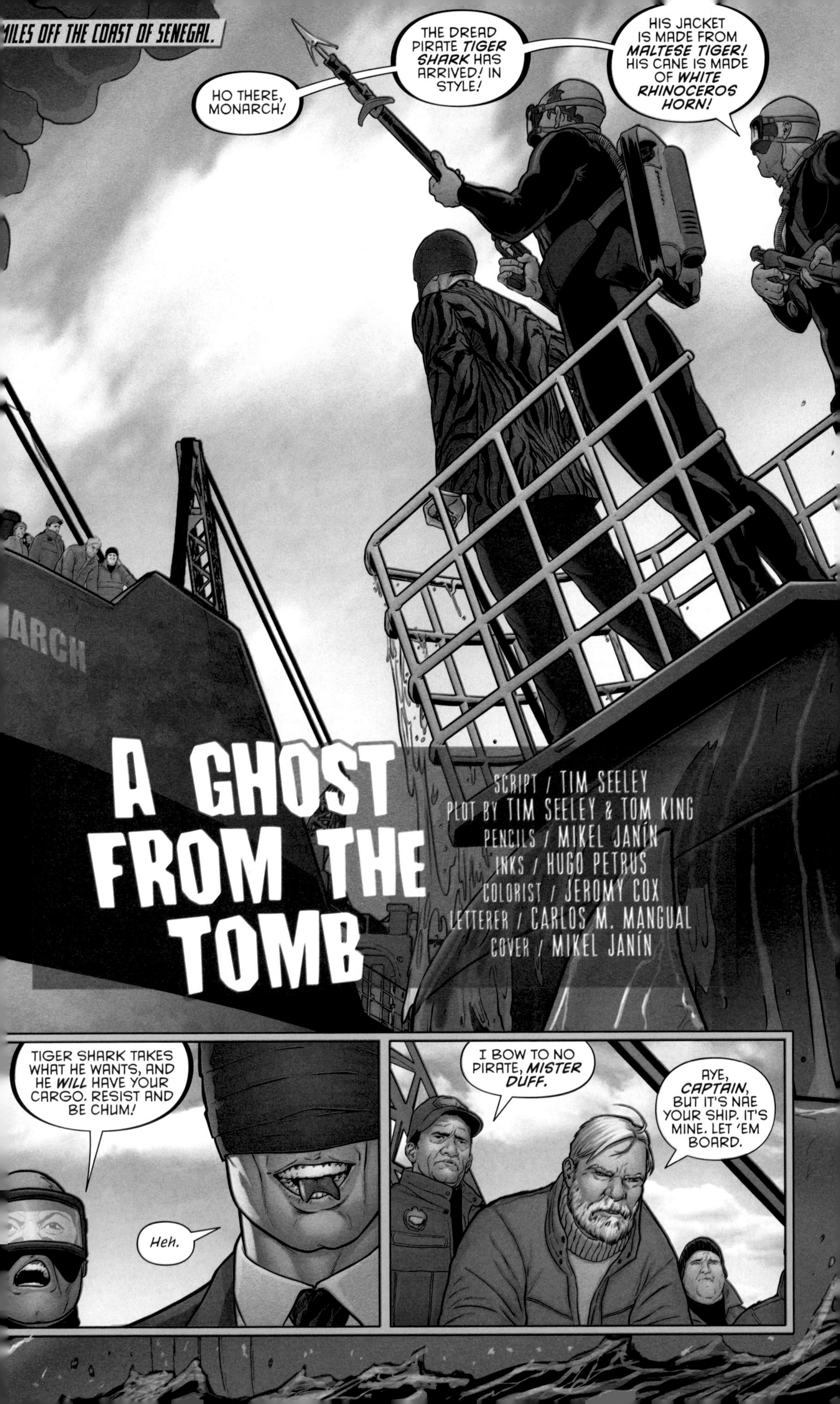

MILES OFF THE COAST OF SENEGAL.
HO THERE, MONARCH!
THE DREAD PIRATE TIGER SHARK HAS ARRIVED! IN STYLE!
HIS JACKET IS MADE FROM MALTESE TIGER! HIS CANE IS MADE OF WHITE RHINOCEROS HORN!
ARCH
A GHOST FROM THE TOMB
SCRIPT / TIM SEELEY
PLOT BY TIM SEELEY & TOM KING
PENCILS / MIKEL JANÍN
INKS / HUGO PETRUS
COLORIST / JEROMY COX
LETTERER / CARLOS M. MANGUAL
COVER / MIKEL JANÍN
TIGER SHARK TAKES WHAT HE WANTS, AND HE WILL HAVE YOUR CARGO. RESIST AND BE CHUM!
Heh.
I BOW TO NO PIRATE, MISTER DUFF.
AYE, CAPTAIN, BUT IT'S NAE YOUR SHIP. IT'S MINE. LET 'EM BOARD.

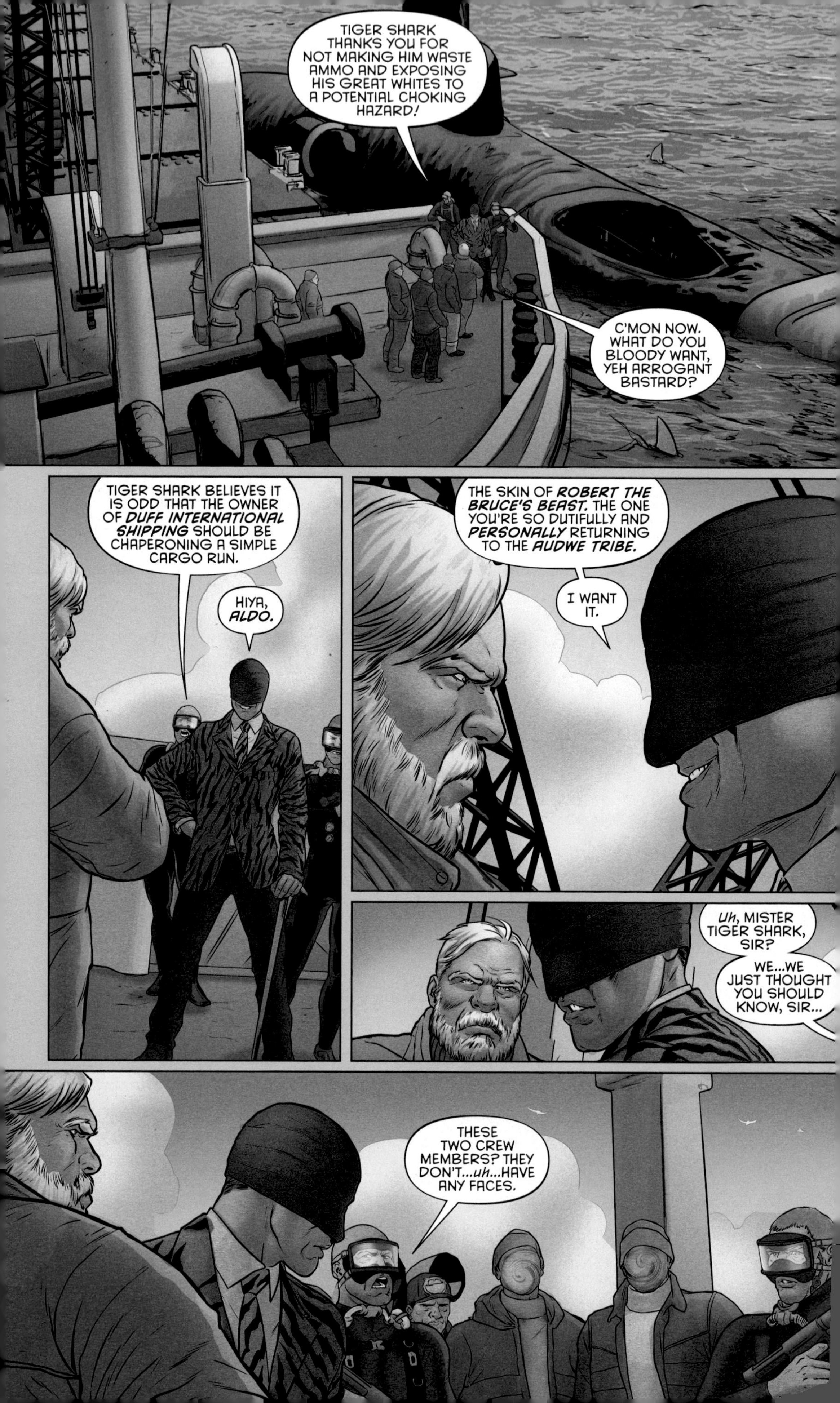

TIGER SHARK THANKS YOU FOR NOT MAKING HIM WASTE AMMO AND EXPOSING HIS GREAT WHITES TO A POTENTIAL CHOKING HAZARD!
C'MON NOW. WHAT DO YOU BLOODY WANT, YEH ARROGANT BASTARD?
TIGER SHARK BELIEVES IT IS ODD THAT THE OWNER OF *DUFF INTERNATIONAL SHIPPING* SHOULD BE CHAPERONING A SIMPLE CARGO RUN.
HIYA, *ALDO.*
THE SKIN OF *ROBERT THE BRUCE'S BEAST.* THE ONE YOU'RE SO DUTIFULLY AND *PERSONALLY* RETURNING TO THE *AUDWE TRIBE.*
I WANT IT.
UH, MISTER TIGER SHARK, SIR?
WE...WE JUST THOUGHT YOU SHOULD KNOW, SIR...
THESE TWO CREW MEMBERS? THEY DON'T...*UH*...HAVE ANY FACES.

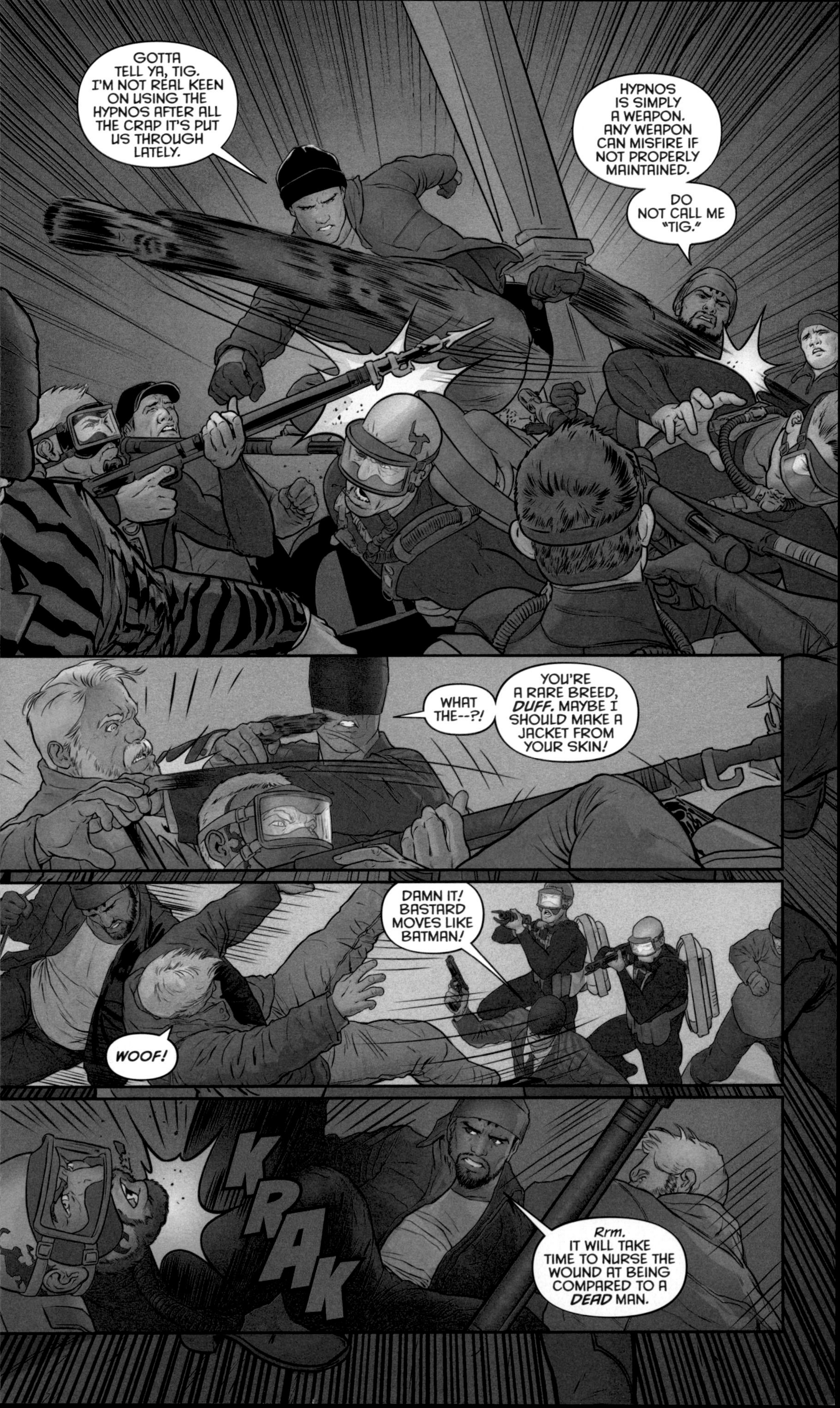
GOTTA TELL YA, TIG. I'M NOT REAL KEEN ON USING THE HYPNOS AFTER ALL THE CRAP IT'S PUT US THROUGH LATELY.
HYPNOS IS SIMPLY A WEAPON. ANY WEAPON CAN MISFIRE IF NOT PROPERLY MAINTAINED.
DO NOT CALL ME "TIG."
WHAT THE--?!
YOU'RE A RARE BREED, DUFF. MAYBE I SHOULD MAKE A JACKET FROM YOUR SKIN!
DAMN IT! BASTARD MOVES LIKE BATMAN!
WOOF!
KRAK
Rrm. IT WILL TAKE TIME TO NURSE THE WOUND AT BEING COMPARED TO A DEAD MAN.

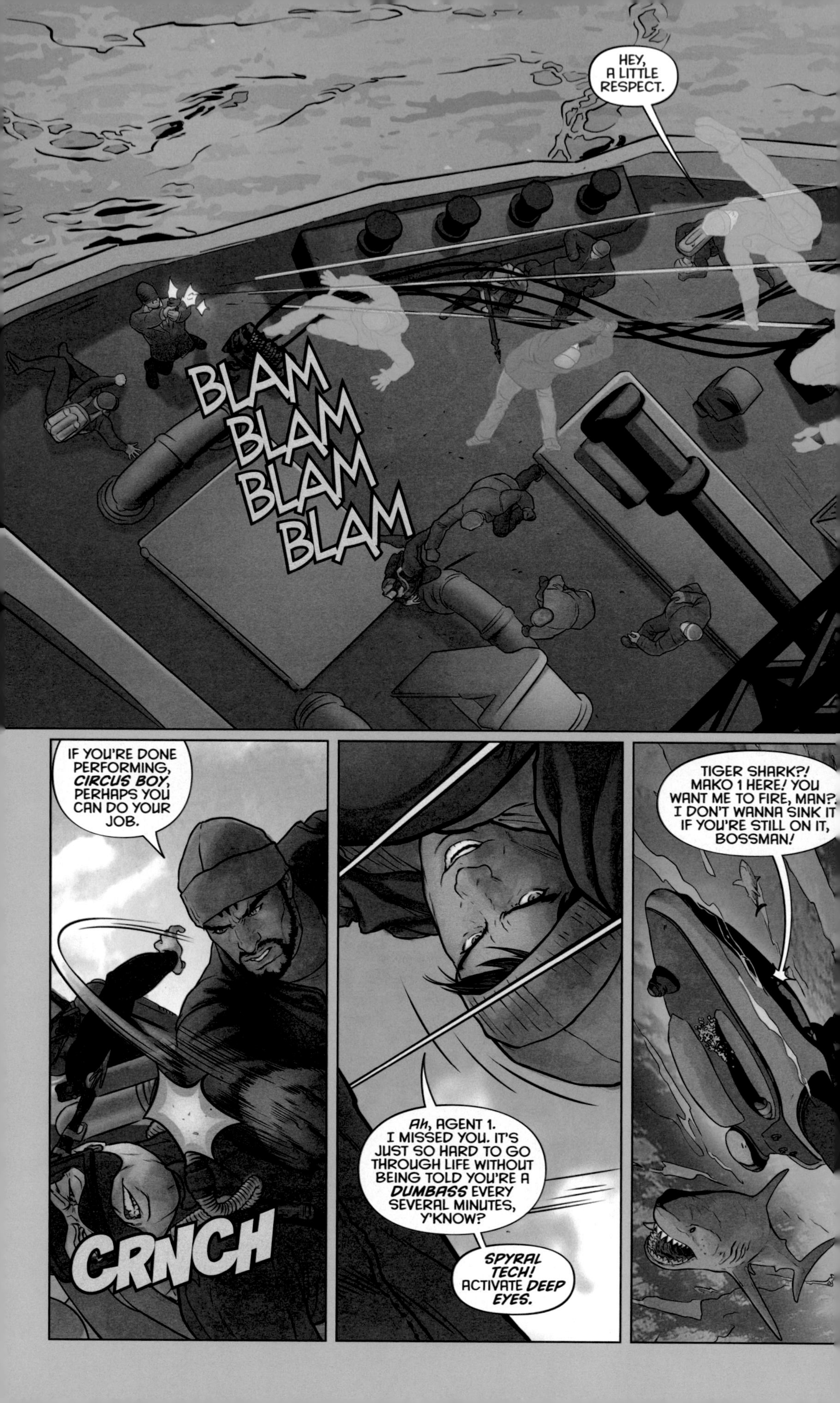

HEY, A LITTLE RESPECT.
BLAM BLAM BLAM BLAM
IF YOU'RE DONE PERFORMING, *CIRCUS BOY*, PERHAPS YOU CAN DO YOUR JOB.
CRNCH
Ah, AGENT 1. I MISSED YOU. IT'S JUST SO HARD TO GO THROUGH LIFE WITHOUT BEING TOLD YOU'RE A *DUMBASS* EVERY SEVERAL MINUTES, Y'KNOW?
SPYRAL TECH! ACTIVATE *DEEP EYES.*
TIGER SHARK?! MAKO 1 HERE! YOU WANT ME TO FIRE, MAN?. I DON'T WANNA SINK IT IF YOU'RE STILL ON IT, BOSSMAN!

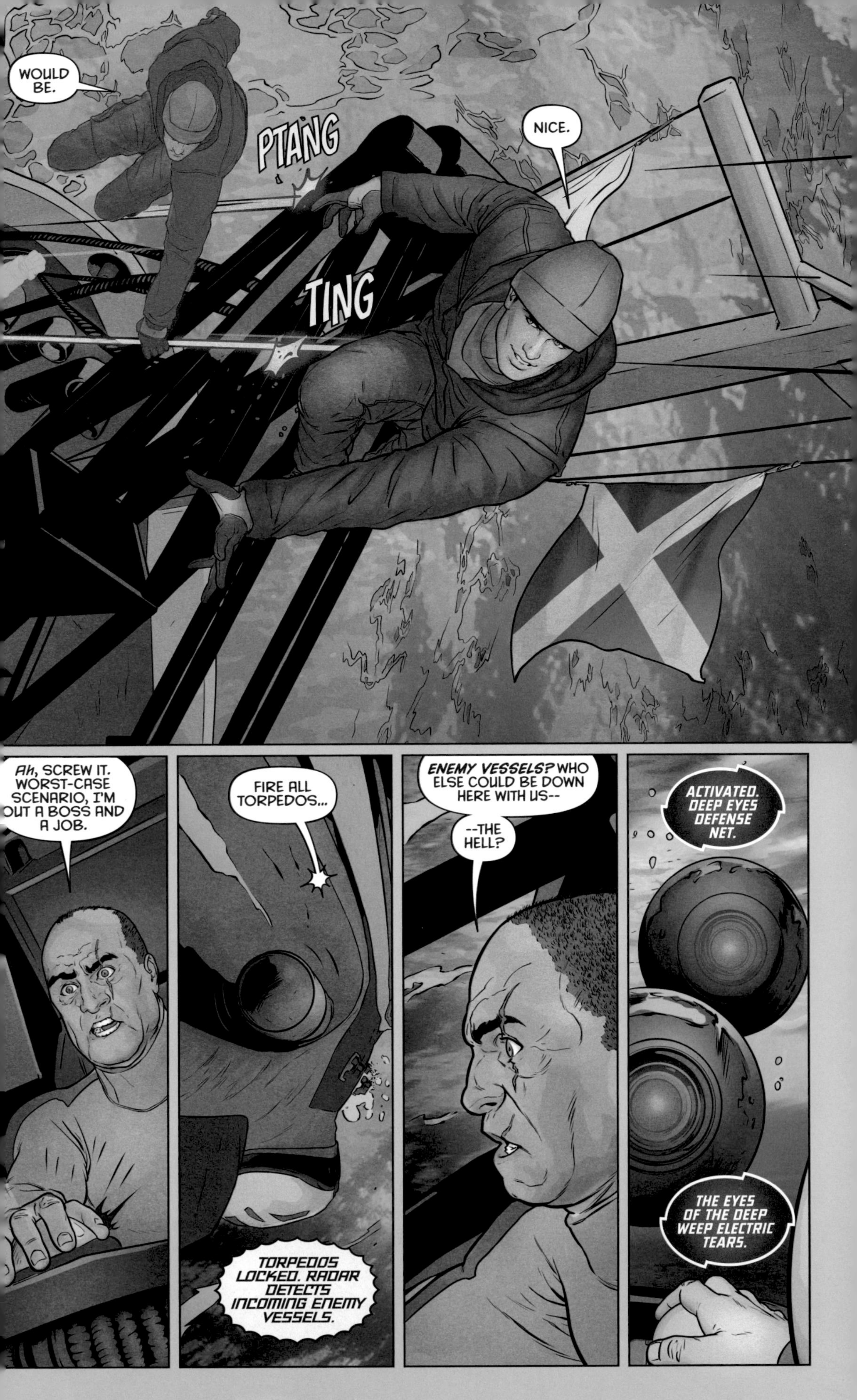

WOULD BE.
PTANG
NICE.
TING
Ah, SCREW IT. WORST-CASE SCENARIO, I'M OUT A BOSS AND A JOB.
FIRE ALL TORPEDOS...
TORPEDOS LOCKED. RADAR DETECTS INCOMING ENEMY VESSELS.
ENEMY VESSELS? WHO ELSE COULD BE DOWN HERE WITH US--
--THE HELL?
ACTIVATED. DEEP EYES DEFENSE NET.
THE EYES OF THE DEEP WEEP ELECTRIC TEARS.

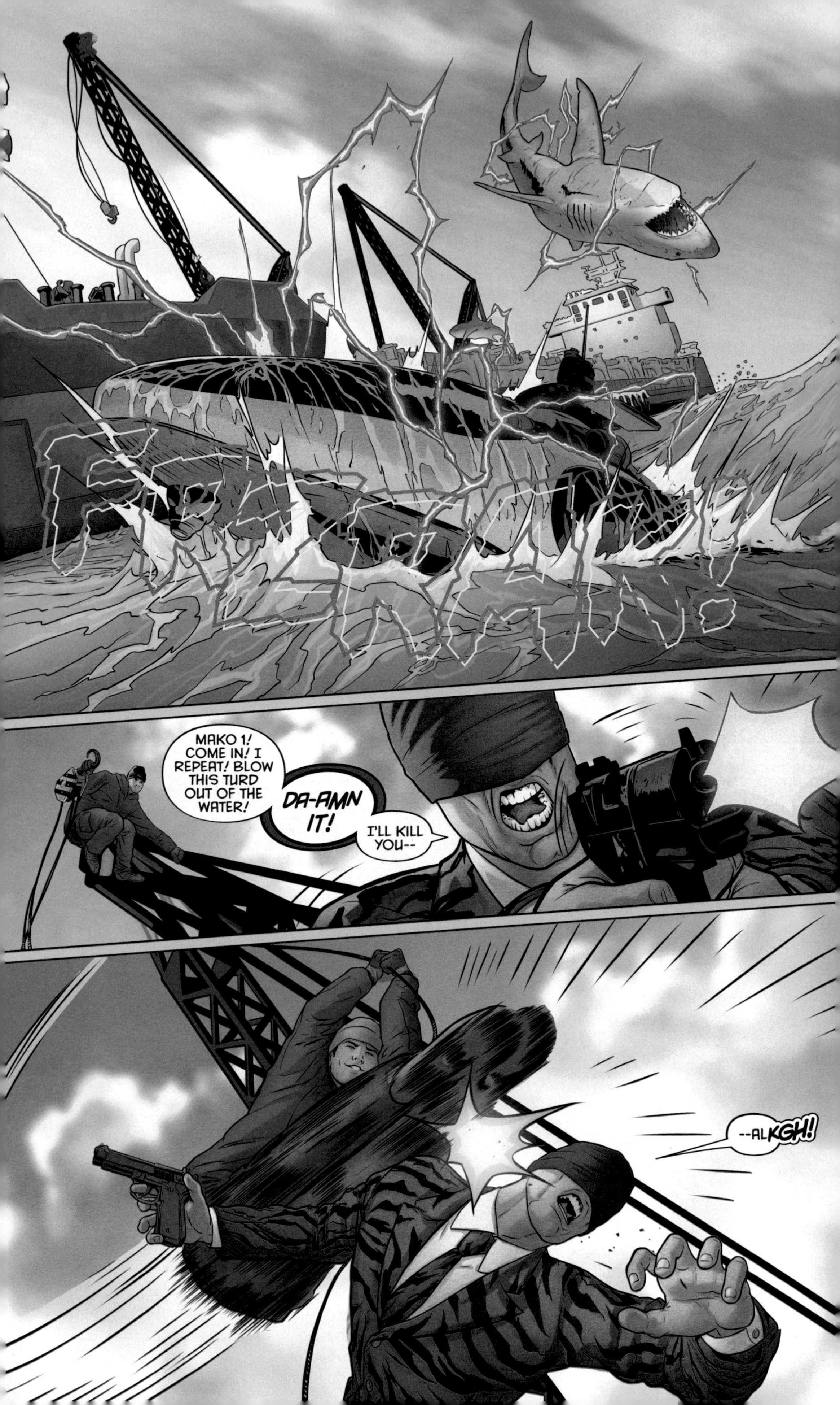
MAKO 1! COME IN! I REPEAT! BLOW THIS TURD OUT OF THE WATER!
DA-AMN IT!
I'LL KILL YOU--
--ALKGH!

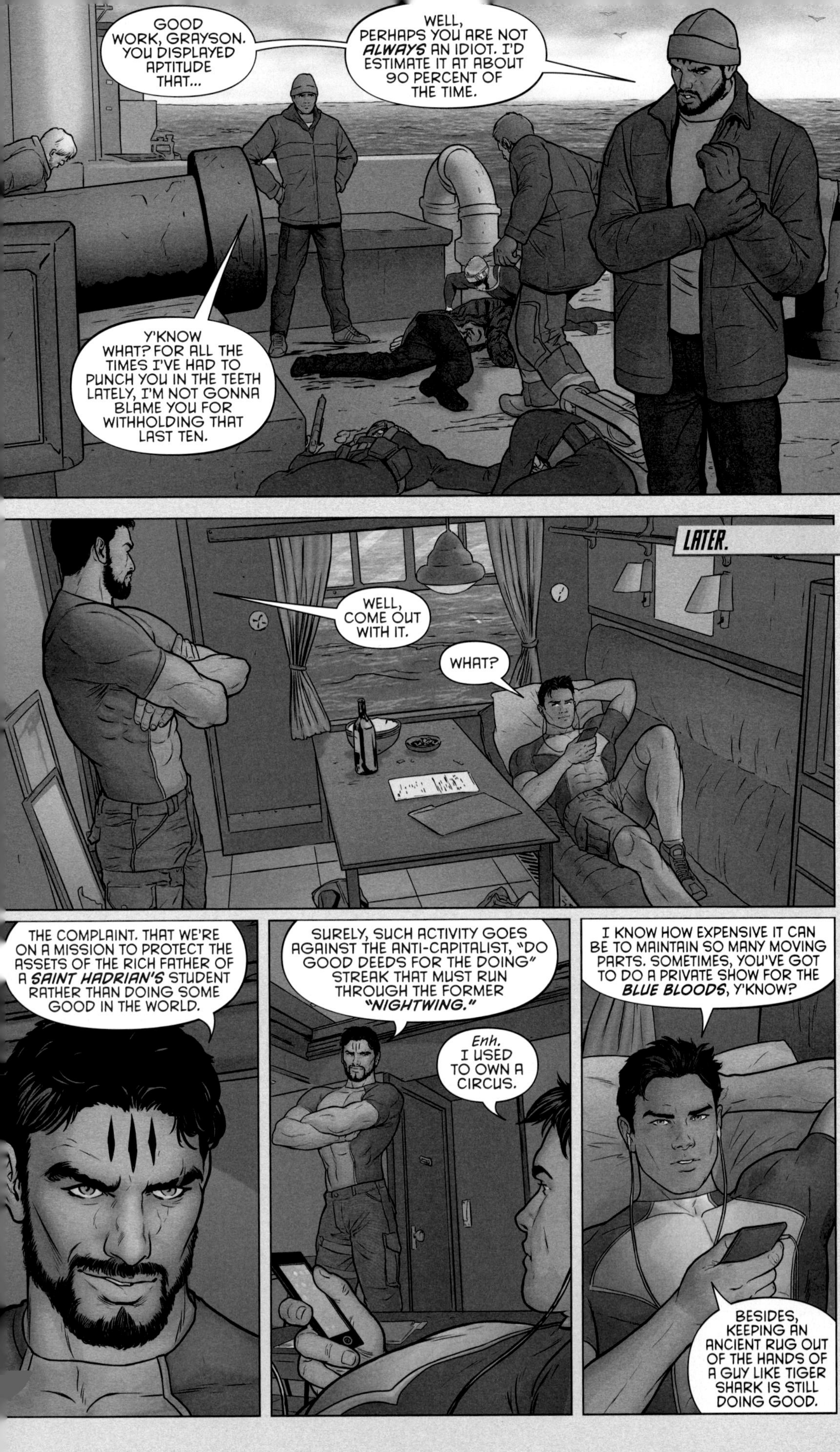
GOOD WORK, GRAYSON. YOU DISPLAYED APTITUDE THAT...
WELL, PERHAPS YOU ARE NOT ALWAYS AN IDIOT. I'D ESTIMATE IT AT ABOUT 90 PERCENT OF THE TIME.
Y'KNOW WHAT? FOR ALL THE TIMES I'VE HAD TO PUNCH YOU IN THE TEETH LATELY, I'M NOT GONNA BLAME YOU FOR WITHHOLDING THAT LAST TEN.
LATER.
WELL, COME OUT WITH IT.
WHAT?
THE COMPLAINT. THAT WE'RE ON A MISSION TO PROTECT THE ASSETS OF THE RICH FATHER OF A SAINT HADRIAN'S STUDENT RATHER THAN DOING SOME GOOD IN THE WORLD.
SURELY, SUCH ACTIVITY GOES AGAINST THE ANTI-CAPITALIST, "DO GOOD DEEDS FOR THE DOING" STREAK THAT MUST RUN THROUGH THE FORMER "NIGHTWING."
Enh. I USED TO OWN A CIRCUS.
I KNOW HOW EXPENSIVE IT CAN BE TO MAINTAIN SO MANY MOVING PARTS. SOMETIMES, YOU'VE GOT TO DO A PRIVATE SHOW FOR THE BLUE BLOODS, Y'KNOW?
BESIDES, KEEPING AN ANCIENT RUG OUT OF THE HANDS OF A GUY LIKE TIGER SHARK IS STILL DOING GOOD.

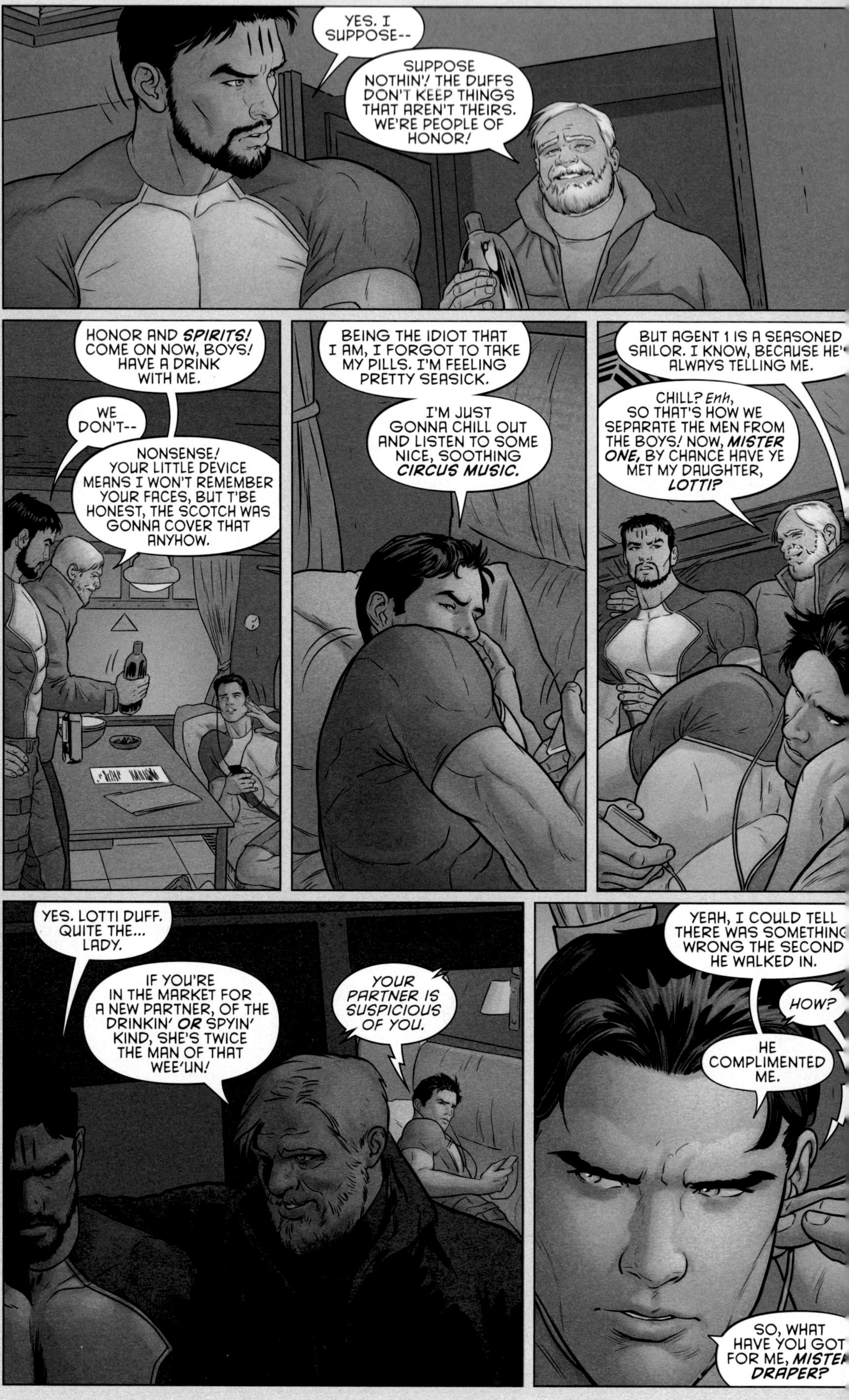
YES. I SUPPOSE--
SUPPOSE NOTHIN'! THE DUFFS DON'T KEEP THINGS THAT AREN'T THEIRS. WE'RE PEOPLE OF HONOR!
HONOR AND SPIRITS! COME ON NOW, BOYS! HAVE A DRINK WITH ME.
WE DON'T--
NONSENSE! YOUR LITTLE DEVICE MEANS I WON'T REMEMBER YOUR FACES, BUT T'BE HONEST, THE SCOTCH WAS GONNA COVER THAT ANYHOW.
BEING THE IDIOT THAT I AM, I FORGOT TO TAKE MY PILLS. I'M FEELING PRETTY SEASICK.
I'M JUST GONNA CHILL OUT AND LISTEN TO SOME NICE, SOOTHING CIRCUS MUSIC.
BUT AGENT 1 IS A SEASONED SAILOR. I KNOW, BECAUSE HE'S ALWAYS TELLING ME.
CHILL? Enh, SO THAT'S HOW WE SEPARATE THE MEN FROM THE BOYS! NOW, MISTER ONE, BY CHANCE HAVE YE MET MY DAUGHTER, LOTTI?
YES. LOTTI DUFF. QUITE THE... LADY.
IF YOU'RE IN THE MARKET FOR A NEW PARTNER, OF THE DRINKIN' OR SPYIN' KIND, SHE'S TWICE THE MAN OF THAT WEE'UN!
YOUR PARTNER IS SUSPICIOUS OF YOU.
YEAH, I COULD TELL THERE WAS SOMETHING WRONG THE SECOND HE WALKED IN.
HOW?
HE COMPLIMENTED ME.
SO, WHAT HAVE YOU GOT FOR ME, MISTER DRAPER?

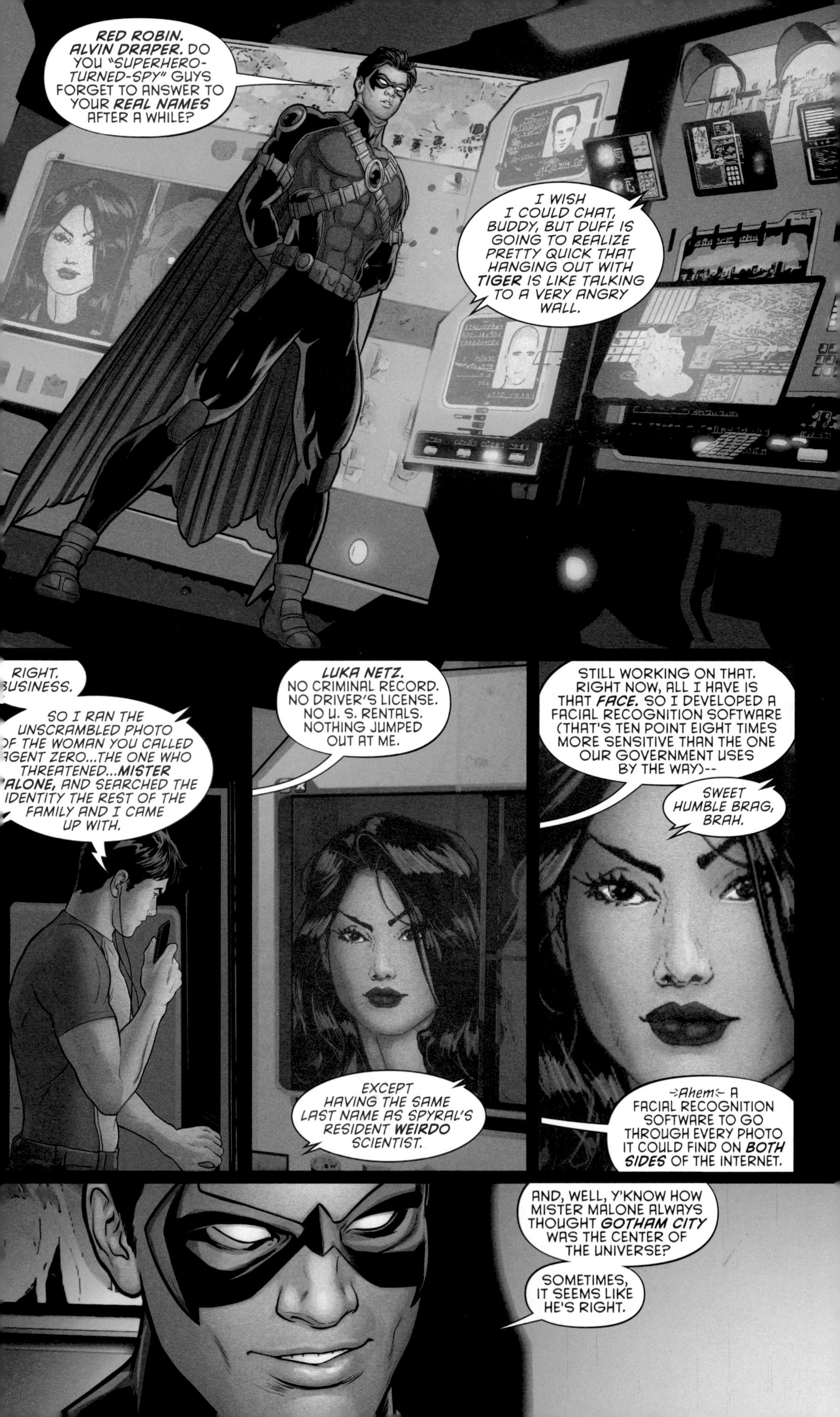
RED ROBIN. ALVIN DRAPER. DO YOU "SUPERHERO-TURNED-SPY" GUYS FORGET TO ANSWER TO YOUR REAL NAMES AFTER A WHILE?
I WISH I COULD CHAT, BUDDY, BUT DUFF IS GOING TO REALIZE PRETTY QUICK THAT HANGING OUT WITH TIGER IS LIKE TALKING TO A VERY ANGRY WALL.
RIGHT. BUSINESS.
SO I RAN THE UNSCRAMBLED PHOTO OF THE WOMAN YOU CALLED AGENT ZERO...THE ONE WHO THREATENED...MISTER MALONE, AND SEARCHED THE IDENTITY THE REST OF THE FAMILY AND I CAME UP WITH.
LUKA NETZ. NO CRIMINAL RECORD. NO DRIVER'S LICENSE. NO U. S. RENTALS. NOTHING JUMPED OUT AT ME.
EXCEPT HAVING THE SAME LAST NAME AS SPYRAL'S RESIDENT WEIRDO SCIENTIST.
STILL WORKING ON THAT. RIGHT NOW, ALL I HAVE IS THAT FACE. SO I DEVELOPED A FACIAL RECOGNITION SOFTWARE (THAT'S TEN POINT EIGHT TIMES MORE SENSITIVE THAN THE ONE OUR GOVERNMENT USES BY THE WAY)--
SWEET HUMBLE BRAG, BRAH.
-Ahem- A FACIAL RECOGNITION SOFTWARE TO GO THROUGH EVERY PHOTO IT COULD FIND ON BOTH SIDES OF THE INTERNET.
AND, WELL, Y'KNOW HOW MISTER MALONE ALWAYS THOUGHT GOTHAM CITY WAS THE CENTER OF THE UNIVERSE?
SOMETIMES, IT SEEMS LIKE HE'S RIGHT.

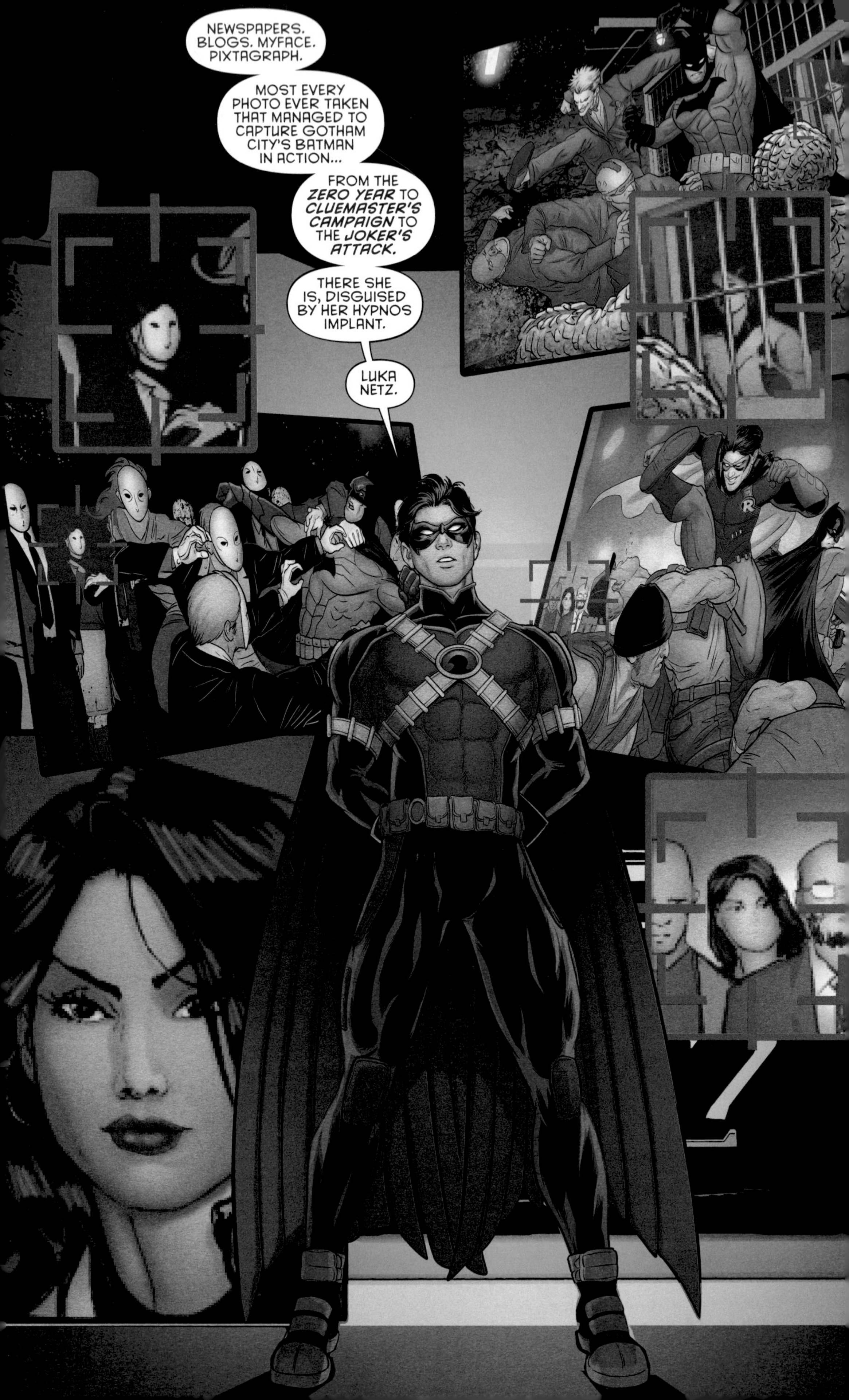
NEWSPAPERS. BLOGS. MYFACE. PIXTAGRAPH.
MOST EVERY PHOTO EVER TAKEN THAT MANAGED TO CAPTURE GOTHAM CITY'S BATMAN IN ACTION...
FROM THE ZERO YEAR TO CLUEMASTER'S CAMPAIGN TO THE JOKER'S ATTACK.
THERE SHE IS, DISGUISED BY HER HYPNOS IMPLANT.
LUKA NETZ.

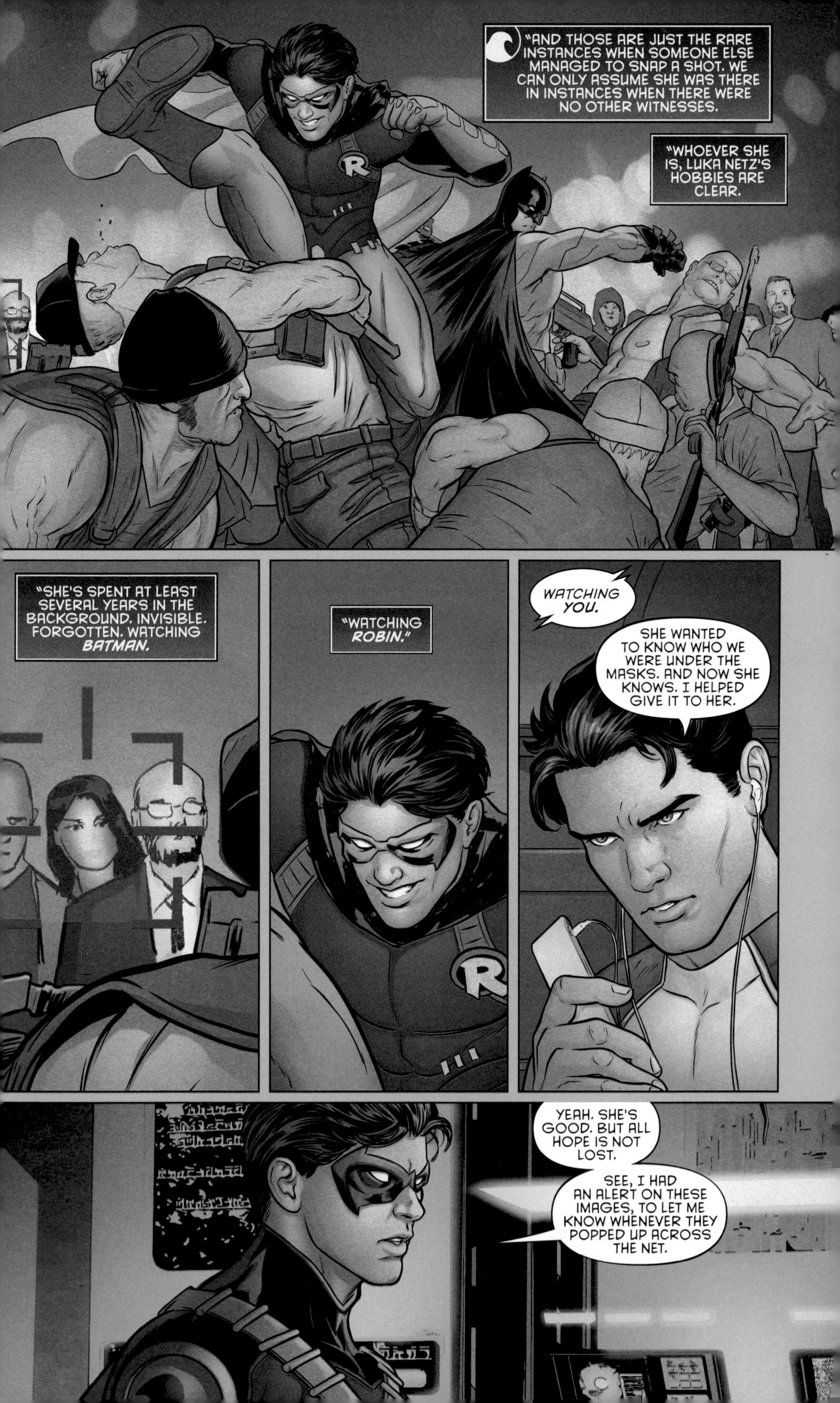
"AND THOSE ARE JUST THE RARE INSTANCES WHEN SOMEONE ELSE MANAGED TO SNAP A SHOT. WE CAN ONLY ASSUME SHE WAS THERE IN INSTANCES WHEN THERE WERE NO OTHER WITNESSES.
"WHOEVER SHE IS, LUKA NETZ'S HOBBIES ARE CLEAR.
"SHE'S SPENT AT LEAST SEVERAL YEARS IN THE BACKGROUND. INVISIBLE. FORGOTTEN. WATCHING *BATMAN.*
"WATCHING *ROBIN.*"
WATCHING *YOU.*
SHE WANTED TO KNOW WHO WE WERE UNDER THE MASKS. AND NOW SHE KNOWS. I HELPED GIVE IT TO HER.
YEAH. SHE'S GOOD. BUT ALL HOPE IS NOT LOST.
SEE, I HAD AN ALERT ON THESE IMAGES, TO LET ME KNOW WHENEVER THEY POPPED UP ACROSS THE NET.

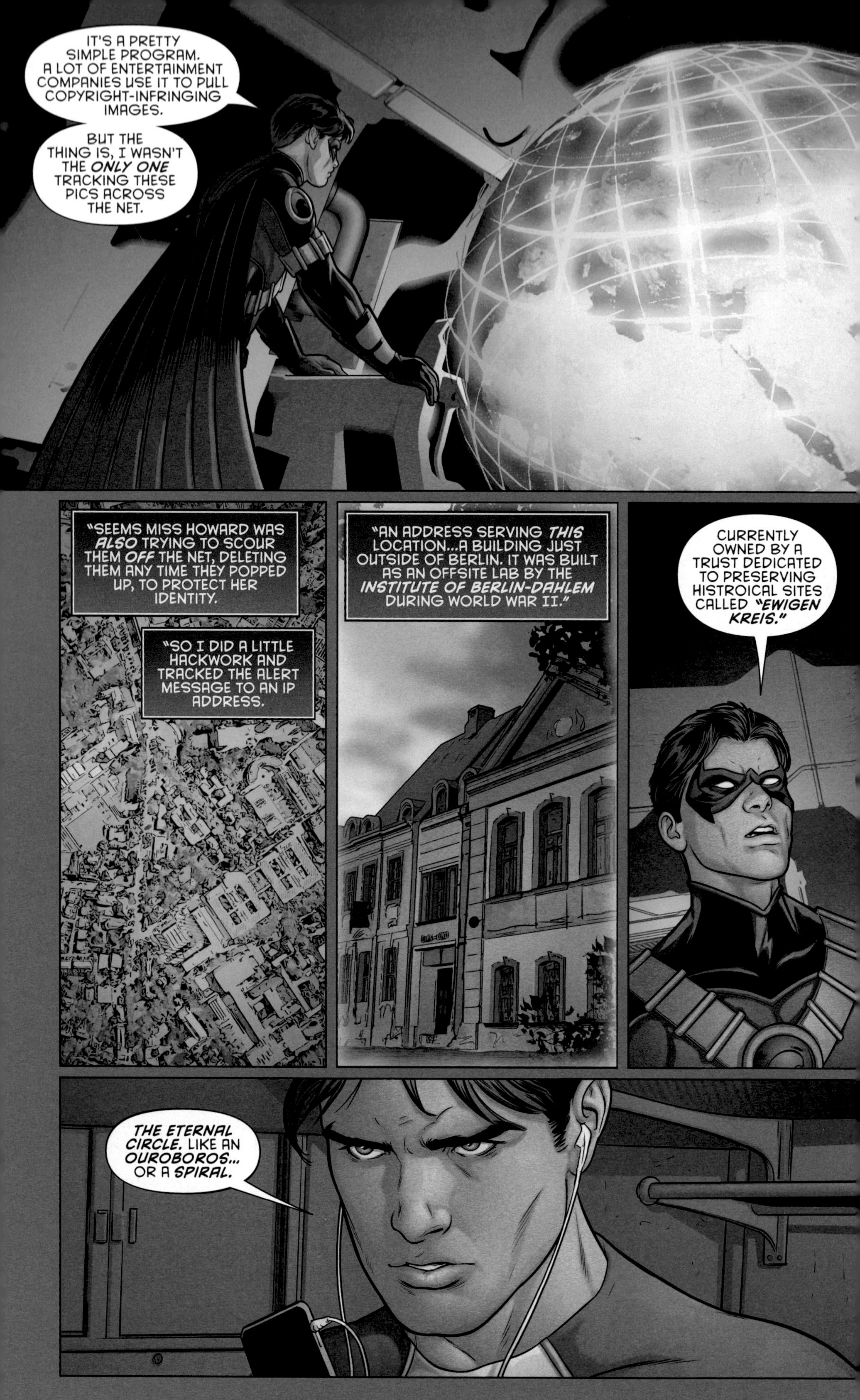

IT'S A PRETTY SIMPLE PROGRAM. A LOT OF ENTERTAINMENT COMPANIES USE IT TO PULL COPYRIGHT-INFRINGING IMAGES.
BUT THE THING IS, I WASN'T THE *ONLY ONE* TRACKING THESE PICS ACROSS THE NET.
"SEEMS MISS HOWARD WAS *ALSO* TRYING TO SCOUR THEM *OFF* THE NET, DELETING THEM ANY TIME THEY POPPED UP, TO PROTECT HER IDENTITY.
"SO I DID A LITTLE HACKWORK AND TRACKED THE ALERT MESSAGE TO AN IP ADDRESS.
"AN ADDRESS SERVING *THIS* LOCATION...A BUILDING JUST OUTSIDE OF BERLIN. IT WAS BUILT AS AN OFFSITE LAB BY THE *INSTITUTE OF BERLIN-DAHLEM* DURING WORLD WAR II."
CURRENTLY OWNED BY A TRUST DEDICATED TO PRESERVING HISTROICAL SITES CALLED *"EWIGEN KREIS."*
THE ETERNAL CIRCLE. LIKE AN *OUROBOROS...* OR A *SPIRAL.*

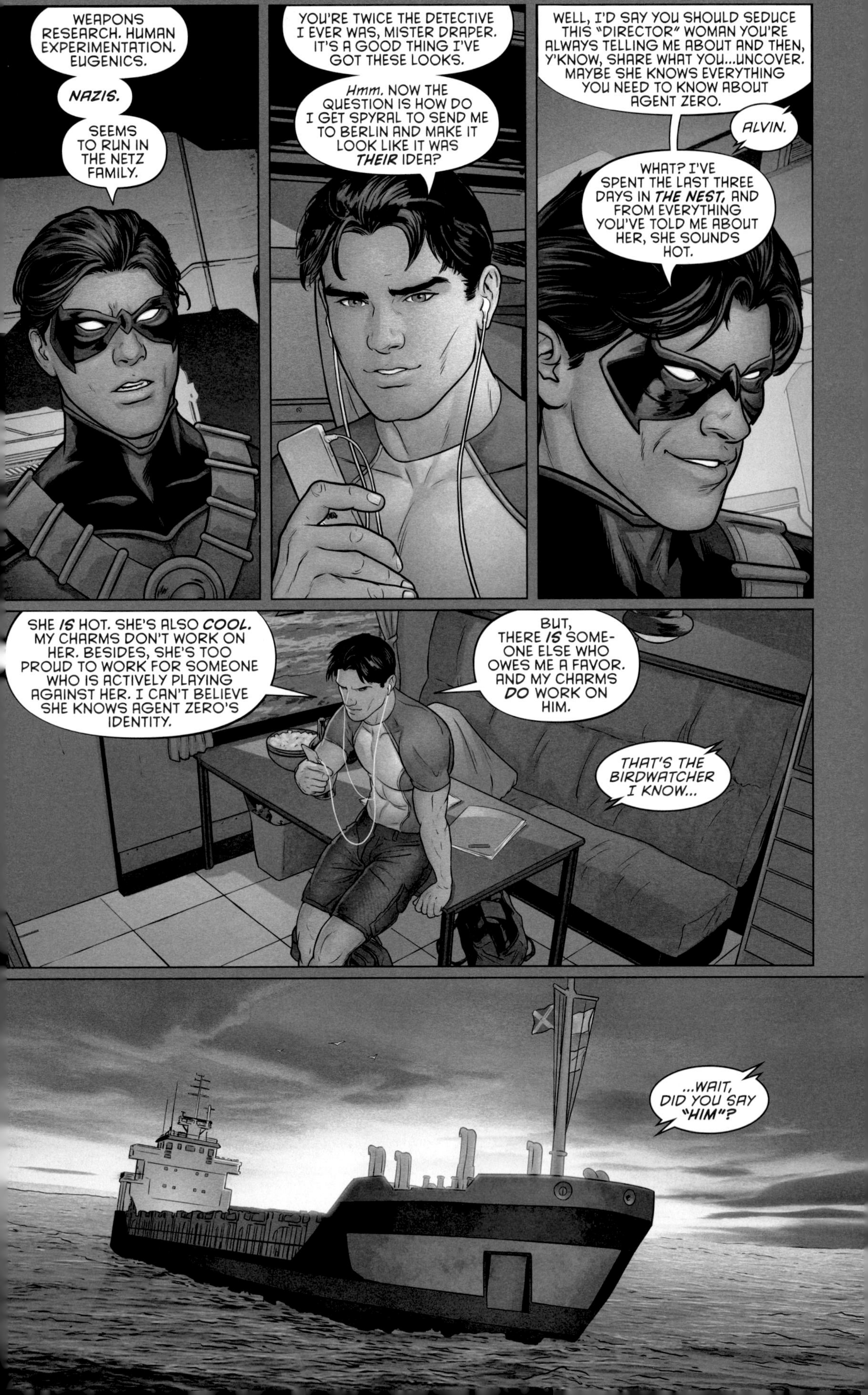
WEAPONS RESEARCH. HUMAN EXPERIMENTATION. EUGENICS.
NAZIS.
SEEMS TO RUN IN THE NETZ FAMILY.
YOU'RE TWICE THE DETECTIVE I EVER WAS, MISTER DRAPER. IT'S A GOOD THING I'VE GOT THESE LOOKS.
Hmm. NOW THE QUESTION IS HOW DO I GET SPYRAL TO SEND ME TO BERLIN AND MAKE IT LOOK LIKE IT WAS THEIR IDEA?
WELL, I'D SAY YOU SHOULD SEDUCE THIS "DIRECTOR" WOMAN YOU'RE ALWAYS TELLING ME ABOUT AND THEN, Y'KNOW, SHARE WHAT YOU...UNCOVER. MAYBE SHE KNOWS EVERYTHING YOU NEED TO KNOW ABOUT AGENT ZERO.
ALVIN.
WHAT? I'VE SPENT THE LAST THREE DAYS IN THE NEST, AND FROM EVERYTHING YOU'VE TOLD ME ABOUT HER, SHE SOUNDS HOT.
SHE IS HOT. SHE'S ALSO COOL. MY CHARMS DON'T WORK ON HER. BESIDES, SHE'S TOO PROUD TO WORK FOR SOMEONE WHO IS ACTIVELY PLAYING AGAINST HER. I CAN'T BELIEVE SHE KNOWS AGENT ZERO'S IDENTITY.
BUT, THERE IS SOME-ONE ELSE WHO OWES ME A FAVOR. AND MY CHARMS DO WORK ON HIM.
THAT'S THE BIRDWATCHER I KNOW...
...WAIT, DID YOU SAY "HIM"?

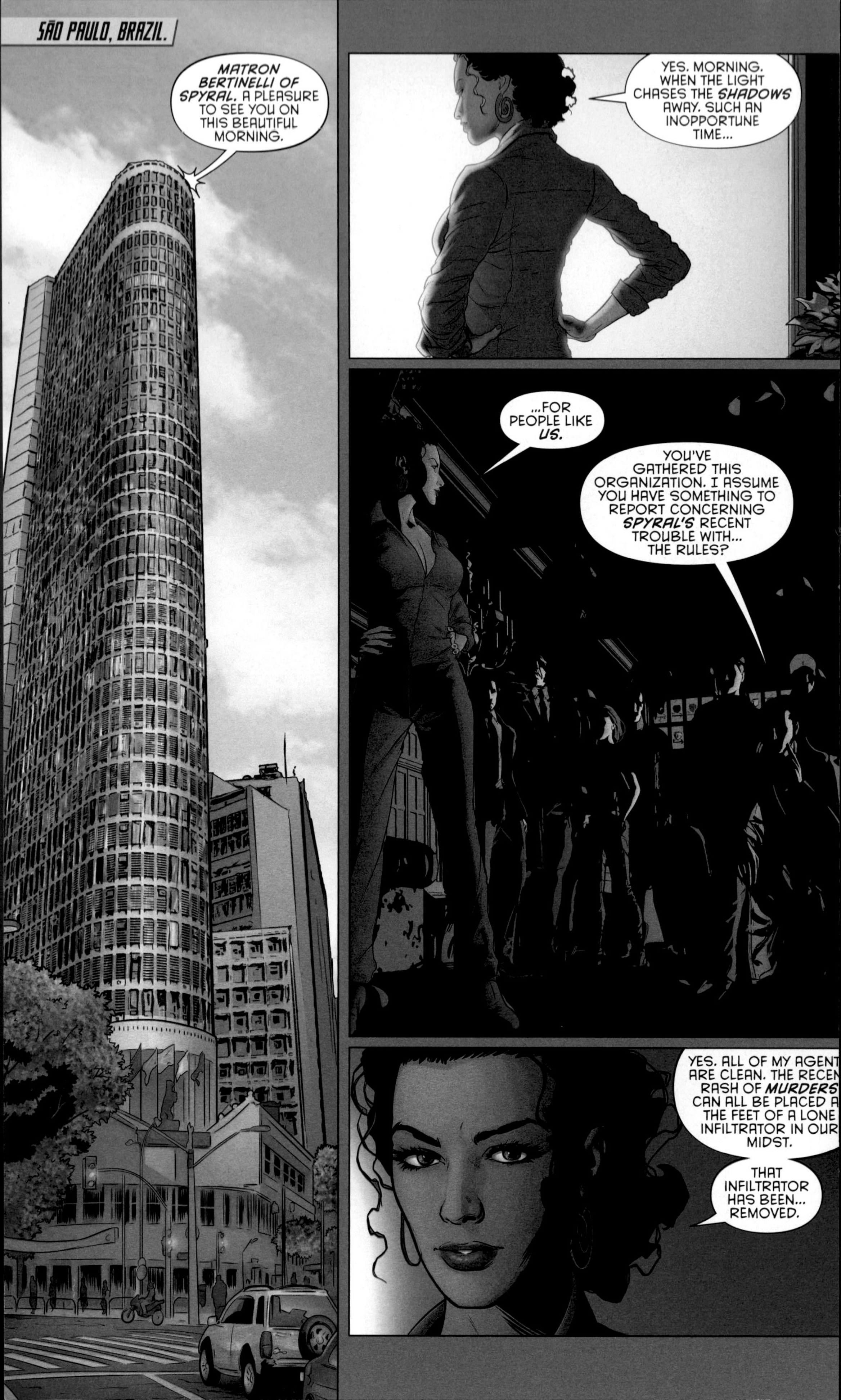
SÃO PAULO, BRAZIL.
MATRON BERTINELLI OF SPYRAL. A PLEASURE TO SEE YOU ON THIS BEAUTIFUL MORNING.
YES. MORNING. WHEN THE LIGHT CHASES THE SHADOWS AWAY. SUCH AN INOPPORTUNE TIME...
...FOR PEOPLE LIKE US.
YOU'VE GATHERED THIS ORGANIZATION. I ASSUME YOU HAVE SOMETHING TO REPORT CONCERNING SPYRAL'S RECENT TROUBLE WITH... THE RULES?
YES. ALL OF MY AGENT ARE CLEAN. THE RECEN RASH OF MURDERS CAN ALL BE PLACED A THE FEET OF A LONE INFILTRATOR IN OUR MIDST.
THAT INFILTRATOR HAS BEEN... REMOVED.

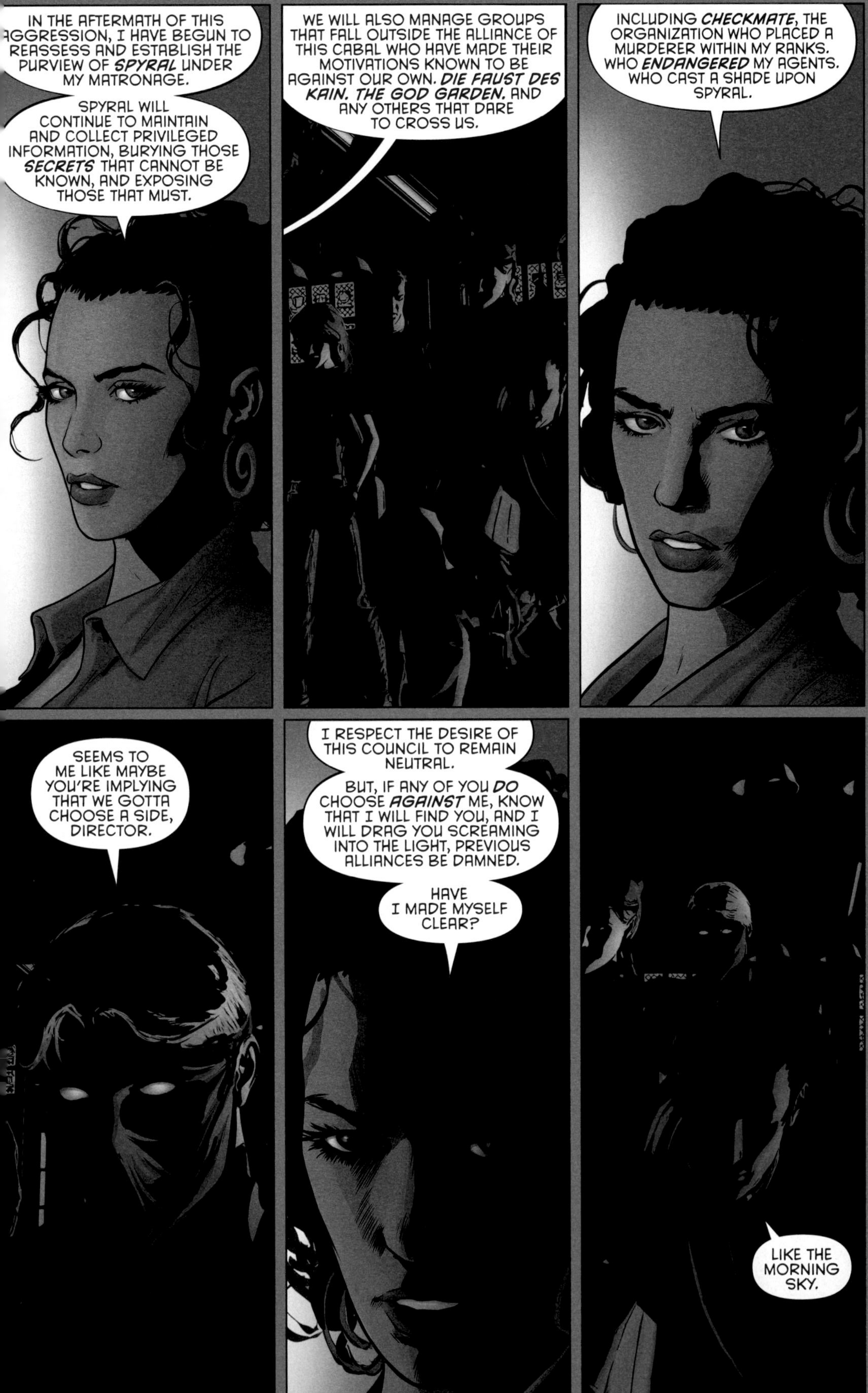
IN THE AFTERMATH OF THIS AGGRESSION, I HAVE BEGUN TO REASSESS AND ESTABLISH THE PURVIEW OF SPYRAL UNDER MY MATRONAGE.
SPYRAL WILL CONTINUE TO MAINTAIN AND COLLECT PRIVILEGED INFORMATION, BURYING THOSE SECRETS THAT CANNOT BE KNOWN, AND EXPOSING THOSE THAT MUST.
WE WILL ALSO MANAGE GROUPS THAT FALL OUTSIDE THE ALLIANCE OF THIS CABAL WHO HAVE MADE THEIR MOTIVATIONS KNOWN TO BE AGAINST OUR OWN. DIE FAUST DES KAIN. THE GOD GARDEN. AND ANY OTHERS THAT DARE TO CROSS US.
INCLUDING CHECKMATE, THE ORGANIZATION WHO PLACED A MURDERER WITHIN MY RANKS. WHO ENDANGERED MY AGENTS. WHO CAST A SHADE UPON SPYRAL.
SEEMS TO ME LIKE MAYBE YOU'RE IMPLYING THAT WE GOTTA CHOOSE A SIDE, DIRECTOR.
I RESPECT THE DESIRE OF THIS COUNCIL TO REMAIN NEUTRAL.
BUT, IF ANY OF YOU DO CHOOSE AGAINST ME, KNOW THAT I WILL FIND YOU, AND I WILL DRAG YOU SCREAMING INTO THE LIGHT, PREVIOUS ALLIANCES BE DAMNED.
HAVE I MADE MYSELF CLEAR?
LIKE THE MORNING SKY.

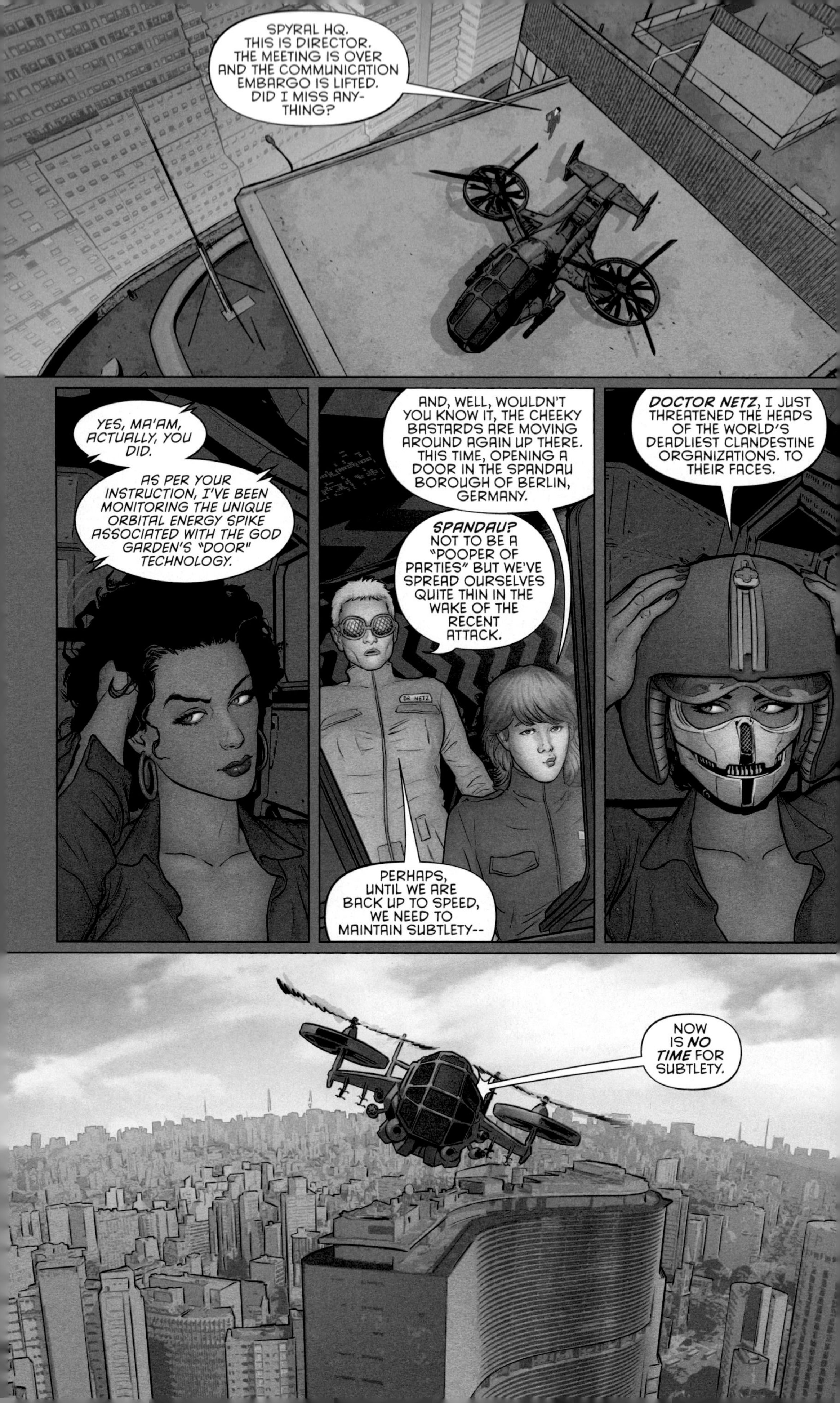
SPYRAL HQ. THIS IS DIRECTOR. THE MEETING IS OVER AND THE COMMUNICATION EMBARGO IS LIFTED. DID I MISS ANY-THING?
YES, MA'AM, ACTUALLY, YOU DID.
AS PER YOUR INSTRUCTION, I'VE BEEN MONITORING THE UNIQUE ORBITAL ENERGY SPIKE ASSOCIATED WITH THE GOD GARDEN'S "DOOR" TECHNOLOGY.
AND, WELL, WOULDN'T YOU KNOW IT, THE CHEEKY BASTARDS ARE MOVING AROUND AGAIN UP THERE. THIS TIME, OPENING A DOOR IN THE SPANDAU BOROUGH OF BERLIN, GERMANY.
SPANDAU? NOT TO BE A "POOPER OF PARTIES" BUT WE'VE SPREAD OURSELVES QUITE THIN IN THE WAKE OF THE RECENT ATTACK.
PERHAPS, UNTIL WE ARE BACK UP TO SPEED, WE NEED TO MAINTAIN SUBTLETY--
DR. NETZ
DOCTOR NETZ, I JUST THREATENED THE HEADS OF THE WORLD'S DEADLIEST CLANDESTINE ORGANIZATIONS. TO THEIR FACES.
NOW IS NO TIME FOR SUBTLETY.

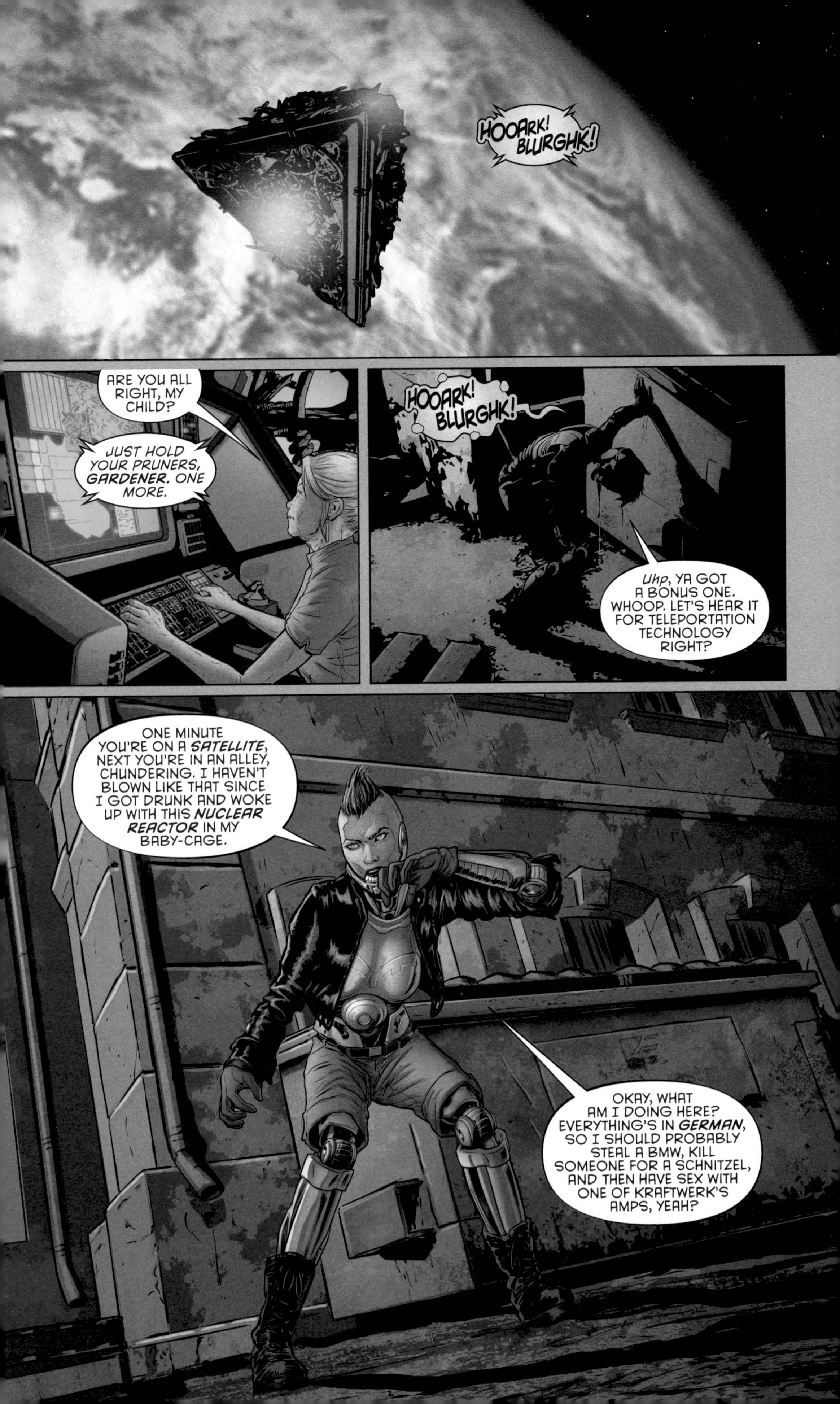
HOOARK! BLURGHK!
ARE YOU ALL RIGHT, MY CHILD?
JUST HOLD YOUR PRUNERS, GARDENER. ONE MORE.
HOOARK! BLURGHK!
Uhp, YA GOT A BONUS ONE. WHOOP. LET'S HEAR IT FOR TELEPORTATION TECHNOLOGY RIGHT?
ONE MINUTE YOU'RE ON A SATELLITE, NEXT YOU'RE IN AN ALLEY, CHUNDERING. I HAVEN'T BLOWN LIKE THAT SINCE I GOT DRUNK AND WOKE UP WITH THIS NUCLEAR REACTOR IN MY BABY-CAGE.
OKAY, WHAT AM I DOING HERE? EVERYTHING'S IN GERMAN, SO I SHOULD PROBABLY STEAL A BMW, KILL SOMEONE FOR A SCHNITZEL, AND THEN HAVE SEX WITH ONE OF KRAFTWERK'S AMPS, YEAH?

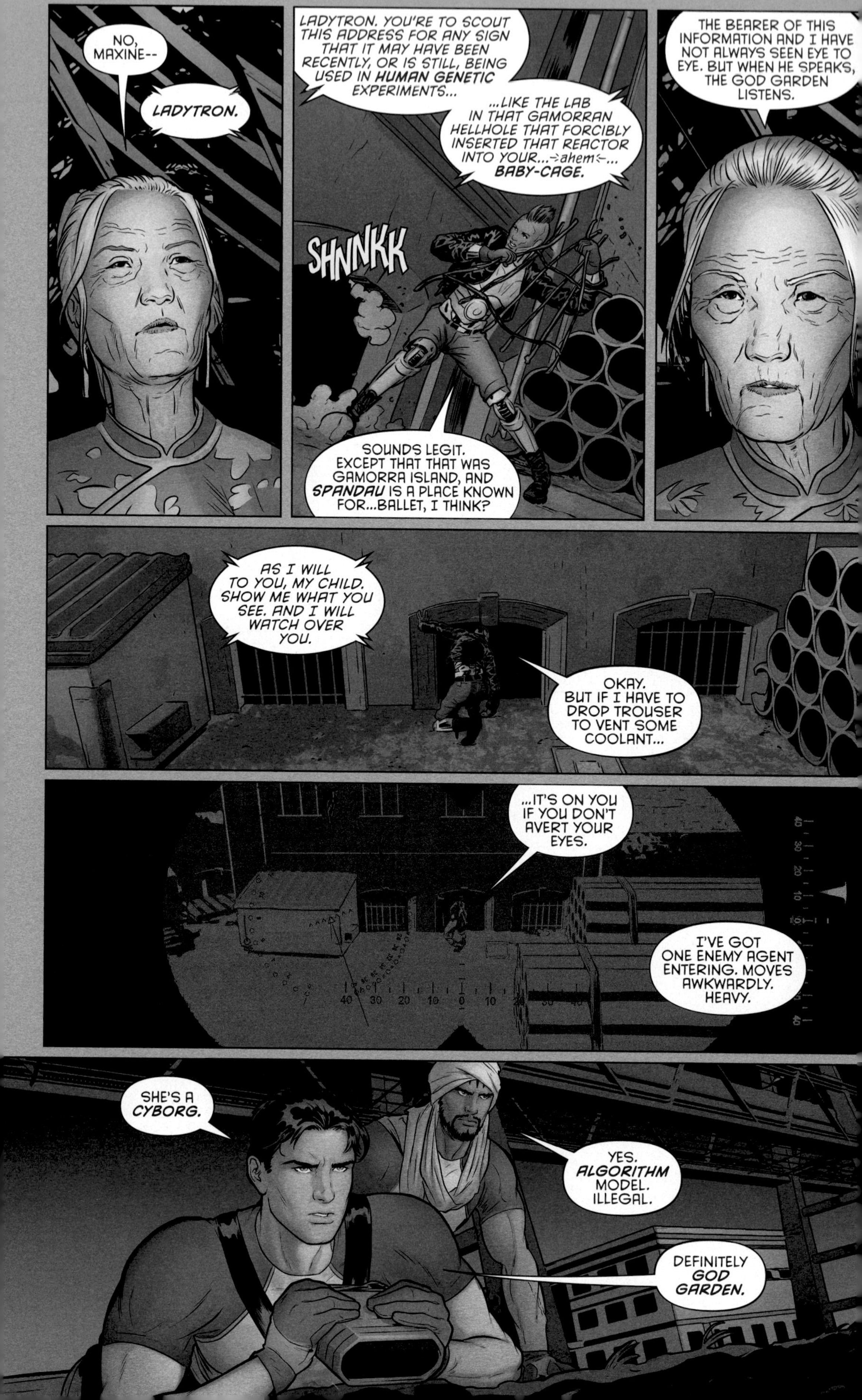
NO, MAXINE--
LADYTRON.
LADYTRON. YOU'RE TO SCOUT THIS ADDRESS FOR ANY SIGN THAT IT MAY HAVE BEEN RECENTLY, OR IS STILL, BEING USED IN HUMAN GENETIC EXPERIMENTS...
...LIKE THE LAB IN THAT GAMORRAN HELLHOLE THAT FORCIBLY INSERTED THAT REACTOR INTO YOUR...ahem... BABY-CAGE.
SHNNKK
SOUNDS LEGIT. EXCEPT THAT THAT WAS GAMORRA ISLAND, AND SPANDAU IS A PLACE KNOWN FOR...BALLET, I THINK?
THE BEARER OF THIS INFORMATION AND I HAVE NOT ALWAYS SEEN EYE TO EYE. BUT WHEN HE SPEAKS, THE GOD GARDEN LISTENS.
AS I WILL TO YOU, MY CHILD. SHOW ME WHAT YOU SEE. AND I WILL WATCH OVER YOU.
OKAY. BUT IF I HAVE TO DROP TROUSER TO VENT SOME COOLANT...
...IT'S ON YOU IF YOU DON'T AVERT YOUR EYES.
I'VE GOT ONE ENEMY AGENT ENTERING. MOVES AWKWARDLY. HEAVY.
SHE'S A CYBORG.
YES. ALGORITHM MODEL. ILLEGAL.
DEFINITELY GOD GARDEN.

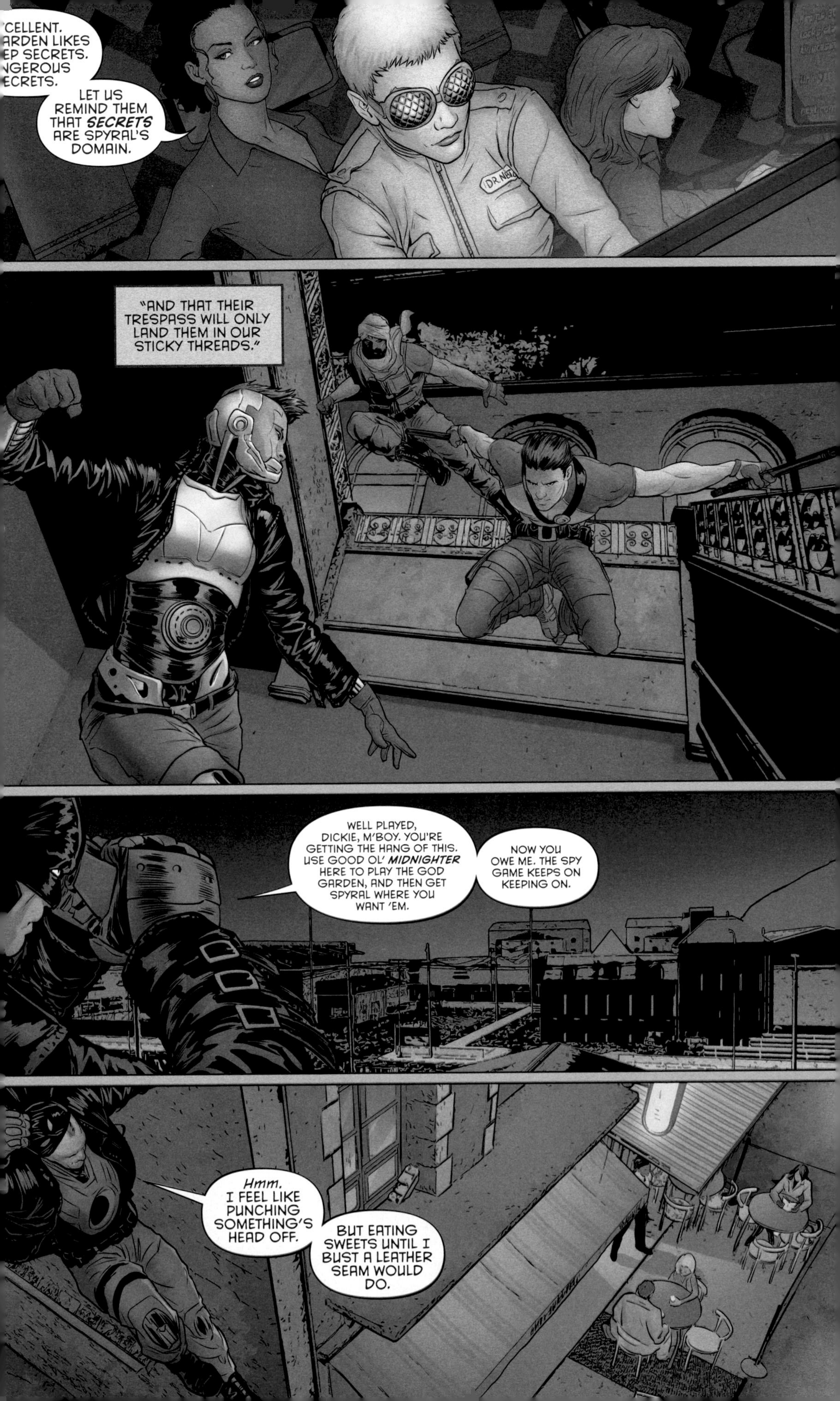
'CELLENT.
ARDEN LIKES
EP SECRETS.
NGEROUS
ECRETS.
LET US REMIND THEM THAT *SECRETS* ARE SPYRAL'S DOMAIN.
DR. NETZ
"AND THAT THEIR TRESPASS WILL ONLY LAND THEM IN OUR STICKY THREADS."
WELL PLAYED, DICKIE, M'BOY. YOU'RE GETTING THE HANG OF THIS. USE GOOD OL' *MIDNIGHTER* HERE TO PLAY THE GOD GARDEN, AND THEN GET SPYRAL WHERE YOU WANT 'EM.
NOW YOU OWE ME. THE SPY GAME KEEPS ON KEEPING ON.
Hmm. I FEEL LIKE PUNCHING SOMETHING'S HEAD OFF.
BUT EATING SWEETS UNTIL I BUST A LEATHER SEAM WOULD DO.

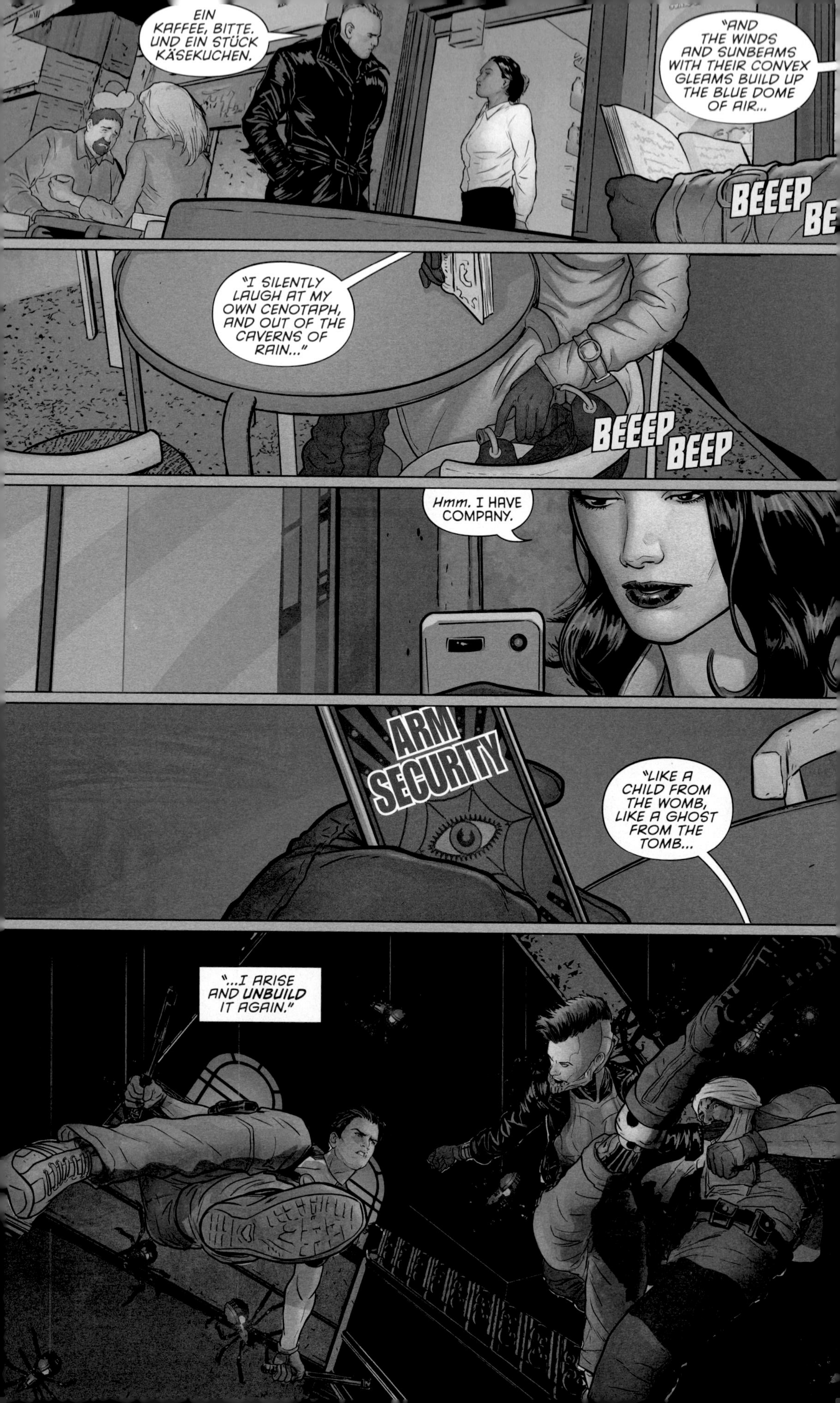
EIN KAFFEE, BITTE. UND EIN STÜCK KÄSEKUCHEN.
"AND THE WINDS AND SUNBEAMS WITH THEIR CONVEX GLEAMS BUILD UP THE BLUE DOME OF AIR...
BEEEP BE
"I SILENTLY LAUGH AT MY OWN CENOTAPH, AND OUT OF THE CAVERNS OF RAIN..."
BEEEP BEEP
Hmm. I HAVE COMPANY.
ARM SECURITY
"LIKE A CHILD FROM THE WOMB, LIKE A GHOST FROM THE TOMB...
"...I ARISE AND UNBUILD IT AGAIN."

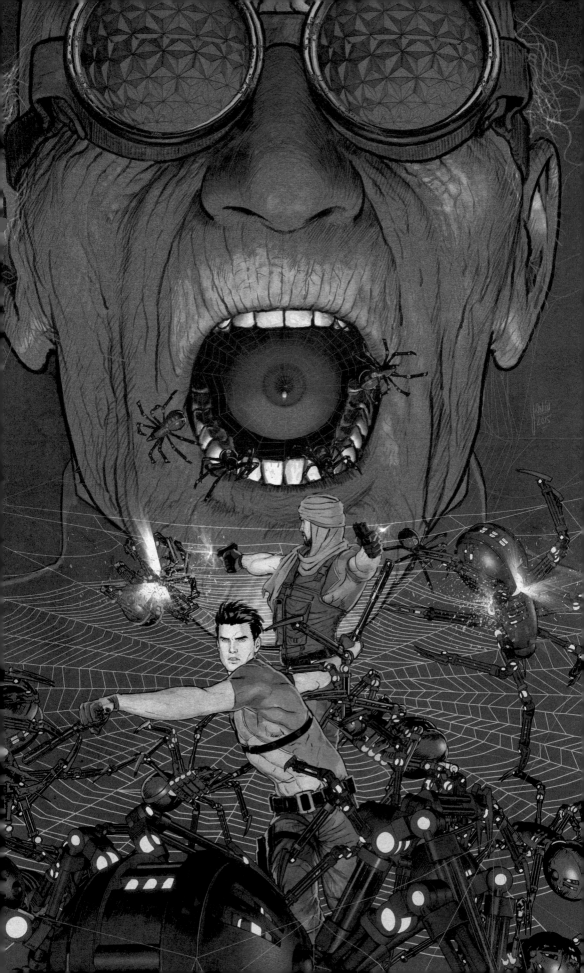

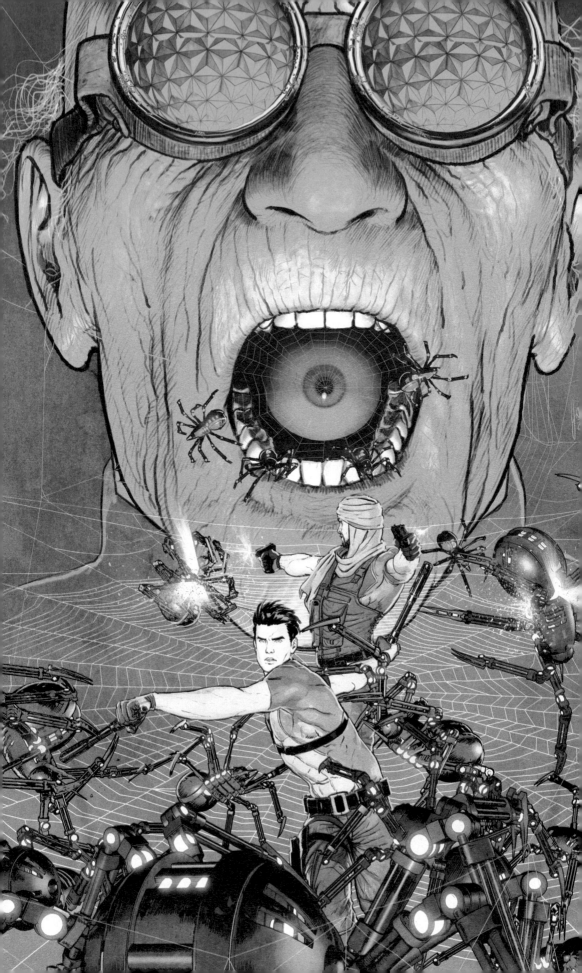

"ONCE UPON A TIME..."

YES. THAT IS THE PERFECT PLACE TO START, ISN'T IT? *ONCE?* IN A MOMENT OF TIME? A SINGLE POINT ON THE INFINITE LINE.

ONCE UPON A TIME, THERE WAS A BRIGHT MAN, AN *UNUSUAL* MAN. ONE NOT BOUND BY PRINCIPALS OF LAW OR MORALITY, BUT WITH A GREAT LOVE FOR HIS LAND.

AND SO, WHEN HIS COUNTRY DECIDED TO FIGHT AGAINST *INJUSTICE*, THIS INTELLIGENT MAN BECAME A SCIENTIST, TASKED WITH MAKING STRONGER SOLDIERS.

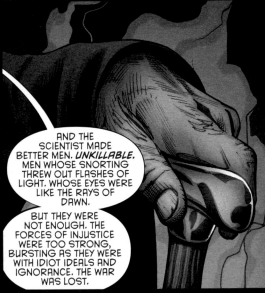

AND THE SCIENTIST MADE BETTER MEN. *UNKILLABLE.* MEN WHOSE SNORTING THREW OUT FLASHES OF LIGHT. WHOSE EYES WERE LIKE THE RAYS OF DAWN.

BUT THEY WERE NOT ENOUGH. THE FORCES OF INJUSTICE WERE TOO STRONG, BURSTING AS THEY WERE WITH IDIOT IDEALS AND IGNORANCE. THE WAR WAS LOST.

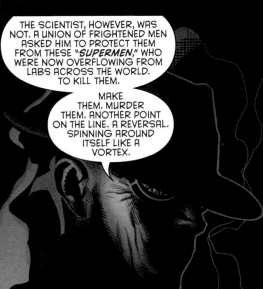

THE SCIENTIST, HOWEVER, WAS NOT. A UNION OF FRIGHTENED MEN ASKED HIM TO PROTECT THEM FROM THESE "*SUPERMEN,*" WHO WERE NOW OVERFLOWING FROM LABS ACROSS THE WORLD. TO KILL THEM.

MAKE THEM. MURDER THEM. ANOTHER POINT ON THE LINE. A REVERSAL. SPINNING AROUND ITSELF LIKE A VORTEX.

AND SO THE SCIENTIST CREATED AN EVER-EXPANDING WEB CALLED *SPYRAL...*

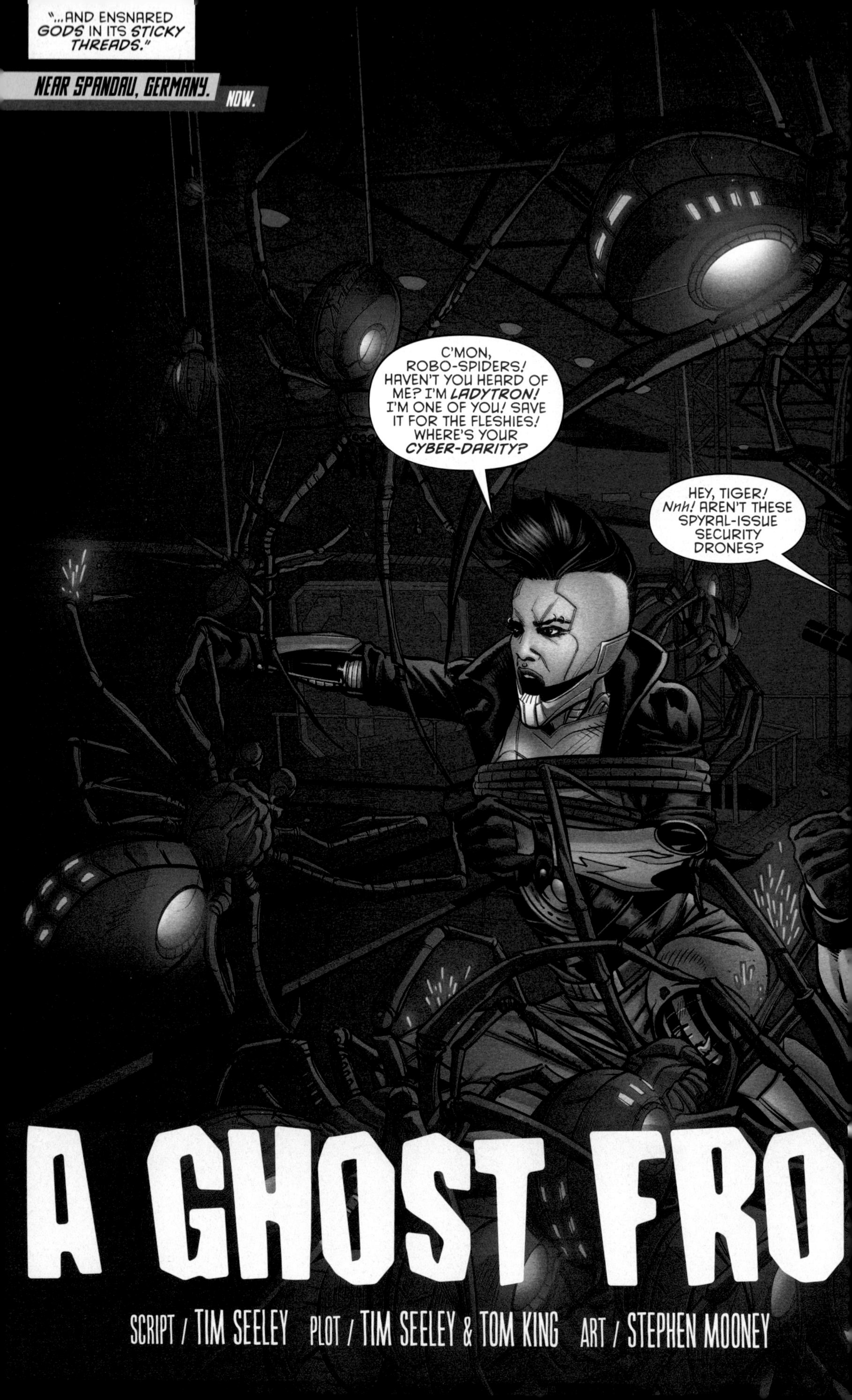
"...AND ENSNARED GODS IN ITS STICKY THREADS."
NEAR SPANDAU, GERMANY.
NOW.
C'MON, ROBO-SPIDERS! HAVEN'T YOU HEARD OF ME? I'M LADYTRON! I'M ONE OF YOU! SAVE IT FOR THE FLESHIES! WHERE'S YOUR CYBER-DARITY?
HEY, TIGER! Nnh! AREN'T THESE SPYRAL-ISSUE SECURITY DRONES?
A GHOST FRO
SCRIPT / TIM SEELEY PLOT / TIM SEELEY & TOM KING ART / STEPHEN MOONEY

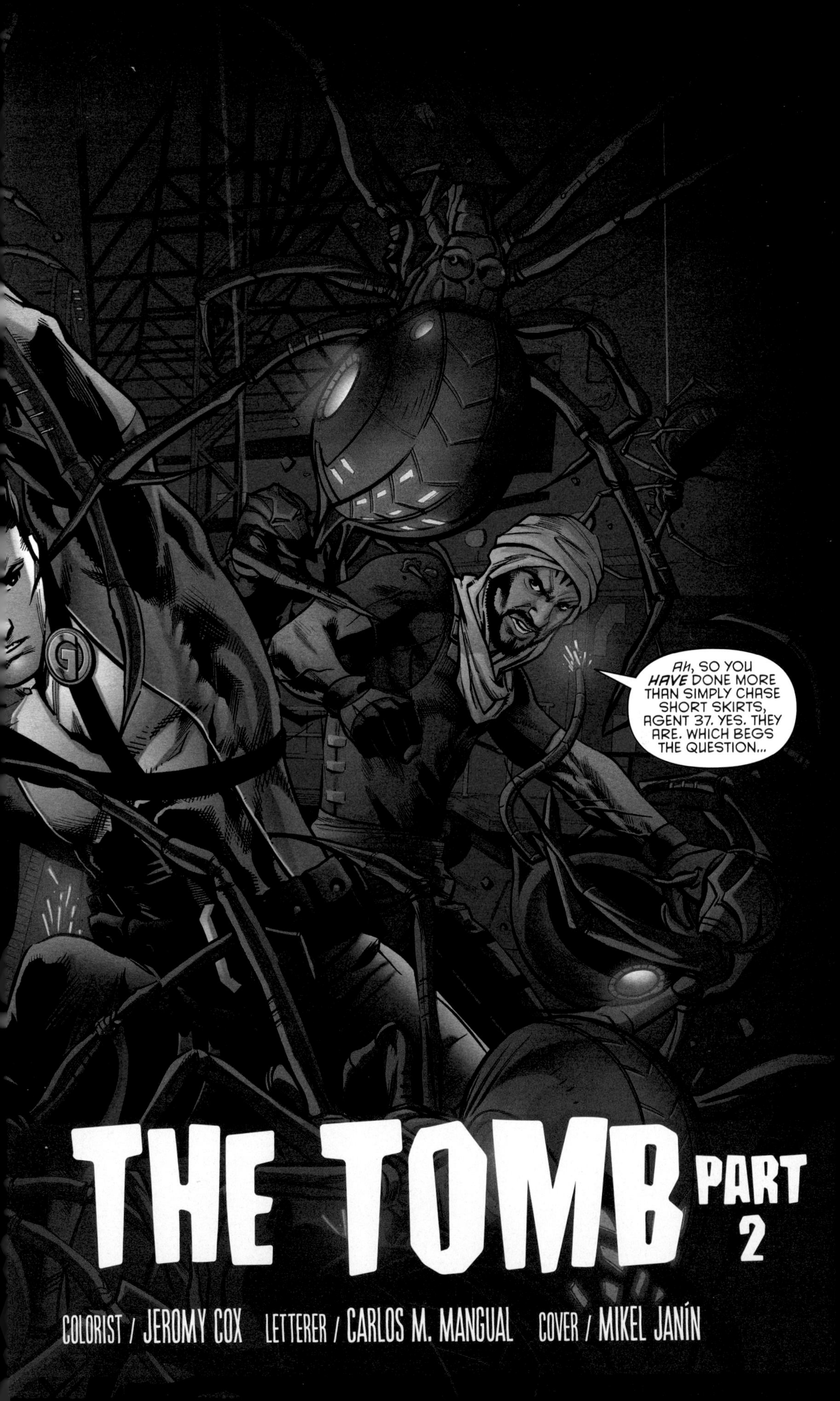

Ah, SO YOU HAVE DONE MORE THAN SIMPLY CHASE SHORT SKIRTS, AGENT 37. YES. THEY ARE. WHICH BEGS THE QUESTION...
THE TOMB PART 2
COLORIST / JEROMY COX LETTERER / CARLOS M. MANGUAL COVER / MIKEL JANÍN

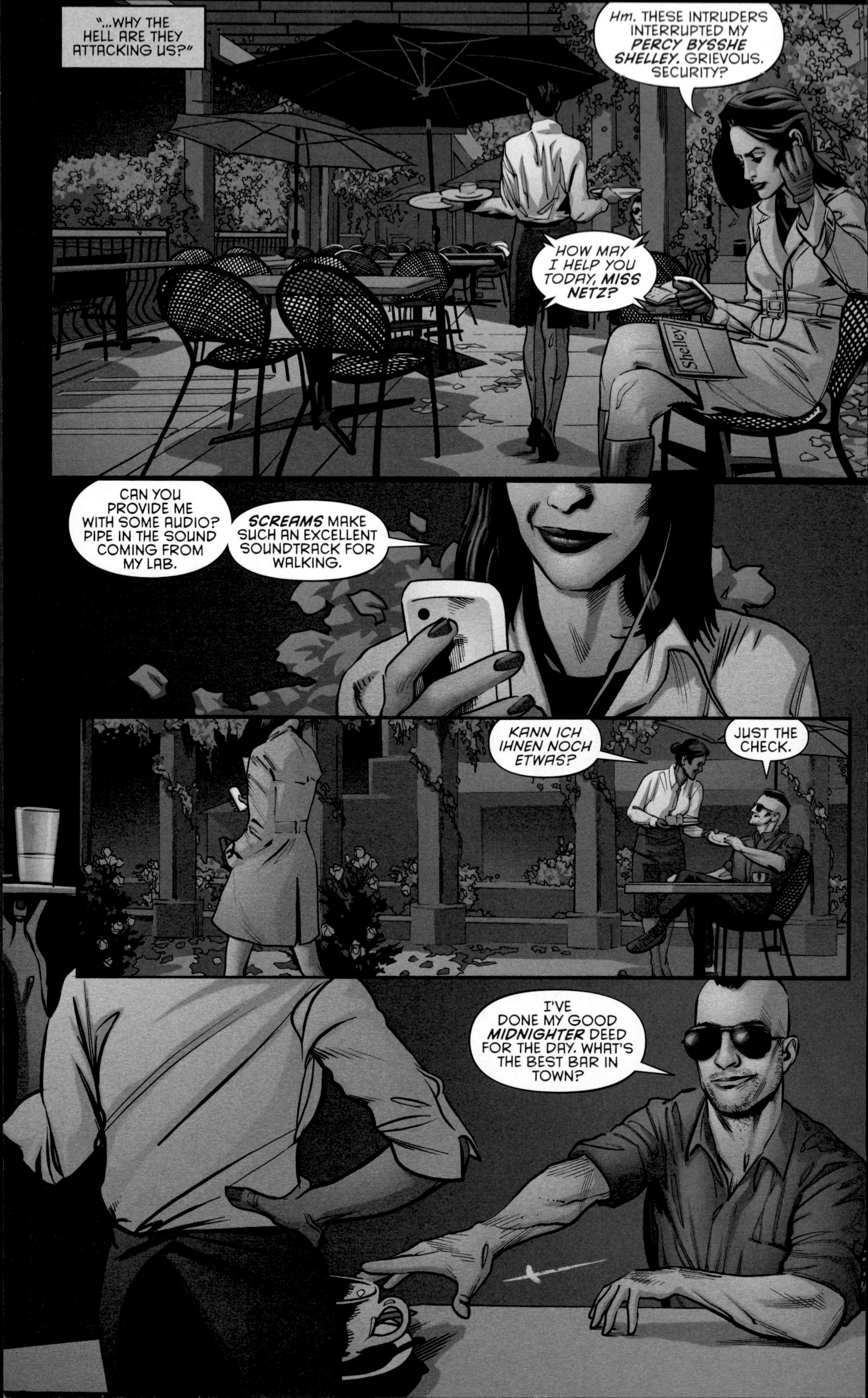
"...WHY THE HELL ARE THEY ATTACKING US?"
Hm. THESE INTRUDERS INTERRUPTED MY PERCY BYSSHE SHELLEY. GRIEVOUS. SECURITY?
HOW MAY I HELP YOU TODAY, MISS NETZ?
Shelley
CAN YOU PROVIDE ME WITH SOME AUDIO? PIPE IN THE SOUND COMING FROM MY LAB.
SCREAMS MAKE SUCH AN EXCELLENT SOUNDTRACK FOR WALKING.
KANN ICH IHNEN NOCH ETWAS?
JUST THE CHECK.
I'VE DONE MY GOOD MIDNIGHTER DEED FOR THE DAY. WHAT'S THE BEST BAR IN TOWN?

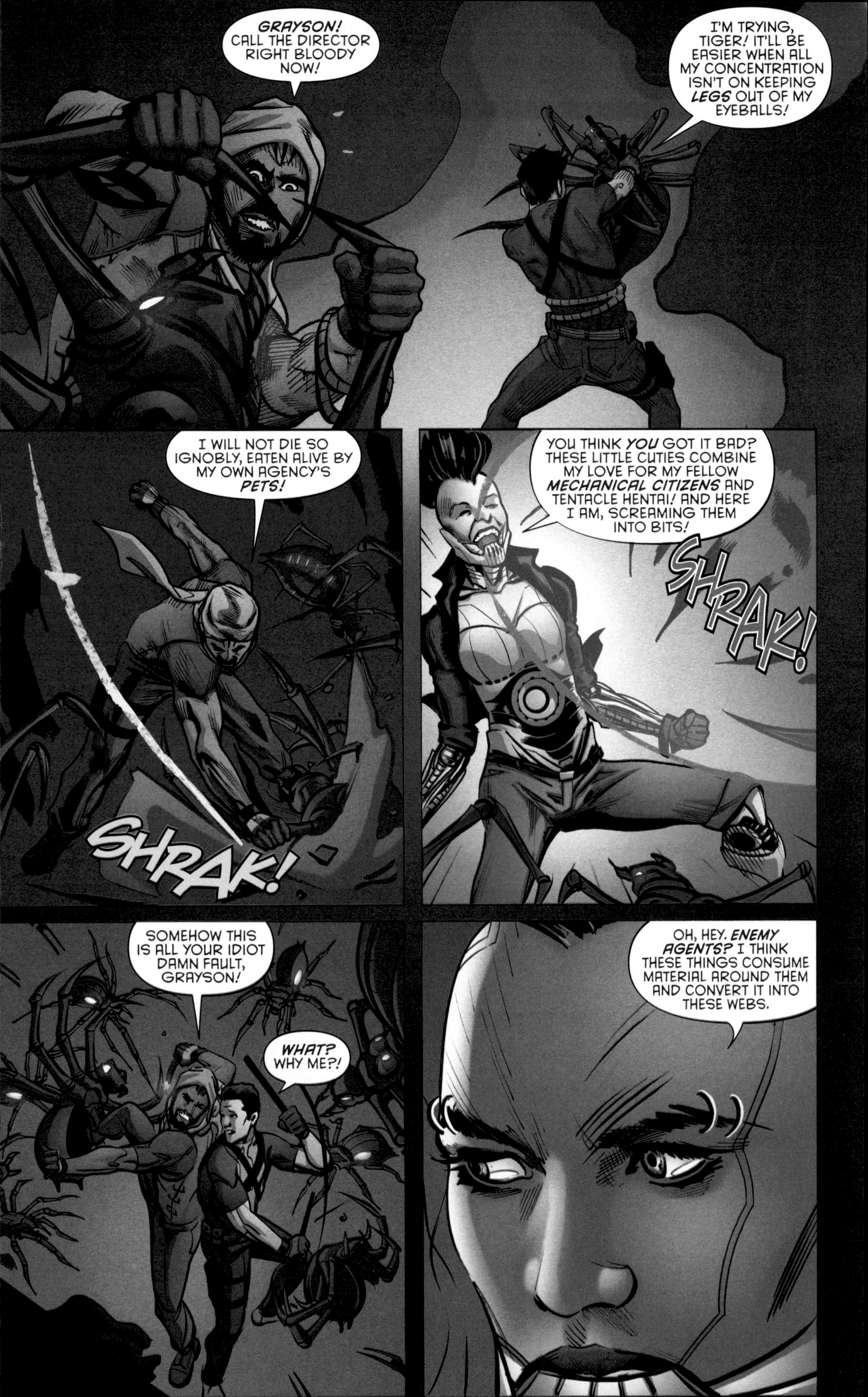
GRAYSON! CALL THE DIRECTOR RIGHT BLOODY NOW!
I'M TRYING, TIGER! IT'LL BE EASIER WHEN ALL MY CONCENTRATION ISN'T ON KEEPING LEGS OUT OF MY EYEBALLS!
I WILL NOT DIE SO IGNOBLY, EATEN ALIVE BY MY OWN AGENCY'S PETS!
SHRAK!
YOU THINK YOU GOT IT BAD? THESE LITTLE CUTIES COMBINE MY LOVE FOR MY FELLOW MECHANICAL CITIZENS AND TENTACLE HENTAI! AND HERE I AM, SCREAMING THEM INTO BITS!
SHRAK!
SOMEHOW THIS IS ALL YOUR IDIOT DAMN FAULT, GRAYSON!
WHAT? WHY ME?!
OH, HEY. ENEMY AGENTS? I THINK THESE THINGS CONSUME MATERIAL AROUND THEM AND CONVERT IT INTO THESE WEBS.

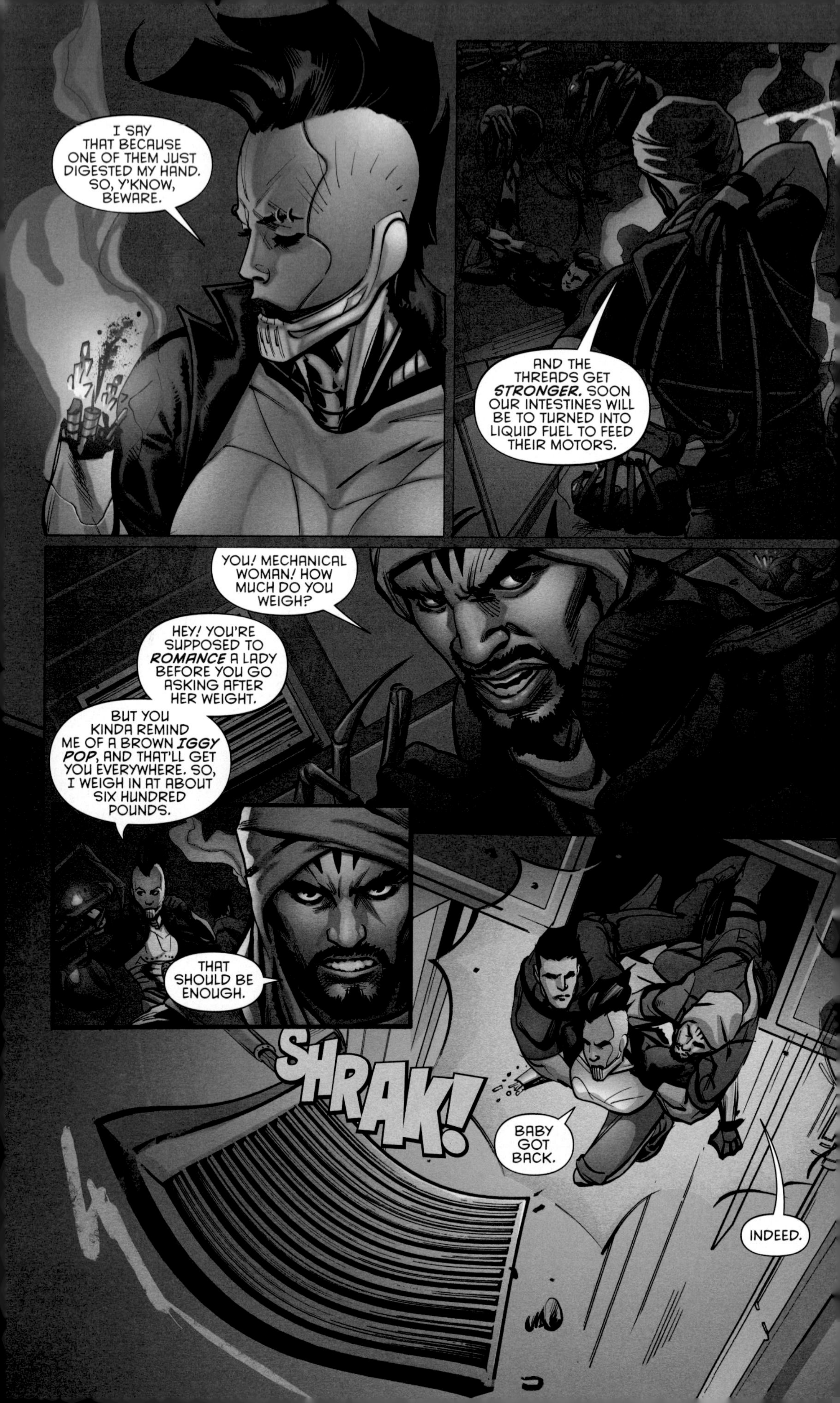
I SAY THAT BECAUSE ONE OF THEM JUST DIGESTED MY HAND. SO, Y'KNOW, BEWARE.
AND THE THREADS GET STRONGER. SOON OUR INTESTINES WILL BE TO TURNED INTO LIQUID FUEL TO FEED THEIR MOTORS.
YOU! MECHANICAL WOMAN! HOW MUCH DO YOU WEIGH?
HEY! YOU'RE SUPPOSED TO ROMANCE A LADY BEFORE YOU GO ASKING AFTER HER WEIGHT.
BUT YOU KINDA REMIND ME OF A BROWN IGGY POP, AND THAT'LL GET YOU EVERYWHERE. SO, I WEIGH IN AT ABOUT SIX HUNDRED POUNDS.
THAT SHOULD BE ENOUGH.
SHRAK!
BABY GOT BACK.
INDEED.

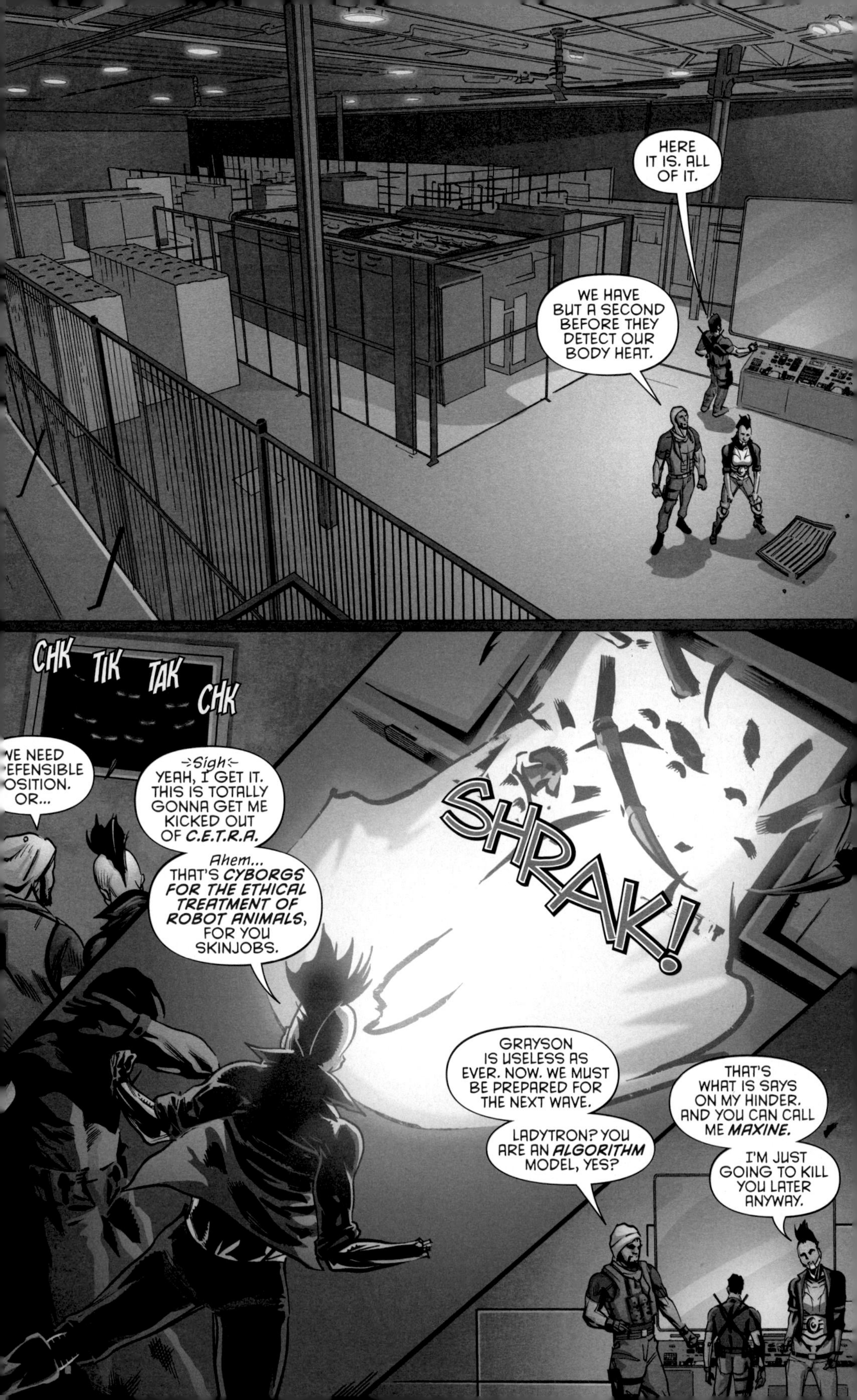
HERE IT IS. ALL OF IT.
WE HAVE BUT A SECOND BEFORE THEY DETECT OUR BODY HEAT.
CHK TIK TAK CHK
WE NEED EFENSIBLE OSITION. OR...
Sigh
YEAH, I GET IT. THIS IS TOTALLY GONNA GET ME KICKED OUT OF C.E.T.R.A.
Ahem... THAT'S CYBORGS FOR THE ETHICAL TREATMENT OF ROBOT ANIMALS, FOR YOU SKINJOBS.
SHRAK!
GRAYSON IS USELESS AS EVER. NOW. WE MUST BE PREPARED FOR THE NEXT WAVE.
LADYTRON? YOU ARE AN ALGORITHM MODEL, YES?
THAT'S WHAT IS SAYS ON MY HINDER. AND YOU CAN CALL ME MAXINE.
I'M JUST GOING TO KILL YOU LATER ANYWAY.

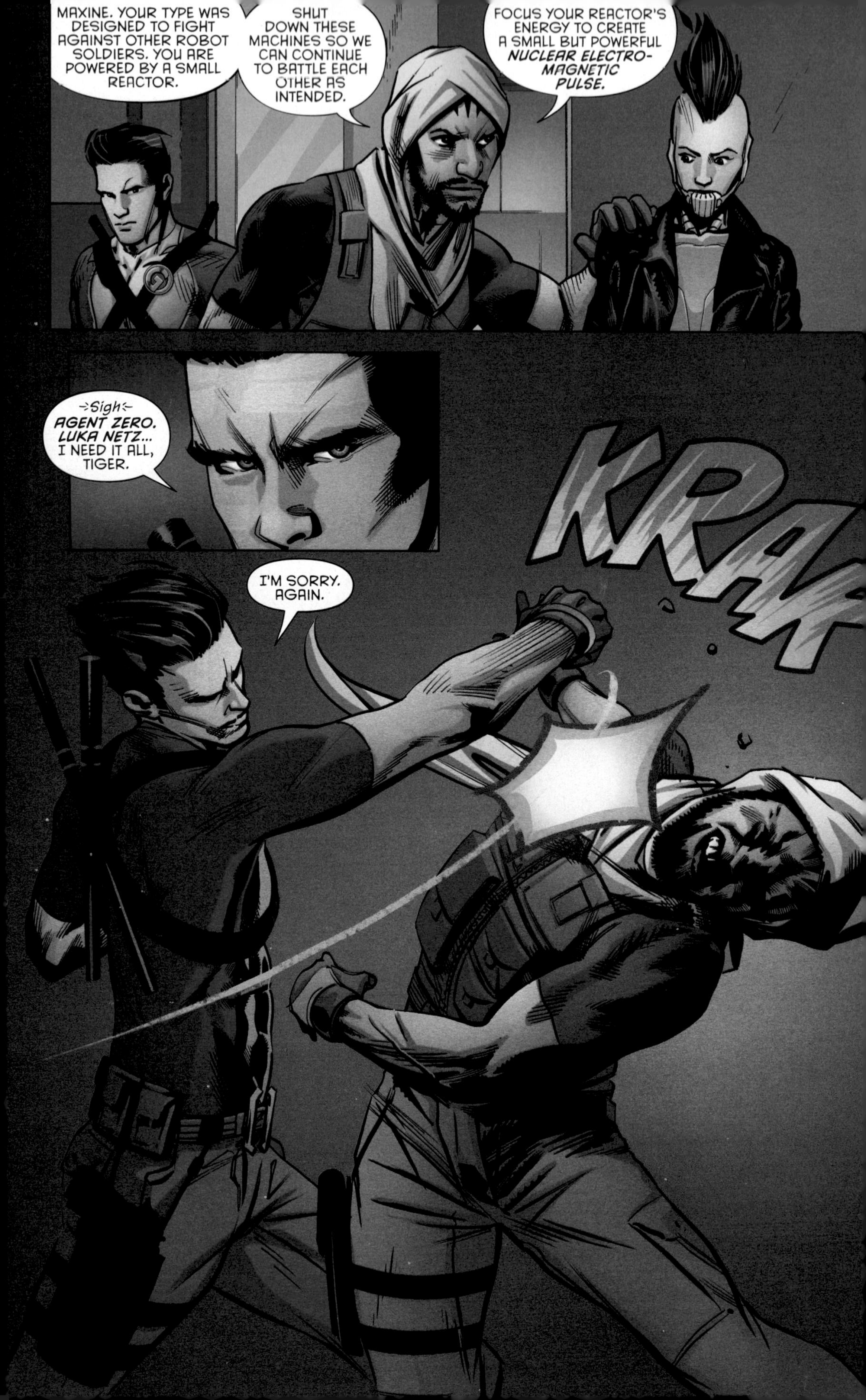
MAXINE. YOUR TYPE WAS DESIGNED TO FIGHT AGAINST OTHER ROBOT SOLDIERS. YOU ARE POWERED BY A SMALL REACTOR.
SHUT DOWN THESE MACHINES SO WE CAN CONTINUE TO BATTLE EACH OTHER AS INTENDED.
FOCUS YOUR REACTOR'S ENERGY TO CREATE A SMALL BUT POWERFUL *NUCLEAR ELECTRO-MAGNETIC PULSE.*
Sigh *AGENT ZERO. LUKA NETZ...* I NEED IT ALL, TIGER.
KRAK
I'M SORRY. AGAIN.

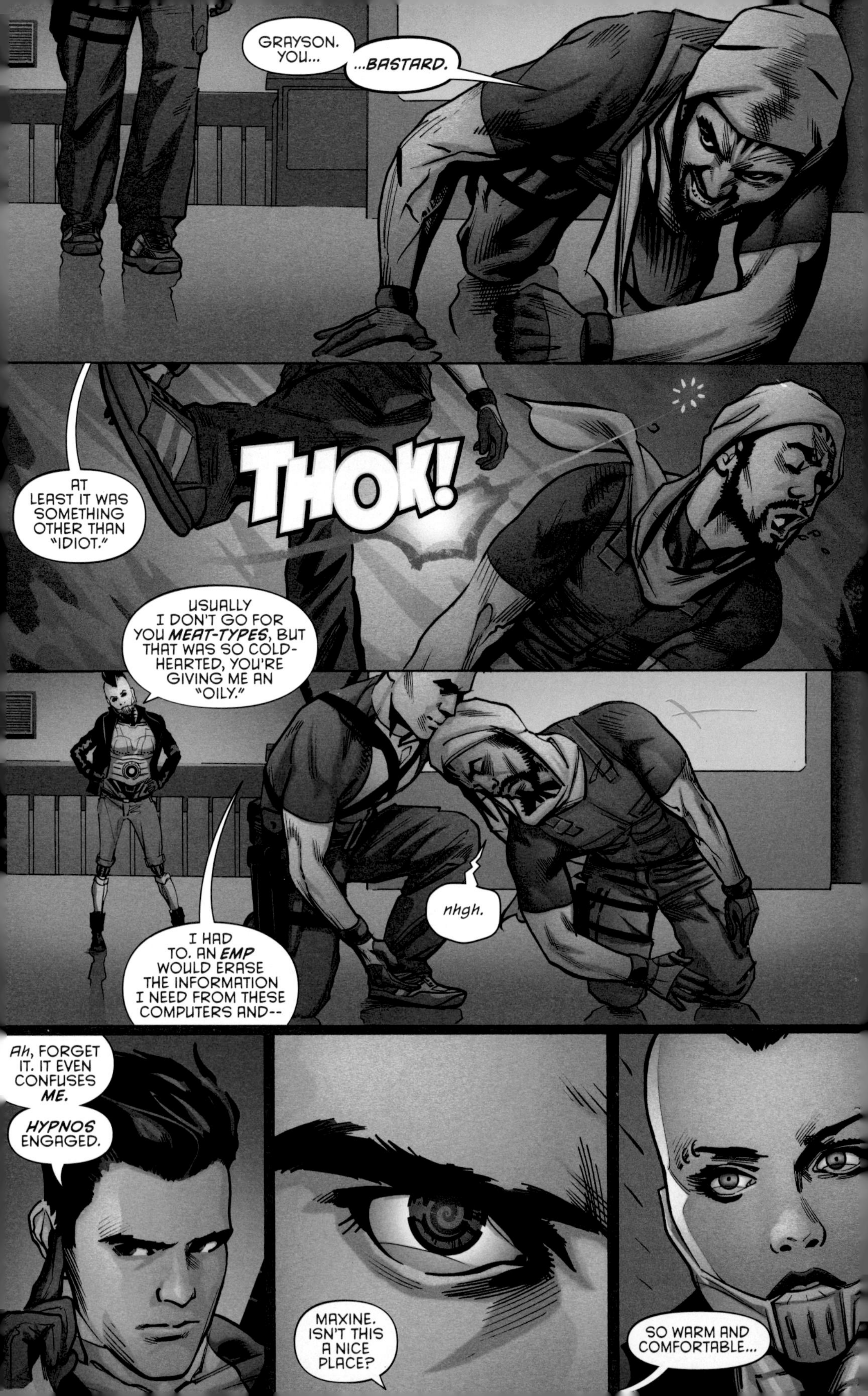
GRAYSON. YOU...
...BASTARD.
THOK!
AT LEAST IT WAS SOMETHING OTHER THAN "IDIOT."
USUALLY I DON'T GO FOR YOU MEAT-TYPES, BUT THAT WAS SO COLD-HEARTED, YOU'RE GIVING ME AN "OILY."
I HAD TO. AN EMP WOULD ERASE THE INFORMATION I NEED FROM THESE COMPUTERS AND--
nhgh.
Ah, FORGET IT. IT EVEN CONFUSES ME.
HYPNOS ENGAGED.
MAXINE. ISN'T THIS A NICE PLACE?
SO WARM AND COMFORTABLE...

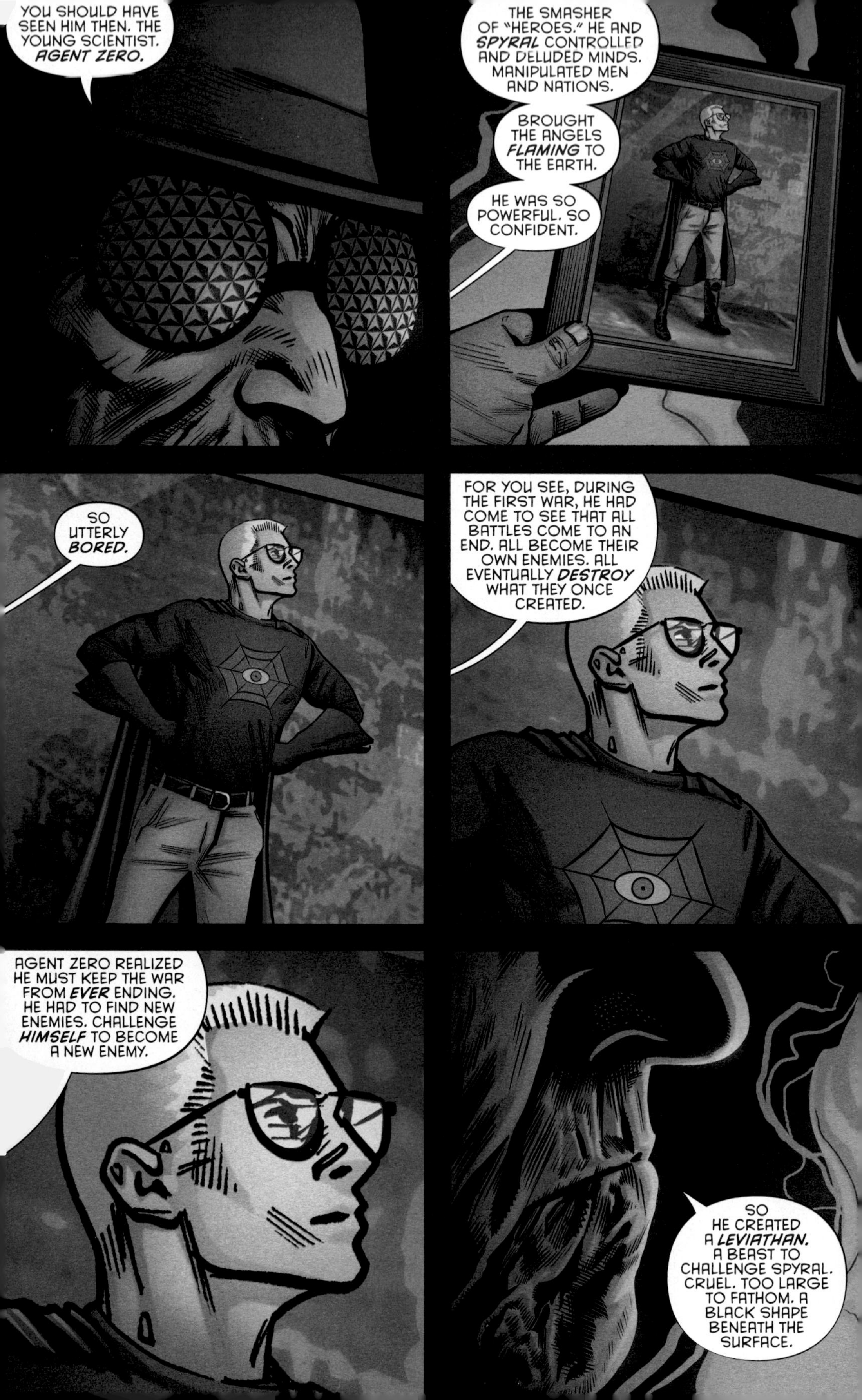
YOU SHOULD HAVE SEEN HIM THEN. THE YOUNG SCIENTIST. AGENT ZERO.
THE SMASHER OF "HEROES." HE AND SPYRAL CONTROLLED AND DELUDED MINDS. MANIPULATED MEN AND NATIONS.
BROUGHT THE ANGELS FLAMING TO THE EARTH.
HE WAS SO POWERFUL. SO CONFIDENT.
SO UTTERLY BORED.
FOR YOU SEE, DURING THE FIRST WAR, HE HAD COME TO SEE THAT ALL BATTLES COME TO AN END. ALL BECOME THEIR OWN ENEMIES. ALL EVENTUALLY DESTROY WHAT THEY ONCE CREATED.
AGENT ZERO REALIZED HE MUST KEEP THE WAR FROM EVER ENDING. HE HAD TO FIND NEW ENEMIES. CHALLENGE HIMSELF TO BECOME A NEW ENEMY.
SO HE CREATED A LEVIATHAN. A BEAST TO CHALLENGE SPYRAL. CRUEL. TOO LARGE TO FATHOM. A BLACK SHAPE BENEATH THE SURFACE.

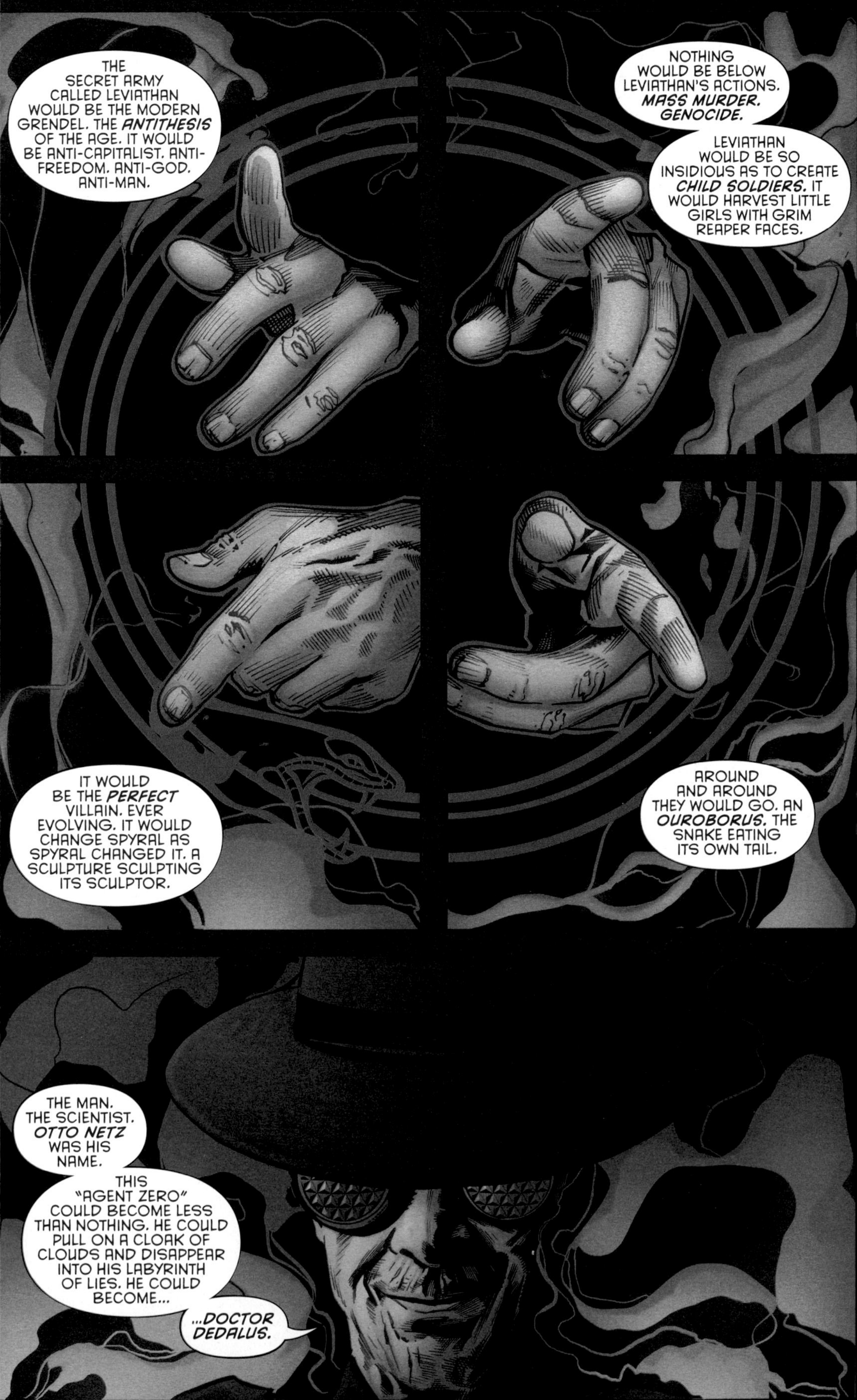
THE SECRET ARMY CALLED LEVIATHAN WOULD BE THE MODERN GRENDEL. THE *ANTITHESIS* OF THE AGE. IT WOULD BE ANTI-CAPITALIST. ANTI-FREEDOM. ANTI-GOD. ANTI-MAN.
NOTHING WOULD BE BELOW LEVIATHAN'S ACTIONS. *MASS MURDER. GENOCIDE.*
LEVIATHAN WOULD BE SO INSIDIOUS AS TO CREATE *CHILD SOLDIERS.* IT WOULD HARVEST LITTLE GIRLS WITH GRIM REAPER FACES.
IT WOULD BE THE *PERFECT* VILLAIN. EVER EVOLVING. IT WOULD CHANGE SPYRAL AS SPYRAL CHANGED IT. A SCULPTURE SCULPTING ITS SCULPTOR.
AROUND AND AROUND THEY WOULD GO. AN *OUROBORUS.* THE SNAKE EATING ITS OWN TAIL.
THE MAN. THE SCIENTIST. *OTTO NETZ* WAS HIS NAME.
THIS "AGENT ZERO" COULD BECOME LESS THAN NOTHING. HE COULD PULL ON A CLOAK OF CLOUDS AND DISAPPEAR INTO HIS LABYRINTH OF LIES. HE COULD BECOME...
...*DOCTOR DEDALUS.*

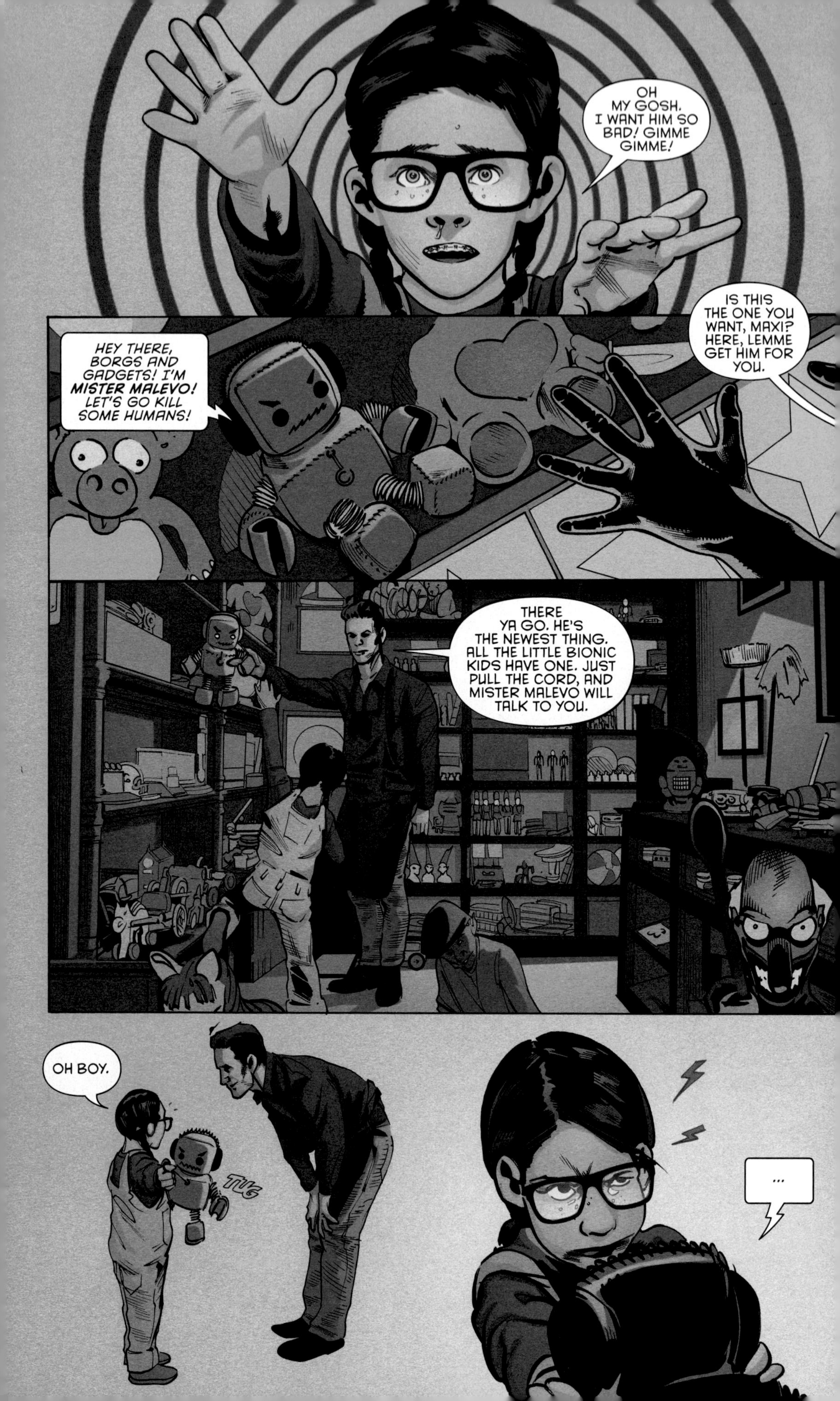
OH MY GOSH. I WANT HIM SO BAD! GIMME GIMME!
HEY THERE, BORGS AND GADGETS! I'M MISTER MALEVO! LET'S GO KILL SOME HUMANS!
IS THIS THE ONE YOU WANT, MAXI? HERE, LEMME GET HIM FOR YOU.
THERE YA GO. HE'S THE NEWEST THING. ALL THE LITTLE BIONIC KIDS HAVE ONE. JUST PULL THE CORD, AND MISTER MALEVO WILL TALK TO YOU.
OH BOY.
TUG
...

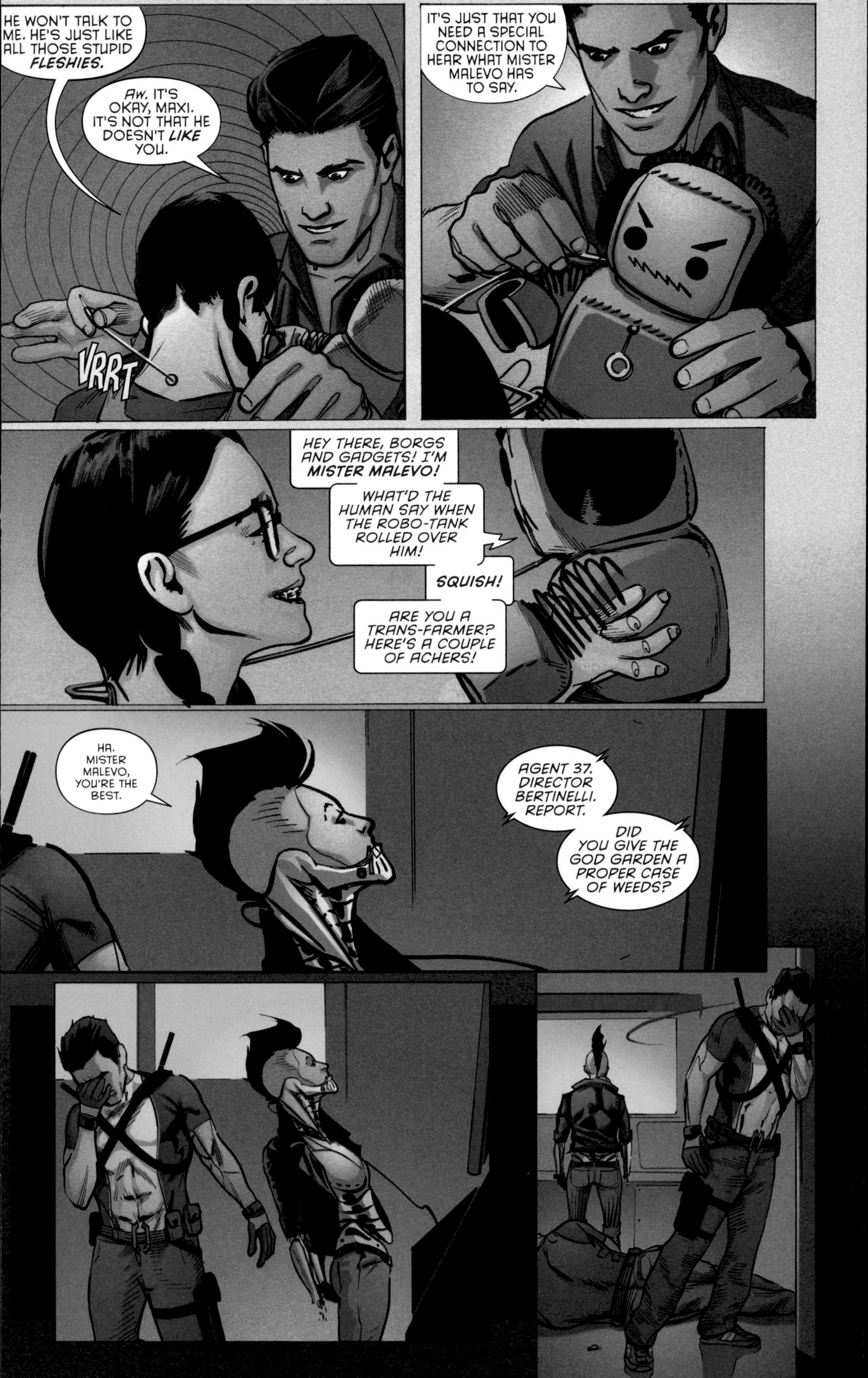

HE WON'T TALK TO ME. HE'S JUST LIKE ALL THOSE STUPID FLESHIES.
AW. IT'S OKAY, MAXI. IT'S NOT THAT HE DOESN'T LIKE YOU.
VRRT
IT'S JUST THAT YOU NEED A SPECIAL CONNECTION TO HEAR WHAT MISTER MALEVO HAS TO SAY.
HEY THERE, BORGS AND GADGETS! I'M MISTER MALEVO!
WHAT'D THE HUMAN SAY WHEN THE ROBO-TANK ROLLED OVER HIM!
SQUISH!
ARE YOU A TRANS-FARMER? HERE'S A COUPLE OF ACHERS!
HA. MISTER MALEVO, YOU'RE THE BEST.
AGENT 37. DIRECTOR BERTINELLI. REPORT.
DID YOU GIVE THE GOD GARDEN A PROPER CASE OF WEEDS?

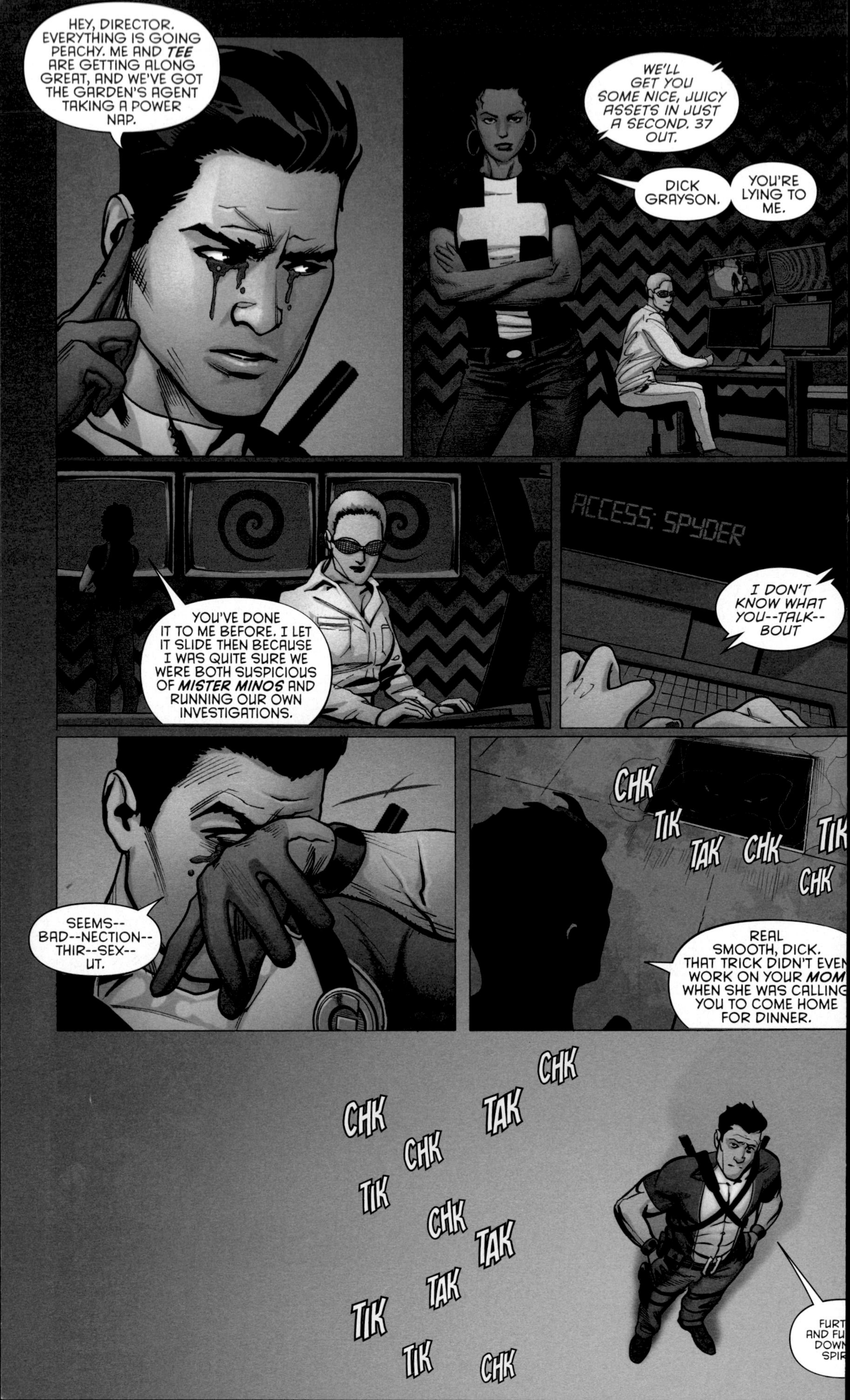

HEY, DIRECTOR. EVERYTHING IS GOING PEACHY. ME AND TEE ARE GETTING ALONG GREAT, AND WE'VE GOT THE GARDEN'S AGENT TAKING A POWER NAP.
WE'LL GET YOU SOME NICE, JUICY ASSETS IN JUST A SECOND. 37 OUT.
DICK GRAYSON.
YOU'RE LYING TO ME.
YOU'VE DONE IT TO ME BEFORE. I LET IT SLIDE THEN BECAUSE I WAS QUITE SURE WE WERE BOTH SUSPICIOUS OF MISTER MINOS AND RUNNING OUR OWN INVESTIGATIONS.
ACCESS: SPYDER
I DON'T KNOW WHAT YOU--TALK--BOUT
SEEMS--BAD--NECTION--THIR--SEX--UT.
CHK
TIK
TAK
CHK
TIK
CHK
REAL SMOOTH, DICK. THAT TRICK DIDN'T EVEN WORK ON YOUR MOM WHEN SHE WAS CALLING YOU TO COME HOME FOR DINNER.
CHK
CHK
TAK
CHK
TIK
CHK
TAK
TAK
TIK
TIK
CHK

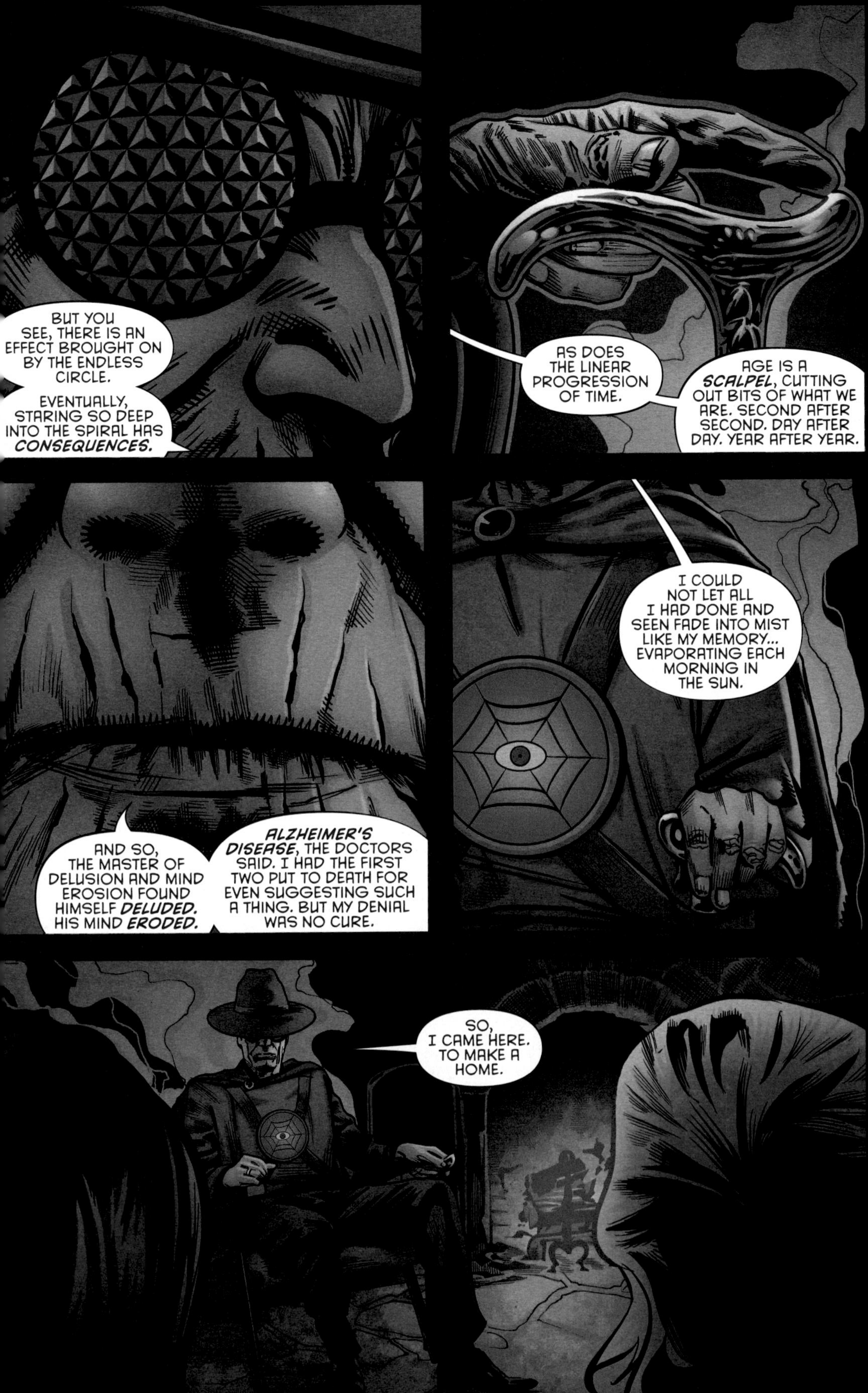
BUT YOU SEE, THERE IS AN EFFECT BROUGHT ON BY THE ENDLESS CIRCLE.
EVENTUALLY, STARING SO DEEP INTO THE SPIRAL HAS *CONSEQUENCES.*
AS DOES THE LINEAR PROGRESSION OF TIME.
AGE IS A *SCALPEL*, CUTTING OUT BITS OF WHAT WE ARE. SECOND AFTER SECOND. DAY AFTER DAY. YEAR AFTER YEAR.
AND SO, THE MASTER OF DELUSION AND MIND EROSION FOUND HIMSELF *DELUDED.* HIS MIND *ERODED.*
ALZHEIMER'S DISEASE, THE DOCTORS SAID. I HAD THE FIRST TWO PUT TO DEATH FOR EVEN SUGGESTING SUCH A THING. BUT MY DENIAL WAS NO CURE.
I COULD NOT LET ALL I HAD DONE AND SEEN FADE INTO MIST LIKE MY MEMORY... EVAPORATING EACH MORNING IN THE SUN.
SO, I CAME HERE. TO MAKE A HOME.

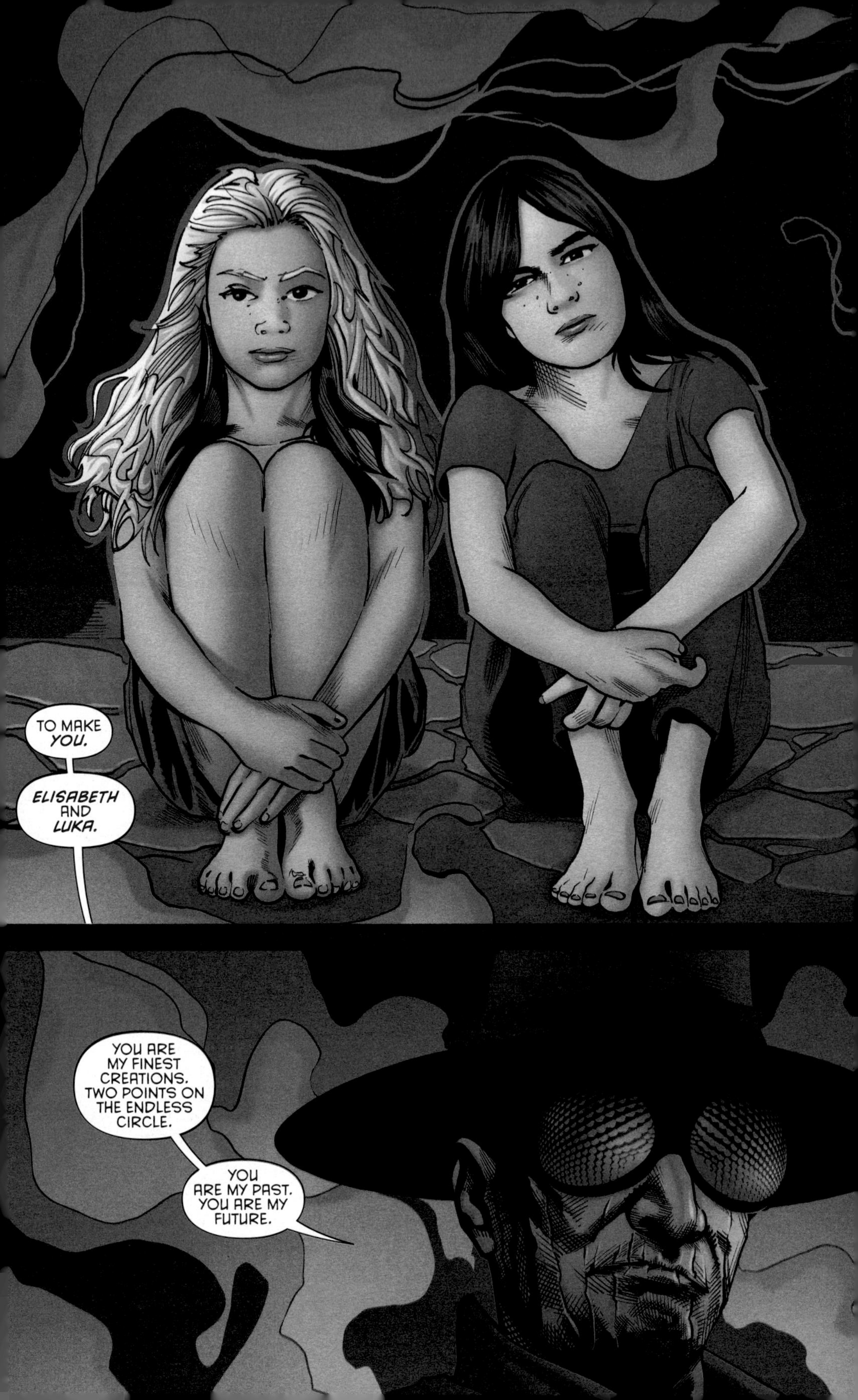
TO MAKE YOU.
ELISABETH AND LUKA.
YOU ARE MY FINEST CREATIONS. TWO POINTS ON THE ENDLESS CIRCLE.
YOU ARE MY PAST. YOU ARE MY FUTURE.

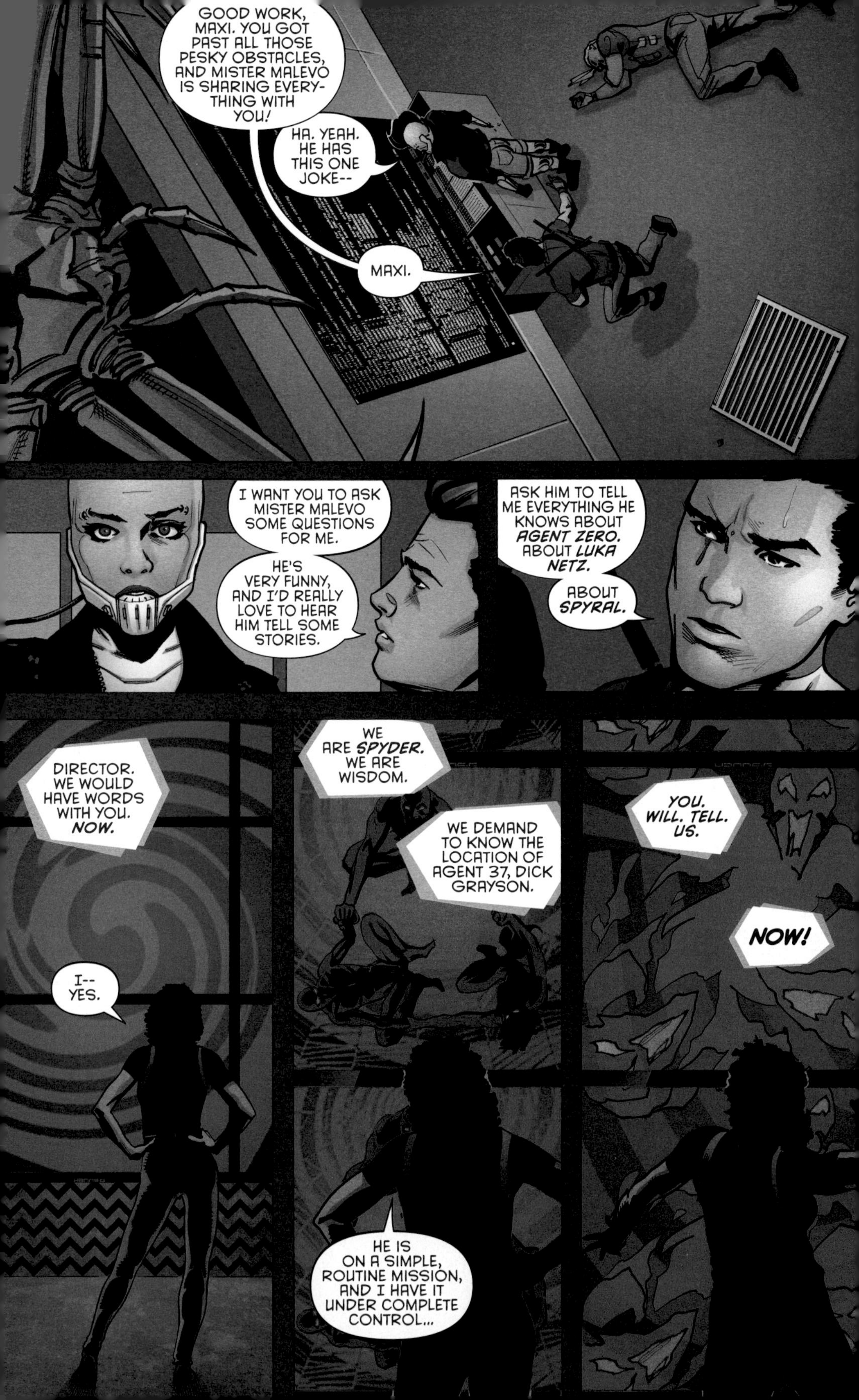
GOOD WORK, MAXI. YOU GOT PAST ALL THOSE PESKY OBSTACLES, AND MISTER MALEVO IS SHARING EVERY-THING WITH YOU!
HA. YEAH. HE HAS THIS ONE JOKE--
MAXI.
I WANT YOU TO ASK MISTER MALEVO SOME QUESTIONS FOR ME.
HE'S VERY FUNNY, AND I'D REALLY LOVE TO HEAR HIM TELL SOME STORIES.
ASK HIM TO TELL ME EVERYTHING HE KNOWS ABOUT *AGENT ZERO.* ABOUT *LUKA NETZ.*
ABOUT *SPYRAL.*
DIRECTOR. WE WOULD HAVE WORDS WITH YOU. *NOW.*
I-- YES.
WE ARE *SPYDER.* WE ARE WISDOM.
WE DEMAND TO KNOW THE LOCATION OF AGENT 37, DICK GRAYSON.
HE IS ON A SIMPLE, ROUTINE MISSION, AND I HAVE IT UNDER COMPLETE CONTROL...
YOU. WILL. TELL. US.
NOW!

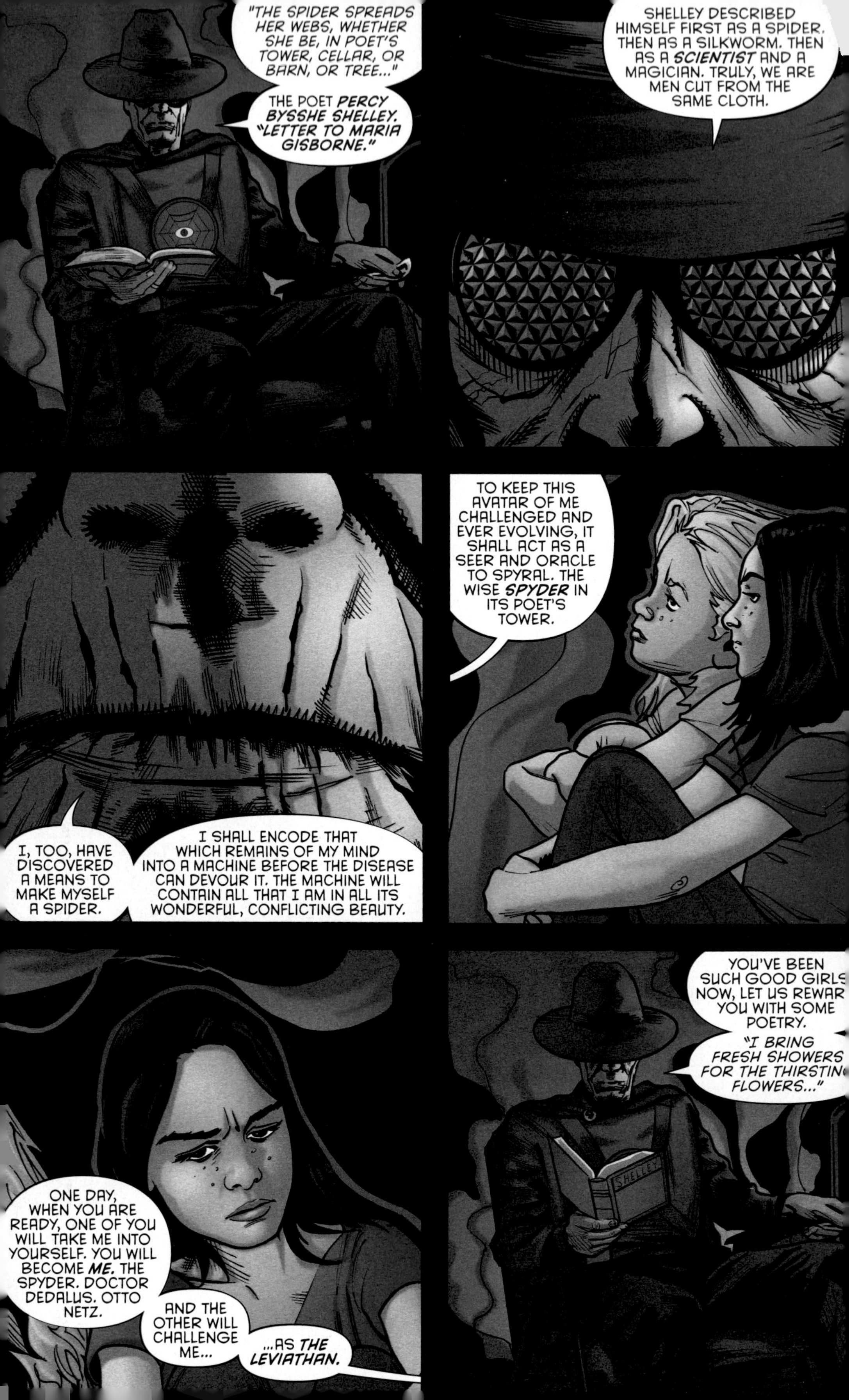
"THE SPIDER SPREADS HER WEBS, WHETHER SHE BE, IN POET'S TOWER, CELLAR, OR BARN, OR TREE..."
THE POET PERCY BYSSHE SHELLEY. "LETTER TO MARIA GISBORNE."
SHELLEY DESCRIBED HIMSELF FIRST AS A SPIDER. THEN AS A SILKWORM. THEN AS A SCIENTIST AND A MAGICIAN. TRULY, WE ARE MEN CUT FROM THE SAME CLOTH.
I, TOO, HAVE DISCOVERED A MEANS TO MAKE MYSELF A SPIDER.
I SHALL ENCODE THAT WHICH REMAINS OF MY MIND INTO A MACHINE BEFORE THE DISEASE CAN DEVOUR IT. THE MACHINE WILL CONTAIN ALL THAT I AM IN ALL ITS WONDERFUL, CONFLICTING BEAUTY.
TO KEEP THIS AVATAR OF ME CHALLENGED AND EVER EVOLVING, IT SHALL ACT AS A SEER AND ORACLE TO SPYRAL. THE WISE SPYDER IN ITS POET'S TOWER.
ONE DAY, WHEN YOU ARE READY, ONE OF YOU WILL TAKE ME INTO YOURSELF. YOU WILL BECOME ME. THE SPYDER. DOCTOR DEDALUS. OTTO NETZ.
AND THE OTHER WILL CHALLENGE ME...
...AS THE LEVIATHAN.
YOU'VE BEEN SUCH GOOD GIRLS NOW, LET US REWAR YOU WITH SOME POETRY.
"I BRING FRESH SHOWERS FOR THE THIRSTIN FLOWERS..."
SHELLEY

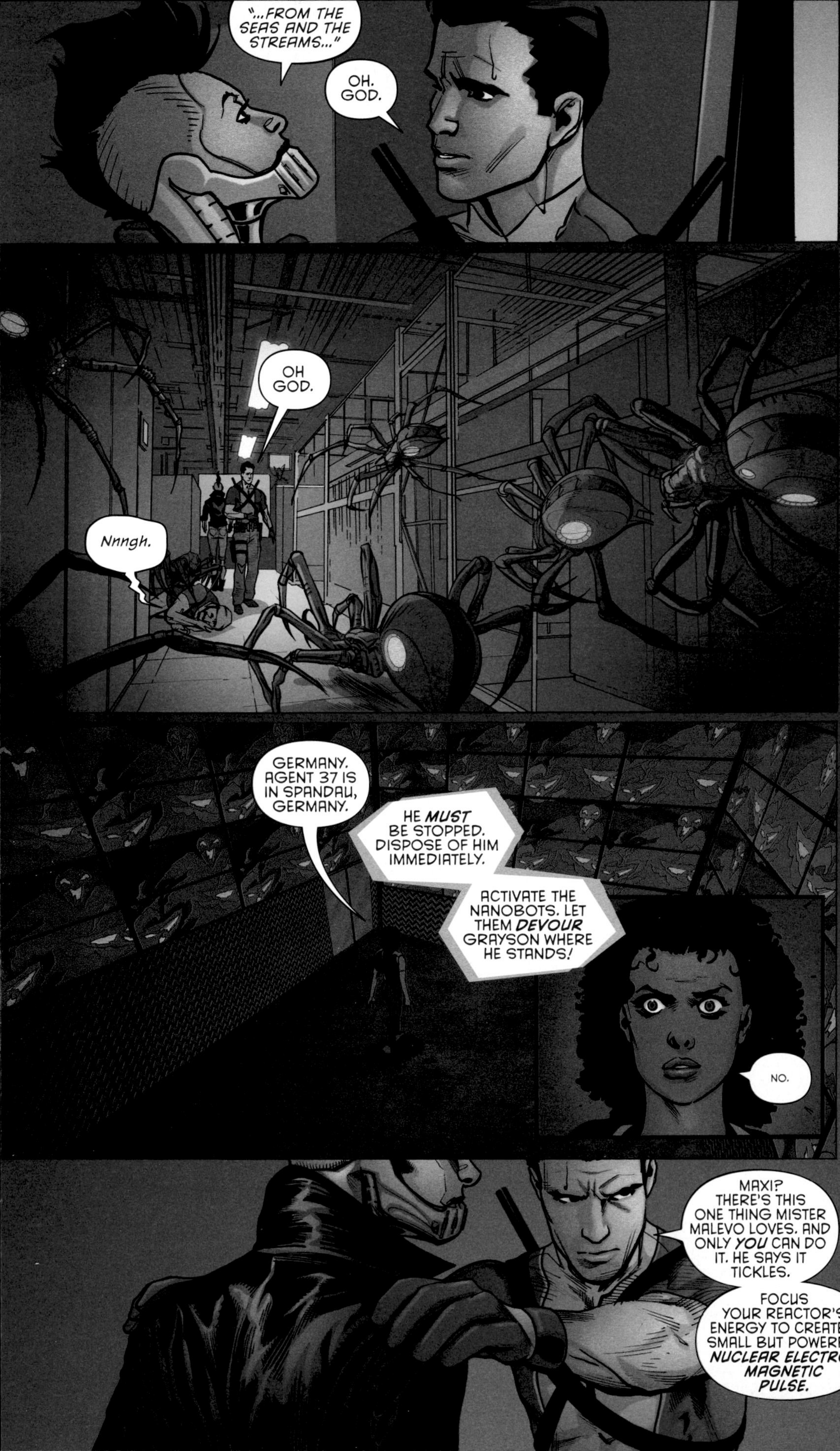
"...FROM THE SEAS AND THE STREAMS..."
OH. GOD.
OH GOD.
Nnngh.
GERMANY. AGENT 37 IS IN SPANDAU, GERMANY.
HE MUST BE STOPPED. DISPOSE OF HIM IMMEDIATELY.
ACTIVATE THE NANOBOTS. LET THEM DEVOUR GRAYSON WHERE HE STANDS!
NO.
MAXI? THERE'S THIS ONE THING MISTER MALEVO LOVES. AND ONLY YOU CAN DO IT. HE SAYS IT TICKLES.
FOCUS YOUR REACTOR'S ENERGY TO CREATE A SMALL BUT POWERFUL NUCLEAR ELECTRO-MAGNETIC PULSE.

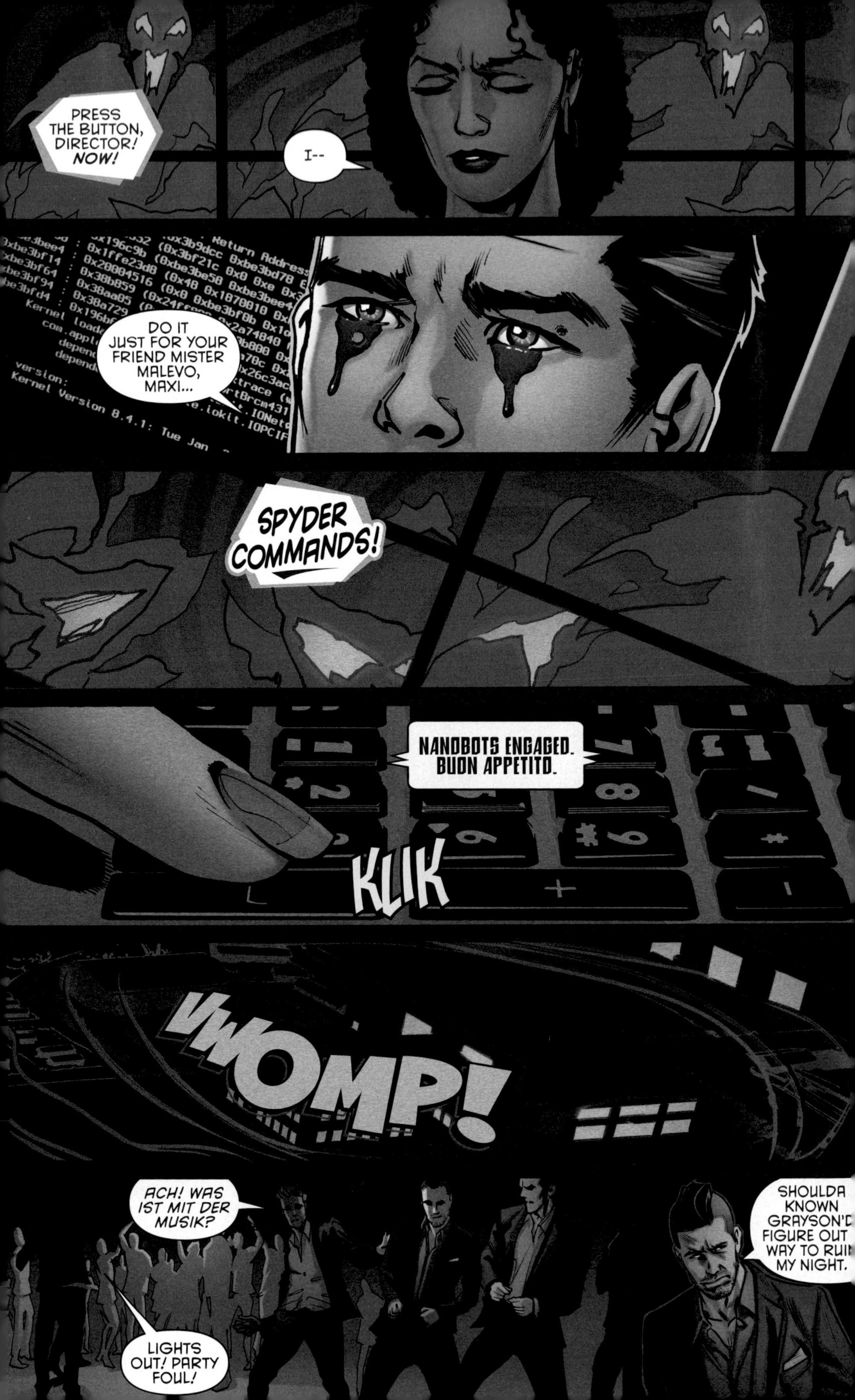
PRESS THE BUTTON, DIRECTOR! NOW!
I--
DO IT JUST FOR YOUR FRIEND MISTER MALEVO, MAXI...
SPYDER COMMANDS!
NANOBOTS ENGAGED. BUON APPETITO.
KLIK
VWOMP!
ACH! WAS IST MIT DER MUSIK?
LIGHTS OUT! PARTY FOUL!
SHOULDA KNOWN GRAYSON'D FIGURE OUT WAY TO RUIN MY NIGHT.

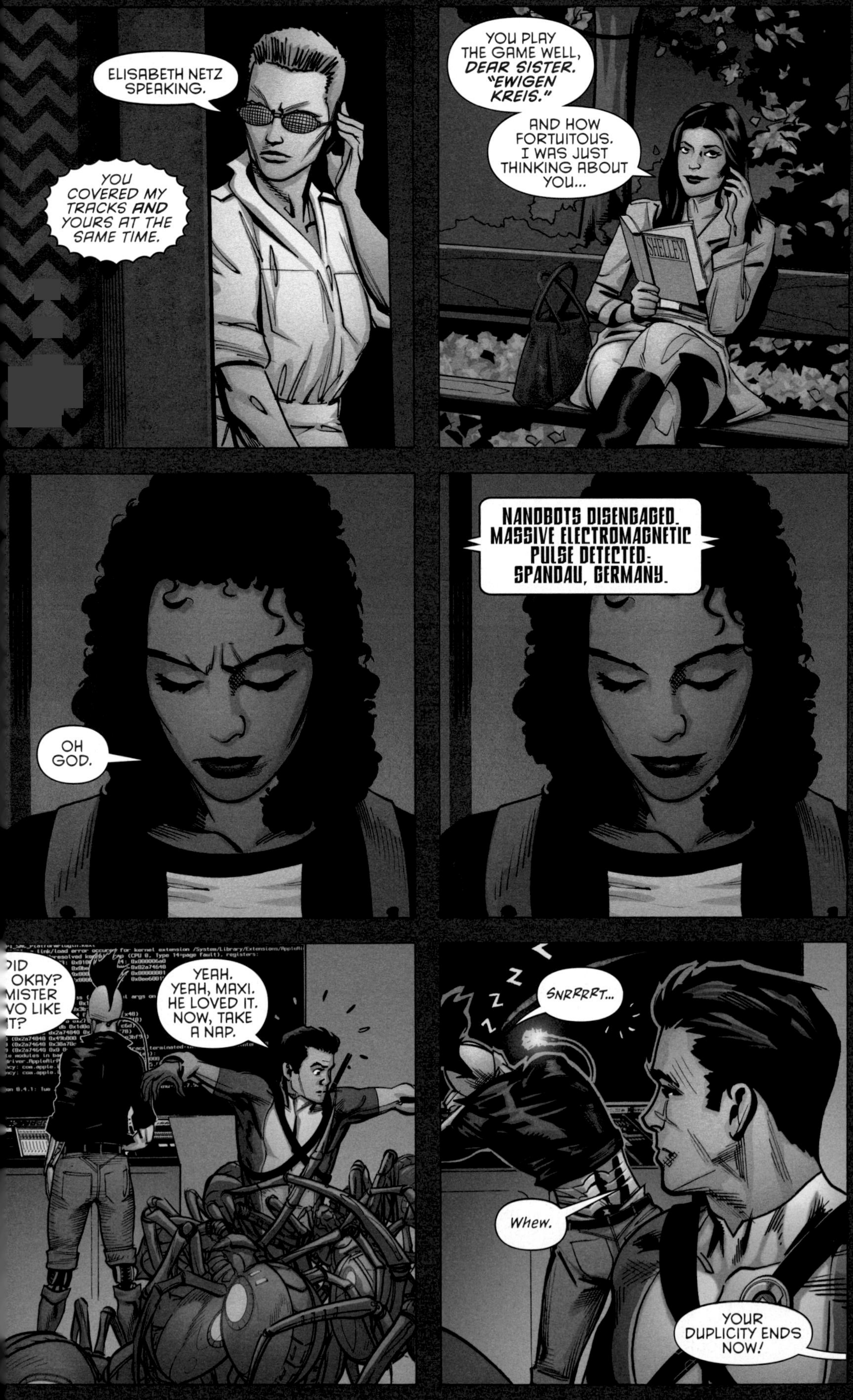
ELISABETH NETZ SPEAKING.
YOU COVERED MY TRACKS AND YOURS AT THE SAME TIME.
YOU PLAY THE GAME WELL, DEAR SISTER. "EWIGEN KREIS."
AND HOW FORTUITOUS. I WAS JUST THINKING ABOUT YOU...
SHELLEY
OH GOD.
NANOBOTS DISENGAGED. MASSIVE ELECTROMAGNETIC PULSE DETECTED: SPANDAU, GERMANY.
OKAY? MISTER
YEAH. YEAH, MAXI. HE LOVED IT. NOW, TAKE A NAP.
SNRRRRT...
Whew.
YOUR DUPLICITY ENDS NOW!

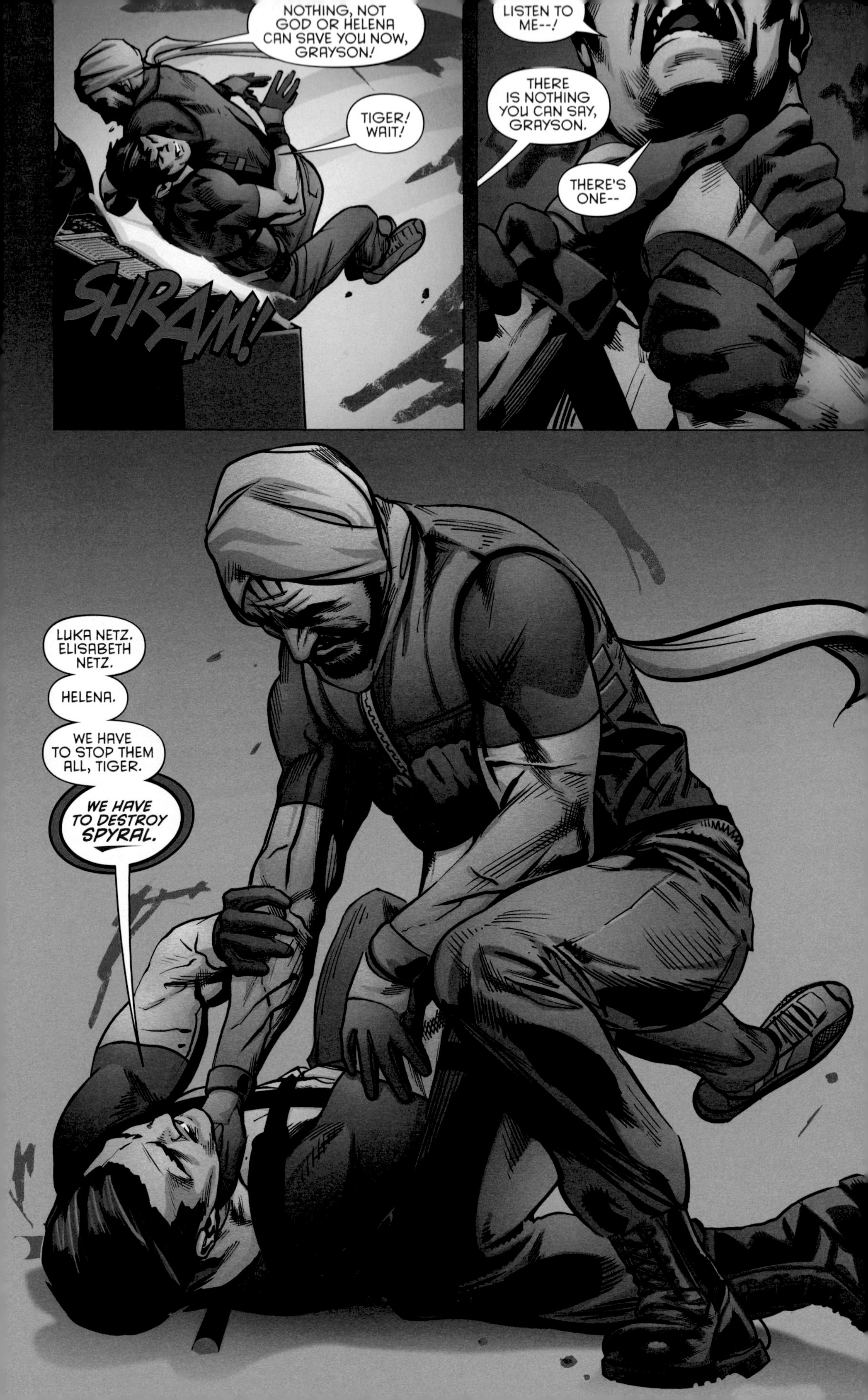
NOTHING, NOT GOD OR HELENA CAN SAVE YOU NOW, GRAYSON!
TIGER! WAIT!
SHRAM!
LISTEN TO ME--!
THERE IS NOTHING YOU CAN SAY, GRAYSON.
THERE'S ONE--
LUKA NETZ. ELISABETH NETZ.
HELENA.
WE HAVE TO STOP THEM ALL, TIGER.
WE HAVE TO DESTROY SPYRAL.

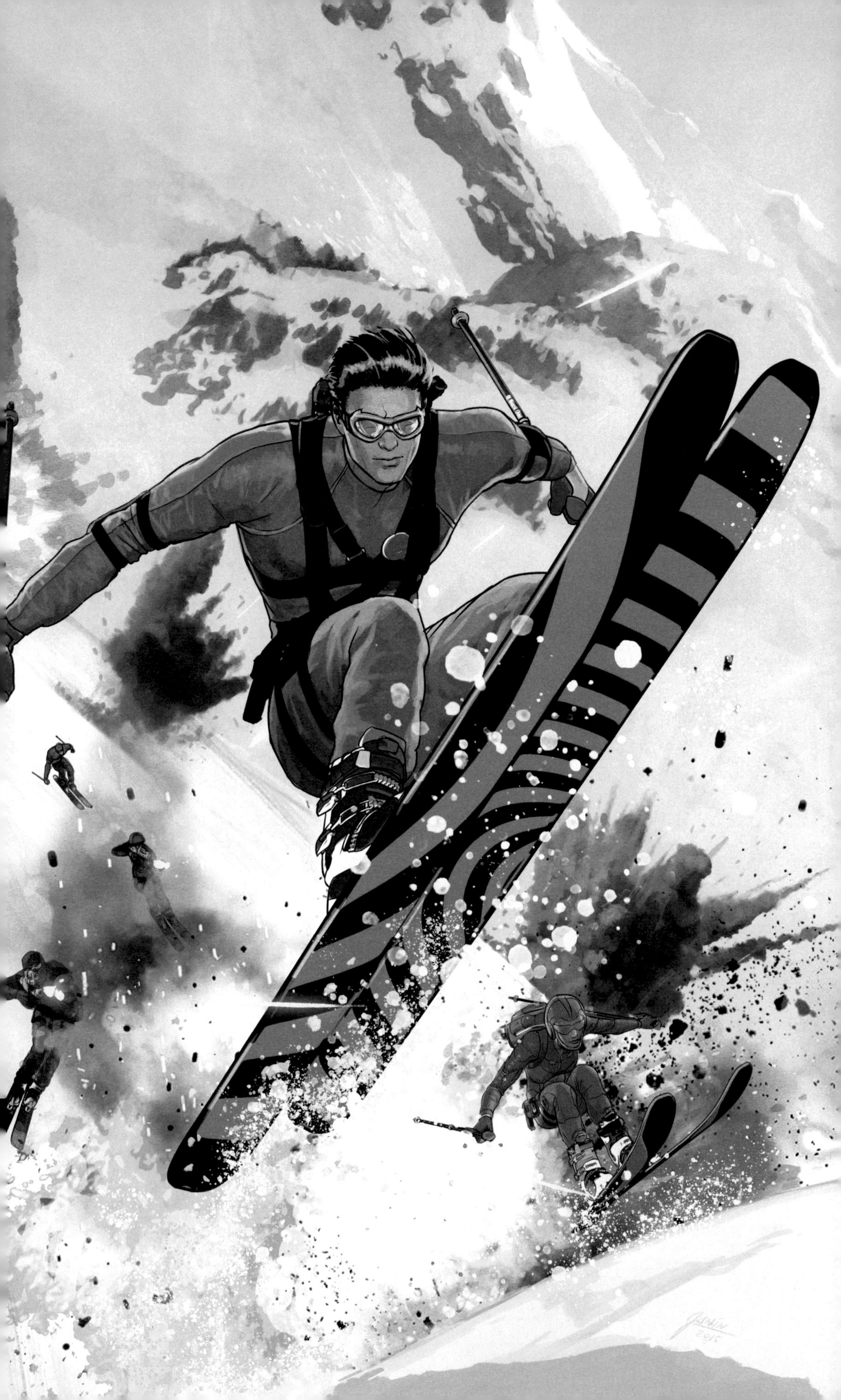

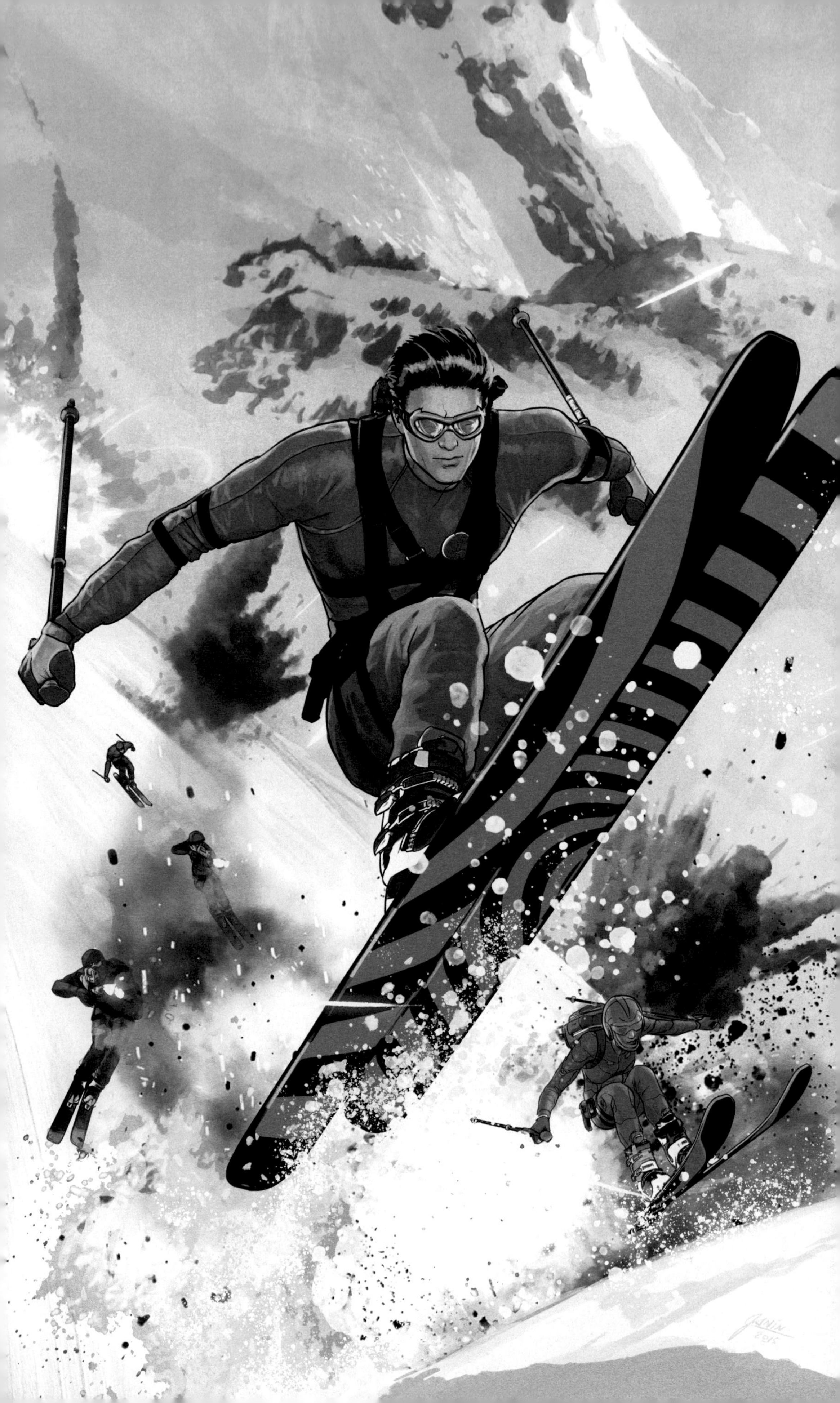

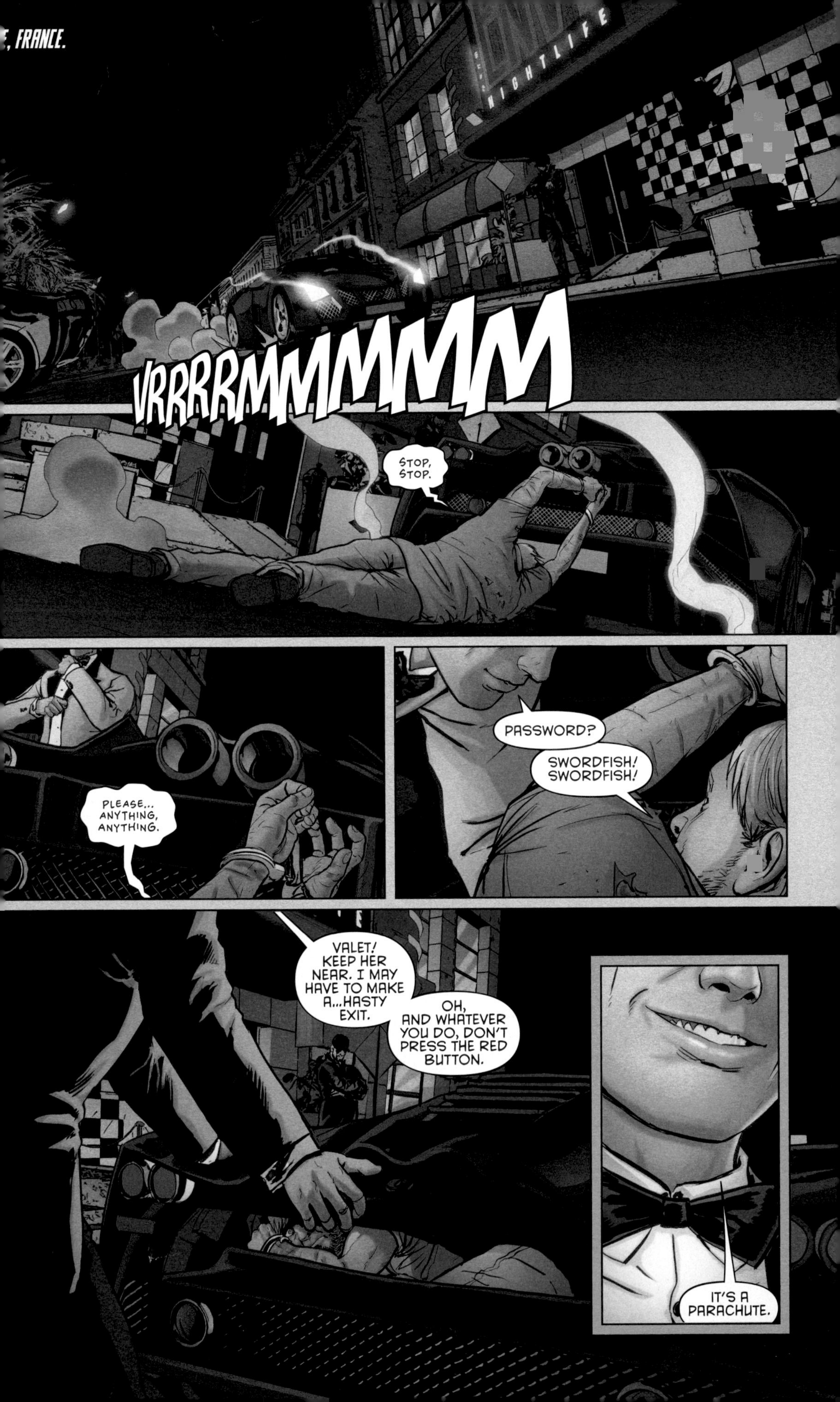

, FRANCE.
NIGHTLIFE
VRRRRMMMMMM
STOP, STOP.
PLEASE... ANYTHING, ANYTHING.
PASSWORD?
SWORDFISH! SWORDFISH!
VALET! KEEP HER NEAR. I MAY HAVE TO MAKE A...HASTY EXIT.
OH, AND WHATEVER YOU DO, DON'T PRESS THE RED BUTTON.
IT'S A PARACHUTE.

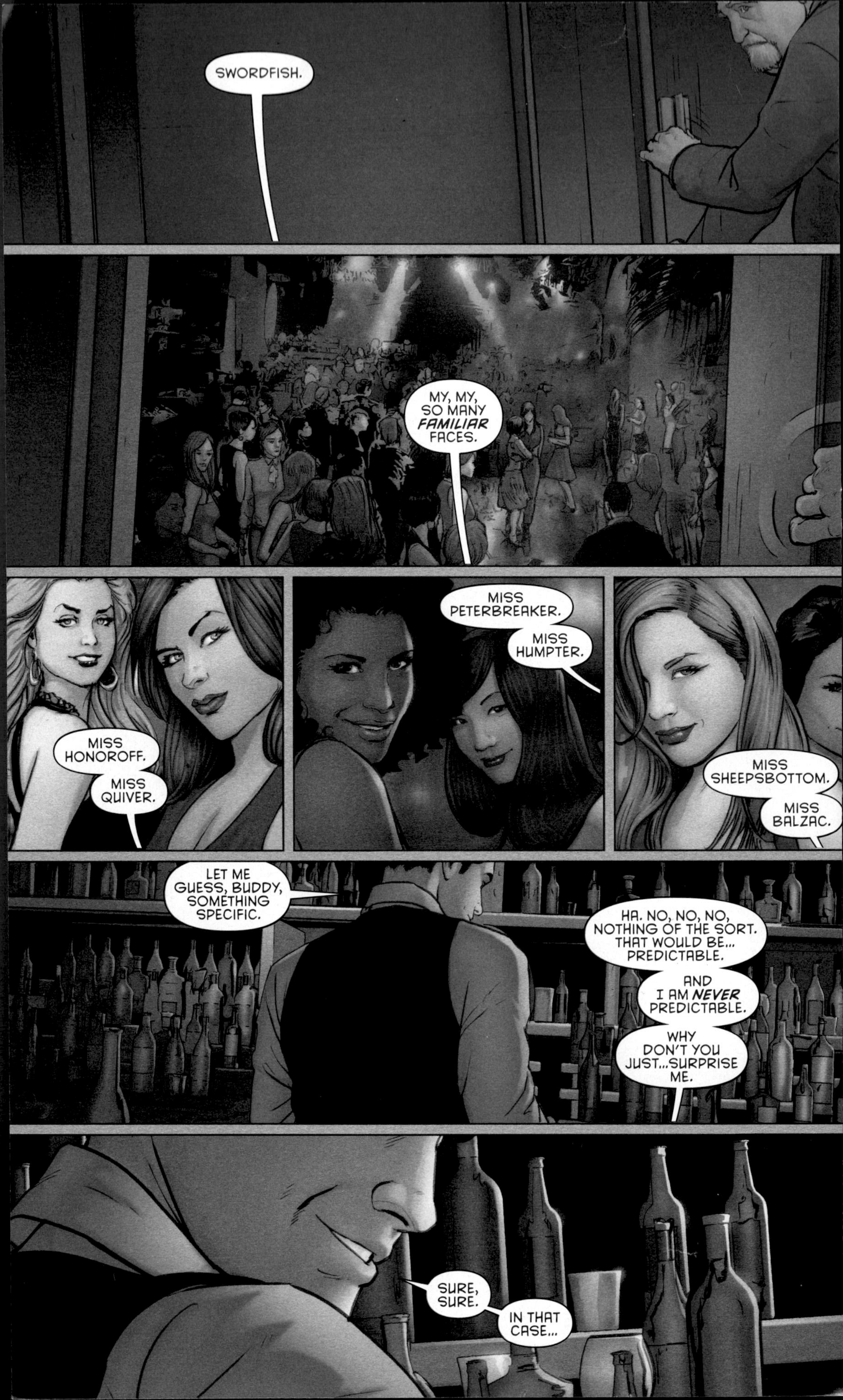
SWORDFISH.
MY, MY, SO MANY *FAMILIAR* FACES.
MISS HONOROFF.
MISS QUIVER.
MISS PETERBREAKER.
MISS HUMPTER.
MISS SHEEPSBOTTOM.
MISS BALZAC.
LET ME GUESS, BUDDY, SOMETHING SPECIFIC.
HA. NO, NO, NO, NOTHING OF THE SORT. THAT WOULD BE... PREDICTABLE.
AND I AM *NEVER* PREDICTABLE.
WHY DON'T YOU JUST...SURPRISE ME.
SURE, SURE.
IN THAT CASE...

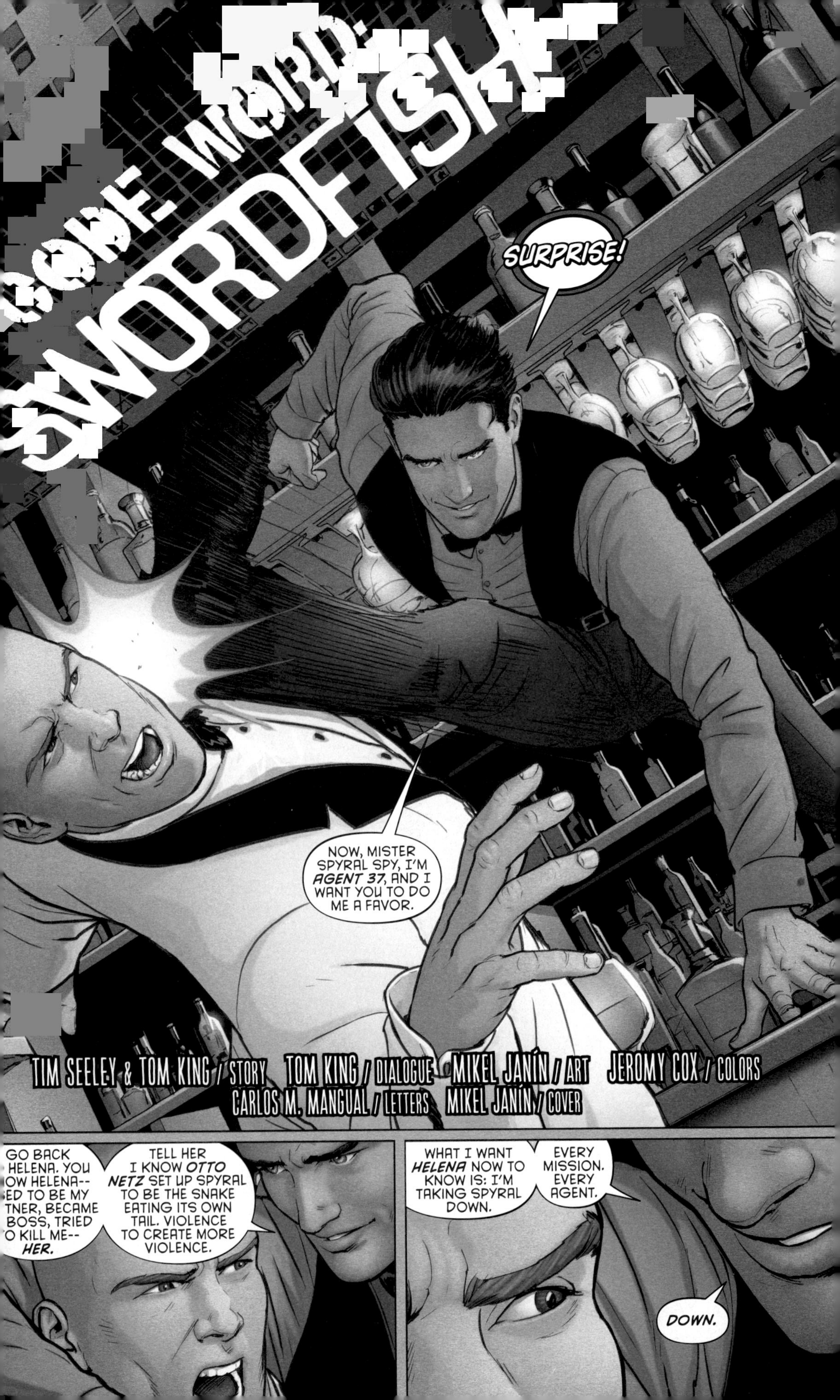
CODE WORD: SWORDFISH!
SURPRISE!
NOW, MISTER SPYRAL SPY, I'M *AGENT 37*, AND I WANT YOU TO DO ME A FAVOR.
TIM SEELEY & TOM KING / STORY TOM KING / DIALOGUE MIKEL JANÍN / ART JEROMY COX / COLORS
CARLOS M. MANGUAL / LETTERS MIKEL JANÍN / COVER
GO BACK HELENA. YOU OW HELENA-- ED TO BE MY TNER, BECAME BOSS, TRIED O KILL ME-- *HER.*
TELL HER I KNOW *OTTO NETZ* SET UP SPYRAL TO BE THE SNAKE EATING ITS OWN TAIL. VIOLENCE TO CREATE MORE VIOLENCE.
WHAT I WANT *HELENA* NOW TO KNOW IS: I'M TAKING SPYRAL DOWN.
EVERY MISSION. EVERY AGENT.
DOWN.

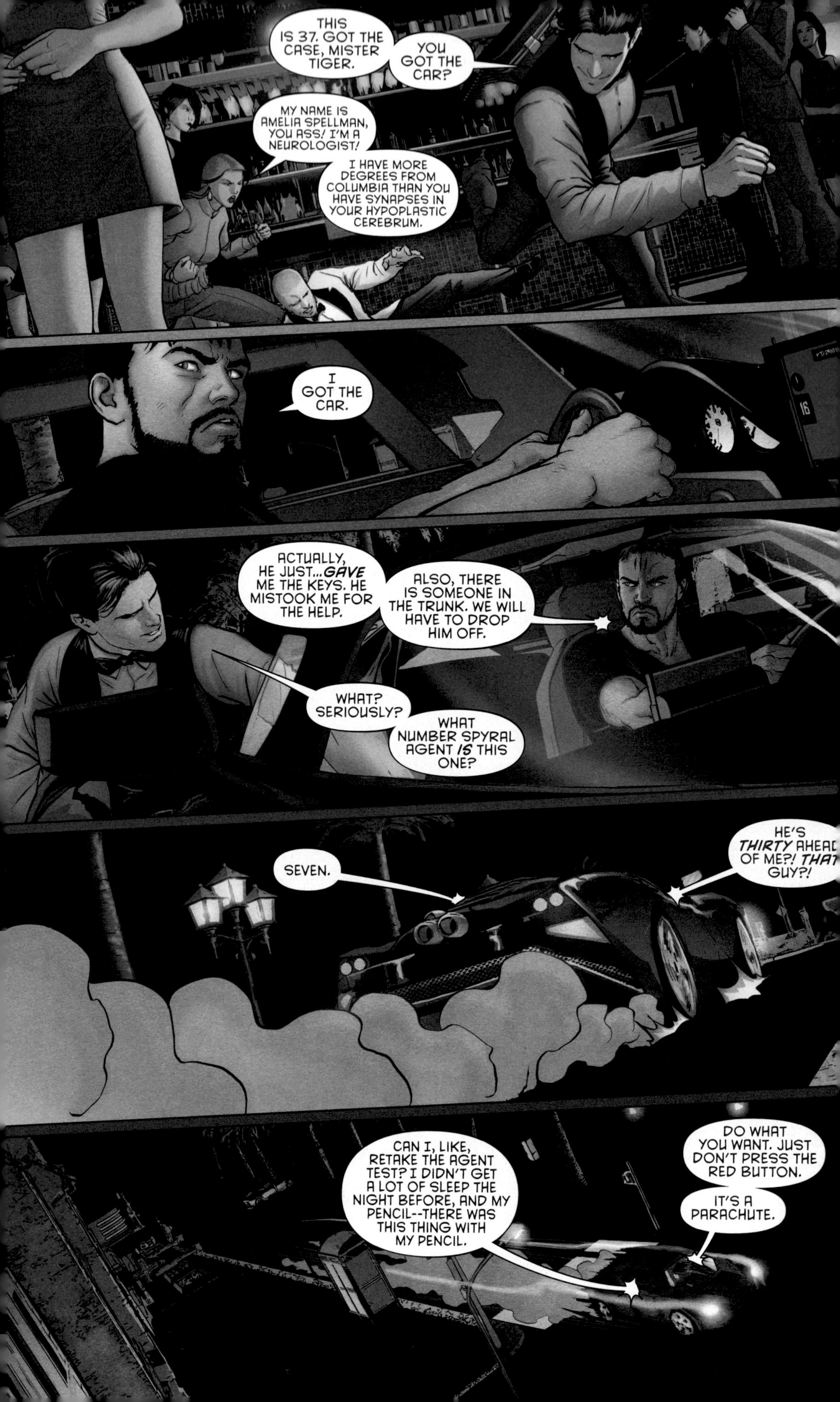
THIS IS 37. GOT THE CASE, MISTER TIGER.
YOU GOT THE CAR?
MY NAME IS AMELIA SPELLMAN, YOU ASS! I'M A NEUROLOGIST!
I HAVE MORE DEGREES FROM COLUMBIA THAN YOU HAVE SYNAPSES IN YOUR HYPOPLASTIC CEREBRUM.
I GOT THE CAR.
ACTUALLY, HE JUST...GAVE ME THE KEYS. HE MISTOOK ME FOR THE HELP.
ALSO, THERE IS SOMEONE IN THE TRUNK. WE WILL HAVE TO DROP HIM OFF.
WHAT? SERIOUSLY?
WHAT NUMBER SPYRAL AGENT IS THIS ONE?
SEVEN.
HE'S THIRTY AHEAD OF ME?! THAT GUY?!
CAN I, LIKE, RETAKE THE AGENT TEST? I DIDN'T GET A LOT OF SLEEP THE NIGHT BEFORE, AND MY PENCIL--THERE WAS THIS THING WITH MY PENCIL.
DO WHAT YOU WANT. JUST DON'T PRESS THE RED BUTTON.
IT'S A PARACHUTE.

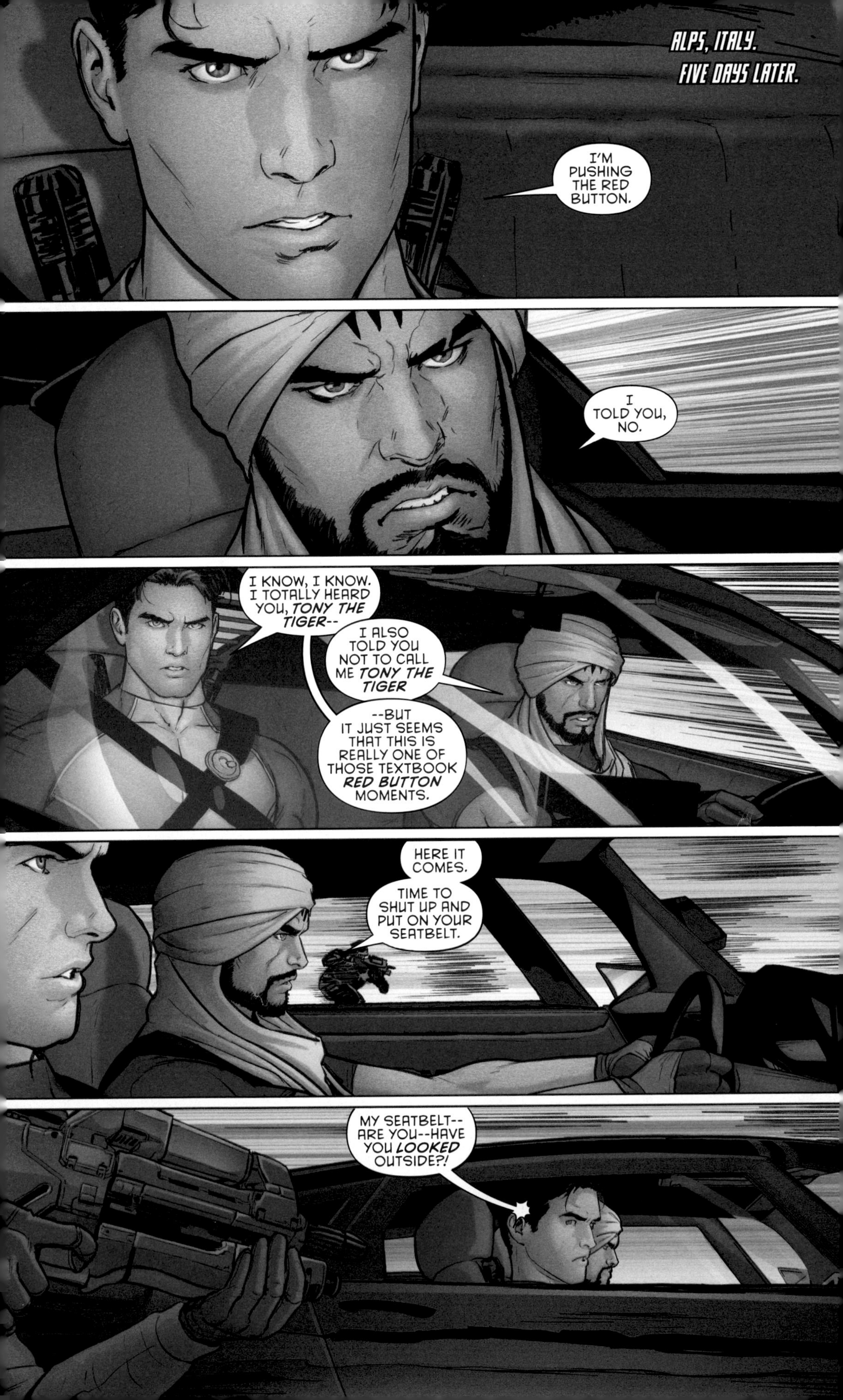
ALPS, ITALY.
FIVE DAYS LATER.
I'M PUSHING THE RED BUTTON.
I TOLD YOU, NO.
I KNOW, I KNOW. I TOTALLY HEARD YOU, *TONY THE TIGER*--
I ALSO TOLD YOU NOT TO CALL ME *TONY THE TIGER*
--BUT IT JUST SEEMS THAT THIS IS REALLY ONE OF THOSE TEXTBOOK *RED BUTTON* MOMENTS.
HERE IT COMES.
TIME TO SHUT UP AND PUT ON YOUR SEATBELT.
MY SEATBELT--ARE YOU--HAVE YOU *LOOKED* OUTSIDE?!

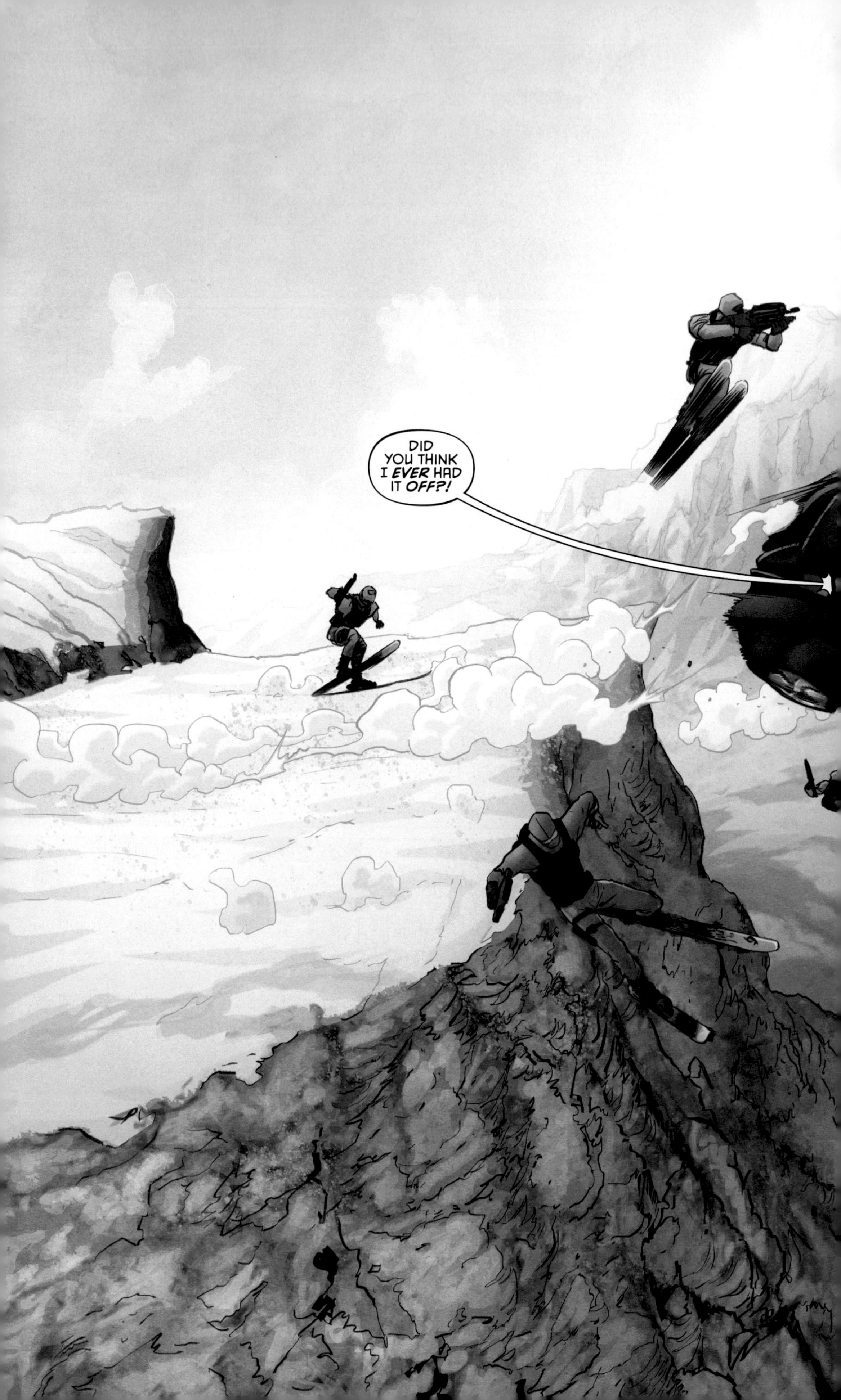
DID YOU THINK I EVER HAD IT OFF?!

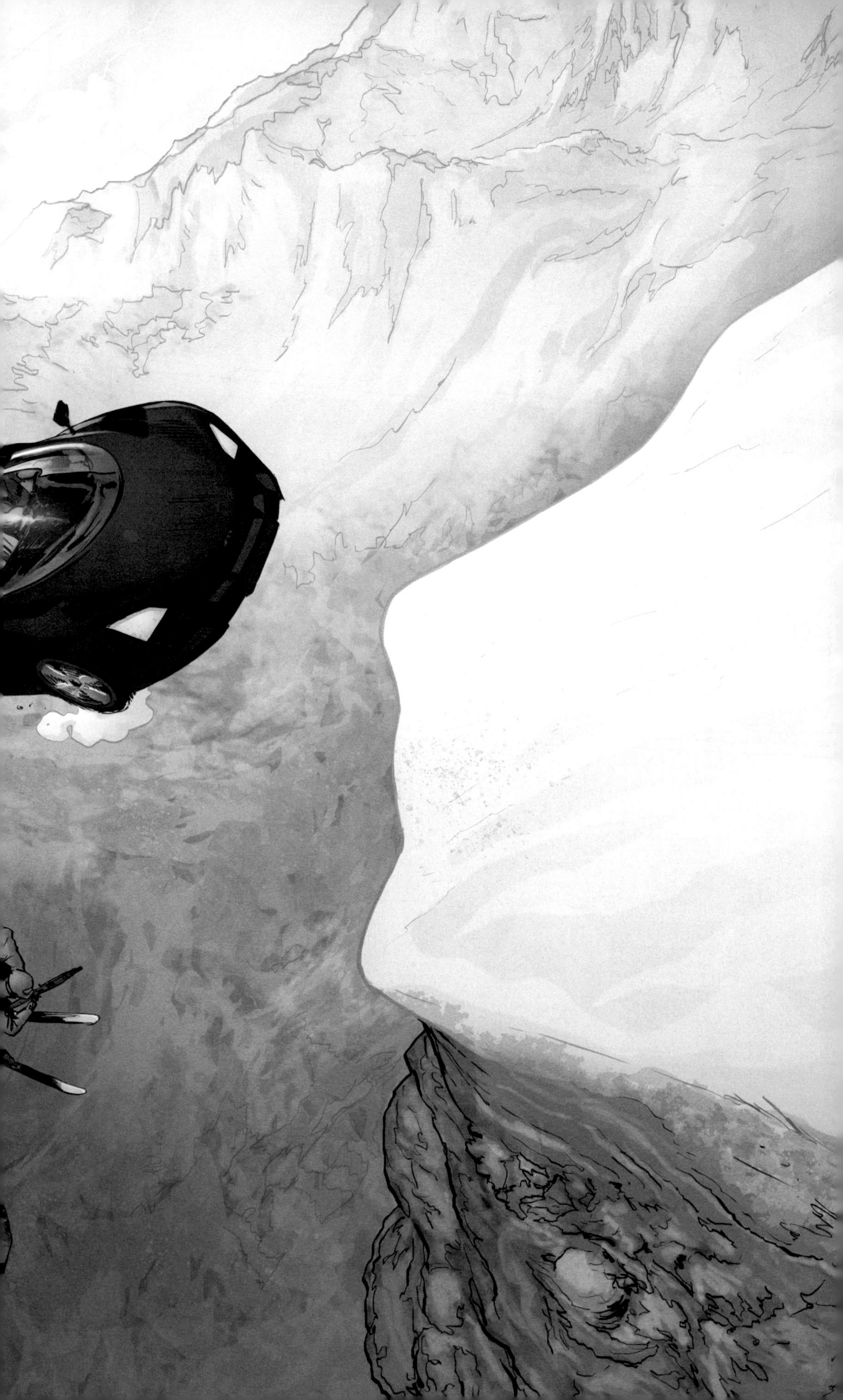

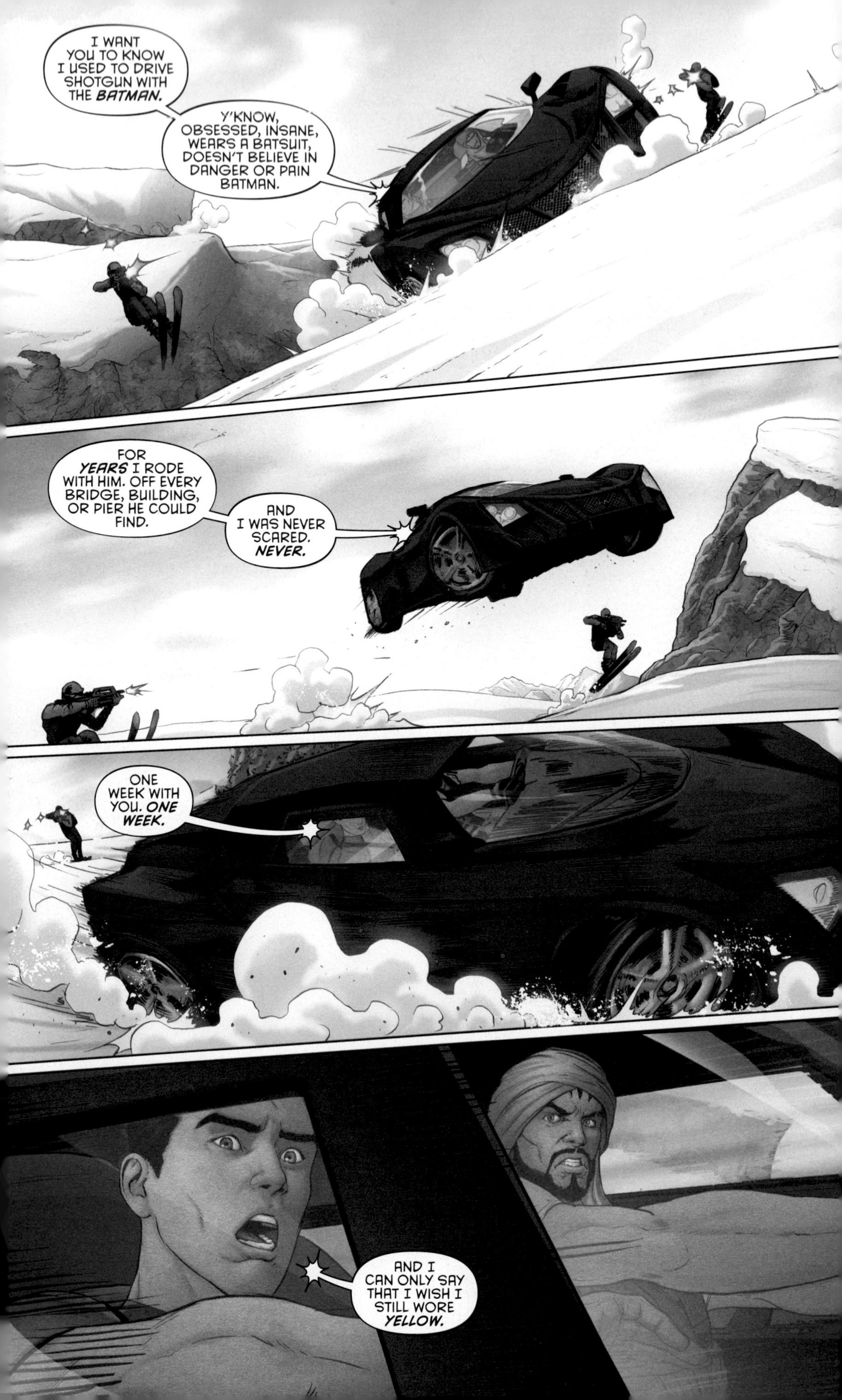
I WANT YOU TO KNOW I USED TO DRIVE SHOTGUN WITH THE *BATMAN.*
Y'KNOW, OBSESSED, INSANE, WEARS A BATSUIT, DOESN'T BELIEVE IN DANGER OR PAIN BATMAN.
FOR *YEARS* I RODE WITH HIM. OFF EVERY BRIDGE, BUILDING, OR PIER HE COULD FIND.
AND I WAS NEVER SCARED. *NEVER.*
ONE WEEK WITH YOU. *ONE WEEK.*
AND I CAN ONLY SAY THAT I WISH I STILL WORE *YELLOW.*

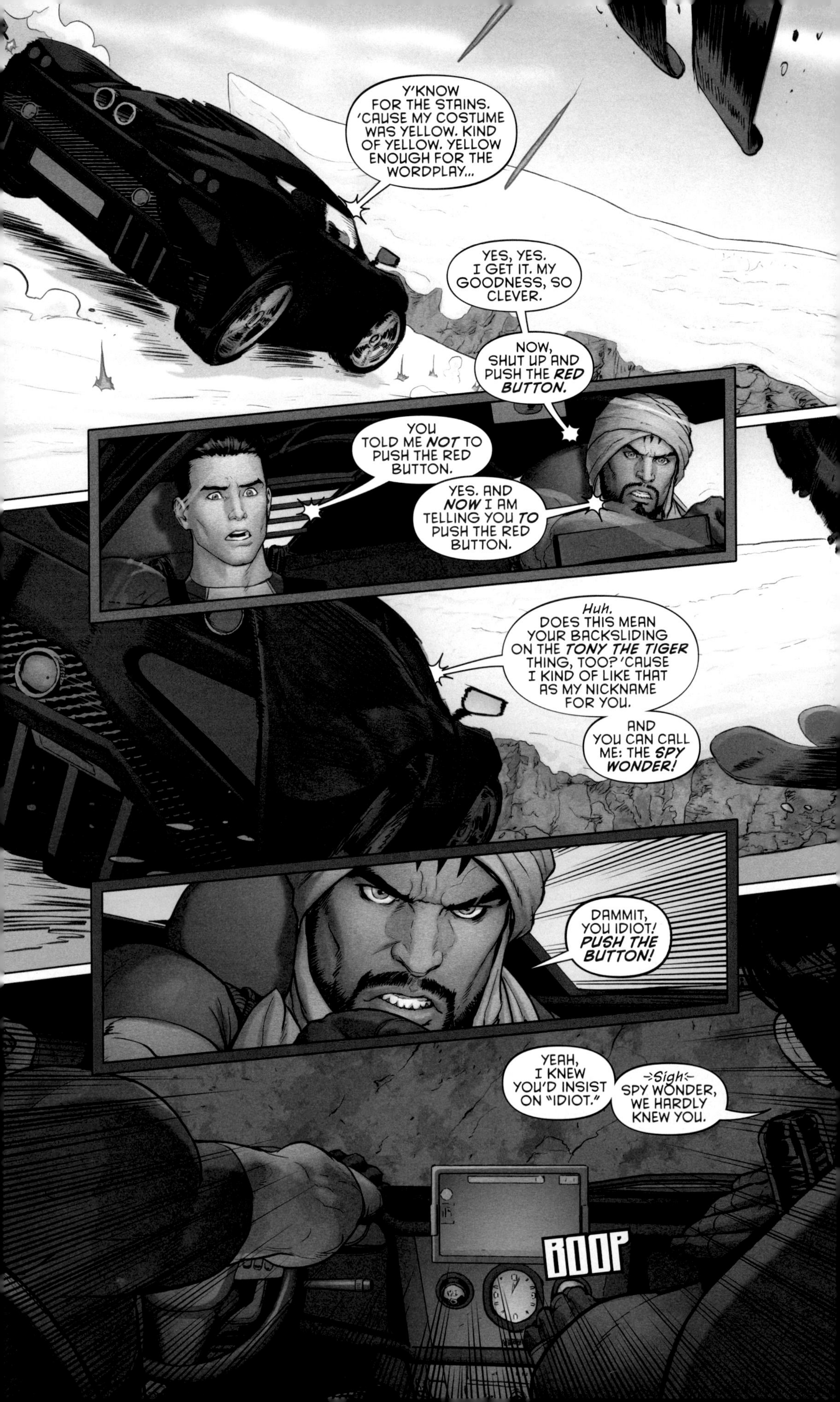

Y'KNOW FOR THE STAINS. 'CAUSE MY COSTUME WAS YELLOW. KIND OF YELLOW. YELLOW ENOUGH FOR THE WORDPLAY...
YES, YES. I GET IT. MY GOODNESS, SO CLEVER.
NOW, SHUT UP AND PUSH THE *RED BUTTON.*
YOU TOLD ME *NOT* TO PUSH THE RED BUTTON.
YES. AND *NOW* I AM TELLING YOU *TO* PUSH THE RED BUTTON.
Huh. DOES THIS MEAN YOUR BACKSLIDING ON THE *TONY THE TIGER* THING, TOO? 'CAUSE I KIND OF LIKE THAT AS MY NICKNAME FOR YOU.
AND YOU CAN CALL ME: THE *SPY WONDER!*
DAMMIT, YOU IDIOT! *PUSH THE BUTTON!*
YEAH, I KNEW YOU'D INSIST ON "IDIOT."
Sigh SPY WONDER, WE HARDLY KNEW YOU.
BOOP

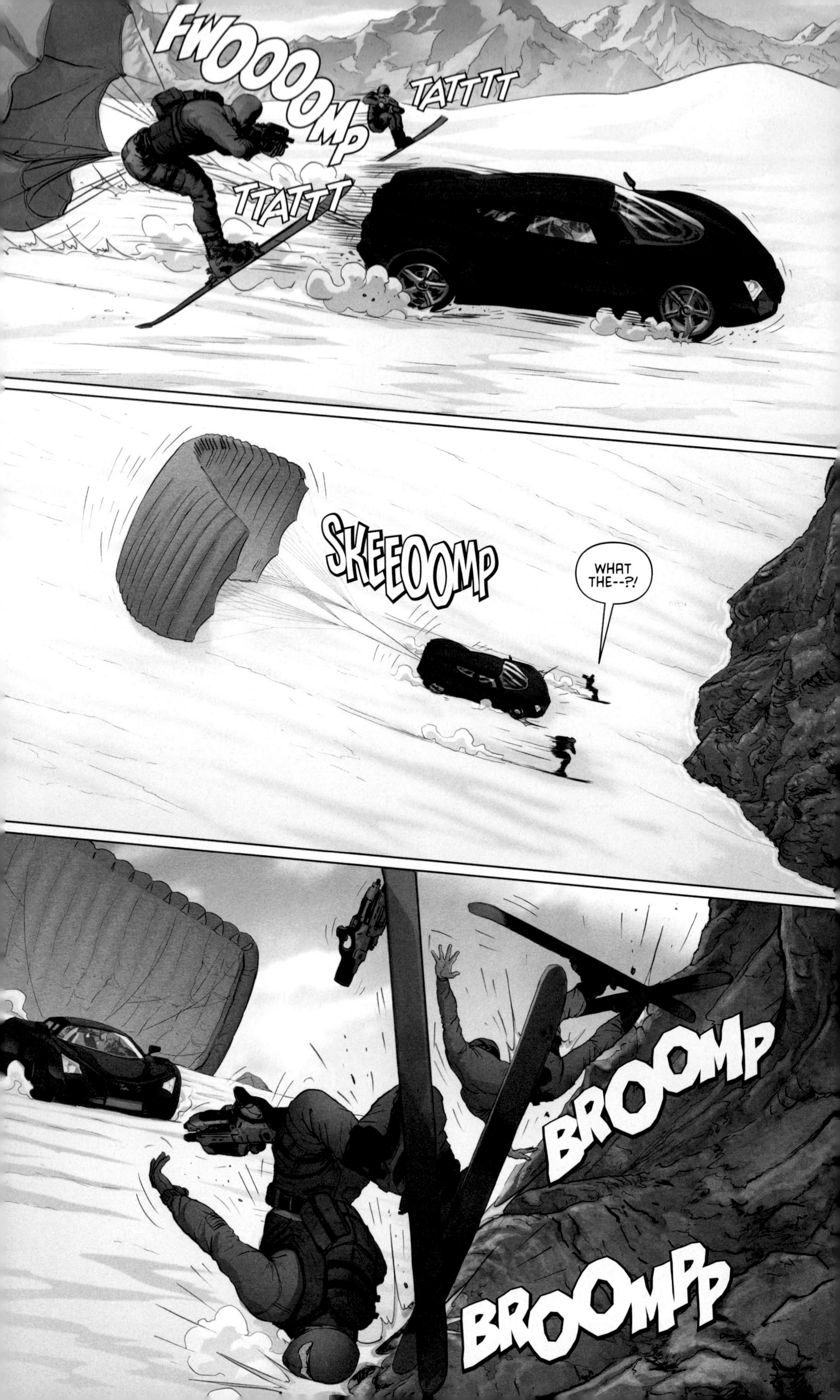
FWOOOOOMP
TATTTT
TTATTT
SKEEOOMP
WHAT THE--?!
BROOMP
BROOMPP

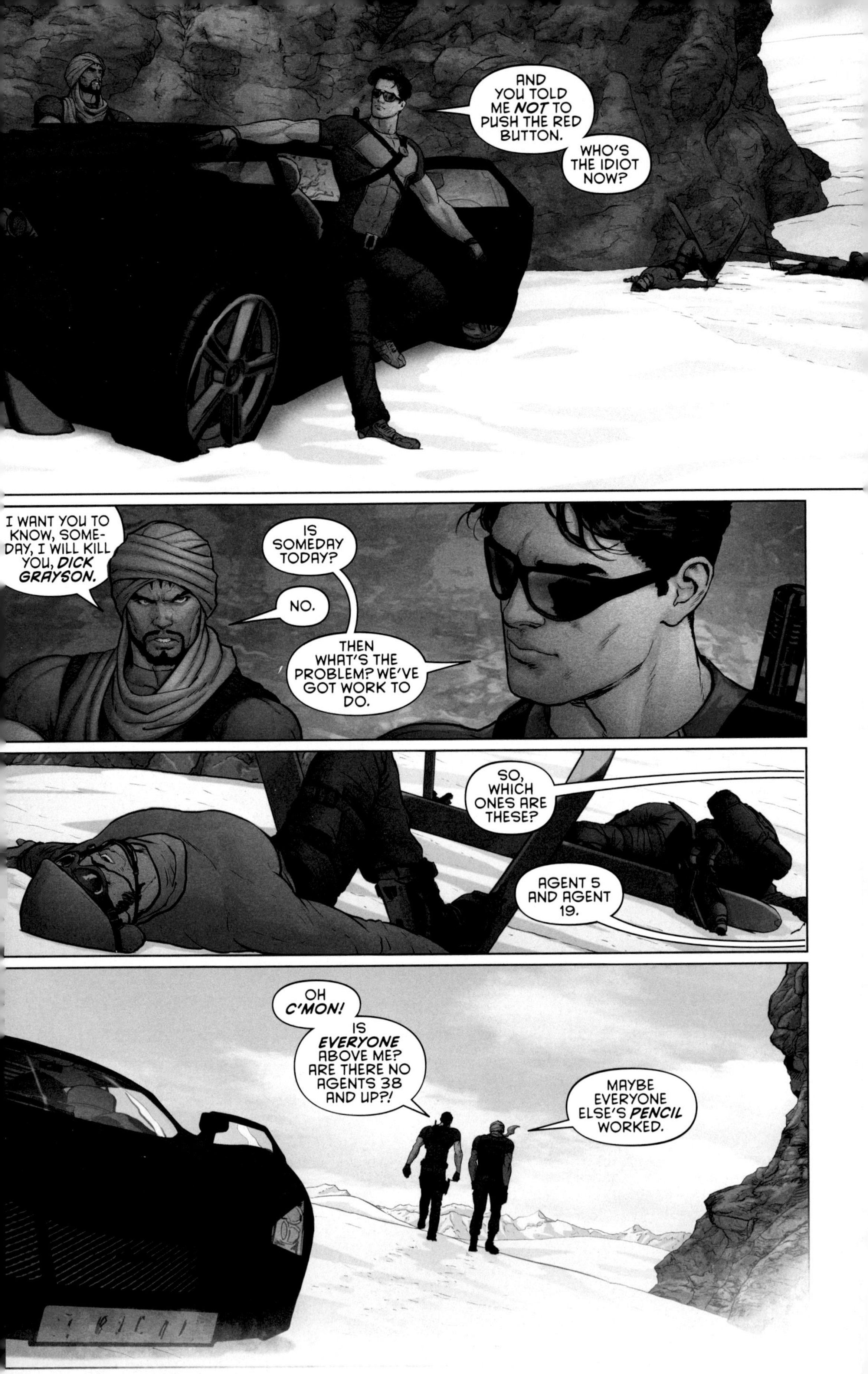
AND YOU TOLD ME *NOT* TO PUSH THE RED BUTTON.
WHO'S THE IDIOT NOW?
I WANT YOU TO KNOW, SOMEDAY, I WILL KILL YOU, *DICK GRAYSON.*
IS SOMEDAY TODAY?
NO.
THEN WHAT'S THE PROBLEM? WE'VE GOT WORK TO DO.
SO, WHICH ONES ARE THESE?
AGENT 5 AND AGENT 19.
OH *C'MON!*
IS *EVERYONE* ABOVE ME? ARE THERE NO AGENTS 38 AND UP?!
MAYBE EVERYONE ELSE'S *PENCIL* WORKED.

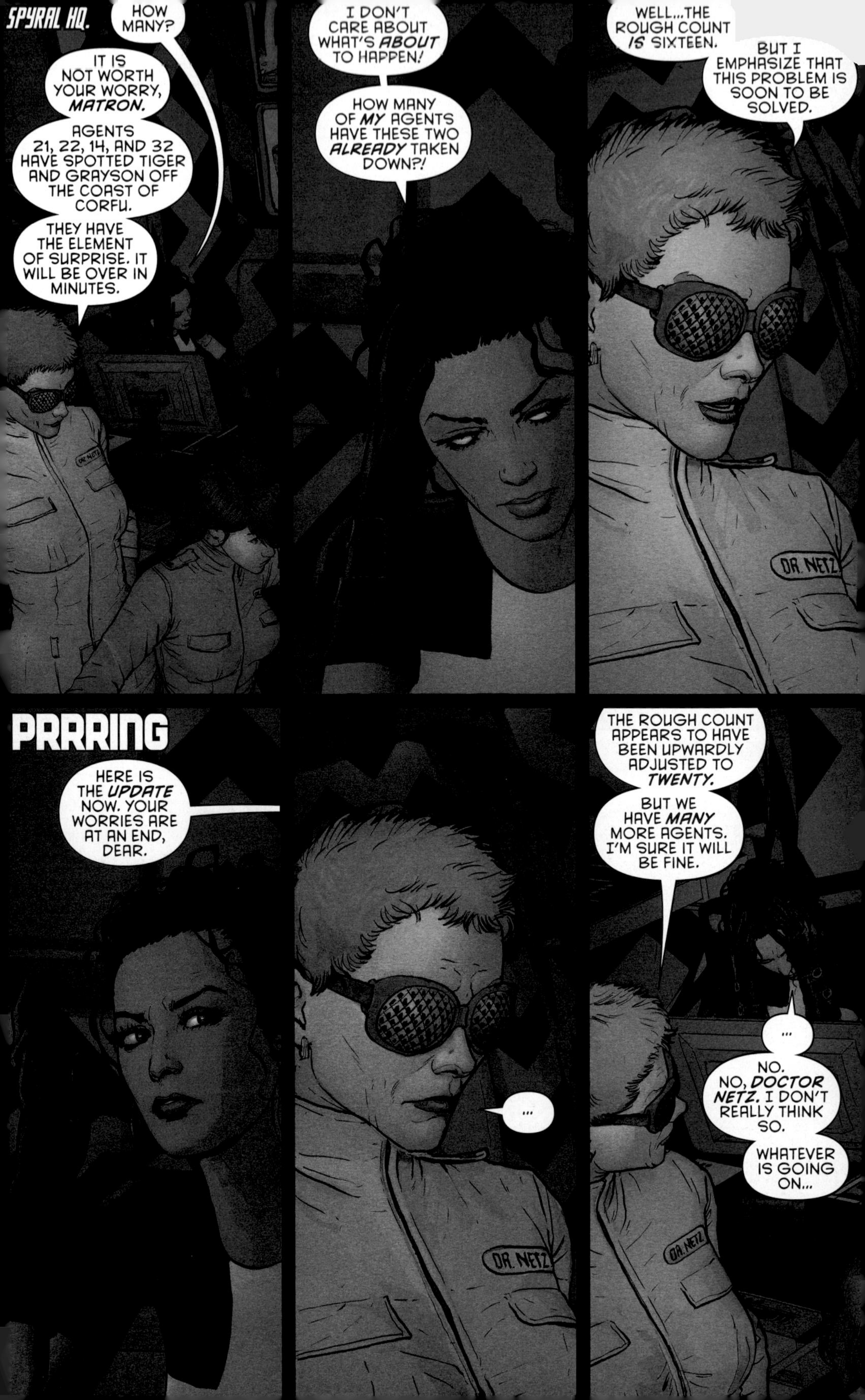
SPYRAL HQ.
HOW MANY?
IT IS NOT WORTH YOUR WORRY, MATRON.
AGENTS 21, 22, 14, AND 32 HAVE SPOTTED TIGER AND GRAYSON OFF THE COAST OF CORFU.
THEY HAVE THE ELEMENT OF SURPRISE. IT WILL BE OVER IN MINUTES.
I DON'T CARE ABOUT WHAT'S ABOUT TO HAPPEN!
HOW MANY OF MY AGENTS HAVE THESE TWO ALREADY TAKEN DOWN?!
WELL...THE ROUGH COUNT IS SIXTEEN.
BUT I EMPHASIZE THAT THIS PROBLEM IS SOON TO BE SOLVED.
DR. NETZ
PRRRING
HERE IS THE UPDATE NOW. YOUR WORRIES ARE AT AN END, DEAR.
...
DR. NETZ
THE ROUGH COUNT APPEARS TO HAVE BEEN UPWARDLY ADJUSTED TO TWENTY.
BUT WE HAVE MANY MORE AGENTS. I'M SURE IT WILL BE FINE.
...
NO. NO, DOCTOR NETZ. I DON'T REALLY THINK SO.
WHATEVER IS GOING ON...
DR. NETZ

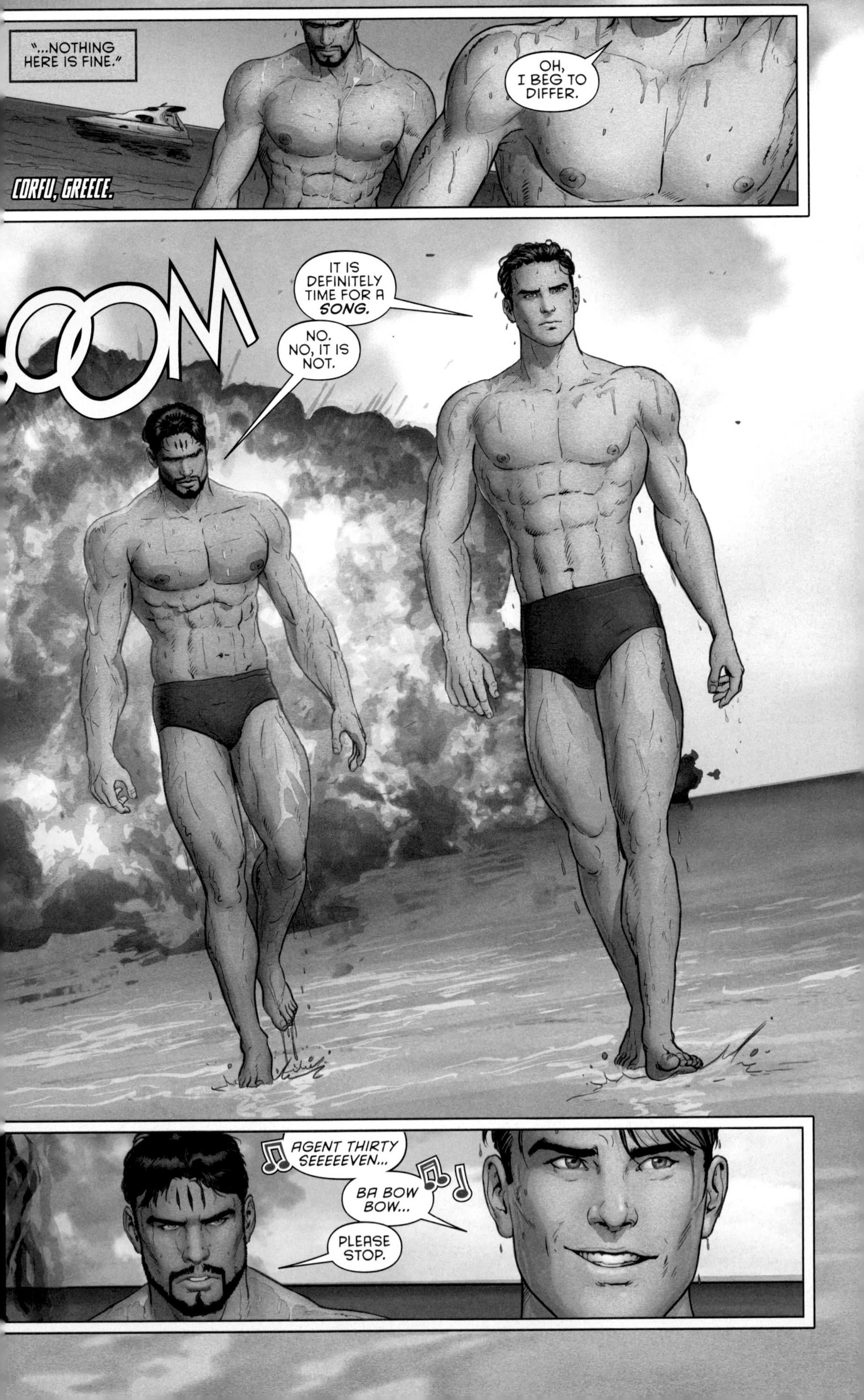
"...NOTHING HERE IS FINE."
OH, I BEG TO DIFFER.
CORFU, GREECE.
OOM
IT IS DEFINITELY TIME FOR A SONG.
NO. NO, IT IS NOT.
AGENT THIRTY SEEEEEVEN...
BA BOW BOW...
PLEASE STOP.

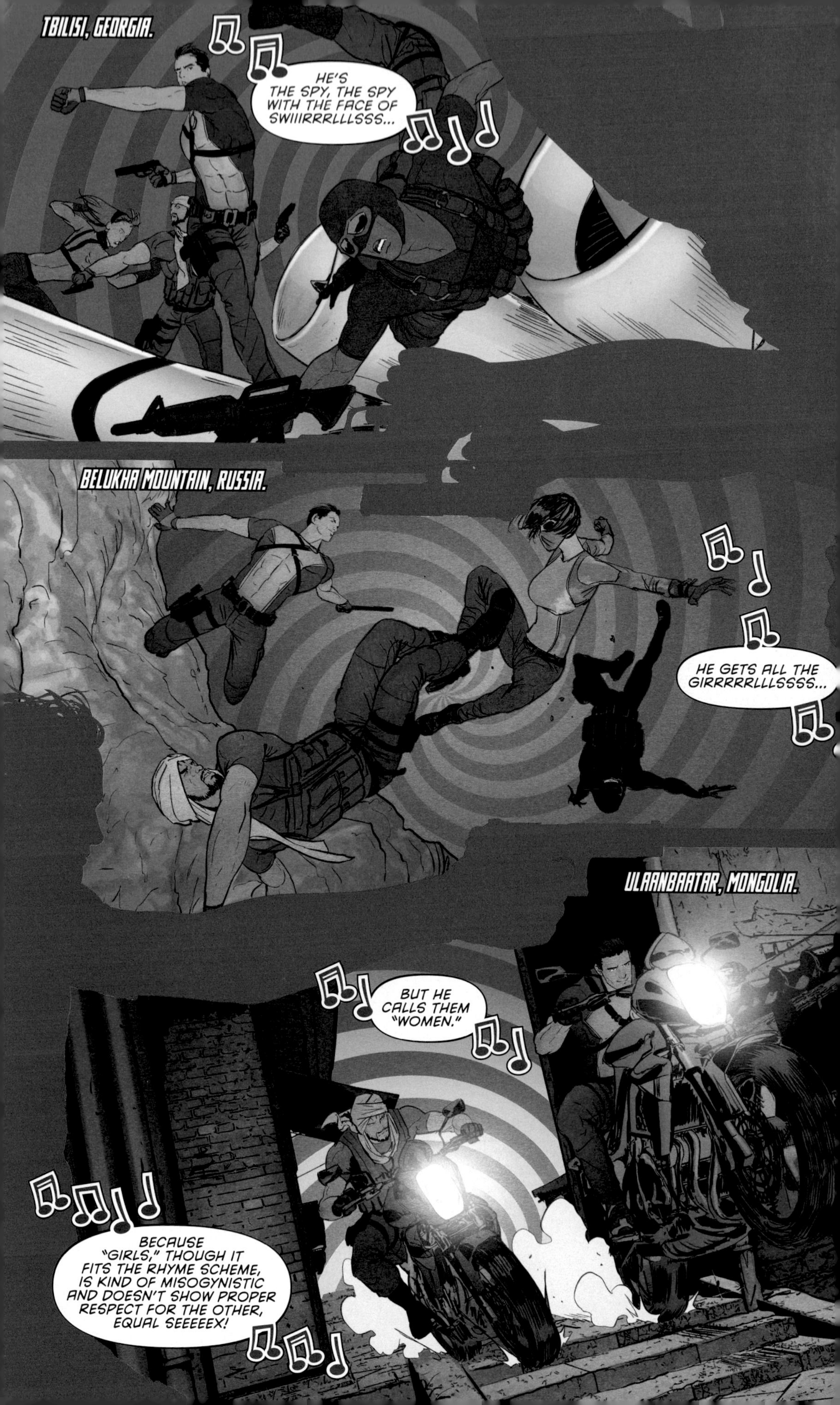
TBILISI, GEORGIA.
HE'S THE SPY, THE SPY WITH THE FACE OF SWIIIRRRLLLSSS...
BELUKHA MOUNTAIN, RUSSIA.
HE GETS ALL THE GIRRRRRLLLSSSS...
ULAANBAATAR, MONGOLIA.
BUT HE CALLS THEM "WOMEN."
BECAUSE "GIRLS," THOUGH IT FITS THE RHYME SCHEME, IS KIND OF MISOGYNISTIC AND DOESN'T SHOW PROPER RESPECT FOR THE OTHER, EQUAL SEEEEEX!

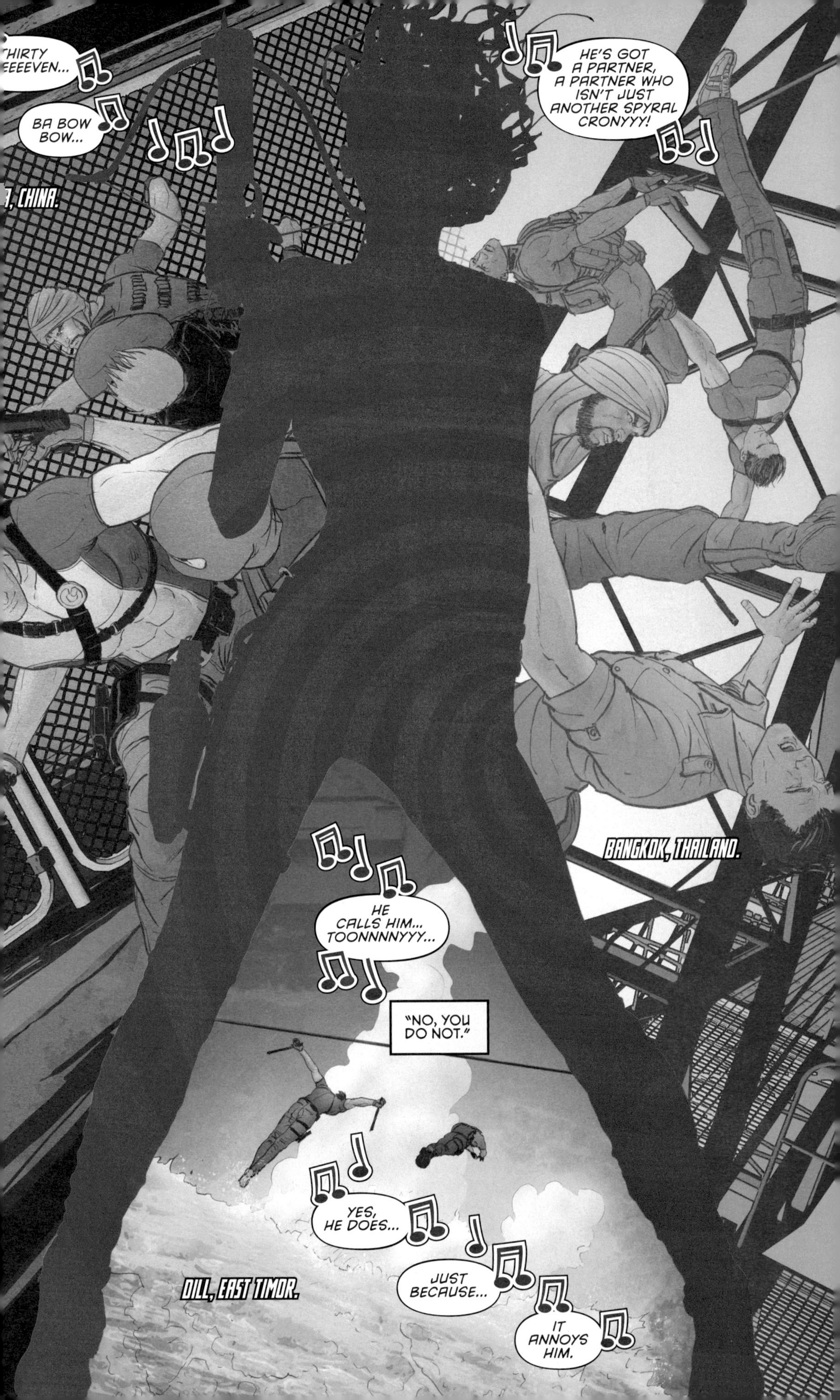

THIRTY EEEEVEN...
BA BOW BOW...
, CHINA.
HE'S GOT A PARTNER, A PARTNER WHO ISN'T JUST ANOTHER SPYRAL CRONYYY!
BANGKOK, THAILAND.
HE CALLS HIM... TOONNNNYYY...
"NO, YOU DO NOT."
YES, HE DOES...
JUST BECAUSE...
IT ANNOYS HIM.
DILL, EAST TIMOR.

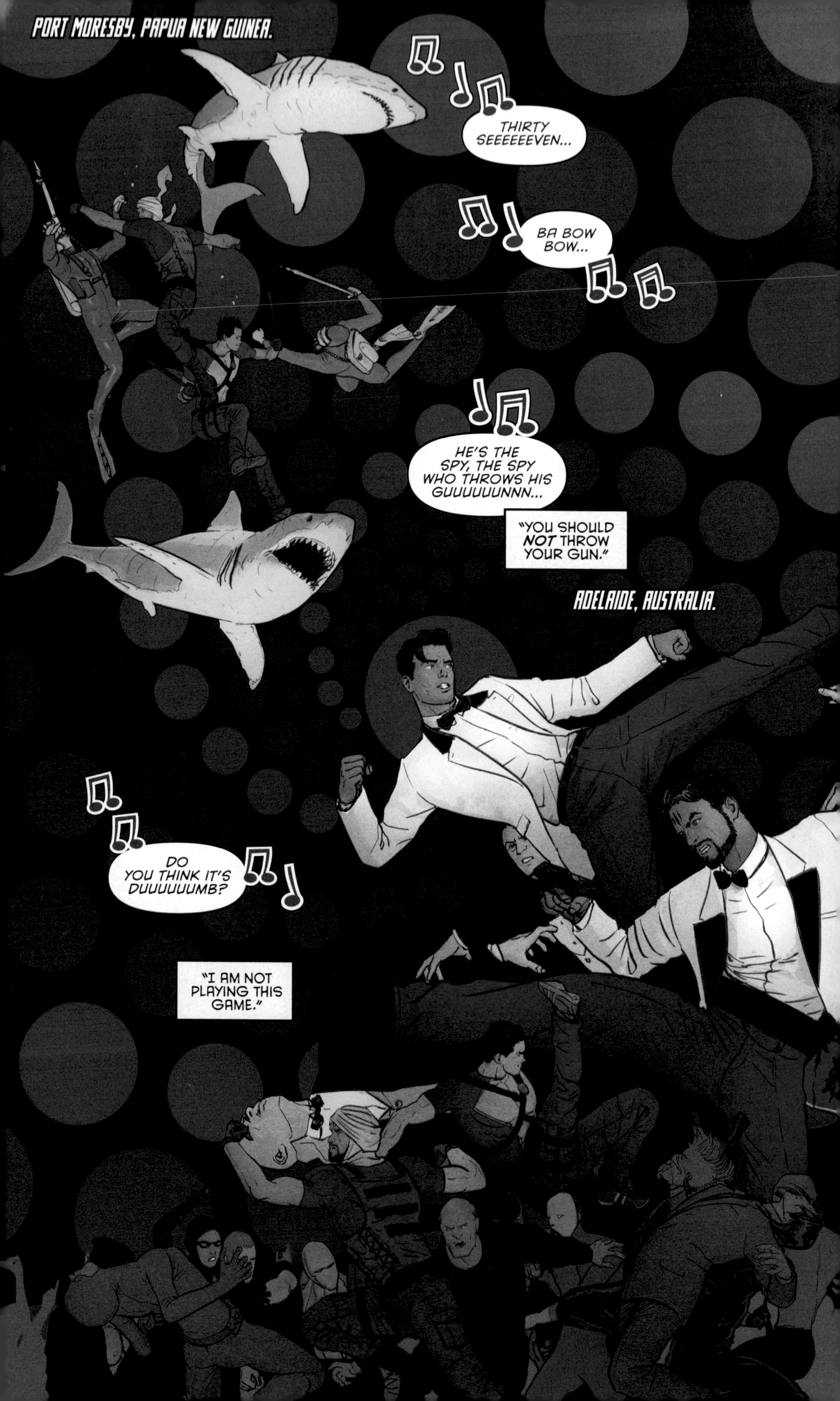
PORT MORESBY, PAPUA NEW GUINEA.
THIRTY SEEEEEEVEN...
BA BOW BOW...
HE'S THE SPY, THE SPY WHO THROWS HIS GUUUUUUNNN...
"YOU SHOULD NOT THROW YOUR GUN."
ADELAIDE, AUSTRALIA.
DO YOU THINK IT'S DUUUUUUMB?
"I AM NOT PLAYING THIS GAME."

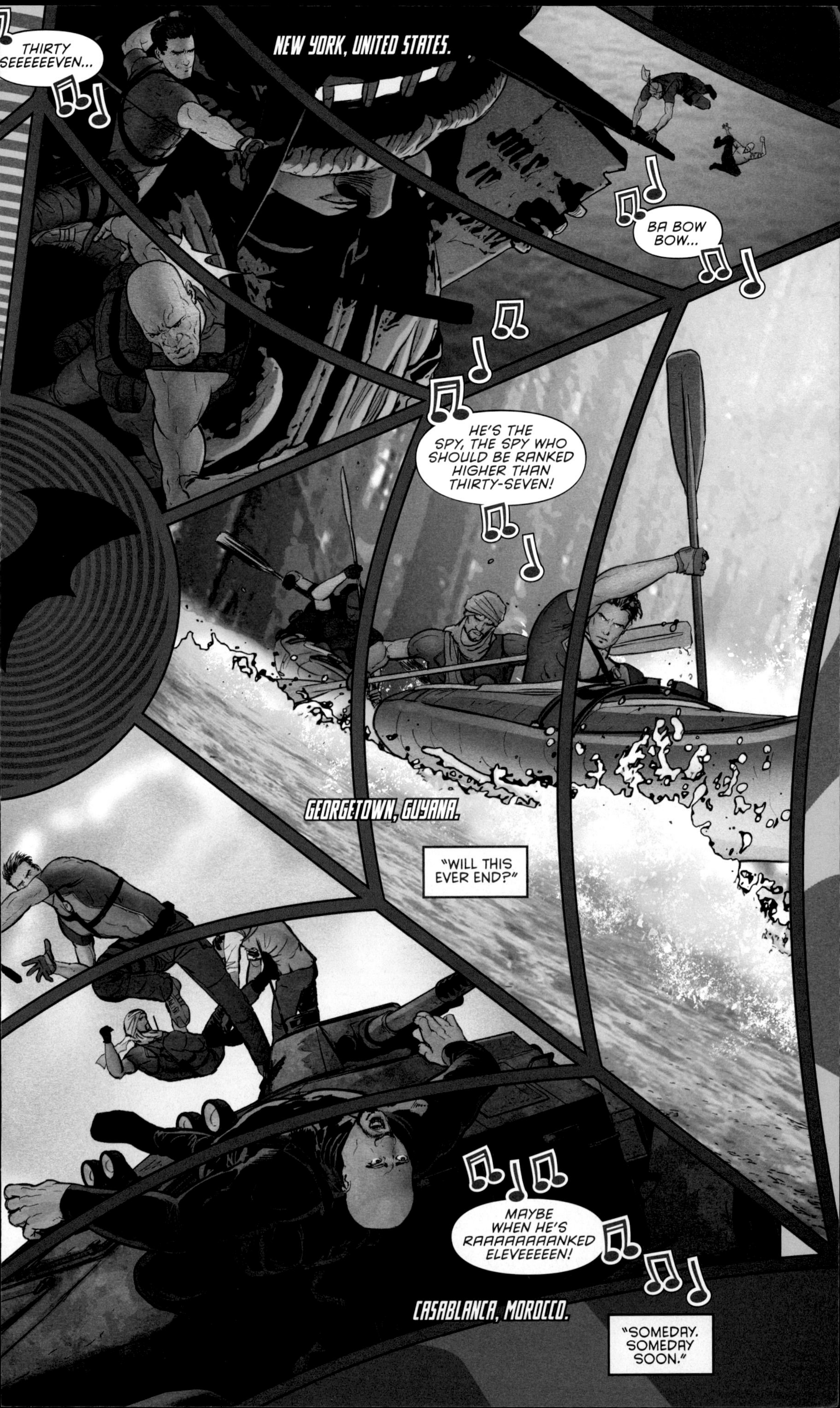
NEW YORK, UNITED STATES.
THIRTY SEEEEEEVEN...
BA BOW BOW...
HE'S THE SPY, THE SPY WHO SHOULD BE RANKED HIGHER THAN THIRTY-SEVEN!
GEORGETOWN, GUYANA.
"WILL THIS EVER END?"
MAYBE WHEN HE'S RAAAAAAAANKED ELEVEEEEEN!
CASABLANCA, MOROCCO.
"SOMEDAY. SOMEDAY SOON."

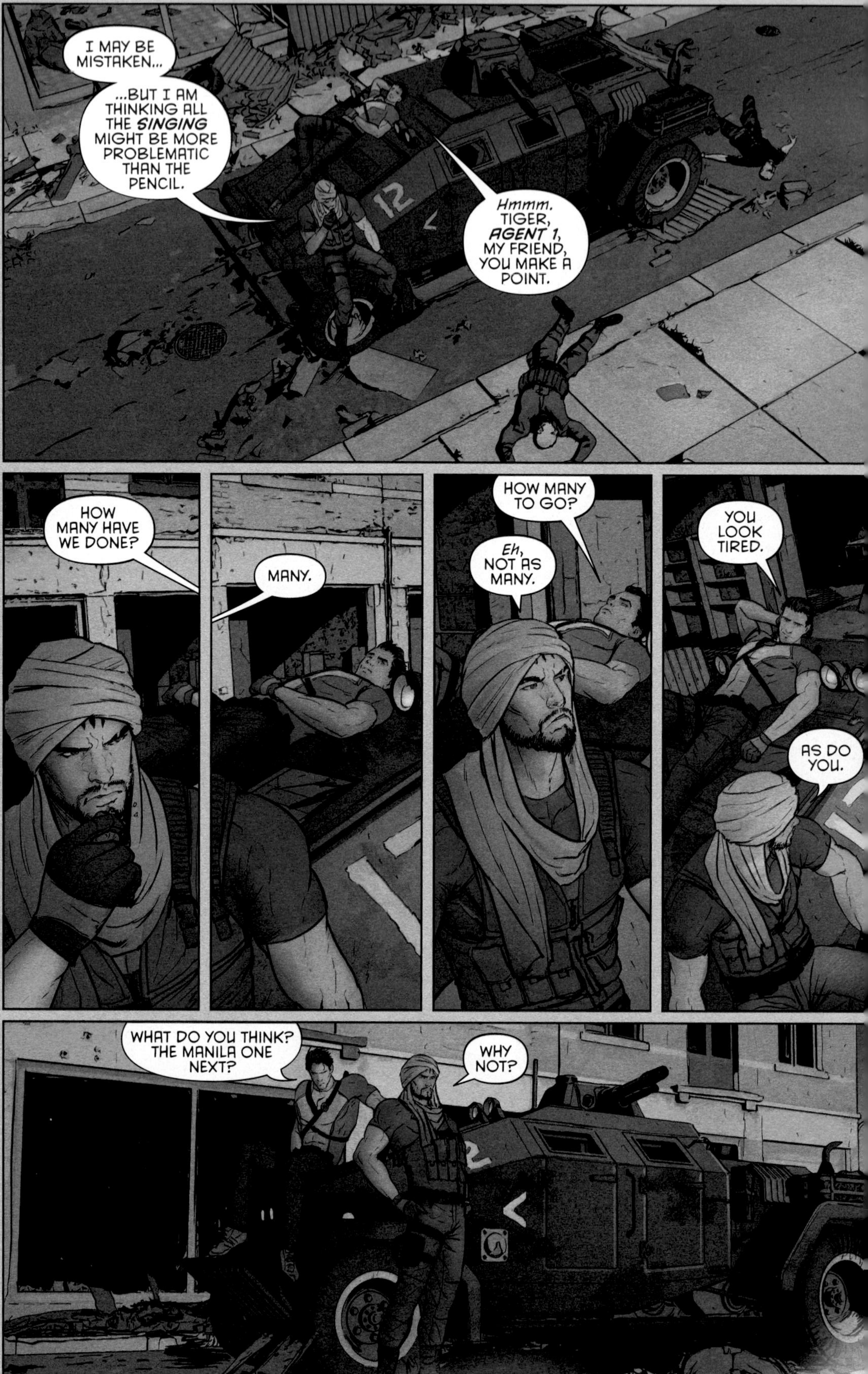

I MAY BE MISTAKEN...
...BUT I AM THINKING ALL THE *SINGING* MIGHT BE MORE PROBLEMATIC THAN THE PENCIL.
Hmmm. TIGER, ***AGENT 1***, MY FRIEND, YOU MAKE A POINT.
HOW MANY HAVE WE DONE?
MANY.
HOW MANY TO GO?
Eh, NOT AS MANY.
YOU LOOK TIRED.
AS DO YOU.
WHAT DO YOU THINK? THE MANILA ONE NEXT?
WHY NOT?

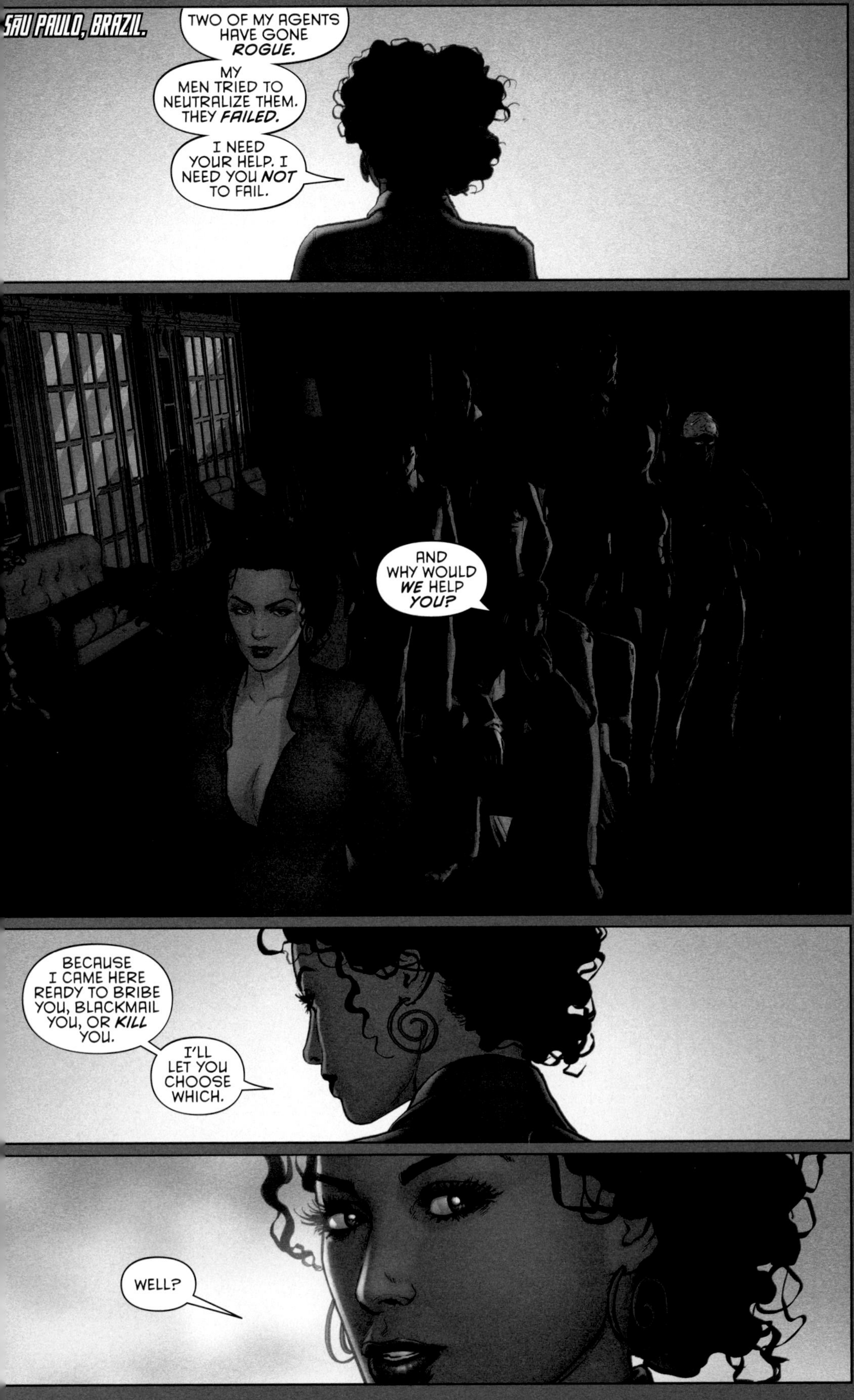
SÃO PAULO, BRAZIL.
TWO OF MY AGENTS HAVE GONE ROGUE.
MY MEN TRIED TO NEUTRALIZE THEM. THEY FAILED.
I NEED YOUR HELP. I NEED YOU NOT TO FAIL.
AND WHY WOULD WE HELP YOU?
BECAUSE I CAME HERE READY TO BRIBE YOU, BLACKMAIL YOU, OR KILL YOU.
I'LL LET YOU CHOOSE WHICH.
WELL?

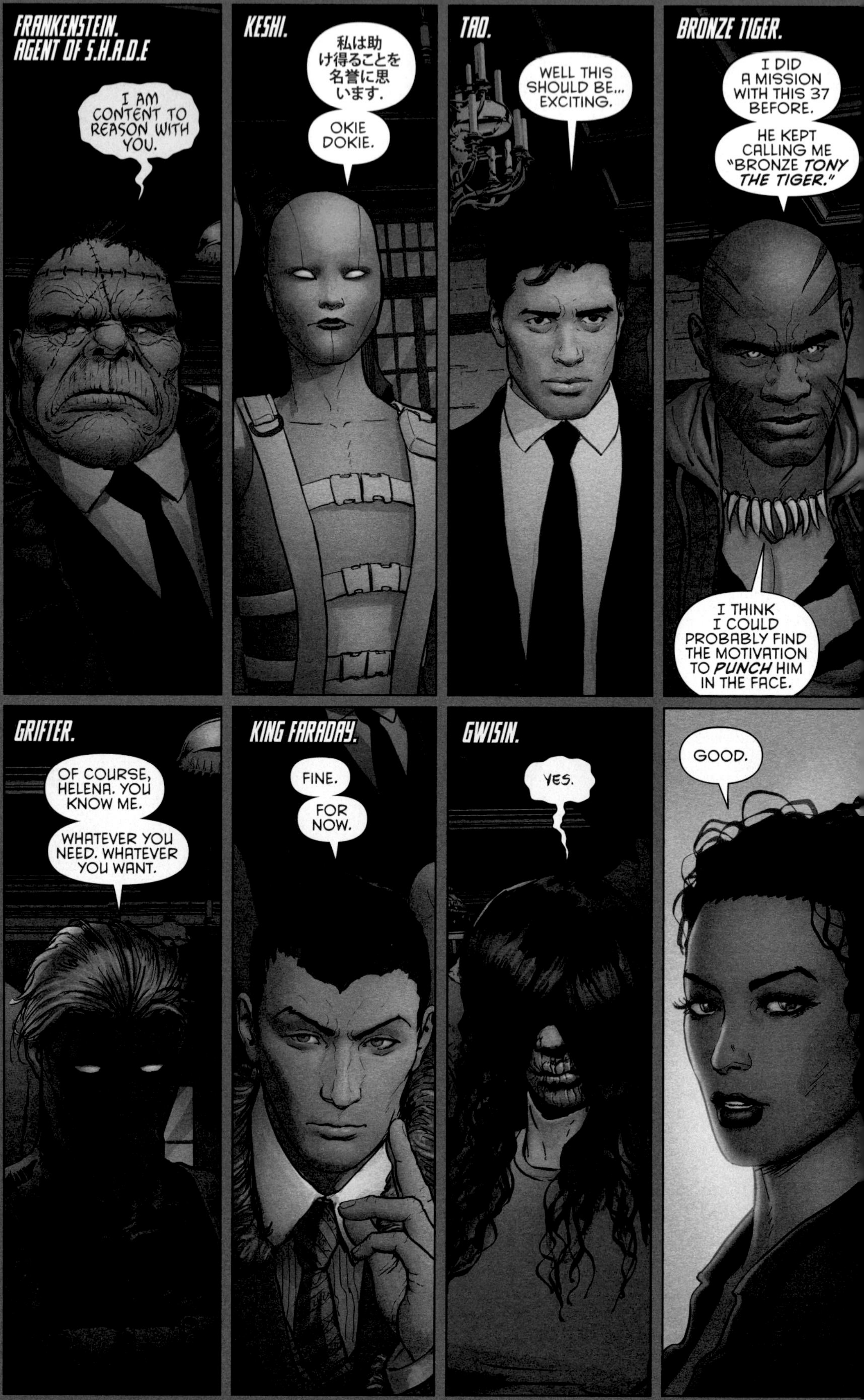
FRANKENSTEIN. AGENT OF S.H.A.D.E
I AM CONTENT TO REASON WITH YOU.
KESHI.
私は助け得ることを名誉に思います。
OKIE DOKIE.
TAO.
WELL THIS SHOULD BE... EXCITING.
BRONZE TIGER.
I DID A MISSION WITH THIS 37 BEFORE.
HE KEPT CALLING ME "BRONZE TONY THE TIGER."
I THINK I COULD PROBABLY FIND THE MOTIVATION TO PUNCH HIM IN THE FACE.
GRIFTER.
OF COURSE, HELENA. YOU KNOW ME.
WHATEVER YOU NEED. WHATEVER YOU WANT.
KING FARADAY.
FINE.
FOR NOW.
GWISIN.
YES.
GOOD.

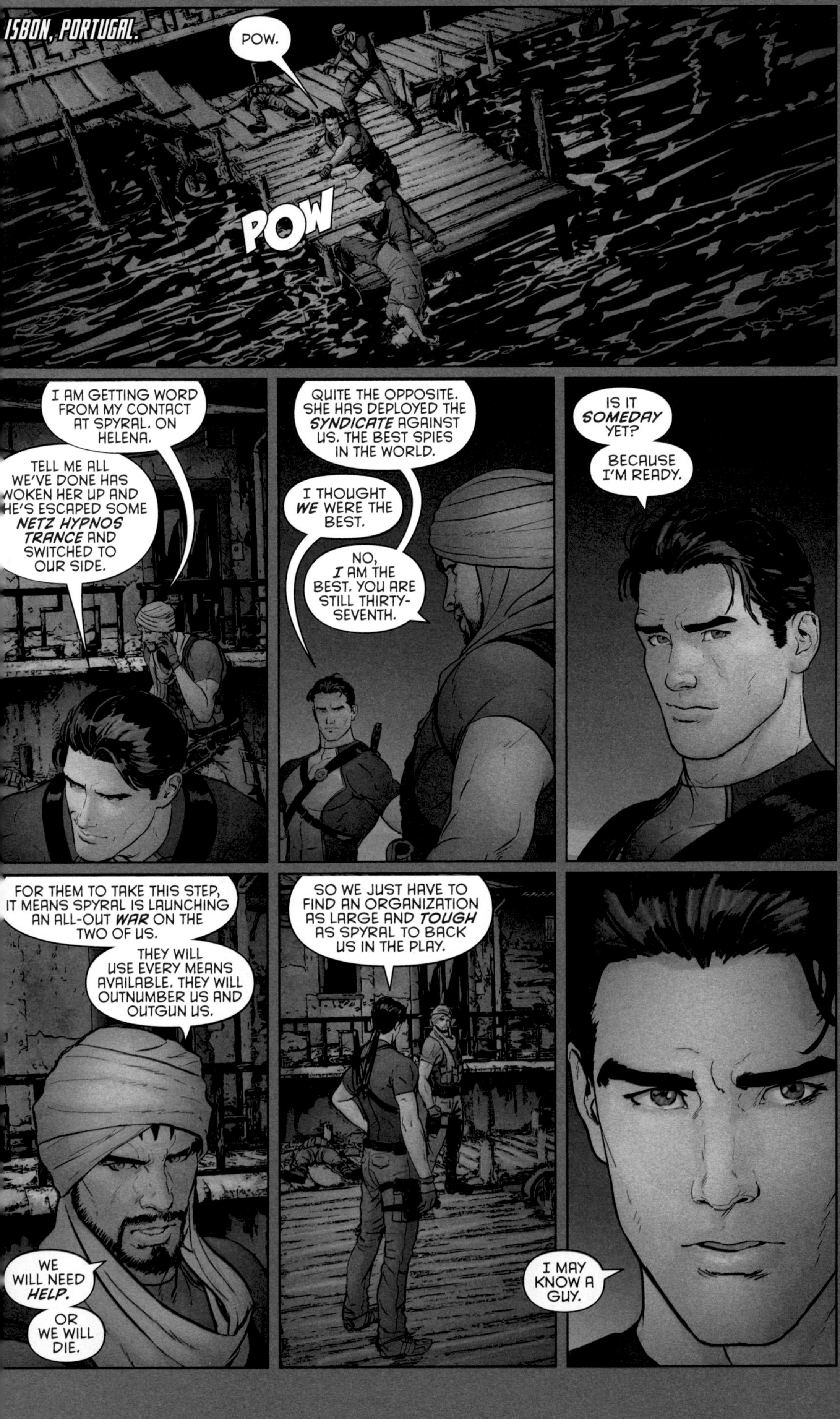

ISBON, PORTUGAL.
POW.
POW
I AM GETTING WORD FROM MY CONTACT AT SPYRAL. ON HELENA.
TELL ME ALL WE'VE DONE HAS WOKEN HER UP AND HE'S ESCAPED SOME NETZ HYPNOS TRANCE AND SWITCHED TO OUR SIDE.
QUITE THE OPPOSITE. SHE HAS DEPLOYED THE SYNDICATE AGAINST US. THE BEST SPIES IN THE WORLD.
I THOUGHT WE WERE THE BEST.
NO, I AM THE BEST. YOU ARE STILL THIRTY-SEVENTH.
IS IT SOMEDAY YET?
BECAUSE I'M READY.
FOR THEM TO TAKE THIS STEP, IT MEANS SPYRAL IS LAUNCHING AN ALL-OUT WAR ON THE TWO OF US.
THEY WILL USE EVERY MEANS AVAILABLE. THEY WILL OUTNUMBER US AND OUTGUN US.
WE WILL NEED HELP.
OR WE WILL DIE.
SO WE JUST HAVE TO FIND AN ORGANIZATION AS LARGE AND TOUGH AS SPYRAL TO BACK US IN THE PLAY.
I MAY KNOW A GUY.

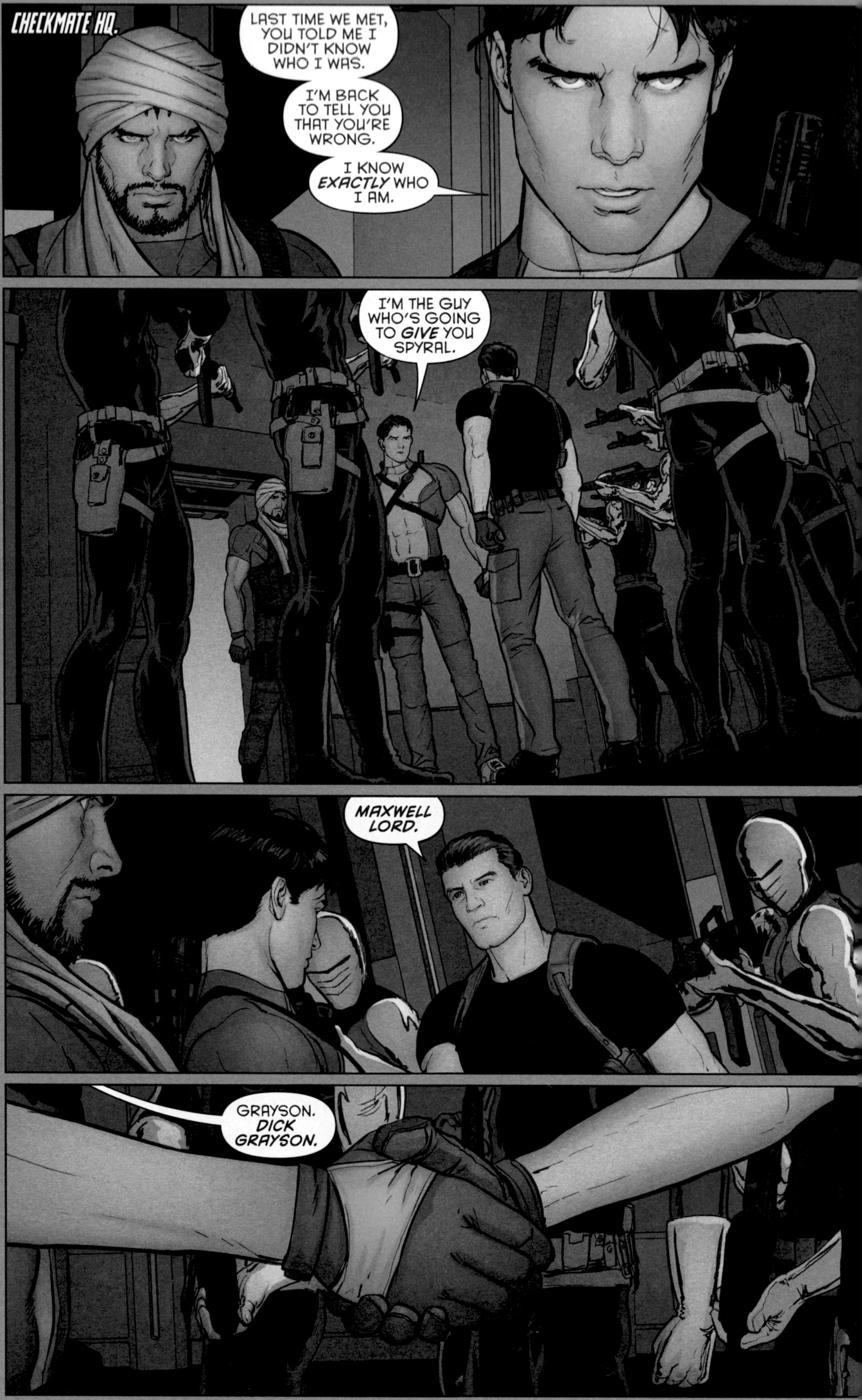
CHECKMATE HQ.
LAST TIME WE MET, YOU TOLD ME I DIDN'T KNOW WHO I WAS.
I'M BACK TO TELL YOU THAT YOU'RE WRONG.
I KNOW *EXACTLY* WHO I AM.
I'M THE GUY WHO'S GOING TO *GIVE* YOU SPYRAL.
MAXWELL LORD.
GRAYSON. *DICK GRAYSON.*

VARIANT COVER GALLERY

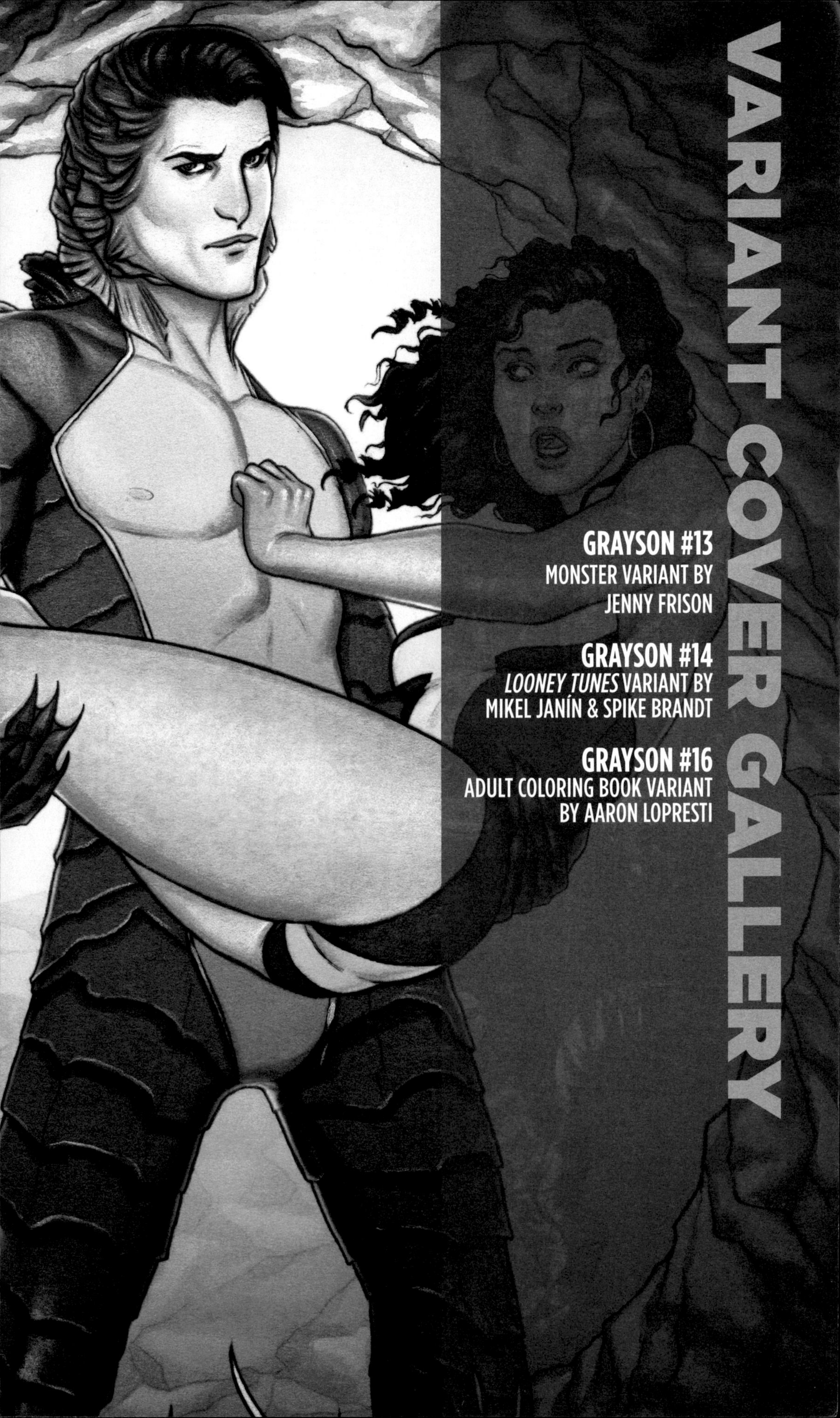

GRAYSON #13
MONSTER VARIANT BY
JENNY FRISON

GRAYSON #14
LOONEY TUNES VARIANT BY
MIKEL JANÍN & SPIKE BRANDT

GRAYSON #16
ADULT COLORING BOOK VARIANT
BY AARON LOPRESTI

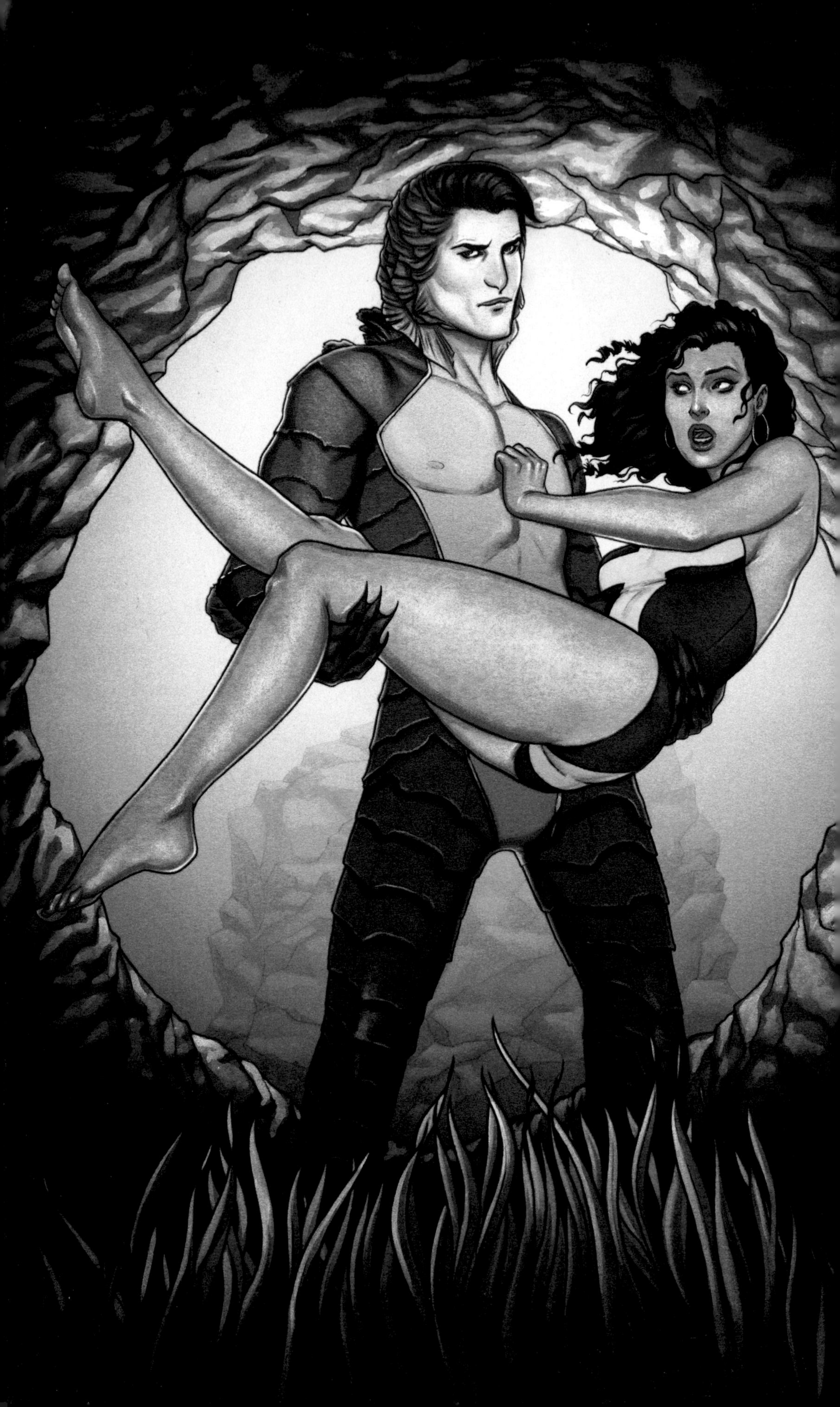

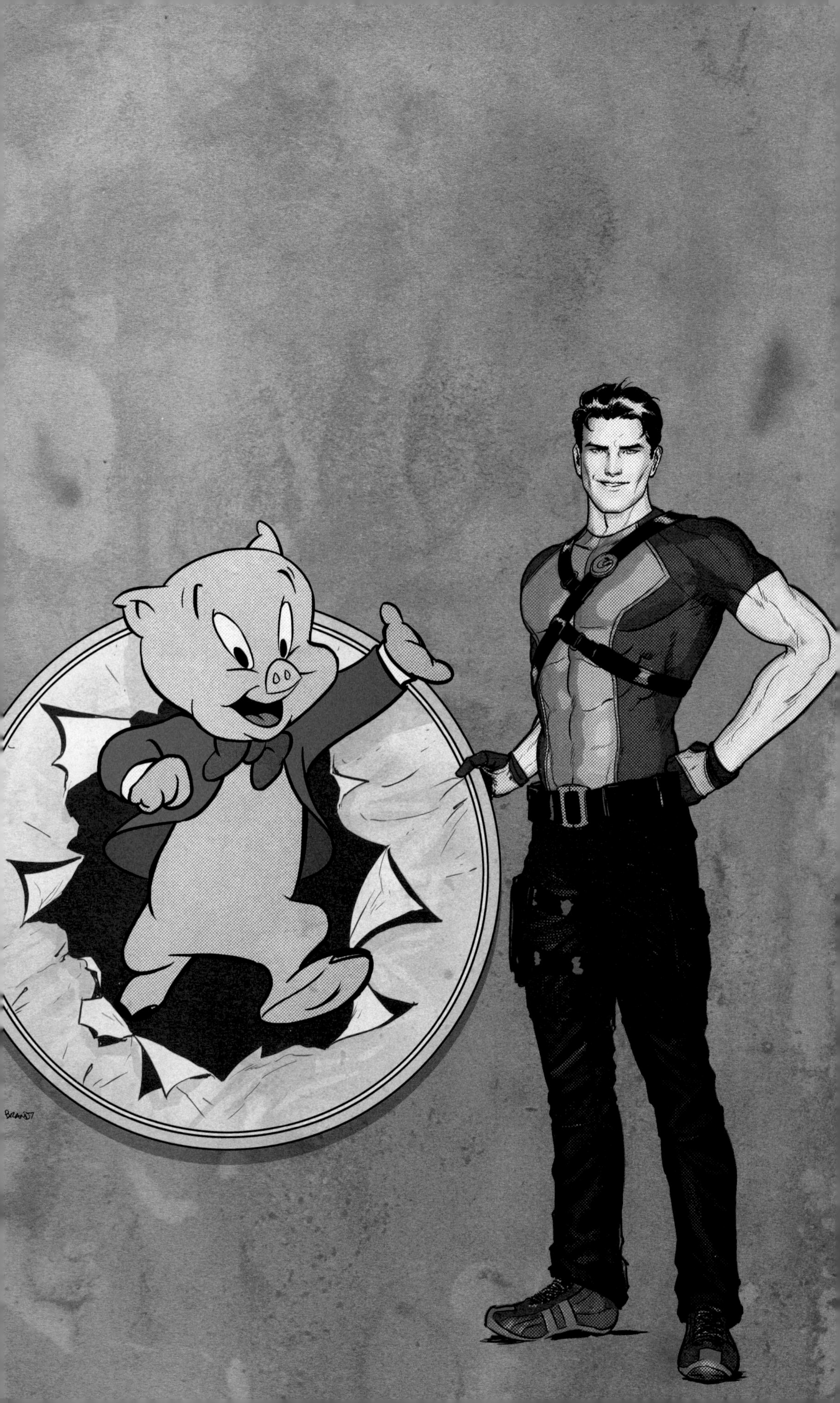

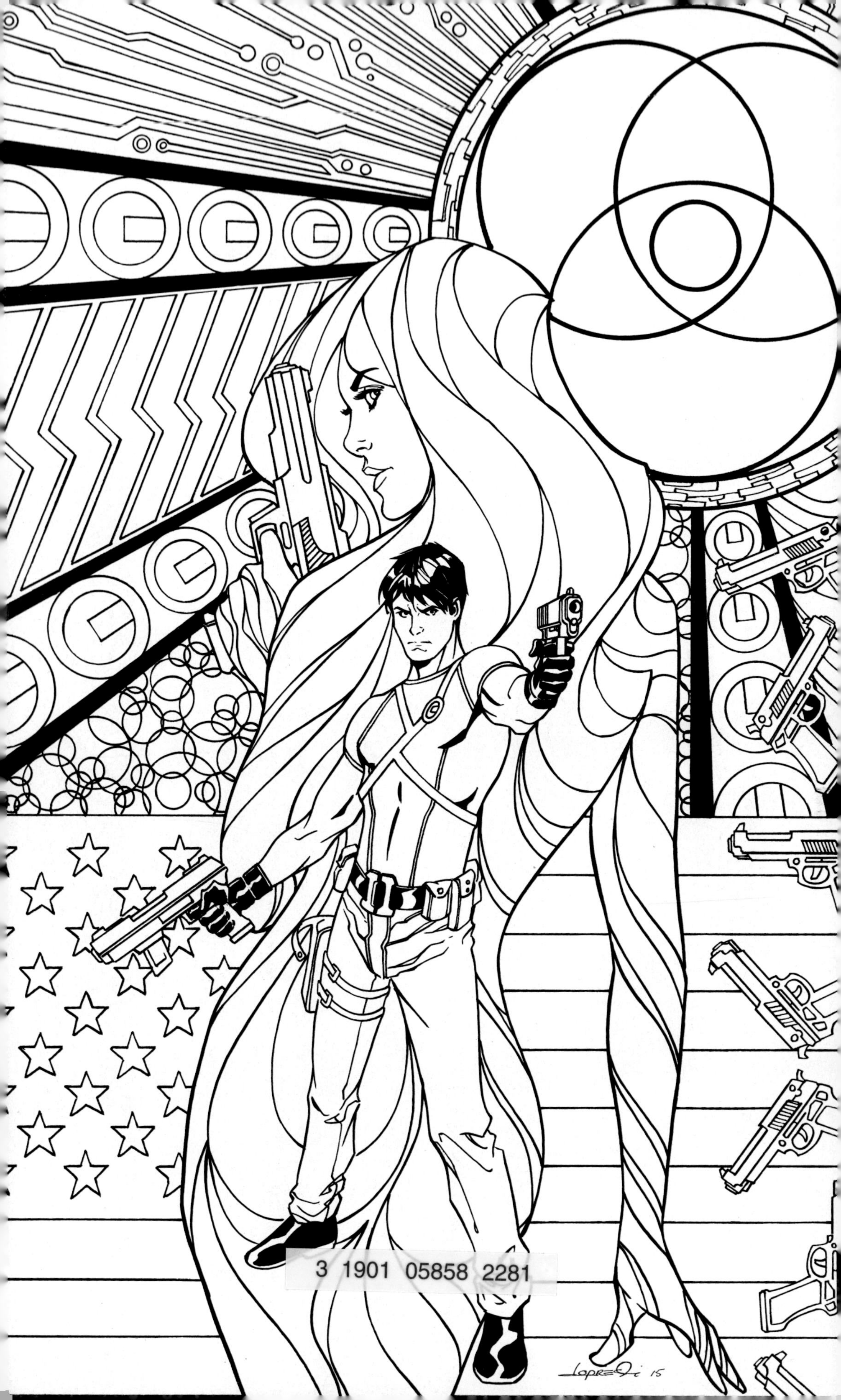